"Every country has its Saviours. He who dissipates the darkness of ignorance by the help of the torch of science, thus disclosing to us the truth, deserves that title as a mark of our gratitude, quite as much as he who saves us from death by healing our bodies. Such a one awakens in our benumbed souls the faculty of distinguishing the true from the false, by kindling therein a divine flame hitherto absent, and he has the right to our grateful reverence, for he has become our creator. What matters the name of the symbol that personifies the abstract idea, if that idea is always the same and is true? Whether the concrete symbol bears one title or another, whether the Saviour in whom we believe has for an earthly name Krishna, Buddha, Jesus or Aesculapius – also called 'Saviour-God', we have but to remember one thing: symbols of divine truth were not invented for the amusement of the ignorant; they are the alpha and omega of philosophical thought."

H. P. Blavatsky

SYMBOLS OF THE
ETERNAL DOCTRINE

SYMBOLS OF THE ETERNAL DOCTRINE

FROM SHAMBALLA TO PARADISE

BY

HELEN VALBORG

COMPILED BY
THE EDITORIAL BOARD OF THEOSOPHY TRUST

THEOSOPHY TRUST BOOKS
WASHINGTON, D.C.

Symbols of the Eternal Doctrine
From Shamballa to Paradise

Theosophy Trust books may be ordered through BookSurge, Amazon.com, and other booksellers, or by visiting:

http://www.theosophytrust.org/online_books.php

ISBN 978-0-9793205-1-4
ISBN 0-9793205-1-8

Library of Congress Control Number 2007902478

Printed in the United States of America

To

Nandini Iyer

Spititual Teacher, Thinker, and

an Inspiration to All Who

Have Had the Great Good Karma

to Learn from Her

.

KRISHNA:

Men say that the Ashwattha, the eternal sacred tree, grows with its roots above and its branches below, and the leaves of which are the Vedas; he who knows this knows the Vedas. Its branches growing out of the three qualities with the objects of sense as the lesser shoots, spread forth, some above and some below; and those roots which ramify below in the regions of mankind are the connecting bonds of action. Its form is not thus understood by men; it has no beginning, nor can its present constitution be understood, nor has it any end. When one hath hewn down with the strong axe of dispassion this Ashwattha tree with its deeply imbedded roots, then that place is to be sought after from which those who there take refuge never more return to rebirth, for it is the Primeval Spirit from which floweth the never-ending stream of conditioned existence. Those who are free from pride of self and whose discrimination is perfected, who have prevailed over the fault of attachment to action, who are constantly employed in devotion to meditation upon the Supreme Spirit, who have renounced desire and are free from the influence of the opposites known as pleasure and pain, are undeluded, and proceed to that place which endureth forever. Neither the sun nor the moon nor the fire enlighteneth that place; from it there is no return; it is my supreme abode.

The Bhagavad-Gita, Ch. XV

CONTENTS

INTRODUCTION

Symbols are as old as thinking humanity. They are of such importance that H. P. Blavatsky, who first brought Theosophy to light in the modern world, devoted whole sections of her great work, *The Secret Doctrine*, to them. Part II of the first volume, dealing with cosmogenesis or the origin of the universe, consists of "The Evolution of Symbolism in its Approximate Order," and Part II of the second volume on anthropogenesis or the Theosophical understanding of human evolution, is "The Archaic Symbolism of the World-Religions."

H. P. Blavatsky agreed with Gerald Massey, the famous Egyptologist that "Mythology was a primitive mode of *thinking* the early thought.... Mythology is the repository of man's most ancient science ... when truly interpreted once more, it is destined to be the death of those false theologies to which it has unwittingly given birth." But she insistently added that "every symbol in papyrus or *olla* is a many-faced diamond, each of whose facets not merely bears several interpretations, but relates likewise to several sciences." Here 'primitive' does not mean 'crude' but rather, as originally the word indicated, 'early' or 'first, prime,' and 'science' has the broad meaning of coherent body of knowledge, broader than the restricted use of the word often found today.

Symbols are embedded in the myths of all nations and times, conditioning and guiding human perspectives on life and the world, enhancing self-understanding, and in general making sense of what lies within and beyond the capacity of rigidly defined concepts and even words to express. Theosophy teaches that each human being is on a long spiritual journey, a path that rises and falls as individuals act and react to situations presented by karma, passing through myriad lives as each soul works out its destiny. Symbols are and have always been crucial to that journey, in part because of their multi-faceted richness of meaning. In this sense, for any individual, a symbol has both an exoteric or public side and esoteric or hidden dimensions. What is exoteric is what an individual can understand at the moment when reflecting on the symbol. What is esoteric are all the levels and layers of meaning and spiritual nuance that are not yet clear to the individual. But what is obscure to one may be clear to another, and yet both may understand, use and meditate upon the same symbol in his or her own way. And symbols can even intimate that which lies beyond all understanding. Symbols are thus always invitations to broader, deeper understanding and awareness, and as such they nurture the spiritual intuition of the seeker. And all are seekers.

Dr. Raghavan Iyer launched the journal *Hermes* in 1975. Widely recognized by the world for his philosophical, ethical and political contributions to India, England and America, he imbued the creation of *Hermes* with a unique blend of erudition and spiritual insight. He envisaged an article in each monthly issue devoted to the elucidation of a symbol and invited Helen Valborg to undertake the long-term commitment to writing them. This she did, each month until 1989, when the journal ceased to be published.

At the beginning of each of these fifteen years, Professor Valborg created a list of possible symbols to be explored and, in consultation with Dr. Iyer, selected the twelve topics that would become the *Hermes* symbol articles for the year. Some are natural symbols, focusing on such things as the elements or animals. Some are based in mythology or religious and shamanistic systems. As an anthropologist, Professor Valborg brings to her investigation of symbols a broad cross-cultural approach and utilizes, along with ethnographic studies, a wide variety of resources from recent scientific research to historical documents and the literature and poetry of various traditions that often elucidate facets of symbolic interpretation.

These eclectic threads are woven into the fabric of Professor Valborg's writing, along with rich and multi-layered references found in theosophical writings. The weave has been created on a loom of analogy and correspondence, reflective of the author's own journey into the realm of symbolic correspondences between the intuitive and the empirical. The breadth of research evidenced in the twenty-eight articles in this volume encourages readers to make the connection between the physical and the metaphysical, the material and spiritual, in attempting to understand symbols and their use. Each is infused with hints and suggestions that reward the intuition of reflective readers, so that they may use these essays in their own spiritual journeys. May new readers find in them wisdom, truth and the inspiration to broaden their own modes of interpretation and understanding.

> Prof. Elton A. Hall
> Boise, Idaho
> October 2007

SHAMBALLA

Behind the ice walls of the Himalayas lie the empty deserts and remote mountains of Central Asia. There, blown clear of habitation by the harsh winds of high altitude, the plateau of Tibet extends north over thousands of square miles up to the Kunluns, a range of unexplored peaks longer than the Himalayas and nearly as high. Beyond its little-known valleys are two of the most barren deserts in the world: the Takla Makan and the Gobi. Farther north more ranges – the Pamir, the Tien Shan, the Altai, and numerous others – break the horizon until they give way to the great forests and open tundra of Siberia. Sparsely populated and cut off by geographic and political barriers, this vast region remains the most mysterious part of Asia, an empty immensity in which almost anything could be lost and waiting to be found.

Edwin Bernbaum

Wandering in a hidden valley beneath the snow-wrapped shoulders of Dhaulagiri, a lone hunter from the region of Dolpo hearkened to the echo of lamas chanting and the beating of drums. Tibetans tell the story of how this simple transient followed the sound of the music towards its source, which brought him to a doorway in a great cliff. Passing through it, he found himself in a beautiful valley adorned with verdant rice fields, villages and a gracious monastery. The people who lived in this valley were peaceful and happy, and they extended to the hunter a warm welcome, urging him to stay. He was delighted with their blissful existence but soon became anxious to go back to his own family and bring them to enjoy the beautiful valley. The residents there warned him that he would not be able to find the way back, but he was determined to leave. As he made his way out through the cliff door, he took the precaution of hanging his gun and his shoes beside the entrance to mark it. Confidently he went to fetch his wife and children, but when he returned to the hidden valley, he found the gun and shoes hanging in the middle of a blank rock wall.

1

It is not easy to find such places, but it is almost impossible to find them again. The hero of James Hilton's saga found the fabled Shangri-La only because he crashed whilst flying over the Great Snowy Range. He was not expecting to discover such a place, and it is difficult to know what peculiar combination of qualities he possessed that would have permitted him entrance into such a lost world. But he was imbued with that which enabled him to record with appreciation and awe the conditions that he found. He described the austere serenity of Shangri-La. "Its forsaken courts and pale pavilions shimmered in repose from which all the fret of existence had ebbed away, leaving a hush as if moments hardly dared to pass." A place out of time, it seemed, where timeless wisdom prevailed; such an aura of wisdom and peace is rarely and only dimly reflected in the world. When the High Lama there asked the hero if the Western world could offer anything in the least like Shangri-La, he answered with a smile: "Well, yes – to be quite frank it reminds me very slightly of Oxford." But of course one need not fly and come close to death in order to find Oxford, for despite its inspiring eminence, it is a child of the world and only points to greater visions of a pure and perfect land.

Who can find such a place? Many dream of going there, and old Tibetan records tell of long and difficult journeys undertaken by some who are vainglorious but successfully accomplished only by Adepts who have the eyes to see it. Having heard stories of a celestial temple atop a mountain in India, a British expedition in the nineteen thirties climbed the sacred peak and, having seen no golden temple, mentioned this to a holy man, who smiled and said, "No, you probably wouldn't have." As such places have been called the birthplace of the gods, it is small wonder that sceptical men would find it difficult to see them. The Greeks believed that only the gods and great heroes guided by Hermes could know Elysium and "only those mortals were translated thither who had come through a triple test in life". This was the Hyperborean land that answered to the pure land of Shamballa where, it is said, the Masters of the Snowy Range assemble every seven years. To find one's way into the presence of such beings must be difficult indeed, and yet many have wondered and dreamed and risked all they had in their efforts to discover the way.

How can anyone begin to find the way to Shamballa? In 1775 the Panchen Lama wrote a detailed guidebook inspired by the vivid experiences and instructions he had received in dreams. This *Shambhalai Lamyig* describes many ordeals and is considered by those who pursue these mysteries to be one of the main sources of information about the place and the journey to it. The other major sources are the *Kanjur* and *Tanjur*, a three-hundred volume set which is considered the sacred Tibetan Buddhist canon. These palm leaves contain the earliest known mention of Shamballa, the Pure Land whose name in Tibetan is *bde'byung* or 'Source of happiness'. The Buddhists say that the Pure Land is not a paradise but a land only for those who are on their way to nirvana. They believe that whoever reaches it or is reborn there can never fall back into a lower state and that it is the only pure land that exists on earth. The Pure Land Doctrine or *Sukhavati* teaches that a Bodhisattva may make a vow of compassion that after he has obtained supreme Buddhahood he will establish a Buddha-field wherein conditions will be conducive to enlightenment. *Sukhavati* is one of the names of the Buddha and is not nirvana itself but a symbol of it, and Japanese Buddhists assert that to be reborn there is to achieve enlightenment. Thus Shamballa is not an end in itself but rather an exalted stage leading to something even more incomprehensible beyond.

The Sanskrit *sham* (happiness) *bhal* (to give) has the same meaning as the Tibetan and this happiness is born of the shedding of illusions. Popular Tibetan tradition suggests that many who reach there are not immortal nor fully enlightened. They retain some of their illusions and failings, but they continually strive to become free of them as they move closer towards rebirth in that blissful place. The kings of Shamballa are enlightened and believed to be an incarnation of a Bodhisattva who is in essence a source of happiness. The Panchen Lama was a king there and will be reborn as such in the future as a channel through which the Buddha-state manifests in the world, as though that office was a reflection of an eternal truth which asserts itself cyclically in time. Just so do other centres appear and disappear like the seven sacred localities where the Kabiri created fire on the island of Samothrace. Such places are reflections of Shamballa which manifest, ripen and become forgotten by humanity. They remain in the world as islands or mountains, but their power is doubted and the aura of transcendence which hovers around their floating headlands and barren peaks is sensed only by the very few.

The most complex and sacred teaching of the Tibetans is the *Kalachakra* (Wheel of Time), which is known only to those initiated into its mysteries. Some have pointed out that in recent years the elaborate enactment of the rituals performed in the presence of uninitiated laymen amounts to a degradation of the teachings of the *Kalachakra* and to the idea of initiation itself. But High Lamas have pointed out that those simple peasants or Westerners who witness such proceedings are indeed initiated at a very rudimentary level. So great is the power of these teachings that even their symbolic ritual enactment is believed to bestow a gift of insight, although it is one which marks only the beginning of a course which will be more fully pursued by very few. It is said that just before his death and final entry into nirvana, the Buddha took the form of the Kalachakra deity and gave his highest mystical teachings to sages and gods. These teachings remained hidden in Shamballa for a thousand years until they appeared in Tibet around the tenth century or after the spread of Buddhism from India to Tibet. Since then they have become the subject of study of those who, like the Dalai Lama, spend their lives as transmitters of the Bodhisattvic source lying at the heart of the kingdom of Shamballa. Their arcane secrets about the final measurements of time and the mode of attaining liberation from the illusions of this world are like the guidebooks to Shamballa itself, difficult to locate and thrice difficult to follow. Like the Pure Land, they can only be found through a process of becoming.

The Greeks spoke of *Asteria*, the Island of Divine Kings, where the gods were born, and *Annwfn*, *Avalon* and *Elysium* are other names given by ancient races to that place which is the source of divinity and bliss. H.P. Blavatsky noted that all the *dwipas*, continents, *lokas*, globes and islands referred to in occult traditions are, in essence, the same as those 'Islands' or 'Lands' constantly referred to in mythology. Understanding mystical geography requires an intuitive and flexible application of the analogical approach involving a broad but imaginative perception of correspondences. One's understanding of time and space must be refined and rendered capable of reflecting the subtleties of patterns emanating from a Buddhic level of consciousness. Thus when anyone asks where Shamballa is, it is not easy to answer. There is a story which illustrates this difficulty in telling of a young man who set off on a quest to find it. He crossed many mountains and finally came to a hermit's cave, and when the hermit asked him where he was going across these wastes of snow, he replied, "To find Shamballa." "Ah well, then," said the hermit, "you need not travel far. The kingdom of Shamballa is in your heart."

> Now over the trackless snowy range I wend my lonely way to Bhota, elsewhere called Tibet, where Dharma's glorious sun pours forth His light and melts the cheerless snows of doubt and pain and sorrow vexing mortal men.
>
> Nineteenth Century Japanese Monk

The *Mahabharata* describes *Uttarakuru*, the land of enlightened Sages, as lying to the north of Mount Meru, although some say it is to be found in the Tarim Basin or in Siberia. Arjuna is described as travelling to Lake Manasasarova and then to Mount Kailas before crossing the Tibetan Plateau leading on to the Kunlun Mountains and Khotan. Some guidebooks place Shamballa far to the north of this, mentioning the polar regions and the North star. Chinese and Tibetan records identify it as the Sacred Island of Adepts which continues to exist in a place well known to them, whether the surrounding topography changes or not. The changes and flow of the earth's history are thus acknowledged, whilst at the same time the changeless nature of Shamballa is suggested.

> In the guidebooks the directions look easy, but when you try to follow them it's difficult: either you lose your way or you get covered with mist.
>
> *A Lama's Warning*

As in the story about the hunter who happened to be at the right place and the right moment to see the door in the cliff, René Daumal showed how the voyagers trying to find Mount Analogue had to wait and watch in the open sea for a mysterious channel to open up in the waves which, if breached at the precisely correct moment, would reveal the island mountain for a fleeting second and enable them to steer their ship in the right direction. The only people who could find it were those who had heard of it and who, despite the fact that it could be found on no map known to geographers or navigators, believed totally in its existence. Some have thought that Shamballa lies on the edge of physical reality as a bridge which connects this world to that which lies beyond it. But as the traveller draws near to it, the directions become increasingly mystical and difficult to correlate with the physical world. Most of the guidebooks establish a physical link between the ordinary world and that of Shamballa, and they start off from well known places like the caves of Ajanta and Ellora or the Hollow Hills of Celtic tradition. There is a physical entrance where people go from time to time and where, as so many traditions would have it, people disappear from ordinary sight. In the Tibetan view, however, the belief persists that everything conceivable could and probably does exist somewhere in the world, whether it has been seen or not. Most lamas firmly believe that Shamballa exists in this world and that the *Kalachakra* may be seen as a symbolic representation of it that can be used to spark the soul's memory rather than as a description of what the place actually looks like.

In *The Secret Doctrine*, Shamballa is said to be an 'island' which still exists as an oasis surrounded by the Gobi Desert, and that this is what is left of a vast inland sea which extended over much of Central Asia. Such an island is linked with each of the Root Races that preceded our own, which were compared by Siddhartha to Four Islands "which studded the ocean of birth and death". But does this mean that Shamballa exists on the physical plane? Is it merely a Utopia, which literally means 'no place', or does it have its roots on earth and its summit (or centre) in heaven, as is said of Mount Meru? If Shamballa is a community of mystics, it may be a secret society scattered around the world, or it may be found only in the heart, as the old hermit suggested. But the idea persists that there is a Shamballa and that it can be found by one who has the eyes to see it. Even so, as the old Tibetans warn: "If the time to go there has not come, everything, houses and all, will be covered by thickets and trees, and all will be of the nature of forest and grassland."

So powerful and tenacious is the idea of Shamballa that some political groups have used it to give a spiritually idealized focus to their otherwise worldly promises. Sukhe Bator, the founder of the modern Mongolian People's Republic, introduced a battle hymn to the simple herdsmen and nomads that he gathered into the mundane fold of twentieth century nationalism. Its refrain urged them: "Let us die in this war and be reborn as warriors of the King of Shamballa!"

The prophecy of Shamballa describes a situation similar to that of Ithaca in Homer's story of Odysseus. Both involve the idea of returning to the source and both places are threatened with barbarian invasion. This prophecy tells of the thirty-two kings that will rule in Shamballa and of the rise of brutal materialism in the world. It says that when the *dungans* have become more troublesome than ever, the Panchen Lama will be born as the son of the king of Shamballa. The *dungans* will lay waste to Tibet, and the people, following the Dalai Lama, will abandon their homeland to set off for Shamballa, where they will be received by the new king. The *dungans* will subdue Asia and Europe and will even try to invade Shamballa, but they will be defeated by the forces of the king and driven back into their own country. This great final battle represents a confrontation between the desire-ridden personality and the Higher Self, where the true 'king' extends his rule over the vestures of the outside world. But the details of the prophecy are so closely mirrored in the shadowy struggles of recent history that it cannot but remind one of the Tibetan world-view which assumes that everything conceivable probably exists in the world. The great battle between truth and ignorance rages at the gates of Shamballa as it does in the human heart, and whole nations and their armies simply galumph along hideously, acting it out on the gross physical plane.

Going home to Shamballa is like the 'journey to the East', to the birthplace of Apollo and Hermes. It is the home of the Sons of Will and Yoga who lived on as remnants of the Third Race, and all of the avatars of Vishnu are said to have sprung from its centre. In the Hindu tradition, *Kalki* will be the last of these avatars, and according to Tibetan calculations, he corresponds to Rudra Chakrin, the last king of Shamballa. Just as Rama possessed the aid of Hanuman in the Ramayana as he fought the barbarian demons, so the king will possess a General Hanumanda who will assist him in that final great battle foretold in the prophecy. The link between Vishnu and Shamballa is also forged in the mysterious teachings of time and cycles, which must be understood at some level in order even to enter upon the battleground. This is inextricably interwoven with the mystery of the Earth itself, who demonstrates these cycles in all her shifts and flows. It is said that at the beginning of human life, only the North Pole of the earth was motionless and dry. This island is a 'skull-cap' which prevails during the entire manvantara of our Round. It is the head of the mother from which pure waters flow, to become foul at her feet. When they return to her heart, they are once again purified, for her heart beats "under the sacred foot of Shamballa". This heart also lies beneath the Sea of Knowledge, which existed where the sands of the Gobi Desert now stretch in desolation and throw up miraged outlines of lost cities as though it were a graveyard yielding forth its ghosts.

The most secret aspects pertaining to the location of Shamballa and the path leading to it have never been conveyed in written form. Gradually these mysteries are revealed orally to those who pass through stages of initiation. The obstacles on the way are many and deadly in their potential to eliminate the seeker from the quest. The *Tanjur* says that "the water from the Mountains of Gold causes death, the water from the Mountains of Silver drives men mad, and the water from the other mountains brings sickness and the loss of skin and hair. But the seeker with the power of mantras will find the waters of these springs beneficial to drink." Even if one can bring about this extraordinary internal alchemy, the great snow mountain wall surrounding Shamballa acts as an inner barrier thrown up by the deeper levels of the mind to keep out the impurities of lower Manas. The peaks take on the wrath of demon guardians and inspire the overwhelming fear that the limitations of the mind might not be transcended. This must be seen through so that the Master within can carry one, soaring over their awesome height. There are many stories concerning the flight of Adepts to Shamballa. Most of them tell of a flight made possible by a wonderful horse, the symbolic nature of which represents the power of transcendence. It is this power which breaks through the bondage of the last doubt, and it is the only way possible to cross over the encircling ring of mountains which engulf an even higher range within. The journey is said to consist of dismaying setbacks long before these mountains are reached, but still some persist, moving ever closer as they catch the signs and omens and make fewer and fewer mistakes.

There are seductive maidens and sirens along the earlier parts of the way to Shamballa, and these must be avoided initially whilst the seeker slowly develops control of the centres of power within him. These are the Calypsos and Dakinis who, in their alluring or monstrous forms, have the ability to side-track a pilgrim indefinitely or to turn him into frozen stone. Thus in the efforts of Perseus to reach *Hyperborea*, the horrid threat of Medusa had to be overcome, but it was only when Odysseus and Perseus, as well as numerous other heroes, could control the negative side of these feminine energies that they could enlist their necessary aid in helping them to realize their goal. In this way, Perseus outwitted the Graiae sisters, who alone could give him the information he needed to slay Medusa. She guarded the edges of the world, the limits of reality that mark the beginning of the Hyperborean realm and paralysed the progress of any seeker who approached and knew not the secret of her nature. Such are the unconscious forces within man which can rise up unexpectedly and cripple him or blind him or even destroy him as he reaches closer within himself towards the goal.

Just as Hermes guides Perseus to *Hyperborea*, so a tutelary deity guides the pilgrim to Shamballa. One lama who had a succession of vivid dreams detailing the journey to Shamballa early on experienced the inability to proceed without a guide. Thus in his dream he sent forth a visualized yogi messenger with this request: "Take this message and go to my father in Shamballa. May my words of Truth, conquering the mountains of dualism, guide you along the way and help you to overcome the obstacles that lie before you." It is difficult to know here who is actually giving assistance to whom, but when one considers that the messenger is actually a counterpart of the lama's Higher Self, it begins to appear that the dialogue between Self and non-self can proceed to a very subtle and abstract level. But the way to Shamballa is dangerous, and the checking and waiting, the devotion and trust, all characteristic of the nature of the *Guruparampara* chain, are essential to getting there, perceiving the great gates and approaching the palace of the king.

The *Kalachakra* states clearly that perfect balance, coordination and a guide are required to follow this Path. And one may move along it, whilst fulfilling these requirements, at different rates of speed. One way of understanding this by analogy is to say that the Hinayana pilgrim shuns poison, the Mahayana pilgrim takes it in small doses to build up immunity, but the *Vajrayana* seeker drinks it neat, realizing that it is an illusion. In this way the *Vajrayana* follower attempts to control and make use of the passions and illusions that keep most people bound to the world of delusion. This is the Diamond Way, the shortest and most dangerous route to Shamballa, pursued only by the foolish or by persons of invincible courage and unwavering clarity of understanding. This mode places emphasis on the control of the vital airs (winds), which at the deeper level of interpretation refers to the *prajna-upaya* or the inseparable unity of wisdom and compassion which constitutes the essence of Enlightenment.

In the *Kalachakra* work *Vimalaprabha*, Tsong-Kha-Pa wrote that the Mahayana has two divisions: *prajnaparamita*, the 'causal' side, and the mantra or side of 'effects', which involves initiation in the *Kalachakra mandala*. These are like two wings of the Mahayana, both sides composing the Bodhisattva vehicle capable of soaring. Tsong-Kha-Pa wrote: "Holding the form of the void is the cause; the fruit is the adherence to incessant compassion. The indissoluble union of voidness (*sunyata*) and compassion (*karuna*) is called 'mind of enlightenment' (*Bodhichitta*). " To achieve this realization of and blending of the masculine and feminine sides, the *Tantra* called the *Vajrapanjara* teaches that: "If the void were the means (*upaya*), there would be no Buddhahood, because the effect would be no different from the cause." Contemplation of Voidness has been taught by the Buddhas to ward off the adherence to a lower self, but this must be joined to the awakening of the means in the *mandala* initiation so that the disciple may begin to realize within himself the thirty-two characteristics of the Master and the eighty minor marks of the Lord. In this way the means, or awakened powers, are under the tutelage of the Guide but can provide the energy necessary to complete the journey to Shamballa.

In the *Kalachakra* initiation the disciple stands at the eastern gate and is reborn into the *mandala*. He is purified with water and begins to merge, in stages, with the central deity. One is reminded that everything in a *mandala* exists in relation to its centre. The passage through different dimensions symbolized by a series of concentric circles and squares has meaning only in its movement towards the centre. Each circle represents a stage of initiation, a level of consciousness, and the initiated identifies completely with each part of the *mandala* pattern as he advances. Finally, "when the yogi identifies himself with the deity of the central syllable, the features that issue from it come to symbolize the hidden parts of his mind. The *mandala* spreads his inner world out before him where he can recognize and become aware of it." Such a person then synthesizes these elements back into the centre, awakening a flow of awareness and energy within himself.

The gates of Shamballa in the *Kalachakra mandala* face the cardinal points. The eastern gate represents *shraddha* (faith) which is preliminary to all the rest. The southern gate is *virya* (the four right eliminations or strivings). The western gate is that of *dharma-pravicaya* (mindfulness generated by knowledge of the doctrine and the four bases of magical power). The northern gate represents samadhi (control of the five faculties and powers). As one moves through these gates, the Diamond Line (or turning of the wheel by the power of mantra) awakens soul recollection and strengthens the practice of *dharma*. At each stage all of the ornaments represent collections of virtues enabling a closer approach to the central palace, which symbolizes knowledge and the erection of an edifice of consciousness. All of the myriad details in the *mandala* pattern can be interpreted as orifices, organs and chakras within the human body, every one of which is the seat of passion and illusion or potentially alchemized energy.

Like a lotus opening, the *mandala* of Shamballa symbolizes the macrocosmic and microcosmic, the awareness of power and the power itself. In an exoteric interpretation it represents the cosmology of the universe whilst teaching the mysteries of time, astrology, mathematics and the cyclic pattern of forces. From a more esoteric point of view it demonstrates the flow of the masculine cause and feminine effect merged in an active realization of balance. The passage of time becomes identical with the flow of energy in the body. At its highest level this leads to the unification of wisdom and compassion and the potential to create, at some level, a Buddha-field. Having transcended the fear of losing himself, the disciple discovers a gem-like awareness in the depths of his mind. The ego becomes a transparent window transforming the view of the world, enabling a glimpse of the Pure Land that looms ahead. As one approaches closer to the goal, the eight noble pathways leading to the lotus centre increasingly converge into the disciple's consciousness. Like psychic channels, they merge into a powerful basis for Buddhic wisdom and the horse and the rider become as one, soaring over the last obstacles to the Sacred Isle where the deer is ever safe.

In Tibetan tradition it is said that the Water Eye can see the world, but the Flesh Eye only a distance of eighteen days' walk. The God Eye reveals hidden things and places, like the door in the cliff, whilst the Wisdom Eye penetrates to the core of things and is capable of opening the Buddha Eye that can discern the ultimate reality. Before the pilgrim can find the beginning of the way to Shamballa, he must be filled with the light of the God Eye. At the end of the great journey, the gates, the palace and even the king may merge as a drop into the Great Void, but the idea, the *mandala*, the raft, cannot be abandoned until the island shore is reached. Like a window on the edge of the world, the glorious and serene kingdom of Shamballa waits. Veiled in mists and hidden beyond all the snowy ranges with their precipitous passes and laboured chasms, it looms and waits for those who have the eyes to see it. The door in the blank cliff wall, the opening in the mind, offer themselves only for a moment. Grasp that moment and move onwards.

> The way appears but fleetingly,
> The vision lasts not long.
> But lifetimes lived in time
> Are as ashes to this flame.
> O dreamed of Shamballa,
> I come to thy Pure Land.

Hermes, November 1981

THE TETRAKTYS

Pythagoras establishes Unity as the principle of all things and said that from this Vnity sprang an indefinite Duality. The essence of this Unity, and the manner in which the Duality that emanated from it was finally brought back again, were the most profound mysteries of his doctrine; the subject was sacred to the faith of his disciples and the fundamental points were forbidden them to reveal.

Fabre d'Olivet

The golden light of the candles blurred into incense-laden shadows which thickened in the corners of the small village church. The walls displayed the flickering images of saints whose bodies oozed dampness from the sodden earth outside. Their sad eyes gazed from the gloom, their faces boldly Hellenic with narrowed noses and arching brows. Only their pose lacked the distinctive fluidity of pagan heroes and sages. Muted thus, and obscured by the shadows and soot, they witnessed the re-enactment of an ancient ritual laden with arcane symbolism and mystery. An old priest with tangled grey hair knotted behind his decorated crown stood before a low square altar hewn from the native rock and bedecked with hierophanies displayed for the occasion. To his left and his right in front of him stood a bride and a groom, their bowed heads crowned with wreaths of white satin ribbon and flowers. The mended and altered gown of the young bride was darkened at the seams with the yellowing of a previous generation, but the fresh flowers of her crown reflected the soft glow of the candle. It shone in response to its companion which encircled the buoyant locks of the groom's unruly hair. Behind them stood a row of witnesses in a horizontal line of maids and men. They created a threshold separating the actors of the ritual mystery and the gathered crowd, which stood in dusky silence, transfixed by the illuminated scene.

In a small darkened dome of the church, the Angel Gabriel looked down upon them. His practised eyes, gazing from the orbs of a peeling fresco, traced the lines of the pattern below him. The old priest was the apex of a triangle that stood before the square. The hierophanies, arranged in a mystic triad upon the altar, marked its prototype and the line of witnesses formed its base. The bride and groom stood at the left and right angles of the triangle, and a radiant satin ribbon connecting their crowns strengthened the suggestion of their union. As the apex of the triad, the old priest acted as a solitary liaison between the altar and the couple. Only he understood the use of the sacred objects and the names that would enliven their power. Only he could make the gestures that would transmit their spiritually unified essence in the unification of the man and woman before him. Old and grizzled as he was, his heart was filled with the sanctity of this responsibility, and his gnarled hands imparted faithfully the blessing from on high. Smiling, Angel Gabriel saw the hidden current of light flow through the humble priest and unite the simple pair. He knew that from their merger another triad would be born, another division and union in an endless chain of such, and he laughed as he withdrew. The crowds below sighed and, at the completion of the ritual, mingled and mused upon former weddings and those yet to come. They wept in recalling and comparing notes on dowries and bride-wealth. They gossiped and speculated upon the prospects of the newly-weds and basked unconsciously in the luminousness of the magic that had just taken place.

Simple villagers that they were, how could they know that millennia before their time the ancients, perhaps even some of their own Greek ancestors, had openly recognized this magic in an oath taken by disciples of Pythagoras. Being unfamiliar with such mysteries and sensing their presence only through an intuitive understanding of recurring patterns in nature, they did not realize the significance of the triad and the square. They glimpsed the beauty of spiritual transmission through union but could not grasp the immensity of the pattern nor its noumenal source. If in a dream an ancient ancestor came to them and spoke that sacred oath, their soul's memory might be aroused, but would they recognize the symbol of the Tetraktys? Would they know that it had been represented in their humble village church?

> By Him who gave to our Soul the Tetraktys
> Which hath the fountain and root
> Of ever-springing Nature.

The real significance of the Tetraktys is suggested in the portion of the Pythagorean Oath which describes it as containing "the fountain and root of ever-springing Nature". It is not merely symbolic of static relations, such as might be imagined to exist between priest and bride and groom, but enshrines the cosmogonical movement of life "evolving out of primal unity, the harmonized structure of the whole". In this way it is a fountain of ever-flowing life. It is also the measure of all things. The One becomes the many without losing its essential Unity, expressed in a bond of proportion running through manifestation. Porphyry tells us how followers of Pythagoras swore by the Tetraktys given by their Teacher as a symbol applicable to the solution of problems in nature. They believed that the nature of all things could be grasped through the decad as expressed in the symbol of the Tetraktys. They asserted that it would be impossible for the orderly and universal distribution of things to subsist without it. Resulting from an infinite series of quaternaries was a world geometrically, harmonically and arithmetically arranged, containing the entire range of number, magnitude and form. The Pythagoreans thus used an Oath with a key which applied to the assimilation of all things into number.

One of the epithets used to describe the Tetraktys was 'key-bearer of Nature1. As the wise Platonist Thomas Taylor observed: "It is a God after another manner than the Triad, because in the triad the first perfect is beheld, but in the tetrad all mundane natures are comprehended according to the causality principle. From its all-comprehending nature likewise, it is a manifold, or rather, every divinity. As, too, it causally contains all mundane natures, it may very properly be called the fountain of natural effects. Because likewise it opens and shuts the recesses of generation, it is denominated, as the anonymous author observes, the key-bearer of Nature, as is also the mother of the Gods, who is represented with a key." Opening and shutting the recesses of generation, the Tetraktys stands like the altar before the bridal couple, containing all the potential effects which will manifest partially and idiosyncratically in the microcosmic process of meiosis resulting from their union.

It is said that the One, by Itself, does not "exist". Only when It is united with the Monad and duad is Being produced. The One is No-number. It is the primary, undifferentiated soul of the universe, and numbers arise from it by a process of 'separating out', not as a collection of units built up by addition, but as minor souls, each possessing a distinct nature with certain mystical properties. The interblending of these distinct natures produces infinitely complex harmonies distinguished by the Greeks as replicating tetrachords consisting of three intervals and four sounds. They believed that the multiplex expression of these conveyed the music of stars and planets, and ultimately every expression of the replicating duad. The Pythagorean School, pursuing lines of thought akin to the teachings of Orpheus, considered the problem of the One and the many in terms of 'the Fall' of the human soul from the One. In myth it was said that the reign of Aphrodite, the Age of Love, was a state of bliss whose end was heralded by the Great Oath of the gods (the Tetraktys). Putting "trust in strife", certain daemons were then banished by the gods and caused to mix, as a cross within a circle, the two streams of love and strife.

Love and strife – the Higher in the lower. Surely this is what awaits the rustic bride and groom. They bask for a moment beneath the reign of Aphrodite, whilst the greater part of their life involves the struggle to keep body and soul together and in harmony. But in the sacred moment of their union, the united ray of their Higher Self illuminates their vestures and empowers them with the ultimate creativity of their inner nature. The primary maxim of the Delphic Oracle was "Know Thyself", and Iamblichus tells us that the most difficult question posed by Pythagoras to his pupils required them to understand the Delphic Oracle as the Tetraktys. In terms of 'the Fall', one can grasp the idea of the Self enveloped in the strife of the lower vestures, but the Self that is to be 'known' is the Oath or Word itself, which initiates the strife inherent in the duad and its endless progeny.

The duad doubled is four, or the tetrad, which when doubled or unfolded, is the hebdomad. Thus four retorted into itself results in the first cube, which is a fertile number. Philo Judaeus pointed out that four is the virgin number related to the sacred Tetraktys, whereas the seventh power of any number is a square and a cube. This potential fertility is expressed again in terms of 'the Son' of the immaculate Celestial Virgin, who, born on earth, becomes humanity. The triad becomes the Tetraktys, the Perfect Square and six (seven)-faced cube on earth. Though tracing this unfoldment from the plane of the abstract to the particular is difficult, students of Pythagoras began by identifying two basic quaternaries: one through addition (of the first four numbers) and a second through multiplication (of even and odd numbers starting from Unity). Odd numbers, symbolizing the limit and formal principle of universe, were set along one side of a triangle (3 - 9 - 27), whilst even numbers, or those which represented the tendency to divide according to their own nature, were arranged along the other side (2 - 4 - 8). In this way, by virtue of the numbers from this Tetraktys, growth proceeds from the point to the line, to the surface and the solid cube. It is these numbers which, in the *Timaeus*, Plato identifies with the human soul.

There is a third Tetraktys which takes its point from the second and has the property of constituting any curved or plane magnitude through point, line, surface and solid. The fourth Tetraktys is comprised of the elements – fire, air, water and earth; the fifth is the pyramid, octahedron, icosahedron and cube; whilst the sixth involves the seed (point), growth (line), the quality of width (surface) and that of thickness (solid). According to Theon of Smyrna, the seventh Tetraktys is composed of man, family, village and city; the eighth of thought, science, opinion and feeling (parallel to Plato's Divided Line); the ninth of the four faculties of judgement; the tenth of the four seasons; and the eleventh of the four ages of man. From above below, each of these descending levels of the Tetraktys unfolds through odd and even (male and female) pairs in a process of multiplication that is ever true to the principles laid down by the first Tetraktys.

As Creator, the Tetraktys is the divine numerical series of one to four. In this sense numbers are gods. "But", asked Hierocles, "how does 'God' come to be four?" We are told that Unity, the Absolute One, possesses within it the potential aspect of Absolute Motion which, radiating as the Great Breath, manifests the duad, the doubling of Unity. This, accompanied by Infinite Space-Matter, comprises three, which is the first number having a beginning, middle and end, thus expressing multitude. From this springs Fohat, the number four which is sacred to Hermes and to the Oath of the gods. This four is expressed in the four syllables (one hidden) of the AUM. It is said that when the Ain-Soph manifested Itself in the First Logos, the latter uttered the first word of his name, a syllable of four letters. This was followed by second, third and fourth syllables which intoned the number of Deity manifested. One added to two, added to three, added to four, equals ten or the figured representation of ten as a triangular number. Four and ten were the numbers of divinities to the Pythagoreans. In The Sale of Philosophers Lucian represents Pythagoras as asking a prospective buyer to count. When he had counted to four, the philosopher interrupted, "Lo! what thou thinkest four is ten, and a perfect triangle, and our Oath." Perhaps it is for this reason that the triangular-shaped) (delta) is the fourth letter of the Greek alphabet, for the delta represents the issuing forth of the river of life which proceeds from the Monad till it arrives at the divine Tetrad, the mother of all things; the boundary is the sacred Decad.

In Plato's dialogue of his name, Timaeus, a Pythagorean from the Italian city of Locri, speaks of the Tetraktys as a double four (an odd and even series of numbers) forming the cosmic psyche. These were produced by the Dyad (identified with Rhea or Isis) or the flow of the universe involving matter in a constant state of flux. It was held that the Tetraktys "completed the process of fluxion whereby physical objects are produced from points, lines, surfaces and solids". In this process the Dyad produces even numbers by multiplication and odd numbers by functions of limit, which acts to stop, equalize and stabilize the propensity of the Dyad to multiply. Pythagoras, in placing even and odd sequences on either side of the Tetraktys, revealed his awareness of this necessary interaction even in the construction of the World Soul.

Between two square numbers there is one mean proportional number. This odd third number acts as the 'lock' or binder between what may be called the building blocks of the universe. This role cannot be played by even numbers which, when they are divided, are empty in the centre and therefore weak. Thus, in the building of the square, the odd number is always master. It moves beyond the Dyad to the three and the four and, eventually, the cube. The Dyad contains the One from which issues the Three (the Three-in-One). Put in a slightly different way, "Matter is the vehicle for the manifestation of soul on this plane of existence, and soul is the vehicle on a higher plane for the manifestation of spirit, and these three are a trinity synthesized by Life which pervades them all," From *Parabrahm* the Three-in-One issues forth. It is the Tetraktys (the Three and One) from which radiates the One in many – the Dhyani Buddhas. It is the Four-Faced Brahmā, the *Chaturmukha* (the perfect cube) "forming itself within and from the infinite circle". Brahmā is thus *Hiranyagarbha, Hari* and *Shankara*, or the Three Hypostases of the manifesting Spirit of the Supreme Spirit – the one plus three which equals four. The Greeks identified this Tetrad as the first manifest deity, and Orpheus said that all of the intellectual orders of gods were "astonished on surveying this deity unfold himself into light from mystic and ineffable silence".

The one macrocosm is eternally hidden in the Absolute. The entire universe is a "microcosmic projection of that one and only macrocosmos". Every microcosmic reflection follows its parent – projecting itself and becoming the macrocosmos to its offspring. The Ray from the Concealed Deity falls into primordial cosmic matter, resulting in the Divine Androgyne or First Logos, which, projecting further, becomes the Second Logos or Tetraktys. From *Parabrahm, Mulaprakriti* emerges as the basis of objective evolution and cosmogenesis. Projecting forth, the First Spiritual Logos provides the basis of the subjective side of manifest being and the source of all individual consciousness. This highest Logos is expressed through Force, which is transformed into the energy of the supra-conscious Logoic thought, which is infused into objectivization. This Primal Impress defines the laws of matter, which are synthesized in the Second Logos or Tetraktys. In its universal form and idea the three become four, but still the Tetraktys is the formless square giving forth only the idea of universal order.

In this one can see the results of the first creation depicted in the *Linga Purana* as *Mahat-Tattwa*, in that it is primordial self-evolution of that which had to become   (Divine Mind – the Spirit of the Universal Soul or *Maha Buddhi*). The intelligible world proceeds out of the Divine Mind as the Tetraktys reflects upon its own essence and on its beginning. Once one, twice two, and a tetrad arises. At its top is the essence of Light which illuminates the world of Deity without burning. Its base becomes the square platform of a pyramid, rooted in the world. Looked at once again, this mystery is that of the double Tetraktys: the Higher and the lower. The Higher or Macroprosopus is the Absolute Perfect Square within the circle 'Pass-Not'. The lower Microprosopus is the manifest Logos who passes through the circle and becomes the triangle in the square which is sevenfold – the square which is a cube, which unfolds and becomes the cross of flesh.

The Higher Tetraktys, whilst containing the noumenon of the potential square, is yet in essence the Triad out of which the Tetrad emerges. *The Secret Doctrine* describes how the point that appears in the circle emanates the first three points, connects them with lines and thus forms the noumenal basis of the second Triad of the manifest world before retiring into the silent depths of the circle. Thus the one contains three which, together, possess the potential quaternary. The emanation from the three points is the Monadic reflection in the phenomenal world of its invisible Logoic parent. It is this Monad which then becomes the 'parent' apex of the lower triad, the mother and son composing its lower angles. At the baseline they are unified on the universal plane of phenomenal, productive nature, just as they were unified in essence at the apex in the causal realm. By the same mystic transmutation which is mirrored in the marriage of the bride and groom, they – triune – become the Tetraktys.

Plato called the Higher Triad 'Intellectual' and compared it to its lower intelligible counterpart. The Tetraktys, it is said "subsists at the extremity of the intelligible triad. . . . And between these two triads (the double triangle) . . . another order of gods exists which partakes of both extremes". The key idea here is that the Tetraktys 'subsists', which is to say, 'is kept in life', at the apex of the lower triad as the Monadic soul of mankind expressed as the One in the many. In its synthesis it bears the potential qualities of the Dhyani Buddhas or gods of "another order" and is the Higher Tetraktys. Expressed in the phenomenal world, it becomes the Seven Dhyanis out of whom issue the scintillas or souls in the form of Monads, atoms and gods.

The Ray of the Higher Triad falls, and from its point a lower triad emanates. But even as this is resulting in phenomenal expressions, the lower triad has become inverted, pointing away from the triangle above. This is the downward-pointing triad of Vishnu, who is called *Bhutesa*, 'Lord of the Elements and All Things', and *Viswarupa*, 'Universal Substance or Soul'. This second creation proceeds along the triple aspect of *ahankara*, 'I-am-ness', which first issues from Mahat. This *ahankara* is first pure, then passionate and finally rudimental. When this last occurs, the second hierarchy of Dhyan Chohans appears – the Seven Rishis who are the origin of form. The down ward-pointing triad thus contains the reflected point of the Logoic Ray and so it is shown as overlapping and being overlapped by the up ward-pointing triangle which contains the essence of the same Logoic point. This is the symbol of the interlaced triangles called the six-pointed star, which powerfully illustrates the dynamic relationship between Vishnu and Shiva, or Hari and Shankara, within the golden circle of Hiranyagarbha. In the centre of the upward- and downward-pointing triads is the six (hexagon) and one (point) or seven, which is man. One of the Masters of Wisdom has said that "The two interlacing triangles are the *Buddhangams* of creation. They contain the 'squaring of the circle', the 'philosophical stone', the great problems of Life and Death, and the mystery of evil."

The Tetraktys is thus the three made four and the four made three. Put very simply, the upper Triad emanates the Quaternary (symbolizing by itself the sexless 'Heavenly Man') which becomes a septenary by emanating from itself the three principles of the lower nature, thus forming the Decad or total Unity of the universe. One can see this as separate units of 3, 4 and 3, but in trying to understand the Tetraktys, it is important to remember that the Triad of the Inner Man is the Three Hypostases of Atman, and Its contact with Nature and man is the Fourth, which makes it a Tetraktys or the Highest Self. The upper and lower triads are not separate, but their very existence on the heavenly and terrestrial planes is made possible by the connecting Monadic 'link', which makes in turn a quaternary out of either and carries forth the principle of Unity into generation. This is connected with the squaring of the circle, for this greatest of all mysteries takes place at the edge of the 'Ring Pass-Not' as it does within the Golden Egg of Brahmā and within every egg made fertile on the worldly plane. The key to understanding the squaring of the circle is concealed in the androgynous nature of the Logos, whose Ray becomes the Tetraktys in man. He who is fully informed by this is an Adept, a Master-magician incarnate.

Pythagoras, knowing these mysteries and being such an Adept, attempted to act as a Demiurge, informing those around him who desired to open their minds and hearts to the Higher. That this is a difficult task was borne out by the hostility his efforts aroused in many. But he was wise in the ways of both worlds, and he united in a marriage which produced an offspring, who later (at the death of her father), like a ray projected from the familial triad, went out into the world safeguarding the precious truths that had been entrusted to her. Brave and true, Theona was the indispensable keeper of the flame and embodiment of the Sacred Oath. The sweet bride standing in the dimly lit church does not possess her wisdom and courage, but she is conscious of its spiritual presence hovering over her, symbolically emanating from the altar through the priest and uniting her to the rustic lad by her side. In her simple fashion, she dreams that her son will be a prince amongst men, a gifted and gentle person, and maybe one through whom the Demiurgos speaks in noble accents.

> The Divine Tetraktys was esteemed
> By wise men who beheld in dreams
> Its emanation from the Three-in-One.
> And since the Inner Man of all
> Basks in Its Monadic light,
> Even the lesser dream bears
> The impress of its sacred projection.

Hermes, March 1982

THE ALTAR

I ask thee of the earth's extremest limit,
*   where is the centre of the world, I ask thee.*
I ask thee of the Stallion's seed prolific,
I ask of highest heaven where Speech abideth.
This altar is the earth's extremest limit;
*   this sacrifice of ours is the world's centre.*
The Stallion's seed prolific is the Soma;
*   this Brahman highest heaven where Speech abideth.*

Rig Veda I: CLXIV: 34–35

The great southern gate of Pergamon rises up like a brazen shield carved into walls whose foundations are massive cliffs falling away to hot and dusty plains. No foliage softens their imperious profile, no gentle breeze cools their heated flanks. Before the eyes of the traveller white rocks and barren walls pulsate in the vibrations of summer heat. They glare and invade his consciousness with their irradiating and seemingly weightless mass. Like the land all around him, he is parched and moves painstakingly upwards along the path to the great door. He moves his hand quickly from its metal handle, which burns him as he revolves the smaller pedestrian entrance inward and steps into a broad stone courtyard. On three sides the walls loom and towers cast a darkened shadow across the gleaming flagstones beneath his feet. Overbrooding the promontory entrance-way to Pergamon, they also look down upon a fountain where travellers may refresh themselves and wash away the heat and dust. Rested and cooled, the traveller emerges from the courtyard and ascends the broad stairs leading to the expansive lower *agora* which separates the House of Consul from several gymnasiums and from the temples and treasure-houses of the lower acropolis. His eyes rest thoughtfully upon the Doric columns of the temple of Athena, and they delight in the graceful Ionic symmetry of Demeter's abode.

He muses, thinking of the ancient Thracians and Phrygians whose artistic genius and sense of the dramatic had been matched with a keen awareness of the military strength afforded by the rocky outcrop upon which the city was built. He was aware that Lydians, Macedonians and Greeks had all been drawn to this kingly seat and had each left their architectural stamp upon the temples and altars and public houses. He knew also that they had been drawn to more than the seat of worldly power, for the land of the Pergamenes was known to have been sacred to the Kabiri of old, whose Mysteries were celebrated here. He knew all of this and yet none of his patiently acquired knowledge could prepare him for his first glimpse of the Great Altar that rose upon the terraced slope above the upper *agora* of Pergamon.

It stood in the centre of a platform paved with marble, its forty-foot height supportive of the most complete representation of the Greek pantheon ever sculpted in one place. Atop the crowning entablature, which extended out to two wings on either side of the great central steps, were twelve magnificent life-sized figures of gods and goddesses. The weary traveller was flooded with awe, for he recognized in their exquisite forms craftsmanship that matched the finest sculpture of Praxiteles of Athens or Myron of Thebes. His wonder increased as his eyes moved more carefully, taking in the design of the structure and its artistic details. He realized that the structure was at least one hundred feet deep and well over one hundred feet wide. Twenty-five steps, each seventy-five feet wide, were cut into the huge podium to a thirty-foot depth so that the wings continued to protrude on the sides whilst one mounted to the central platform and Ionic colonnade. As he ascended, he found himself at the base of the podium of the altar, which rose to the height of three or four men above him and included a crepidoma of five steps supporting a base ornamented with a cornice. Above this was another moulding serving as a frame for the most magnificent frieze he had ever beheld.

He, a traveller, who had lived in many lands and fought wars alongside Lydians, Persians and Greeks, gazed in astonishment at the great entablature which adorned all sides of the enormous altar. All the gods, giants and monsters of the three worlds were depicted, locked in myriad expressions of the legendary Gigantomachy, the Great War in Heaven between the kindred and followers of Zeus and the Titans of a previous age. On the eastern side he identified the rising Olympians carved in faithful detail, their valiant expressions matched by their frightening arms. On the western side various divinities of land and sea joined in the struggle, whilst the Titans were banished to the south. Moving slowly around the great altar, his eyes lingered over every agonized and victorious expression while his steps paced off close to four hundred and fifty feet. Numerous serpents adorned the bottom of the frieze, coiling through the powerful movements of death, triumph and immortality. Whilst he stood engulfed in the grandeur of the entire structure, the Mysteries of the Kabiri unfolded before him. He felt himself swept up the altar steps to the place of sacrifice, where a great fire was being prepared. Kneeling before the flames, he felt his heart rise within him and fly up through the battlefield of the gods. Like smoke, he drifted and smouldered, he fought on every side. And like a spark which escapes into a rarer atmosphere, he transcended the struggle, finding himself in a realm of timeless quietude where flame and smoke, spark and essence of fire, were one.

There is, in the altar, a sense of Divine Presence which promises reunion and integration with the Deity. Written on a set of sixteenth-century English altar rails, the words "I will wash mine hands in innocency so will I compasse Thine altar O Lord. Create in me a clean heart O God and renew a right spirit within me" expresses this well. God is present as a witness in the altar. It is the point wherein meet the worshipper and that which is worshipped. In most traditions, offerings and sacrifices are presented on the altar in supplication, recognition and sometimes in thanksgiving to God. But an altar may be raised to receive a god, as in ancient China, where they were built by certain emperors along the banks of the Lo and Ho rivers. Gods would appear in the form of glorious green or yellow dragons, who would ascend the altars and display divine instructions for the kingdom, written in figures upon their backs. In temples, cathedrals and churches, altars are usually placed at the east end of the structure, before the rising sun, and they are often raised above the level of the sanctuary by a symbolic number of steps. In the Christian church the rise of one step usually marks the separation between the choir and the sanctuary, whilst the altar itself is commonly approached by three steps.

Altars are the meeting-point with Deity, but they are not necessarily confined to one sanctified spot. In the worship of Ishtar, small movable prayer-altars were used by individual worshippers in ancient Canaanite shrines, whilst an example of what must be the most portable altar in the world may be found in the American Indian Sacred Pipe. Super-altars are used in Christian rituals when they are placed upon already consecrated high altars for special festivals, whilst some lesser side altars, like the Vedic *dhisnyas*, were merely heaps of earth covered with sand on which the smaller fires were placed. Easily moved, built and destroyed, these altars were, nevertheless, focal points for sacred communion. Their varied shape does not detract from the shared theme of their function, and it may be, as some historians have suggested, that the earliest altars were pillars or movable idol-images of deities. The Hebrew *masseba* might answer to this, and Semitic people engaged in blood sacrifice would attempt to bring the blood into direct contact with the deity by daubing it on the cairn or image believed to be the dwelling place of the god. Sailors of the ancient Mediterranean world used to perform the old fireless sacrifice at the feet of the brazen pillars of Herakles at Gades, believing that their prayers were conveyed through the pillars directly to the god.

Whatever its form, at the altar the deity is witness, and so countless men have stood, like young Cyrus and the Persian nobleman Orontas before the Lydian altar of Artemis, and sworn an oath of friendship. Xenophon and his Ten Thousand passed by here long after this took place and mourned the loss of friends in war. But the power of Lydian altars was renowned, and later still, Pausanias observed that "the Lydians, who are called Persians, have religious precincts in the city of Hierocoesareia at Hypaepa. Within each sanctuary there is a building and in the building there is an altar with ashes atop. But the colour of the ashes is not normal. When the priest has entered the building and heaped up dry wood on the altar, he first puts a diadem on his head and then chants foreign incantations, incomprehensible to Greeks, to some god or other, reciting from a book. It is required that the wood be kindled without fire, and that the bright flame gleam from the logs."

> The great world's altar stairs
> That slope through darkness up to God.

> Alfred, Lord Tennyson

People dedicate altars to a god because they have received assistance, but gods have indicated their holy places to men in myriad ways. Lord Shiva, pursuing the capricious Vishnu in feminine disguise, is said to have scattered his semen as he ran through Aryavarta. Wherever the precious fluid fell, a *lingam* arose as a place of worship, and men, in wonderment, erected beautiful temples where pilgrims still come to venerate the highest life-giving power in the universe made manifest. The *lingam* is part of the altar where they place their offerings of flowers, and the *yoni* at its base is the vessel of sacrifice which holds the Logoic flame.

In the Pawnee creation myth, Tirawa, the Chief of Heaven, and Atira, his spouse and Sky Vault, overbrooded the birth of a son to the Sun and Moon and a daughter to the Morning and Evening Star. With the formation of the earth by the elemental gods, these children were placed upon its surface and bidden to awake. To them was born a son, and they realized that they would have to labour to care for him. To aid them in this, they were instructed and given the first lodge and its altar, as well as the fire to burn and the power to speak in prayer. Such a gift was the buffalo head, used as an altar in the Cheyenne Sun Dance, and the Dakota Sacred Pipe given by White Buffalo Cow Woman. These divine gifts provide a contrast to the notion of the Altar of the Earth erected at the Temple of Heaven in ancient China. Here the altar was identified with the throne upon which the emperor as Son of Heaven would personally intercede with the gods on behalf of his people.

This is similar to the Christian idea that the altar was the earthly representative of the throne of God. To the right of it was the place of honour because God had said, "Sit thou on my right hand." The gospel is supposed to be read on this side and the epitaph of Christ is kept there. In both these examples, the altar is made by man to represent something identified with Deity instead of being, in themselves, gifts of God. Perhaps the concept of the altar as a tomb illustrates a mixture of these ideas, for it combines the notion of God's gift to the world with sacrifice and intercession. Indeed, many altars are in the shape of a tomb or sarcophagus, like those of the martyrs placed by their Christian brethren in recesses in the catacombs of Rome. Secreted under arched canopies hewn out of the rock by burial teams, the faithful prayed at such altars, hoping that the spirit of the martyrs buried within the sarcophagi would intercede with God on their behalf and give them strength to endure their own persecution. Thus, the spirit of God enters the world, is martyred and entombed before it is released to join its Father in Heaven. Men worshipping at the altar-tomb are attempting to receive this spirit and merge their being with it as it is merged with its source.

Another powerful symbolic interpretation of the altar lies in its identification with a table upon which a meal is spread for God. The Mayans constructed their altars so that the sun would descend upon their tops at midday in order to consume the sacrifice. Thus, they said, the fires arose at noon and things of this earth were transported to heaven. The Egyptian hieroglyph for altar was 🕎 or *hetep*, which means both 'altar' and 'offering'. They believed that the altar possessed the power of transmuting the offerings laid upon it and turning them into spiritual entities of such a nature that they became suitable food for the god Osiris and his spirits. This belief is very old and widespread in the world, as can be witnessed by the common ritual of offering food to the household god as well as the many first-fruit ceremonies where the first and best of the harvest is placed upon an altar table dedicated to the deity. Early Christian altars were often referred to as 'Christ's Board' in remembrance of the communion table laid out for Jesus and his disciples at the Last Supper. For this reason the Eastern Orthodox Church continues to use the wooden table form for its altars to this day.

In the rest of the Christian world wooden altars were gradually replaced by heavier ones of stone, some of which resembled a tomb, some a communion table. For the most part, the stone slab tops were very plain and were commonly marked with five crosses at the corners and the centre. These symbolize the five wounds of Christ, and at the consecration of the altar a little fire is made at each one of them and they are smeared with sanctified oil. Though the bareness of the altar signifies penitence, an amazing array of ecclesiastical service has become standard accompaniment to altar ritual. Chalices, patens, cruets, pyxes, censers, chrismatories, crosses and candles are all used in conjunction with cloths and varying coloured frontals which change with the liturgical season. As the altar became more loaded, it increased in size until the whole church treasury could be displayed on festal days. The pomp and ceremony of such rituals easily obscured the idea of sacrifice, and for many Christians the brocade frontal of the royal throne became much more interesting than the linen altar cloth which represented the shroud of Christ.

In Chinese as well as Hebrew and Christian altars, there was often a cavity in which relics were placed before being sealed with an inset of stone. In many traditions it is believed that there is contagious power in the remains of saintly people, and the consolidation of that power within an altar has been conceived of as beneficial to the communion with God. The more numerous the relics, the greater the benefit. One descriptive parchment enclosed within an early English altar informs us that on December 7, 1214, the altar was dedicated to the honour of St. John the Baptist and that the relics placed therein were numerous indeed. They included portions of the vestures of Christ and the Virgin Mary, the bones of John the Baptist, St. Peter and St. Paul, some blood of St. Stephen, the bones of ten masculine saints, ten feminine saints and four martyrs, and the oil of St. Nicholas! Clearly, the emphasis here was on the altar as a tomb and on the powers of intercession believed to be possessed by exemplars of religious faith.

The ideas of intercession and appeasement were mixed in the various practices of blood sacrifices known to man. The Vedic horse sacrifice was based upon the belief that the prayers of the priest could be conveyed heavenward by the spirit of an animal believed to embody the elemental powers of the gods. Human sacrifices involved the giving up of man's most treasured gift by proxy in the hope that this supreme gesture would inspire the Deity to reciprocate in a shower of rain or assistance of some sort. The descriptions by the Spaniards of scenes witnessed at Aztec sacrificial altars reflect their horror of this practice. The great beauty of the altars was lost to them in the confusion and shock which they felt in the presence of the awesome gods Huitzilopochtli and Tezcatlipoca, whose grim countenances looked down upon the bloody remains of burning human hearts. The Aztecs would, no doubt, have been equally horrified with the knowledge that Christians dismembered their saints and used the separated remains as relics, but the main theme in both practices is intercession.

At the heart of the symbol of the altar is the theme of sacrifice. More fundamental than all the ideas of intercession and appeasement, sacrifice is the most direct means of establishing reunion with the Source of all that lives. In attempting to merge the fire and its smoke with the source of the spark, man builds a sacrificial fire upon the altar and prays in phrases that may be similar to the beautiful words of the *Rig Veda*:

> May we adore thee in thy loftiest birthplace,
> And, with our praises, in thy lower station.
> The place whence thou issued forth I worship:
> To thee well kindled have they paid oblations.

> *Rig Veda* 11:IX:3

The "loftiest birthplace" is the heavenly solar fire, whilst the "lower station" refers to the firmament where Agni is born as lightning. The place where "thou issued forth" and are "well kindled" is the altar where the sacrificial fire burns. Sacrifice performed in this manner is the outer symbol of an inner work, the inner exchange between gods and men, man giving what he has and the gods giving in turn the "horses of power", "the herds of light", and "the heroes of strength".

> That which refuses to give itself
> Is still the food of the Cosmic Powers.
> The eater eating is eaten.

The altar is the meeting-point of sacrifices from above and from below. The archetypal sacrifice from above sets the stage and hands down to the human race the legacy of the greatest and foremost Law of Nature. In Hindu myth the Altar of Brahma called *Samantapanchaka* is said to rest atop Mount Himavat. Upon it a great sacrifice was performed from which came into being a creature the colour of the blue lotus, with sharp teeth, slender waist, enormous strength and at whose birth the whole earth trembled and the ocean rose in great waves. This being was *Asi*, 'the Sword', who was born to protect the gods. It was passed down from Rudra to Vishnu and to Marichi, who turned it over to the Seers from whence it passed to Vasava, the world Guardians, and finally to Manu in the shape of the Law. Thus, sacrifice is the first law and lays the basis for all other patterns operating in the interdependent universe. Owing to this fact, and as man is capable of being intelligently involved in this process, man must live by sacrifice in order to become more godlike. One of the Sanskrit words for altar means, literally, 'udder', referring to the generous flow of milk from the Akashic abode of Vach on high. Man's greatest task is to become a pure part of that generous flow.

The more exacting Sanskrit word for altar is *vedi*, a feminine term describing the shallow bed dug in the sacrificial court which will contain the fire during a ritual ceremony. Being narrow in the middle, it is like a woman's waist; hence the term *vedi-madhya* ('having a *vedi*-shaped waist'). One of the names of Draupadi was Vedi-Sambhava, she who was born or produced of the altar, and her marriage to the five Pandavas took place in a *vedi-ka* or *vedi*-shaped open pavilion prepared for weddings. Draupadi exemplifies sacrifice. Her life reminds us of the sacrificial *yoni* at the base of the *lingam*, and it is fitting that the kindled flame of Agni should begin here with the feminine sacrificial side of Nature. In the bosom of the Mother, the Law of Sacrifice reigns supreme, and it is in this aspect of his own nature that man must find the kindling to nurture the altar fire.

The Vedic fire altar is the world centre, the "earth's extremest limit", "the uttermost end of the world". The clay from which it is built represents the earth, the water with which it is mixed are the primeval waters, and the lateral walls mark the farthest extent of the ocean of space. The altar is based upon three circular perforated bricks or stones symbolizing the three worlds, the lowest being related to *Agni*, the middle intermediate to *Vayu*, and the highest to the 'Eye' opening upward to heaven, the realm of *Aditya*. The continuous opening running through these levels is both a passage for the ascending fire and a corridor to the higher world, leading out of death and darkness into immortality and light. Made of three hundred and sixty-five bricks, the fire altar represents time materialized, and the sacrifice itself restores the whole to an original timeless unity, an ever new beginning.

The principal elements brought together on the Vedic sacrificial altar are kindling for the divine flame, the offering of *ghrita* (clarified butter), the *soma*-wine and the chanting of the Sacred Word. *Ghrita* is the precious yield of the Cow of Light and symbolizes the rich clarity that comes to the illuminated mind. The kindled fire represents the unification of Light with the Power within man. It symbolizes the communication and interchange between the mortal and the Immortal, the flame growing to become the force of Divine, supra-mental Truth. *Soma*-wine is the immortal delight, the *ananda* which is the very basis of existence. Expressed as sense-mentality in man, the secret delight in existence is translated into terms of sensory awareness. When *soma* is distilled, purified and intensified until it becomes luminous and full of energy, then and then only does it become the food which can be sacrificed to the gods. The Sacred Word binds all these elements together at the altar, focussing them in an expression of illuminated Thought which is formed in the heart, shaped in the mind and arises out of the soul.

The soul is the altar upon which the Divine Flame of *Agni* burns. Inherently pure and untouched by the impurities upon which he feeds, *Agni* rises in the *vedi*-nature of man and forces evil towards goodness, burning in order to purify, destroying in order to save. When the body of the *sadhaka* is burnt up with the heat of *tapas*, it is *Agni* which roars and devours all that attempts to obscure and envelop the soul. Without this Divine Fire, the sacrificial kindling will remain as dead wood upon the altar of the soul, which will remain hidden, wrapped in cold and hard stone. The uttermost limit of the world is to be found at its centre and there, at that heart, must the altar be prepared. There, on the very edge of things material, does man face the presence of the God within. This is why he must make a burning-ground of his heart whilst raising the altar of his soul like a pillar of light shining within him, irradiating all around him. Thus did the Holy Kabiri teach the initiates of Pergamon, and thus did the Vedic sages exemplify by their lives of sanctified sacrifice. Man is a suppliant soul whose greatest and most beautiful purpose in living is to make of one's whole life an altar-place of devotion to Krishna, a sacrificial burning-ground for the sacred Fire of Shiva within.

> The world is the altar
> Of our lifelong session of sacrifice.
> Let us be great souls
> And sacrifice like the gods.

Hermes, August 1982

THE RAVEN

Then, this ebony bird beguiling my sad fancy into smiling
By the grave and stern decorum of the countenance it wore,
"Though thy crest be shorn and shaven, thou ", I said, "art
  sure no craven,
Ghastly, grim, and ancient Raven,
      wandering from the nightly shore:
Tell me what thy lordly name is on the Night's Plutonian
  shore!"
Quoth the Raven, "Nevermore."

Edgar Allan Poe

When the Tower of London was bombed during the Second World War, all of the ravens that had lived therefor centuries flew away. It had long been believed that when they deserted their nesting place, that place itself became doomed, and, according to legend, if they deserted the Tower of London, the whole of England would fall. This dire calamity was narrowly averted by a quick-witted Winston Churchill, who imported a large supply of young ravens from Scotland and Wales and clipped short their wings.

The precaution was wise, for the raven has been hastening away from thickly settled areas for many hundreds of years. There is no arctic island too remote to be visited by it in the summer, and the great shadowed loneliness of the boreal forests finds an animated complement in the bird's solitary flight across the verdant desolation. Bird of omen, the raven delivers portents from a dark and far-off land and yet bears a profound symbolic message which has inspired warriors and shamans, prophets and poets, all over the world. Many have written, like George Peele, of "the fatal raven, that in his voice carries the dreadful summons of our death", and legion are the tales of its insatiable appetite and ravenous ways. But equally numerous are the rich traditions which associate the bird with heroes and solar gods and the light of the sun itself. Between two wings of a most ambivalent nature, the raven has soared and plummetted its way through human history. It "peeps forth from the mists of time and thickets of mythology as a bird of slaughter, a storm bird, a sun and fire bird, a messenger, an oracular figure and a craftsman or cultural hero".

According to popular Christian interpretation, Edgar Allan Poe's famous poem about the raven casts the bird in the role of messenger reporting from the devil to the man who has sold his soul in a vain attempt to recover his dead love. This interpretation is in accord with the symbolism attached to the raven within the Judaeo-Christian and Islamic traditions, where the raven is often characterized as a veritable incarnation of sin. The raven sent out from the ark of Noah represents unrest and uncleanliness and is associated with the fall of Spirit into that which is impure and enjoys carnage. Added to this is the idea of deceitfulness and cunning, due to the fact that the raven did not return to the ark until the waters had dried up from the earth. The raven had defected from its entrusted duty of locating land and had fed its insatiable appetite upon the floating carrion instead. Even the cry of the raven, "Cras! Cras!" ("Tomorrow! Tomorrow!"), is seen in these traditions as standing for spiritual procrastination on the part of the sinner. As St. Augustine said: "I tell you, when you make a voice like a raven you destroy yourselves." The sinner was warned that the eyes of such as he would be picked out by the ravens of the valley or by the very devil himself.

In its blackest-seeming role the raven is shown as thriving on bloodshed, panic and war. Old Norse poetry is filled with references to the raven who is eager for the carrion remains of war. But in the Nordic tradition, as in that of the Celtic and Teutonic, the 'Raven of Battle' was the name given to the hero associated with the goddesses of war (the Valkyries). Ravens assisted in the work of the Valkyries and flew to do their bidding, and some notable birds gained great fame for saving the lives of warrior-heroes. They would sit atop the warrior's shoulder or on his helmet and attack the eyes of any adversary. Others would hunt and peck away the eyes and flesh of the fallen, leaving only bones and scraps to tell the tale. The Zoroastrians of Persia observed this habit of the bird and thought of the raven as pure because it removed pollution from the face of the earth, whilst for this same reason the Jews and Christians considered it impure.

Another characteristic contributing to the ambivalent nature of the raven's reputation is the widespread belief that the black raven was once white. When the raven did not return to Noah in his ark, it was turned black as sin for its defection. Greek tradition maintains that when Apollo's raven revealed to him the fateful news of the infidelity of the beautiful Thessalian nymph Koronis, the heart-broken god cursed the bird and turned his white plumage raven-black. Myths of American Indians, Eskimos, Arabs and Jews also contain equally quaint stories depicting this radical mutation, causing one to ponder the significance of the contrast between white and black in time, as well as in terms of the condition that might be symbolized by the presence and absence of light. Equally mysterious is the fact that even within the Christian tradition, where the raven's character has been especially blackened, the bird is associated with solitary saints whose lives are white with purity and who have received help and succour from attentive ravens. When the prophet Elijah hid from the wrath of Ahab, he was fed by ravens at the command of the Lord, and it was a raven who brought food and protected St. Benedict from the poisoned loaf.

Despite its association with saints, the largely negative focus upon the raven in Christianity does reflect the Semitic obsession with purity and pollution and a Manichaean stress upon dualism, There is considerable focus upon clean or unclean animals to eat or to be sacrificed, and detailed instructions are given as to how to avoid unclean lives. The raven is depicted pecking out the eyes of a dead man, whilst the white dove flies back with the olive branch. The raven loves the gore of the battlefield, whilst the dove unfolds its snowy wings in the name of peace and harmony. Even the transformation of the white to the black raven can be interpreted as the passage from a Solar Age of truth and righteousness to a dark age of pollution and sin. Perhaps this is what the ancient Greeks were hinting at in the telling of the myth about Apollo and Koronis, whose loss of innocence is marked by the blackening of the bird. Such a dramatic transition suggests a strong sense of loss, the folk-memory of a fall from grace very much like that associated with the pollution of the Holy of Holies around which revolves the tenacious Karma of Israel.

Seizing upon the raven symbolically to carry this burden has been a relatively easy course to adopt, for its association with warlike adventures was already well developed in classical times by the Mediterranean and Nordic peoples as well as the Hindus and Ceylonese. Two ravens led the expedition of Alexander the Great across the trackless desert to the oasis of Ammon, and many ancient warrior-navigators like the Vikings used to take ravens with them on their innumerable voyages through the fog-bound vastitudes of the seas. Confident that the birds would always guide them to land, they sailed further and further abroad and very often in the cause of plunder and war. The white dove of peace, symbolically linked with the human soul, easily stood in marked contrast to the hoarse croaking raven, whose ominous arrival from across the sea so frequently inspired an anxious watch of the ocean's curve for the cluster of tiny, ever-enlarging ships that might follow.

In the story of the flood described in the Earth-Diver myths of the Woodland Indians, stress is laid upon the importance of the raven sent out by the Sun to measure the size and extent of the new world emerging out of the flood. This is reminiscent of many Siberian traditions like those of the Voguls, who believed that the raven was associated with the Divers in the remaking of the world. It was sent to fly around in progressively longer intervals in order to estimate and report on the increasing size of the emerging earth. The function of marking size and, correspondingly, cycles, is echoed in the Germanic legend about Frederick I Barbarossa, who is said to sleep under Raven's Hill at Kaiserlautern ready to come forth in the last emergency of his country. When a shepherd accidentally stumbled across him in his grotto, he awoke and asked: "Are the ravens still flying around the hill?" When the shepherd told him that they were, the king sighed: "Then I must sleep another hundred years." Attendant of gods and cultural heroes, ravens frequently play a part in the great cycles of the sun and the deluge. Raven mythology in this regard is strikingly homogeneous across Siberia, Kamchatka and into North America, as well as amongst Germanic and Celtic peoples. Such ideas must be very ancient and deeply embedded in the Race mind to have spread so far and lasted so long. Indeed, many thousands of years after a painter at Lascaux depicted a raven standing beside a dying hunter, a statue of another dying hero with a raven on his shoulder was erected to commemorate those executed in the Irish Rebellion of 1916.

> Where bad priests become ravens,
> Bad nuns become crows.

> French Peasant Saying

It has been said that "crows seem to have been all that the raven was, only, as befitting their size, in a lesser degree". And though there is truth to this, both zoologically and symbolically, there has been a traceable deterioration of the image of the crow in recent times. From noticeable tendencies to steal bright objects the general characteristic of cheating has been inferred. To 'rook' someone (the rook being a close relative of the raven and crow) is a term indicating a particularly devious way of setting up someone to be cheated. To have 'crow's feet1 is undesirable, and certainly no one wants to be called an 'old crow'. It is significant that these allusions suggest indirect and feminine qualities as opposed to the warlike masculine raven, but cunning is indeed shared by both birds, though the raven's is most often exhibited singly. Crows tend to work together when embarked upon the business of getting food or taking what they want. Frequently one watches out whilst the other does the job, an arrangement illustrated in an amusing if lurid fashion in the ballad of "The Twa Corbies", where one crow instructs another:

> Ye'll sit on his white hause-bane,
> And I'll pike out his bonny blue een:
> Wi' ae lock o' his gowden hair,
> We'll theek our nest when it grows bare.

The recurring theme of pecking out the eyes has a strange twist to it in the old Celtic belief that blind folk who are kind to ravens will regain their eyesight. The symbol of the eye is very closely connected with the occult symbolism of the solar orb itself. There can be little doubt that the raven's habits provide a link between the sun and its analogous counterpart in man as he goes through the process known as dying. Surely this is why during the Mithraic ceremony in which the migration and purification of the soul after death was represented, there was a flapping of wings and cawing of ravens. The followers of Mithra saw this as a corollary to the first stage of initiation into the Mysteries wherein the raven is regarded as the Messenger of the Sun. Indeed, it was called the Morning Bird of Joy and Light after assisting Beowulf in his spiritual victory over the monstrous Grendel. The Northwest Coast Indians have many myths telling how Raven stole the Sun and brought light to the dark world below. In several of these myths Raven pierces the ball of the solar light with his beak so as to release the spiritual fire from the confines of a heavenly realm. In a striking reversal of this process, the raven, hovering over the corpses of the dead, pierces their eyes and symbolically releases the fluid of life from the confines of the dying body. Perhaps the perception of a correspondence such as this led to the graphic depiction of the Raven of Death with the pinecone and the torch of light and life. The raven carries the orb of light and shows the way back to Valhalla – back to the spiritual source. This is why it is said that the raven makes the complete journey to the end of the earth, to the boundary where the sun sinks into the sea, to the edge of the cycle where time ceases to be measured and the darkness of *pralaya* lies in waiting.

The Tlingit say that in the beginning, before life as we know it, there was no daylight, and Raven-At-The-Head-Of-Nass (the One God) had a house with sun, moon and stars within. There also were two aged men called Old-Man-Who-Foresees-All-Trouble-In-The-World and He-Who-Knows-Everything-That-Happens, whilst Old-Woman-Underneath was the world itself as well as sister to the One God. Though Raven-At-The-Head-Of-Nass tried to prevent his sister from giving birth to a son, she circumvented his intent by swallowing a red-hot stone from which she gave birth to Yetl, the Raven Demiurge of the world. A Haida version of the myth describes how the god tries to destroy his sister's child by putting on a huge hat of rain clouds which flood the earth. Yetl is, nonetheless, born and flies heavenward as the hat of his uncle rises. When he reaches the limit of the sky, Yetl pushes his beak into it, piercing his way to the light. With his beak thus fixed, he pushes down upon the watery hat with his foot until, at last, his celestial uncle is drowned. After the deluge the surviving beings of the former age are transformed into animals, humans are created and the present order of the world is established by Yetl.

The Bringer of Light, Raven is also the Transformer and Trickster. He is half Demiurge and half clown and characterized as greedy, selfish, gluttonous (he never gets full) and, yet, the supreme hero of mankind. He constantly destroys or chases other animals in order to take their food, and though sometimes slain in the myths, he continually returns to the realm of the living to recommence his awesomely autocratic but sometimes clownish role. In the old days people used to leave food on the beaches for Raven and he is still much talked about. But he is not an object of worship, being one of those hero-deities of the past about whom indecorous tales may be told without sullying the spirit of reverence shown to him. The Haida call him Nankilstlas or He-Whose-Voice-Must-Be-Obeyed, because whatever he told of came to pass and the utterance of his word was considered a creative act. The trickster element is closely related to transformation or shape-changing. The raven takes on any form and enters all worlds from dark to light and back again. Transcending the ordinary boundaries between light and darkness, black and white, he glides beyond the confines of worldly morality as well as the appeal of relative truth. As with Lord Krishna in the Hindu epics, what is the blackness of night to the raven is the light of day to mankind, and in their darkness he sees radiating light. Thus, what looks like cunning, trickery, greed and cheating is a kaleidoscopic reflection of something quite different from what it seems to be. The fact that the Semitic traditions have steadfastly failed to recognize such transformational subtleties, which, in fact, indicate levels of reality experienced in spiritual initiation, is explainable only in terms of their having lost the knowledge of the Mysteries, leaving them a two-dimensional perspective focussing back and forth on black and white.

The idea that the Creator might take the form of a raven was not limited to the northwest coast of America. In the *Pymander* of Hermes, Seven Primeval Men are spoken of who are one and the same as those depicted on the Cuthah Tablets containing the Babylonian legend of creation, which was overseen by seven human prototypes having the faces of ravens. These are the Elohim, the Dhyanis and the Manus of other traditions, who represent the races of mankind to unfold on this globe. Such a perspective lends a remarkable significance to the role of the raven as totemic ancestor to a whole clan, as it is to the Raven people of the Haida tribe. Great heroes have been lent a primordial and godlike quality through their close association with ravens by the clans and races who identify with them. Thus it is said that King Arthur visits his favourite haunts in Cornwall and Wales in the guise of a raven, whose shape he assumes when flying from Avalon. The Celtic hero Bran's very name means 'Raven' and the bird was often identified as the familiar of both gods and heroes. No wonder the old Scots say "Nae gude ever cam' o' killin' black ravens", whilst Siberian folk went further and stated simply that anyone killing a raven would soon die. One could never know if the bird they saw was a mere animal or what the Haida call a *sgana quedas*, a werefolk or human being in raven form who is capable of assisting the human race with its magical power.

To raven is to plunder. This is what the word means. To have a ravenous appetite suggests greed and lust and insatiable desires. It is not at all surprising that theologians of the dualistic Semitic traditions should be revolted by the habits of the bird so named. The Greek names for the raven do not detract from this nefarious reputation one bit. 'Αφηδάγος (*adifagos*) means 'glutton', άπληστος (*aplistos*) refers to being 'insatiable', άρπάζω (*arpazo*) indicates 'to seize or carry away', αίμόβορος (*hemovoros*) means 'bloodthirsty', and κόρακας (*korakas*) is the bird's generic name, referring to its unpleasant voice and literally means 'to croak'. Indeed, its hoarse cry seems to match its salacious appetites and can be truly alarming, bellowing forth from a body measuring up to twenty-five inches in length, held aloft in flight by a wing-spread of up to fifty-six inches, and topped off with a very large head and beak. Amongst the biggest of perching birds, the raven is a member of the family Corvidae and distinguishable from the crow by its greater size and shaggier plumage about the throat. Being keen-sighted, extremely sagacious and notably wary, the raven survives by its wits; it has never been protected by law. It is a hardy bird thought to live as long as a hundred years largely on the periphery of populated areas. Shunning man's greater numbers, the raven cleaves to the northerly wild areas where it builds gigantic nests of sticks on the edges of cliffs or the tops of very large trees. Ravens have a spectacular courtship flight involving all manner of aerial acrobatics, the wild twists and tricks of which are largely unwitnessed by humankind. They are noisy and aggressive omnivores who will feed happily on carrion and whose feathers are so black as to cast a purplish iridescence, rendering their total absence of colour a source of indigo light. They are passerine predators and soar like true hawks, their intelligent aim never missing its mark, never blurring the unrelenting nature of their intent.

When a Siberian shaman conjures up the spirit of a raven, the spirit speaks in a human tongue, unlike other spirits which have their own languages. The ability of the raven to acquire human speech is linked by many people to the belief that it is a messenger of the gods. There are many references to talking ravens in classical literature wherein the raven's oratorical talents are usually linked with prophecy. Porphyrius declared that sixty-four different intonations of the raven's cry were interpreted by soothsayers of his day, but Pliny described a raven that uttered whole sentences of several words each whilst "frequently learning still more words in addition". The great fascination of such a talented bird lies in its presumed powers of prophecy rather than its clever ability to mimic. As with the Haida He-Whose-Voice-Is-Obeyed, things uttered were believed to come to pass. The raven spoke of that which was and would be with the same unrelenting intent as it displayed in its action as an insatiable predator. The raven of Apollo did not blur the biting truth of the infidelity of Koronis. It did not miss the target, the eyeball, the scorching sun of truth. Thus, the voice of the raven was dreaded even whilst it fascinated, even whilst it imparted the unwanted truth.

In *A Fable for Critics*, James Russell Lowell suggested that the raven of Edgar Allan Poe was really the bedraggled pet raven called Grip belonging to Charles Dickens. With his own unrelenting brand of critical wit, he wrote: "There comes Poe with his raven like Barnaby Rudge, three-fifths of him genius, and two-fifths sheer fudge." But Poe did succeed in capturing the ominous power of what the Celtics call 'raven's knowledge', which sees and knows all about the living as well as the dead. The unwanted truth, like the doleful knell of unalterable fate, intones throughout the poem.

"Prophet!" said I, "thing of evil! – prophet still, if bird or devil!
Whether Tempter sent, or whether tempest tossed thee here
   ashore,
Desolate yet all undaunted, on this desert land enchanted –
On this home by Horror haunted – tell me truly, I implore:
Is there – is there balm in Gilead? – tell me – tell me, I implore!"
Quoth the Raven, "Nevermore.". . .
"Prophet!" said I, "thing of evil! prophet still, if bird or devil!
By that Heaven that bends above us, by that God we both adore,
Tell this soul with sorrow laden if, within the distant Aidenn,
It shall clasp a sainted maiden whom the angels name Lenore:
Clasp a rare and radiant maiden whom the angels name Lenore."
Quoth the Raven, "Nevermore."

Death, war and endless loss are cold thrusts from the beak of
Karma-Nemesis, but there is never any assurance of comfort in
the bald truth. Like necessity operating under law through nature,
disintegration, loss and death follow as closely upon the heels of birth
and growth and life as does a shining black bird pecking at seeds
dropped along the ground one by one. Its appetite is insatiable and it
never misses a seed. It does not stop to wonder if anyone would like
it to lose the trail or leave a few for a later time. To the rough dweller
of the North who worshipped force instead of aesthetic subtleties,
the sable raven of powerful wing and unyielding nature was an
awesome and admirable creature. The hardships of their lives were
facts unflinchingly embraced and they lived as though they were
agents of Nemesis – standard-bearers of the raven's unwanted truth.
It is not surprising that the more aesthetic southern peoples looked
to the north with dread and combined in their thoughts the raven,
the cold of winter and the boisterous savagery of the barbarians who
descended from those boreal wastes from time to time.

To the Norsemen the raven was the emissary of the Supreme Odin,
god of force, intellect and initiation. It is not surprising then – "that
a bird black as night and its mysteries, a familiar of the lightning-
riven pine and the storm-beaten crag, a ghoulish attendant of battling
men and feasting on their slain, muttering strange soliloquies, and
diabolically cunning withal" – that such a creature should have

appeal to Odin's Vikings. Did not that god bear the name of Raafna Gud ('Raven-god') and did he not have as ministers two ravens called Hugin and Munin ('Reflection' and 'Memory') who ranged everywhere and reported to him all that was and was to be? These ravens, then, were the emblem of the Vikings, their standard on the banners carried by them and borne by their ships. The Danes called their standard Landeyda ('Land-waster') and believed implicitly in its miraculous virtues. They said that if they were to win a fight, the raven in the midst of their flag would flutter, as if it were alive. Britain and other lands came to know only too well that dread flag. In the words of James Thomson: "The Danish raven, lured by annual prey, Hung o'er the land incessant." Ravens on the battlefield were seen as men and birds and both seemed to lust after the carnage of it all. In the blackened soil of such fields the Ravens of the Valkyries ('the Choosers of the slain') pecked out the eyes of those selected to die and to cross the Rainbow Bridge to Valhalla.

Victims of such onslaughts could never have shared this sense of glory in such a death, and indeed no people are so pure in motive as to justify their acting as collective instruments of Divine Will. But a faithful though worldly reflection of the great mythic struggles involving the pledge of Odin's eye to gain knowledge, and the ceaseless battles with the forces of the nether world, were often mirrored in the attitudes of the Vikings as well as of others who shared in the broader Eddie mythical tradition. The loss of an eye or both eyes was commonly associated with initiation into a life of spiritual vision. In myths the raven loses an eye and then imparts magical craftsmanship. Man loses an eye to the world only to understand hidden things which are revealed to him. In the Irish sagas the god Lug was father of the raven-hero Cuchulainn, whose eye was struck out whilst dying, and Lug himself, along with Odin, Ogmios and Tochmarc Etaine, were all one-eyed gods and heroes gifted with spiritual sight and magical craftmanship. The eye that remains with the world is the eye of Time but the eye that is pledged is that of Eternity, the orb of Prophecy filled with the pure wisdom-light of the sun. The raven flies to and fro between the solar orb of eternal life and the dying eyes of man in time. He mercilessly pecks away at the delusions formed like veils over the cornea's shield until he penetrates to the darkness of the pupil's cavity and releases the invisible light within.

Odin the Raafna Gud was, like Brahma in the Hindu tradition, born in and out of time. He, like the raven, knows this and the other worlds, and thus, the past and future are one to him, and the cycles of life reduced in complexity to a simple circle whose centre is everywhere. How prophetic, then, are the songs of the three Norse goddesses "to whom the names of Odin whisper of the past and the future, as they flutter around their abode of crystal beneath the flowing river". They tell of the renewal of the world in terms of the past which is yet to be. The unwanted Truth is told and its insatiable desire to express itself may produce terror and loathing in one who is not prepared to give up all to its insistent glare. In anguish, Poe's protagonist attempts to release himself from the compelling fate embodied in the raven's presence.

> "Be that word our sign of parting, bird or fiend!" I shrieked
>   upstarting:
> "Get thee back into the tempest and the Night's Plutonian shore!
> Leave no black plume as a token of that He thy soul hath spoken!
> Leave my loneliness unbroken! quit the bust above my door!
> Take thy beak from out my heart, and take thy form from off my
>   door!"
> Quoth the Raven, "Nevermore."

The raven will not take its beak from out his heart through which, in the poem, his eye has seen. The loss of love is the loss of a dream replaced with the cold light of an arctic dawning. That which knows the beginnings and endings of vast cycles does not pause to embalm the fancies of a lover's romance. Whatever essence of truth lies at its core will rise like the Bird of Joy and Light when the delusive and earth-bound elements are abandoned in the field. The raven's beak pierced the heart of the eye just as it pierced the heavens in the Haida myth, boring its way through the firmament to the realm beyond the world where the blackest dark is pregnant with iridescent light. The soul reaches up and rests between the great bird's arching wings. But they are black! And the neck of this raven bird is not long and sleek but thick and ragged to the touch. The Raven warns its rider: "It is not into a dream we fly but over fields of soon-to-be-broken illusions and openly wanton carnage right to the end of the world. Be sure you are ready for alt this before choosing to come with me." "I come," the soul replies, "because of all the hopes and fearful desires that have bound and tried to consume me, there is one which, beyond them all, is far greater." "And what is that?" asked the Raven. "It is the desire to know what is and what will be. To know the Truth which is True through all time and space. To see the future in the past and the beginning in the end. To fear nothing and hope for nothing but welcome utterly the penetrating light of Eternal Truth." "So be it. Then come along," quoth the Raven, "and ye shall know it ever more."

Thus, the black wings arched aloft and began their wandering to the edge of the world – to the limits of *manvantara* and the beginnings of *pralaya*, where black becomes white and black as night again. Whispering of the past and future, hoarsely echoing the prophecy of antique ages yet to come, the great bird courses on along the current of primeval wisdom flowing out of the precosmic Source of all. He is one of the raven-faced Host of Dhyan Chohans beyond which all is darkness. He is Odin, born in and out of time, and his great wing traces the feathered edge of darkness slowly receding before the beginnings of a new day.

> In larger spheres the Raven flies,
> Small floods will not detain him.
> His prophecies know broader skies,
> The Earth cannot contain them.
> Nor could his flight be curbed by day,
> But night would fast surround it.
> Blending with his blackened wing,
> Till light could ne'er have found it.
> And yet his hoarsely whispered cry,
> Echoes within my hearing.
> Into the dark woods I would fly,
> Beyond the realm of fearing.
> Soaring, beyond the realm of time.

Hermes, December 1982

THE SWORD

Here beginneth the story of the sword, the anvil, and the marble stone, and of how that sword was first achieved by an unknown youth, until then of no renown, whether in arms or of estate.

So hearken unto that which I have hereinafter written.

The Story of Arthur and His Knights

When Sir Kay's sword broke on Sir Balamorgineas' helmet during the great tournament, he sent his younger brother, Arthur, to fetch another from their father's pavilion. Finding no sword there, Arthur's thoughts rushed to that which he had seen thrust into the anvil before the cathedral nearby. In his innocent youth he did not know the significance of this mighty weapon nor, surely, did he possess any clue which might have suggested that it was Merlin who, by his magic, caused it to be placed there. He approached the block of marble and laid his hands on the hilt. Bending his body over it, he drew upon the sword with all his strength and it came forth in his hands with marvellous ease. The brilliance of the mystic blade was so intense that he covered it with his cloak and hastened to his impatiently waiting brother. But when Sir Kay saw the sword, he was astounded. A cunning arose in his heart wherefrom he conceived the desire to take advantage of Arthur's simple innocence and claim the deed of having extricated the sword from the stone.

Destiny, however, would not be denied its rightful king and the test posed by Merlin could not be met by the ambitious Sir Kay. When Arthur confessed to their noble father that it was he who had pulled forth the blade, the old knight told him how, eighteen years previously, Merlin had set a meeting with him at the postern gate of Uther-Pendragon's castle. He explained to him that when they had met at midnight, Merlin gave a swaddled infant into his care to raise as though he were his own son. "Nor have I until now ever known ought of who was thy father; but now I do suspect who he was and

47

that thou hast in thy veins kingly blood. And I do have it in mind that perhaps thy father was Uther-Pendragon himself. For who but the son of Uther-Pendragon could have drawn forth that sword as thou hast done?" After repeated but vain attempts to draw the magic sword, the other knights gathered there came to see that only Arthur could draw forth and return it to the stone. Most of them bowed down and willingly accepted him as their new king, but there were those who persisted in questioning his credentials and would not join in support of him. Thus the drama of the struggle between knightly heroes and the forces of evil was set, at the centre of which the wondrous sword Excalibur was destined to play a decisive role.

Perhaps the old Roman belief that the iron sword could ward off evil lingered in the British Isles and inspired some of the legendary powers attributed to Excalibur, but others in the world have held similar beliefs. In the Islamic tradition the sword is symbolic of holy war against the infidel and of man against his own evil. This belief was equally shared by the Christian knights who fought against them in the bloody crusades. For the Grail Knight it was seen as an instrument of good in overcoming evil. In myth the sword is believed to possess supernatural powers when found under the earth or submerged in water, where it bears a close association with mystical beings like the mysterious Lady of the Lake. In the hand of this Lady or embedded in earthly stone, the sword is masculine, asserting the power of protection, authority, justice and courage. Some traditions single out the western straight-bladed instrument as solar and masculine in distinction to the Oriental curved blade, which could be thought of as lunar and feminine, but the more widely recognized feminine attribute is the scabbard in which the sword is sheathed. The sword in itself is symbolic of psychic and spiritual decision as well as physical extermination, relating to lunar as well as to solar principles in its ability to cut through and penetrate. Its power to wound is also its power to liberate and manifest the superiority of strength and courage over prevarication and self-defense. The hard steel of its blade suggests the transcendental toughness of the all-conquering spirit and the inviolability of the sacred. Its fierce cutting edge speaks of discrimination, spiritual decision and the penetrating power of the intellect. As in the case of Excalibur, in the right hand the sword is capable of dividing good from evil and carving out in precise design the character of the hero's struggle for the Grail. What to earlier races had been a sword god to be sacrificed to became an instrument to be wielded as a mighty human power.

Very famous swords have names and, like Excalibur, are addressed as 'he' as though they had a life and power of their own. Their origins are shrouded in mystical wonder, as in the case of the divine sword of Japanese Shintoism called *Kusanagi*. Being one of the three sacred objects of the imperial regalia, this mighty blade was discovered by Susanowo-no-mikoto, the storm god of the early Shinto pantheon. In the ancient Nihongi the account is given of how this god descended from heaven and proceeded to the headwaters of the River Hi. There he found an old man and woman weeping because all their daughters but one had been devoured year after year by an eight-forked serpent. This great heavenly serpent controlled the rainfall affecting the crops and had been exacting its gruesome payment from those on earth in this manner. The power to initiate the rain lay in a brilliant lightning sword hidden in its tail, and when Susanowo-no-mikoto slew the marauder and cut it into pieces, he discovered it lying there in all its potent splendour. Being profoundly awed by this precious and powerful instrument, he sent it up to heaven to become the property of the Shining Deity, who is Light herself.

The *Kusanagi* sword (like the sacred mirror and jewel regalia) thus came to find its source in the possession of its prototype, which is this bright and overmastering heavenly light. It is fitting that *Kusanagi* became part of the royal regalia, as the Imperial Dynasty itself is considered to be *Hitsugi* (*hi* = light, sun, fire; *tsugi* = succession) or light succession'. Of these sacred objects, the sword is believed to be the dwelling-place and symbol of *ara-mitama*, or the 'rough spirit' of the goddess of light, whilst the mirror is the dwelling-place of *nigi-mitama*, her 'gentle spirit'. The former is lightning, the latter is the sun, whilst the third (the jewels) represents the moon. Together they form a triad of wisdom, benevolence and courage. The lightning fire of the sword symbolizes the activated human will and the desire for purification, which can result from the chastening force of the element of fire as well as the cold steel of the blade's decisive edge. Swords patterned after this great weapon were deemed capable of possession only by those who ardently sought after this purity. It has always been held that a suitable offering to the gods had to possess purity, rarity and value. Great swords have all three elements and were sometimes offered by samurai as a votive sacrifice on the altar of their own spiritual aspiration.

The *Kusanagi* sword is called in full *Kusanagi-no-tsurugi*, or 'Grass-mowing sword', because it saved the life of the hero Yamato-Takeru-no-mikoto when his enemies set fire to the grass surrounding him in the battlefield. Many tales depict the desperate attempts made to steal it but, like other swords such as *Doji-giri*, the Monster-Cutter, or those made by Toshiro Yoshimitsu which brought good fortune to the Tokugawa clan, the sword exerted a life of its own and would not be separated from its rightful possessor. Great care went into the making of such swords. Masters, whose rank stood highest amongst the artisans, followed a ritually rigorous discipline whilst engaged in their manufacture. Those few who still exist continue to lead a semi-religious and abstemious life, beginning each day of work with cold ablutions, abstaining from sexual intercourse, liquor or animal food. Their food is cooked over a sacred fire and prayers are offered at each stage of the forging. Several pieces of metal are heated, stretched and folded lengthwise repeatedly. When malleable, the metal, derived from iron ore or sand, is pounded until tempered. Gradually the pieces are fashioned into a blade, involving a repetition of the entire process as many as thirty times. Each time a piece is folded, a smith must exercise great care to see that all air and dirt are excluded so as to ensure against weak spots which can lead to breakage upon use. The proper degree of hardness has to be ascertained in proportion to the exact grade of steel, and the blade is carefully baked with a covering of clay paste for the final tempering. For these final and most critical operations, the smith dons the court noble's ceremonial costume and the smithy becomes, for the time being, a sanctuary whose approach is hung with the Shinto straw rope to ward off evil influences. In this atmosphere the blade is, at last, quenched in water of a suitable temperature, after which it is polished for two weeks.

Like the mediaeval swords of the Occident which were painstakingly categorized according to design, the Japanese sword has evolved minute variations on a central functional pattern. Points of blades can be divided into four types, but these in turn can be separated into ten classes according to their tempered lines as well as whether their ridge lines are raised or flat. On the blade itself many elements suggest identifiable categories: there are eight types of grooves, four types of groove ends, twenty-six types of tempered lines with names like frog-shaped or clover-tree flower. There are five types of back or top ridges, several classifications of curves, four types of tangs, five tips of tangs and twelve patterns of file marks on tangs. This is only the beginning of the categorizing process which then goes on to consider the hilt and all its parts and clearly captures the rapt attention of only the connoisseur.

Perhaps one of the reasons why the classification of swords has absorbed some is because of the special status ascribed to the owner of the weapon as well as its own symbolic power. To carry a sword in mediaeval Europe was the prerogative of knights and high dignitaries. In China the founders of ancient cities wore them, and they were called "the living soul of the samurai" in Japan. An emblem of his virtue, valour and strength, the sword was believed to have the power to "stiffen" his resolution and guard him from any temptation to unworthy deeds. The icy purity and self-restraint of its metal, as well as the energy and the zest of the fire that helped to forge it, were transposed as characteristics attributable to its owner.

In Europe the sword was the emblem of higher forms of knighthood, leaving the lance to represent the lower classes. It was "a most noble weapon which once had high significance in the minds of men, and fulfilled the most vital and personal service in their hands". The average weight of the mediaeval sword was two to three pounds, and it was balanced carefully according to its length. The knightly sword was derived, via those of the Vikings, from the long iron ones of the prehistoric Celts which were used before and during the Roman period. These evolved (around A.D. 900) to be about thirty inches long and two inches wide at the hilt. The old Norse swords, which were very beautiful and wonderfully made, were used for a lifetime and passed down for often over a century in duration. Excellent swords of later centuries continued to be made at famous weapon-making firms like those in Milan, Passau, Augsburg, Cologne or Bordeaux.

Aside from museum and private collections, the appearance of these can be verified in the wonderfully accurate sculpture that graces such edifices as the cathedrals of Chartres, Notre Dame de Paris, Freiburg, Naumburg, Canterbury and St. Mary's Church at Warwick. Short and long swords, sabres, rapiers and cutlasses are all depicted, including the double-edged sword whose dual powers symbolized the inverse currents of creation and destruction in manifestation. A treatise on the "Ordinances of Chivalry" in the Hasting's manuscript (c. 1450) explains "how a man schal be armyd at his ese when he schal fighte on foote". . . i.e.: "He daggere upon hys righte syde. And then hys shorte swerde [from the Old Norse sverth] upon hys lyfte syde in a rounde rynge all nakid to pulle it out lightli . . . and then hys long swerde in his hande."

The sword and the tree symbols have been entwined as long as their parallel theme of war and peace. Whereas the sword represents spiritual evolution, the tree has to do with involution and proliferation instead of physical extermination. The Word of God, the appearance of lightning and the implacable justice of universal law are all capable of being symbolized by the sword. Indeed, the sword of Damocles, which represents danger in the midst of seeming prosperity, seems to relate to the impersonal and awesome justice capable of cutting to shreds the delusions harboured by those ignorant of the mysterious causes and effects of karma. Such swords are like the penetration of spirit into the world, and initially play the part of gods or their attributes. In the book of *Genesis* a flaming sword was placed in Paradise to keep man out.

> And the Lord God said, Behold, the man is become as one of us, to know good and evil: and now, lest he put forth his hand, and take also of the tree of life, and eat, and live forever . . .   Therefore the Lord God sent him forth from the garden of Eden . . . and placed Cherubims, and a flaming sword which turned every way, to keep the way of the tree of life.
>
> *Genesis* 3:22–24

Here the involution of the spirit of God into the world has taken place, but self-conscious intelligence has been 'stolen'. To use this intelligence to achieve immortality requires coming to terms with the flaming sword that protects the tree, not a task easily contemplated. Here again the sword is in the hands, as it were, of God and seems remote from the human grasp. It is like the ancient Hittite sword god struck into the stone as a portent of the earth's fertility and of rebirth through death. Only under very special ritual circumstances may the king alone draw it from its stony scabbard so as to represent and uphold the Law of God to His people in the world. Thus did the fertility of divine power enter into the mortal realm, but individual men had no right to try to touch it or to do ought but make humble sacrifices to its worldly form. Conscious immortality was not for unregenerate men, and even kings merely passed down their borrowed power through the sword god to their successor when they died.

The death and resurrection of kingship was linked with the annual cycles of winter and spring. The rebirth through death which vitalized a people was ritualized in ancient sacrificial practices wherein the sword slowly shifted from its implacable station in the stone into the hands of dancers and mummers, who dramatized the death and resurrection of a central character through the highly stylized use of their swords. Thus, in the sword dances of Northern England, the morris dance of the Midlands and the South, and the mummer's drama of England and Scotland, which are ancient rites preserved until fairly recent times, the focus was upon this theme of death and resurrection by sword. Such sword dances (which were also practised elsewhere in Europe) provide a link between the ancient worship of divinity manifested through the sword and the enactment of this cyclic rite by ordinary villagers who temporarily wield the sword in their own hands. The next shift which places the sword more firmly in the grasp of man marks the beginning of the Heroic Age. Instead of the latter-day collective dilution of the most ancient mysteries taking the form of country drama and dance, the Heroic Age was marked by the extraordinary courage and effrontery (in the eyes of the gods) of individual heroes engaging in the quest for their own immortality. From the sword of involution linked up with the protection of the tree and all the edicts that form the cornerstone of Brihaspati's power, the process of self-conscious evolution emerged.

The heroes of evolution step out from the fearfully worshipping mass of humanity and begin to acquire their own flame-tempered swords. Typically they are raised in secrecy, unknown by the world, and like Theseus, they must extract a sword from the stone before becoming a true king. The drawing of the sword can be seen as emblematic of the extrication of the hero out of the impersonal ritual of cyclic recurrence. To initiate this, a god like Odin may plunge a sword into a tree-pillar to be drawn only by his mortal heir, Sigmund. In the case of Galahad, the unknown youth saw a sword fixed in stone floating down a river. Only he could draw it forth and set it in his empty scabbard. Of the four knights gathered at Camelot who later achieved the Grail in varying degrees of reality, he alone received the coronation "amongst the spiritualities", repeating at the end of the Arthurian era the king's experience at its beginning. When such an age wanes, the sword is no longer to be found placed in the stone by a god or a Master Magician, but it is sometimes handed down broken. In mediaeval legends the broken or buried sword, which marks a state of destruction and decay, often appeared as the inheritance which had to be reconquered by personal valour. Thus, as a youth, Siegfried discovered the pieces of the sword *Balmunga*, which Odin had stuck into the pillar to be drawn by Siegfried's father, Sigmund. Mime, the blacksmith, was unable to reforge it, but Siegfried succeeded in doing so. In the Arthurian legend, Gawaine was likewise given a broken sword, but he was unable to repair it completely, symbolizing his inability to penetrate to the core of his undertaking.

The Quest is brought powerfully to life in the great epics of the *Ramayana*, the *Iliad*, the *Odyssey*, the *Aeneid* and the *Holy Grail*. Knights dedicated to the discovery of the Grail, or even to the salvation of Jerusalem, carried their swords like a cross of righteousness. Where the blade and the guard conjoined, the vertical and horizontal symbols of life and death were linked in the form of a cross. Indeed, the guard was called the Cross, and inscriptions on them and on the blade were so placed that they could only be read if the hilt was held uppermost. Inscriptions such as *"Cristus Vincit"* and *"Cristus Imperat"* assert the presumed sanctity of their fervently sought-for victory. But the quest for the Grail involved a more inward struggle leading to an uncharted condition in a land only known by the name of Truth. The hero of this quest assumes a stance which can be portrayed as one of active spiritual aggression. To paraphrase William Blake, he will not cease from mental fight, nor will his sword sleep in his hand. All becomes the highest embodiment of a chivalrous code from which there is no relaxation.

At this point the powers of discrimination and decisiveness become paramount. The Buddhist tradition stresses that they cut ignorance at its roots. "As the sword cuts knots, so should the intellect pierce the deepest recesses of Buddhist thought." Manjusri, as the embodiment of wisdom, is shown carrying the sword of discernment in his right hand. Its point emits the light of the indestructible *vajra* which destroys the heterodox mind and drives away the enemies of Dharma. The hero cannot simply reach out and grasp the sword that stands in the garden of paradise. He must reach within the stone, within the sevenfold anvil of his own being, in order to draw forth a weapon which is capable of cutting through to the goal. Like the swordsmith, he must heat, stretch and fold the substance of his nature over and over again so that its layers merge and melt into perfectly tempered pieces, to be gradually fashioned into a blade. Each time the heating and stretching and folding takes place, he must be very careful to make sure that all the tiny air pockets and bits of dirt are excluded. Even one small inclusion of such impurities can ruin the forging of an otherwise well made sword. It may be capable of cutting a fine line of discrimination, but when the pressure of piercing decisiveness is called for, it will break. All of the care and reverence shown by the Japanese master sword-maker are analogous to the inner preparation the hero must make in order to draw forth his sword. He is unknown to the world because he does this within himself in silence. It is only when he has drawn the sword and begins to exercise the faculty of his higher Divine Will that men are surprised and suddenly sense the presence of a higher intelligence acting in the world.

Excalibur takes its name from *ex*, meaning 'out of', and *calibre*, which means 'the weight of character, standing or importance of something'. It signifies being out of or beyond all calibration or ability to gauge the excellence of. There are no empirical or worldly indices that can be used to describe or compare this sword. When Merlin took Arthur to the Lake of Enchantment, he saw rising from the waters a woman's arm "exceedingly beautiful and clad in white samite, and the hand of this arm holdeth a sword of such exceeding excellence and beauty that no eye hath ever beheld its like". The raven-haired Lady of the Lake tells Arthur that no man may win the sword unless he be without fear and beyond reproach. She calls forth a boat whose brass prow is fashioned in the shape of a woman's head and whose sides bear the wings of a swan. Thus, through the agency of Buddhi, which bears him up over the waters of chaos, Arthur reaches his sword. He learns that its sheath is Faith, which possesses the power to protect its owner's life, whilst the sword is Truth, only to be used in serious battle. Through the grace of his *Buddhic* nature, the pure-minded Arthur won his sword, but his greatest trials lay before him, including the treachery of the evil Morgana le Fay, who, deluding his trusting mind, succeeded in obscuring his higher intuition, causing him to lose his sword's protective sheath of faith.

In stealing the sheath and throwing it into the lake, Morgana demonstrated the danger of the lower psychic mind which continually measures things in terms of the fragmented world and cleaves to likes and dislikes even in the presence of universally recognizable goodness. Arthur's goodness needed to be alloyed to the cool steel of discrimination and the impersonal probes necessary to expose the convolutions of the lower mind in oneself and in others. To do this the Higher Will must be activated and used without hesitation or timidity. In the words of the Lady of the Lake, the wielder of this sword must be without fear and beyond reproach. He must be pure and selfless in motive and, grasping the laser sword, he must let its blade thrust home. There is a great distinction made in fencing between the parry (defence) and the attack. "A fencer, even though he possesses a perfect mechanism, will never be developed except through the execution of scientific or reasoned movements, based principally upon the theory of attack." The parry is nothing more than a corrective measure, remaining only a passive factor. The attack involves the imagination, whilst the parry is merely instinctive.

The hero who would reach the Holy Grail must sharpen his sword with the powers of discrimination and decisiveness and be prepared to venture if he would strike to the core of Truth. He does not sit back and soak in Arthurian legends, waiting for someone else to win the fight. He does not wait for someone else to prove to him that good can triumph over evil, that faith and love can vanquish despair and hatred. He does not participate in anxious vicarious contests, sweated through by mere observers who stand on the sidelines, laying bets and waiting for the outcome. Instead, the true hero has sized up the contenders. He has recognized them for what they are and fully grasped that they are within himself and not out there on the tournament field or the battleground. He has quietly cherished his quest throughout the ages, and, arriving at this time in human history, he knows that the world can no longer expect to be uplifted in its dead weight and carried along by the Christs or Gandhis. He is showing the way for each individual to cut away ignorance and impurities of mind, to cleanse the heart of every power to wound by piercing to its diamond core. He parries only out of compassion, never out of self-protectiveness, and is always prepared to dare, to grasp the sword of Truth and attack the muddle of rationalizations and obscurations that cloud men's minds and hearts. With his brilliant and nobly drawn sword he points out the way across the lake to the outstretched arm, to the marble stone and anvil, to the sacred smithy's shop where the secret forging will be done. He is our Grail Knight, our Odysseus and Galahad, our Manjusri. He is our heroic and eternal Higher Self.

> The dancers moved encircling
> Round the body of the Fool.
> But the young lad on the edge
> Of the wildly laughing throng
> Slipped away to the river's edge,
> Where before his wondering gaze
> A beauteous Lady rose
> And presented him a sword.

Hermes, February 1983

THE PENTAGRAM

It becomes the task of the fifth Hierarchy – the mysterious beings that preside over the constellation Capricornus, Makara, or "Crocodile" in India as in Egypt – to inform the empty and ethereal animal form and make of it the Rational Man.

The Secret Doctrine, i 233

Ask anyone to draw a star and they will almost always draw a pentagram. True, there are those few who might respond with a four-pointed figure; the Dakota painted these on their ghost shirts. But if someone mentions a star, most people think of a pentagram without really knowing the reason why. It may occur to one to wonder why pentagrams are called stars. Why are stars called "stars" and made to look like pentagrams? Is it because they are bright, shining and fiery, which is the meaning of the Greek word *aster*? That they are figures with radiating points? This seems a simple explanation, but their generally spherical shape is not lost in radiation, which suggests a less obvious connection with the pentagram. Perhaps the fact that they occasionally "fall" or that they are thought to have so profound an influence upon human destiny has something to do with it. Do pentagrams "fall" or "shine" even symbolically? Why was the pentagram the great αἴαμγιν (enigma or riddle) of the Pythagoreans, their ἀριστοσυμβολου (highest symbol) whose occult meaning remained hidden even whilst it was expressed as a sign of recognition amongst initiated members of the Brotherhood?

Ἀγςοτηρτ⊠μυ⊠ ⊠δημίς ⊠ίσίτω

ΠΛΑΤΟΝ

Only he who is familiar with geometry shall be admitted here.

Plato

Iamblichus wrote that the sign of the pentagon was so jealously guarded that when the Pythagorean Hippasus published a construction

58

of spheres made up of twelve pentagons, his impiety was thought to be responsible for his subsequently perishing in a shipwreck. For a similar act, Hippocrates of Chios was expelled from the fraternity which persisted in transmitting the secret as part of a whole body of esoteric cosmological and philosophical studies. The pentagram continued to be passed down in secret through the centuries long after Pythagoras and the Pythagoreans were gone. It was kept alive as an occult paradigm for architects and master masons (transmitted from father to son or adopted son) as a secret recognition symbol, and as an actual element of magical ritual. Architects and physicians took an oath of secrecy mirroring that taken by the privileged followers of Pythagoras in antiquity.

The symbol of the pentagram has played a significant role in scholarly discussions concerning the question of the survival of Pythagoreanism after the fourth century B.C. Some who argue that centres continued to flourish after this time refer to pentagrams on buildings and stones in various Mediterranean sites, whilst numismatists point to the abundance of coins bearing the pentagram design which were used in Italy as well as Syria, Gaul and Spain until several centuries AD. Some scholars have tried to show a connection between Pythagoreans and Celtic Druids of Gaul through such coins, which are also similar to certain types used in the British Isles during the second century B.C. These pentagrams may be taken as evidence for a continuous Pythagorean influence in the ancient world, or, since most of them on coins were small signs outside the central design, they can be interpreted as merely indicating trade or profession. Such was the case under Roman rule, where a small pentagram on a coin represented the "Builders" (Masons).

The case for the continuance of Pythagorean thought need not rest upon such limited empirical evidence. Neo-Pythagorean and neo-Platonic ideas stimulated and affected pre-Christian and Christian thinking in many more archetypal ways, from philosophical considerations to architecture and design. Arcane knowledge was passed down through the Stone Masons from the *Collegia Opificum* during the Roman Republic to the architectural workshops of the Benedictine monasteries and the secular medieval guilds of Builders and Masons who revered Pythagoras and Hermes as revelators of the secrets of geometry to the human race. The predominant ratios in Egyptian, Greek and Roman architecture were based upon divisions of five or ten within a controlling circle of orientation. This naturally introduced the theme of the Golden Section and displayed the Pythagorean secret of constructing a pentagon in a circle for elevations as well as for plans.

The pentagon and its element, the pentagram, were treated with geometric precision, as they related to the mystery of cosmic manifestation and its reflected structuring in the world. But some claim that the secret recognition sign of the Pythagoreans was drawn as a flowing figure. They assert that it was not an equiangular uniform figure but, instead, one which resulted from the division of the square by the acute-angled triangle and the placing of the sacred cut so as to halve the square. This introduces the square as a parent figure rather than the pentagon or a circle and suggests more complexities concerning the meaning and origin of the pentagram. Was the pentagram originally a geometric figure emerging from the pentagon to gain elevated cosmic significance leading to its association with the stars and planets? Or, was it originally a slanted, long-legged design signifying merely the microcosm as man? A more deductive approach raises the question of whether the pentagram is self-evident in the cosmic process. Is this why it is said to be endless in its design? Why does the *Book of Dzyan* say that Aditi, the Great Mother, lay with the pentagram in her bosom, ready to bring it forth?

Since Pythagoras studied mathematics in Babylon, many believe the pentagram to have originated there, going back as far as the Uruk IV period (*c*. 3000 B.C.). By the same token, his apprenticeship in India could suggest a South Asian origin for the idea and, indeed, the ancient Vedas reveal hints of this. One of the oldest known meanings ascribed to the symbol is the idea that it represents the quintessence acting upon matter. In its parent form it is the square of matter overbrooded by the one apex whose fiery pyramidal point high above is free from any disturbance in the tetrad below. It symbolizes the four limbs controlled by the head, the four fingers controlled by the thumb, and four cardinal points related to their centre. Once the pentagon is formed, the pentagram joins its vertices and emphasizes the five in an unending interplay of triangles. In this guise the pentagram represents "the spirit of life eternal and the spirit of life and love terrestrial – in the human compound". It signifies the *hierosgamos,* or the union of the principle of heaven (3) with that of the mother (2), and it is the symbol of marriage and generation, the bringing together of the masculine and the feminine in an endless "lover's knot" which ceaselessly delivers itself.

The structural symmetry of the pentagon is a common characteristic in Nature, and man is a perfect illustration of it. He combines all of the cosmic elements at the microcosmic level, so that earth, air, fire and water are overbrooded by Spirit, forming the fifth and topmost point of the pentagram, which represents the head seated in control over the limbs. The Pythagoreans associated this form with health and referred to the pentagram as 'αΧιγΧ or "Health" itself, a practice which clearly revealed their recognition of the importance of man's upright position, the supremacy of his thinking principle over the body and the significance of an ideal balance and symmetry in his structure. This corresponds with an upright and geometrically equiangular pentagram whose balance was believed to be fundamental to the harmony basic to good health.

A central theme running through these classical ideas is that man combines in his nature heaven and earth and possesses the means, through intelligent spiritual control, of maintaining his own microcosmic health and harmony in relation to the greater balance of forces in the macrocosm. Each individual was believed to be potentially capable of unlocking the mystery of the pentagram within and releasing the healing flow of divine love that was his birthright. With the eclipse of the Classical Age and the obscuration of the ancient Mysteries, the symbolic emphasis surrounding the pentagram shifted. Increasingly, the archaic belief in its power to protect began to dominate and man was no longer seen as being in control of his own destiny. In this narrowing mental environment the Pythagorean pentagram found its way as an apotropaic sign (one which could turn away or contain evil spirits). From late antiquity through the Middle Ages and Renaissance into the eighteenth century it persisted. Goethe's Faust drew a pentagram on the thresholds of his room in an effort to protect himself from Mephistopheles, and countless people whose lives might never have inspired great literary portraits took precaution by painting the symbol on thresholds and utensils critical to their livelihood. Frightened by what they perceived as external forces of evil expressed in mental and physical disease as well as collective chaos, people strove to barricade themselves through a reliance upon vicarious atonement and lower magical practices. These sometimes took the form of grey or black magic, and the medieval pentagram came to possess a questionable reputation, having been used to contain and transfer evil as well as to repel it.

This twisted symbolic usage represents the lowest fall of the exercise of divine intelligence associated with the pentagram, and it is only through veiled myths and legends that its spiritually occult meaning was preserved. Thus, when Gawain sustained faith in the five wounds of Christ during his quest for the Grail, he was keeping faith with *the god in man*, symbolized by the stigmata on the head and four limbs which formed a pentagram. Like the shield of an unknown Attic warrior of the fifth century B.C., Sir Gawain's shield is said to have borne a pentagram called "the endless knot", which symbolized much more than the power to repel evil. It represented the five "precious things" expressed in five ways through his wits, his fingers, his faith, his purity and virtue, as well as the merging of heaven and earth. In the evolution of the Arthurian cycle, Gawain was the first knight to bear such a shield. From him it passed in legend to Parsifal, Lancelot and to Galahad, who finally succeeded in discovering the Grail. But the myth paled in the glare of nineteenth century materialism.

The old geometrical symbols were resurrected in a cold utilitarian sense, consonant with the new scientific awareness of the world and man's increasing ability to manipulate the physical forces operating in it. The pentagram and pentagon were seen as no more or no less interesting than any other geometrical shape, even whilst the old notion that it described a star continued to persist in common lore. It is this diminished and confused understanding of the symbol which prevails in its modern usage, although children who draw five-pointed stars across the celestial borders of their early artistic endeavours probably intuit more about the symbol's intrinsic meaning than do people who vigorously wave all the star-spangled flags of the world.

Pythagoras, seeing that there are five solid figures ... said that the
Sphere of the Universe arose from the dodecahedron.

Aetius

For Pythagoras as well as for all Initiates of the Greater Mysteries,
the cosmic progression from the One to the many was seen in terms
of a hierarchy of Spirits. From the One Flame arose the Divine Fire of
Daiviprakriti expressed through *Fohat* as Fire and Ether or the Atma-
Buddhic prototype of the incarnating Monads. From this Duad come
the Triads, the Atma-Buddhi-Manasic prototype, and the Tetrad or
essence of human consciousness in which lies the germ that will fall
into generation. Then emanates the Fifth Group of Dhyanis connected
with the Dragon *Makara*, which is the Dragon of Wisdom or *Manas*,
the Human Soul, mind and intelligence. This cosmic hierarchy
ultimately expresses itself in twelve phases of manifestation. *Brahman*
the First is followed by the AUM or Logos, the androgynous *Brahm*
(*Purusha*), the Tetraktys represented by the Four Faces of Brahmā, the
Five Dhyanis (*Jivatma*) linked with the five mystical vowels uttered
by Brahmā, which became the *Panchadasa* and are followed by the
Astral Light of the Virgin Mother. These are followed by the *tattwas*
or subtle elements, thirty-six in number, and the universe in thought,
which is the eighth level, involving the microcosm subjectively
perceived. Then emerge the nine Prajapatis from whom proceeds the
tenth, which is the shape of the material universe in the mind of the
Demiurgos – the Dodecahedron. After this come the fourteen *lokas* and
the five elements, which simply give dimension and substance to the
structure already manifest.

The Fifth Hierarchy is identified with the Dragon of Wisdom or
Makara, whose name signifies five (*ma*) fingers (*kara*) or sides (*karam*),
and which readily expresses itself as the five-limbed, five-principled
symbol of thinking, conscious man. The *Makaram* are said to be
esoterically a hidden mystical class of *devas* whose name is an anagram
for the Kumaras, the sons of Rudra-Shiva. It is significant that another
meaning of *kara*, besides the five-fingered hand, is the star-shaped
figure connected with the scorpion-sting of Scorpio (Shiva). This
Fifth Hierarchy of Dhyanis contains in itself the dual attributes of the

spiritual and physical aspects of the universe (*Mahat*, the Universal Intelligence, and the dual nature of man). They are the Five Kumaras who gained exemption from passion and have the soul of the five elements in them, with water and Ether predominating. Thus, their symbol is both fiery and aquatic, signifying the great sacrifice wherein they take up an earthly abode for an entire *Mahayuga*, during which they exchange their impersonal individualities for individual personalities.

These Five Dhyanis, containing the spiritual and physical aspects of the universe, represent the two poles or the number five doubled, which gives the sacred decad and the tenth sign of the zodiac or *Makara*. Encompassing the dual five, the pentad is the symbol of marriage, dividing the ineffable number ten into two equal parts. This relates to the fact that five alone is the binary symbol of the two sexes *separated*, a subject whose profound mystery is associated with the lighting up of *Manas* and the making of man, the microcosmic pentagram. The *Makaram* are called *thasathisa* or "faces of the universe", which are bound by the pentagons of the dodecahedron. Before the zodiacal signs of *Kanya* (Virgo), *Thula* (Libra) and *Vrischikam* (Scorpio) were separated into three, Virgo and Scorpio were combined into one eighth sign, *Makara*, which was identified with the eight-faced octahedron. This involved a doubling of the tetrad (Tetraktys reflected), describing the universe in thought or subjectively perceived. With the emanation of the Fifth Hierarchy, Virgo and Scorpio split and there was a fall and separation of the sexes. *Makara* was no longer eight-faced but ten, made up of two parts. It now represented both macrocosm and microcosm as external objects of perception. This is why it is said that in Capricorn (*Makara*) the vehicle of the new man will be built.

Makara-Ketu is *Aja* (the Unborn) and *Atma-bhu* (the Self-Existent). *Aja* is the First Logos, the desire that "first arose in IT, which was the primal germ of mind", that which "connects entity with non-entity", or *Manas* with *Atman*. In the first stage *Manas* is with *Atman*. In the second stage Brahmā issues the Mind-born Sons who, in the Fifth and Ninth Creations, become the Kumaras. Thus, *Manas* descends along a Ray emanated through *Makara* cosmically, and individually with each new birth, and it withdraws in like manner with physical dissolution.

The Egyptians believed that *Makara* drew the quintessence from the life lived at the end of it, and Platonists held that the souls of the dead ascended into heaven through the constellation *Makara*, which they called "the Gate of the Gods". The Five Dhyanis are thus a door or a link connecting entity with non-entity, creating self-conscious man, whose dual nature is microcosmically echoed in the separation of the sexes on the physical plane, the latter being the delusive, externalized expression of what every human being combines in his or her inner pentagrammatic nature wherein the true lover's knot is to be generated.

The Triads become Pentagons on earth.

How did the androgynous triadic hierarchies become the Five Dhyani Buddhas who are the *Jivatma* in man? One might ask, how did a geometric solid made up of three-sided figures become a solid made up of five-sided figures? Again, how did the icosahedron, which represents the astral light (noumenal universe), become the dodecahedron, or the manifest physical universe? If we examine models of the two forms, we may observe that, in the process of conversion from the three to the five, the vertices of the pentagons are to be located in the centres of the triads, and the lines of the edges of pentagons cross the edges of triangles so as to be always perpendicular. Another way of visualizing this is to "Describe a sphere about an icosahedron; let perpendiculars be drawn from the centre of the sphere on its faces and produced to meet the surface of the sphere. Now, if the points of intersection be joined, a dodecahedron is formed within the sphere." If we examine a model of an icosahedron, we can discover that the five is already inherent in its structure in the form of the pentagons containing five triangles, which are visible on any side.

In this combination of triad and pentagon, the icosahedron represents microcosmically the Higher Triad of the Inner Man as well as the potential natural man. If we count the triads, there are five above and five below with ten in between. The triads in between face up and down, creating a tension of equal attraction and repulsion between the upper and lower pentagons. They form a buffer separating the higher and lower potentials, which is a requisite condition of the hidden astral universe. With the dodecahedron, the pentagons become the faces, the five made manifest, combining the Higher Triad with *prana* and the *linga sharira*. It is through this marriage that the rational man comes into being. The dodecahedron represents an expansion of the pentagon in three-dimensional space, and in its multiple expression there is no "buffer" separating the upper and the lower. Instead, the whole is made manifest in the pentad itself, which is a primary number divisible by unity only.

The pentagram is an element of the pentagon, joining each vertex to its opposite side. The ratio of the line between two neighbouring vertices of the pentagon and the longer line joining two of its opposite vertices is equal to Ø or the sacred Golden Ratio so valued by the Pythagoreans. This proportion is intimately associated with the regular pentagon and pentagram, so much so that the construction of the pentagon is based upon the Golden Section. Because of the connection between the Golden or Ø Series and *homothetic* growth, and between the Golden Section and the pentagon, it is not surprising that there is a preponderance of pentagonal symmetry in natural forms such as flowers, all fruit blossoms, leaves and starfish, as well as in the proportions of the human body. Whilst never appearing in the inorganic crystalline systems, pentagonal symmetry plays a predominant role in the shape of living organisms and in the patterns of their growth. This is known as *gnomonic* growth, which is *homothetic* growth by *intussusception* or *imbibition* (from inside outwards) as opposed to *agglutination*, which is simple addition from outside of identical elements, as with minerals.

The symmetry involved in this wonderful process is one of dynamic proportionality, not at all like the static concept of symmetry that developed in medieval times, which was based on arithmetic. This pristine sense of symmetry is closer to analogy or "the impression given by that which remains similar to itself in the diversity of evolution". The principle of analogy is common to both art and science and has to do with the permanent similarities. It is found at the base of eurhythmy (of or in harmonic proportion) and modulation in the arts of space as well as musical harmony. It also dominates literature, where metaphor is only a condensed and unexpected analogy. Such intuitive perception of similarity was the source of Shakespeare's metaphors and Leonardo da Vinci's insight into the laws of Nature, so beautifully expressed in his pentagrammatic drawing of man within the cosmic circle.

Pentagonal symmetry cannot be (for purely arithmetical reasons in angular distribution) associated with equal divisions of space or homogeneous point-lattices, but fits in perfectly with the seemingly asymmetrical pulsations of living growth. This reminds one of the assertion made by some scholars that the Pythagorean pentacle was not an equilateral, uniform figure and that it was drawn as a free-flowing figure whose bottom legs were of unequal length, as were the arms and head. It may be that these drawings were merely imprecise, or they could have been meant to reflect the flowing dialectic of imbibitional growths which emanate from the ideal framework of the more noumenal inner pentagram. From an archetypal perspective, however, the irregular pentagram represents the disproportion of mental perversity, which is bound to affect health adversely. Looking at the larger picture, it may be assumed that the seeming asymmetry of *gnomonic* growth in particular instances is balanced off in a greater symmetry operating at the universal level. It is this greater balanced symmetry which the man of perfect health is capable of reflecting.

> Man is his own star and the soul that can
> Render an honest and a perfect man
> Commands all light, all influence, all fate.
> Nothing to him falls early, or too late.
> Our acts our angels are, or good or ill,
> Our fatal shadows that walk by us still.

> John Fletcher

The legend of Sir Gawain has been Christianized, but the original story involved the theme of magician in combat with magician. The pentagram on his shield was a key capable of releasing the higher magic through the five fingers of his mind and hand, capable of awakening him with a fiery Scorpio sting to a Shiva-like awareness of the task at hand. Just so must any man or woman make the journey to self-conscious godhood. In the preparation for the quest, an affirmation of identity must be declared, setting the stage for combat and revealing itself in the pentagram on the shield. This affirmation, this strong act of will, is the greatest defence against the indwelling adversary, and it must be held firmly upright at all times. If the pentagram becomes inverted in one's consciousness, it will draw all the forces of death and witchcraft associated with a perverse prolongation of the Fall. But if its "head" is always held uppermost, one begins to realize in consciousness one's celestial prototype. Only as a five-pointed star can man become a living link between the celestial and terrestrial, an *antaskarana* bridge capable of spanning the noumenal and phenomenal worlds. The up ward-pointing apex of his higher Manasic intellect becomes capable of penetrating the luminous vessel of *Buddhi,* and the mystic marriage between the star and the crescent can take place. In this way do pure knights and initiates ascend to the threshold of *Makara,* the Gate of the Gods, the place of birth of the spiritual microcosm and death of the physical universe.

It is said that the mystery of the pentagram must be mastered before the hexagram can be understood. The quest for the full realization of one's humanity necessitates a courageous adherence to Truth, Love and Beauty with such unswerving purity of mind and heart as to render one a true *Brahmachari,* an unsullied virginal reflector of the Dhyani-Kumaras. When the seeker has become a true *Satyagrahi,* overcoming any division between the higher and lower pentagrams, he will have merged in spiritual wedlock the progeny of the binary number five. With Higher *Manas* fully activated, the marriage with *Buddhi* can take place and the androgynous state exemplified by the Great Initiates of the Sixth Round be approached. Thus may the human pentagram become circumscribed by a hexagram within a circle, and the Knight-Initiate joins the ranks of those who tirelessly serve in the Army of the Builders, whose compassionate design serves as a timeless pathway leading to the perfect symmetry of Truth.

> In the breast of Aditi I blaze;
> Invisible fire beating,
> Pulsating star unseen.

I am the five sacred words of Brahm,
The sparks of Shiva's Seed.
I am the virgin offspring of Truth,
The promised Light of Mind.
Seek ye the Dragon's Gate,
O thou of Lesser Face.
Be thou a bridge onto the Greater Shore.

Hermes, March 1983

THE OWL

There was an old owl liv'd in an oak,
The more he heard, the less he spoke;
The less he spoke, the more he heard,
O, if men were all like that wise bird!

Punch, 1875

Still and solitary, the owl sits in the tree as though frozen in time, a piece of corrugated bark merged into the dapples and designs of the forest. A silent-seeming foot falls softly on decaying leaves and, abruptly, great golden eyes dominate the scene, fixing the intruder with their piercing gaze. He is taken aback by their sudden appearance and made uneasy by the fact that the enormous orbs seem to penetrate through him to his very soul. If he were an Egyptian who had wandered far from his Nile delta to Lebanon's wooded hills, he would surely be gripped with fear, thinking that the sombre bird before him was the *Ba*, or Third Soul, of a deceased, come up from the realm of the dead sun. If the intruder were a Mayan, a Zapotec or an Aztec, he would tremble with foreboding, believing that his time had come. But an ancient Minoan or a Greek who came upon that spot would have looked up with receptive eyes to behold a wise counsellor and protector. For them the sight of an owl was a good omen, which pointed the way through darkness to light.

The darkness to be penetrated is, however, awesome, and many people have associated the apparently disconcerting habits of the owl with the darkness of death and evil. Wherever Christian ideas have come to dominate, there has been a strong emphasis on evil, whilst most other parts of the world continued to identify the owl with night and often the personification of death. The link with darkness readily overlaps into one with stillness and the quietude closely associated with wisdom. Though Chaucer and Spenser wrote of the owl as the prophet of "wo and myschance" and "death's dreadful messengere", and Shakespeare referred to owls as the "comrades of ghosts" and

70

bringers of ill omen, farmers were continually aware that the large-eyed avian destroyed rodents harmful to their crops, whilst hardly ever harming a valued animal. Owls are not scavengers, nor do they specialize in feeding on carrion, as do the great birds of prey so often associated with death. Thus there is an ambivalence and a mystery to the owl, who is symbolic both of wisdom and of death, of all that which is associated with Light and also that which is connected with Darkness.

After Deukalion's flood, Zeus commanded Athena to assist Prometheus in calling forth a new race. Archaic Greek art forms illustrate how they fashioned the new man out of the silt left by the flood waters. From the richest and purest essence culled out of the material of the old, a new human vesture was prepared by the Hellenic deity most intimately linked with the lighting-up of the mind-principle in man and the owl-goddess of wise counsel and fearless combat. Athena assisted in this birth with all the creative potency at her command, whilst remaining chaste and aloof from the material itself, like her quietly withdrawn namesake perched high above the teeming forest bed. In his epic prose, Homer continually refers to Athena as *glaukopis*, meaning "bright-eyed" or "owl-faced", which is derived from γλαυξ (*glaukos*, meaning "owl"). referring to the owl's glaring eyes. The goddess soars in an all-seeing flight of poetry through Homer's melodious lines:

> I begin to sing about Pallas Athena,
> Renowned goddess, with bright eyes, quick
> Mind, and inflexible heart, chaste and
> Mighty virgin, protectress of the city, Tritogeneia.
> Wise Zeus himself gave birth to her from his
> Holy head and she was arrayed
> In her armour of war, all
> Gleaming in gold, and every one
> Of the immortals was gripped
> With awe as they watched

Zeus was counselled by Gaea and Uranus to swallow his wife Metis, as they feared that the children she was destined to bear would surpass him in glory. First of these was to be the keen-eyed maiden Athena, equal to her father in might and good counsel. In springing from her father's forehead, she emerged with a thunderous cry manifesting fully the masculinity of her mind, while her virginity shone through the grace and grandeur of her female form. Among her many by-names, Athena was called Promachos, "she who fights in the foremost ranks", and Alalcomenes, protectress "who repulses the enemy". In her peaceful guise she was protectress of industries, arts and all things basic to civilization, and she was Pronoia, "the far-seeing", wise counsellor of the assembly. Sexually unapproachable, she was Valkyrie-like in her steadfast protection of heroes like Herakles, Perseus and Odysseus. The owl so closely identified with her (often called Minerva's owl after her Roman counterpart) is the nocturnal *Athene noctua*, whose barred and speckled plumage can still be spotted along the rocky bluffs and acropolis of ancient Greek cities. Commonly known as the "little owl" (*glaux*), members of this species were so plentiful in the city of the goddess that any needless task came to be referred to as "taking owls to Athens". At the Acropolis in Athens, owls flew unmolested in and around the Parthenon, the Erechtheum and the temple of Athena Nike.

Though the forty-foot statue of the goddess in the Parthenon depicted a powerful, helmeted maiden with spear and shield, it was believed that Athena could assume the form of her owl and did so at the Battle of Marathon in 490 B.C. In *The Wasps*, Aristophanes credited this owl with raising the morale of the Athenians:

> With rage our lips we swallow'd; while the darts so thick did fly,
> They seem'd to form a coverlid between ourselves and sky.
> But Pallas sent her night-bird; and as the owlet flew
> Across the host, our armies hope and joyous omens drew.
> So by the help of Heaven, ere yet the day did close,
> We shouted word of victory, and routed all our foes.

The Athenians came to be identified so closely with the owl that the Samians, during a temporary victory over them, branded the foreheads of their Athenian prisoners with the figure of the large-eyed bird. Almost all Hellenic coins (except for the smallest) produced during Athenian supremacy between the Persian and Peloponnesian Wars had owls on them, often with the helmeted goddess on the obverse side. So auspicious was this symbol that to say "there goes an owl" was to acknowledge a success, a sentiment played upon adroitly by Agathocles, who, while attacking the Carthaginians, released numbers of birds to encourage the troops.

With Apollo, Athena acts to support heroes who take up their fate actively, as in the case of Odysseus or Orestes, where she sees to the latter's acquittal, as dramatized by the great Initiate and playwright, Aeschylus, in the *Oresteia*. By outwitting the Furies and bringing Orestes before the court of Aereopagus (which she created) in Athens, the owl-goddess silenced an older order of gods and the practice of blood-feuding ("eye for an eye, tooth for a tooth"), which was a residual aspect of an outdated order in a primitive society. The owl-goddess closes a chapter involving the unavenged death of Clytemnestra and introduces the qualities of reason and choice into the concepts of morality and justice in a new order. This association underlies the link that symbolically relates the owl with the mind and with wise and deliberate action. The idea of the lighting-up of the mind has often been symbolized by lightning, and in the owl this is particularly related to the luminosity of its penetrating gaze. Europeans (in Germany until the nineteenth century) nailed dead owls to buildings, believing that their brilliant eyes would sympathetically attract lightning and thereby spare the structure itself. Perhaps a more telling relationship was shown by the Chinese of the Shang Dynasty, to whom the owl was a patron sage who monitored the propitious time for making mirrors and swords. In attempting to think of an ideal symbol for wisdom, it is difficult to imagine anything better than these two reflective and incisive instruments.

The earliest symbolism attached to the owl in general stresses the characteristic of sagacity. Its piercing, highly focussed eyes, its ability to stay awake at night and its gift of seeing in the dark are all qualities meriting such an association. The idea of the "wise old owl" has survived into our own century, where to be "owlish" is to be studious, bookish and, maybe, intelligent. It is undoubtedly because of its presumed intelligence that the owl figures so predominantly in the divination practices of many cultures. It is not taken as coincidental that the bird should sit on a particular side of a tree, or hoot at a particular moment or fly alongside a ship at a certain angle. The coming and going of owls has been widely linked with the beginnings and endings of things, even, sometimes, of life itself. It matters not that the owl behaves as befitting a bird of prey; to many his contemplative stillness, his gravity of mien and precision of action far outweigh such mundane aspects of his character.

> In the ruins of an old castle a treasure-seeker observed an owl
> catch and devour a mouse: "Is that fitting for the philosophical
> favourite of Minerva?" taunted the intruder. "Why not?"
> replied the owl; "because I am fond of quiet meditation,
> can I therefore live upon air? Though I am well aware that
> mankind frequently condemn die learned to such a diet."
>
> *Fables: Aesop's and Others*

The owl has been around for at least sixty million years. It began to develop in the Tertiary Period, after the last of the great dinosaurs had disappeared, when mammals had begun to proliferate along with their predators, including birds of prey. The forerunners of the modern owl evolved in the Miocene period (ten to twenty-five million years ago) and eventually achieved such variations as the elf owl, which is sparrow-sized, and the very large eagle owl of Eurasia, which grows to thirty-three inches in length. A thirty-thousand-year-old Aurignacian cave in France contains petroglyphs of what are recognizably snowy owls that must have been the focus of magical and religious practices. It was only much later, with Aristotle and then Pliny the Elder, that the owl was considered as a subject of natural history. In the eighteenth century Linnaeus placed the owl in his *Systema naturae*, distinguishing thirty-one earless and nineteen eared owls, whilst modern ornithologists recognize one hundred and thirty-two species-types, which are divided into two families within the order *Strigiformes*. Adapting to so many habitats, it is no wonder that the owl is almost omnipresent in the world. As one writer put it, the screech owl is found "screaming, snoring and hissing in almost every country of the world". Even so, it is the owl's remarkable prowess as a hunter and its stillness which, more than any other characteristics, are responsible for its widespread and enduring survival. Its wonderful stillness along with its camouflaged colouration render it often invisible, and it is expert at the art of decoy when it conies to protecting its nestlings. It will even fly to the ground and utter a cry sounding like an injured rabbit to throw a predator off the path. A wise old bird indeed.

The owl possesses two extraordinarily developed senses: those of vision and hearing. Its eyes are very large, far larger than what they appear to be on the outside, where only the iris and the pupil show. They are tubular in shape rather than spherical, taking up so much room in the skull that they sacrifice almost all mobility. Over the lens is a nictitating membrane (a third eyelid) especially developed to shield the highly sensitive retina from excessive brightness. The owl sees better in semi-darkness than we can see in daylight. An unusually large pupil dilates to let more light enter the eye so that it sees at a hundredth of man's need of light, thus making the maximum use of small amounts of light in natural darkness. Despite all claims to the contrary, the owl can see very well in the daytime, having even then, like other birds, powers of vision far superior to our own. As it wings slowly along a bluff or sits in dignified surveillance of the land, the owl is far-sighted, and it relies on tactile feathers to guide it while subduing prey or feeding.

Looking at the structure of the eye itself, one notices immediately that the cornea and the lens are very large, allowing more light to enter the eye. To accommodate this, the lens is much rounder and can focus light over the short distance to the retina without loss. The retina of the owl's eye is covered with light-sensitive rod cells, the density of which is many times greater than in the human eye, whilst the colour-sensitive cones are not so abundant. Rods are particularly adapted for nocturnal vision, which is why man, who has fewer rods that are placed only around the periphery of the cones, tends to look askance (at an angle) at objects in poor light. The owl can hunt with deadly accuracy, using its eyes in any kind of natural darkness, but in a totally blacked-out environment it relies entirely on its power of hearing. Experiments with barn owls placed in a completely lightless room (where they are watched with infra-red equipment) show that the birds would unerringly pounce upon their prey the instant the slightest sound was made. Many owls rely upon sound more than sight in hunting and can pick up a frequency as high as 20,000 cycles per second, as compared to 8,500, which is the highest audible pitch for humans. It can truly be said that owls are not alone in having well developed auditory organs, but they are unique among birds in the degree to which their hearing has developed.

Owls have large ears, one tending to be larger than the other, so as to increase their binaural efficiency in locating sources of sound. They are covered with flaps which are very mobile and can open and close and change in shape at will so that the owl can concentrate on sounds coming from any quarter. The shape of the flaps affects the shape of the facial disks, which open up when the owl is alerted. The disks themselves have an acoustical function in gathering and concentrating sound, much like the parabolic reflectors used by sound specialists. Little wonder that the owl prefers to remain still and very quiet. It is listening intently to a world of sound that stretches far beyond anything that we humans can experience on the physical plane. The owl is a superb listener, and to aid him in his task he has evolved wings covered and edged on the outer margins with velvet-soft, sound-deadening filaments. Air streaming over these does not produce audible vibrations, and their broad shape permits the owl to glide soundlessly and leisurely, without stalling or abruptly altering its course. The experience of seeing one of these great-eyed birds gliding in absolute silence through the darkened air is awesome. If we bear in mind the occult lore concerning the meaning of their appearance at certain times and places, the arrival of a white Siberian owl in California can assume an unexpected significance. One such may have appeared, though only a Sage could realize why and interpret correctly the meaning of its remarkable migration. Hovering along the roadside verge, the ghostly form, moving in complete silence with its enormous golden eyes intently focussed, would swerve and dip and disappear. In such a manner are messages delivered between great Rishis, Bodhisattvas and Adepts who, like the owl, can see beyond the curtain of what, to most men, seems darkness.

In his delightful tale "The Owl Who Was God", James Thurber joined a long line of literary figures who have falsely accused the owl of day-blindness. Perhaps Thurber can here be excused because of his humorous wit. Holding up two claws, a secretary-bird approaches an owl and asks him how many he sees, to which the owl replies, "Two!" Then the secretary-bird asks for an expression meaning "that is to say" or "namely". The owl answers, "To wit!" The secretary-bird is impressed and asks why a lover calls upon his love, and the owl cleverly answers, "To woo!" News spreads of this great sage-like being and all the birds of the forest claim that the owl is God. They follow him everywhere in the daytime, and when he bumps into and stumbles over things, they do too, until he leads them blindly onto a road where they all meet an untimely end. The moral of this story is not difficult to draw, but its ready reception by generations of readers is largely due to a centuries-old defamation campaign launched against the owl by the Christian church. Whilst it is true that even in the ancient Hindu *Panchatantra* there is reference to the day-blindness of the owl, it is the Christian tradition that associated this idea with turning away from the spiritual and embracing evil. In the words of Samuel Coleridge:

> Forth from his dark and lonely hiding place
> (Portentous sight!) the owlet Atheism,
> Sailing on obscene wings athwart the noon,
> Drops his blue-fringéd lids, and holds them close,
> And hooting at the glorious sun in Heaven,
> Cries out, "Where is it?"

Church fathers likened the Jews, who rejected Christ, to the light-shunning, evil owl, whose habits were unclean but who sustained enormous conceit in its blindness. In fact, the theme of the conceited owl has continually recurred throughout the development of what has been basically a non-intellectual religious movement to the point of very nearly eclipsing the bird's earlier association with wisdom. This was paralleled with an intensification of its identification with witchcraft, heretical philosophies and ghoulish entities who make their home in the darkness of night. One is instantly reminded of all the standard figures in a typical Halloween tableau. Ecclesiastical art throughout Europe depicted the owl in various negative aspects, including one where it is held aloft by an ape riding a goat – all three helpmates of the devil.

The association of the owl with the ape is not completely far-fetched. They both are quite humanoid in their appearance. The owl, having eyes that are set in the front of its head (unlike other birds) and standing so upright while resting, does indeed look like a judge in robes. This is probably one of the reasons one is so startled to suddenly see an owl silently standing, as it were, on the limb of a tall tree. Of course, this impression would quickly be shattered if it began to bob its head up and down in the process of getting a good sighting with its binocular vision.

It would be even more disconcerting if the bird turned its head fully upside down in its efforts or kept a bead on one who circled it below by rotating its head two hundred and seventy degrees without moving its body at all. This striking ability is, no doubt, partially responsible for the macabre circumgyrating heads that have played such a startling role in Christian demonism. It is a relief that not all succumbed to such fearful ecclesiastical melodrama. Some writers and poets succeeded in maintaining a balanced and even benign attitude towards the owl, delighting in its remarkable talents and marking its dignified air. In Edward Lear's jaunty lines, Pussy says to the owl:

> "You elegant fowl!
> How charmingly sweet you sing!
> O let us be married! too long we have tarried:
> But what shall we do for a ring?"
> They sailed away, for a year and a day,
> To the land where the Bong-tree grows,
> And there in the wood a Piggy-wig stood
> With a ring at the end of his nose.

> *The Owl and The Pussycat*

The darkness, so deplored by some and associated with evil by others, is applauded as that which harbours true light by Sages. To put it in another way, light on our plane is darkness in the higher spheres. *The Secret Doctrine* reminds us that the "Body of Light" is the darkness of ignorance, but also that of silence and secrecy. Of the Creations mentioned in the Puranas, the first is that of *Mahatattva*, in which the primordial self-evolution of that which had to become *Mahat*, the Divine Mind or Spirit of the Universal Soul, takes place. This creation witnesses the emanation of Light (Spirit) out of Absolute Uncreate "Darkness", and it is followed by a secondary creation involving darkness, not to be confused with Pre-Cosmic Darkness. This secondary creation belongs to the triple aspect of *Ahamkara* ("I-Am-Ness"), that which first issues from *Mahat*. At this stage, the first shadowy outline of selfhood unfolds, wherein the *devas* who are the originators of form will do their work. This is allegorized in the *Vishnu Purana*, where the creations subsequent to the First are spoken of in terms of the Bodies of Brahmā. Concentrating his mind (Brahmā"s) "onto itself and the quality of darkness (matter) pervading (his) assumed body", he produced the *Asuras* from his thigh, "after which abandoning this body it was transformed into Night". Here, *Asuras* (demons) is derived directly from *asu*, referring to the Breath of God, and indicates several classes of beings, including those which have the power to dispel ignorance, and *Rakshasas*, whose concern it is to preserve the silence and secrecy of truth from profanation.

Thus, in the Creations, darkness follows light and all emanate from that Darkness which is the Ever-Concealed Deity. In the *Book of Hermes*, Pymander appears to Hermes saying, "The Light is me, I am the Nous, I am thy God, and I am far older than the human principle which escapes from the shadow ("Darkness" or the concealed Deity)." This Light refers to the Second Logos, which, whilst preceding the Light of the human (Third) Logos, is itself emanated from the Body of Night, into whose essence the First Logoic ray has withdrawn. This archetypal occult process does not take place in steps through time. In reality, "Darkness radiates Light" continually, and those who have the ability to transcend the brain-mind, which is only able to perceive things in increments of contrast on the gross physical level, experience this regularly. The Day and Night of Brahma are not merely successive cycles, but have to do with planes that coexist. Humans seem to move through them in time, but that too is mayavic because they are simultaneously manifested all along. Time and space, that which seems to separate us in one state from another, is a complete illusion. Man can assume the perspective of the Builder who rested in the darkness of *Paranishpanna* prior to beginning the work of producing "Form from No-Form". Right now, not in time, man can be in that state where Non-Ego, Voidness and Darkness are the *Three-in-One*.

The lower mind of man, the darkness in which the owl is most active, is filled with *bhuts* and evil possibilities. It is heavy and covers one like a leaden cloak. The owl experiences this absence of physical light in a very different way. We know that with its extraordinary sight it can see well enough to hunt in natural darkness. It does so, in part, by focussing upon patterns of movement, which it anticipates skillfully. More important, it relies strongly on its remarkable sense of hearing with which it "sees" with precision what the enveloping night holds. In this manner it is vibrantly in touch with an entire environment only very dimly sensed by human beings. The owl not only sees in the dark, but in the daylight as well. It possesses twenty-four-hour vision through which it can participate equally in both aspects of the universal cycle, which we easily see as analogous to life and death as well as to *manvantaras* and *pralayas*. The light and darkness on the other side of darkness in this way coexist for the owl.

It is said that Athena originated in Lemuria at the close of the Third Race. This would correspond with her task of assisting Prometheus to create a new race, for it was during that time that thinking man emerged. Now, just as before that period there had been cycles of development followed by obscuration, so also, after that period, the flood of darkness covered all. Twice, long before the rise of the Third Sub-Race (of the Fifth Race) in Greece, was there darkness covering sunken continents and civilizations dimly remembered. With the impetus of the Hellenic flowering, far-sighted Athena blossomed forth to stir up bright and penetrating beams of consciousness in human beings and teach them how to look beyond the darkened veil of appearances. To them the owl was the symbol of all that is capable of seeing through duality to the core which transcends it. To them the owl symbolized all that was wise. But later people, like the medieval

Christians, scorned the goddess and reviled her owl. For these, what had been a joyful and protective omen became an emblem of evil and death. In the fluctuations of light and dark, the rise and fall of civilizations, what was life for one people at one time became death for another. The occult truth that lies between these apparent opposites is often glimpsed by one who, though vainly seeking it throughout life, discovers it only as death comes. Out of darkness comes light and it existed all the time.

Just as this may happen to an individual, so too with nations.

As Hegel eloquently pointed out, at the collapse of a great civilization, when all is lost, Minerva's owl can appear and reveal the painful truth. He may come in the form of a Sage who might have been overlooked by almost everyone when things were going well. Thus are old cycles brought to a close to be replaced with the new. The Siberian owl carries its message from an old and dying European culture to the seedbed for the new civilization of the future. It is, in part, like a rich swan-song wafted across the darkness separating two continents. There will be those who hear the song and merely give poor and superficial imitations of it, but there will be some who see to the heart of the melody and recognize its original spiritual genius. In order to do this, one must, like the owl, listen at the highest possible level of one's being. Only in darkness, when the appearances of the daylit world have been seen for the illusion they are, can one listen well enough to become wise. The wonderfully large ears of a Buddha or a Gandhi belonged to beings who were profound listeners attuned to the universal sounds of Akashic heights. To see what to do in their lives they had to perceive first the patterns in what is a blinding darkness to others.

The owl has always been associated with death, but for two quite different reasons. To those who saw darkness and death existing fully in light and life, the owl was a symbol of transcendence, whose hooting was a constant reminder of the Oneness inherent in duality. To those who feared darkness and death, the owl's appearance could only strike panic in their hearts. Ill prepared to learn the painful truth, they would see the owl as evil, when in reality he is merely (like the *Rakshasas*) preserving the secrecy and sacredness of Truth from general profanation. The ancient Chinese were very intuitive when they identified the owl as a Sage who monitored the propitious time for making mirrors and swords. The owl's nature perfectly reflects the means by which the human mind can become like a Truth reflecting mirror which, with the sword-like accuracy of the great bird's brilliant gaze, can cut through the layers of endless contrasts to a realm of Absolute Light.

At twilight one glimpses this. This is the moment of Truth. If one is still appearing as nothing in the eyes of others, camouflaged to blend in while listening deeply to the often poignant undercurrent of sound that lies behind the cacophony and bright dazzle of the world, one may discover the thread that connects one's own incarnations and the incarnations of billions with the Logoic Light. One can soar like the owl through darkness and light with equal ease, arriving at last, beyond all boreal forests and the acropoles as we know them, at the pristine origin of Light and Life.

> His silent flight and piercing gaze
> Scatter the rodents from the maze;
> And in devotion to that Sage
> They likewise in their minds did cage
> The rodent-thoughts of worldly wage.
> Entering thus, in stillness held,
> They pierced the dark and Truth beheld.

Hermes, November 1983

THE DOG

The unwearied watch their listening leaders keep,
And crouching close repel invading sleep,
So faithful dogs their charge maintain . . .
They start, they gaze around, watch on every side,
  and turn to every sound.

Illiad, Homer

"Imagine, my little ones, the ancient Grandmother of the Earth. Since the beginning of time she has sat, huddled, on the rim of existence. Humming over and again to herself the most pristine harmony, she tirelessly weaves the great basket called the world. Slowly by day the woven pattern emerges while her dog patiently waits. His eyes never cease to follow her nimble hands, recording and remembering the pattern as it grows. Until she rests from her work at nightfall, he watches and waits and then begins to unravel every strand. The Old One sleeps and the dog unwinds the knotted strands of day. By morning, all has been undone and the patient weaver begins again. She never rises from her task to chase the dog away nor does she fail to feed him from her exhaustless store. Every day and night proceed like those that went before: so it has always been; so it shall always be. We of the Shawnee Tribe have never doubted this, and I have heard it said that others believe it too. Do not the Kato people say that 'when the First Mover was going around the world creating, he took his dog'?"

Satisfied that she had thoroughly made her point, the old story-teller tucked the children in, herself a grandmother finishing up the day. Behind closed eyes the children's thoughts drifted along the rim of the world and explored the details of the tale they had heard. Had the ancient Grandmother existed before the dog? Did the dog exist before the world? Had there always been dogs waiting and watching? They wondered about these things and about the Creator, who took his dog with him when he created the world. The questions merged with dreams for the children, but asleep or awake, anyone might wonder if the dog may have been around forever. It seems to appear always, even in the oldest myths and in quaint scratches on the walls of caves. To the Egyptians and the Greeks the dog was esteemed as a companion of Hermes, who, as the good shepherd, is both messenger and presiding deity of the mind and goes about accompanied by his faithful dog, Sirius, the "all-seeing vigilance". For many people of the world, the dog itself has been a messenger: between the gods and man and between life and death. Revered as a fire-bringer and solar herald, seen by many as the Hound of Heaven, the dog inspires awe, whilst in its guise as harbinger of death it is dreaded and reviled.

Plutarch felt that the dog symbolized the conservative and watchful principle of life and, like Plato, characterized it as a philosopher. This perhaps suggests a witness who, like the Shawnee Grandmother's dog, existed from the very beginning of things. Apuleius described the dog as "raising his rough neck, his face alternately black and golden, denoting the messenger going hence and thence between the higher and infernal powers". In the Shawnee myth the dog is the unraveller, but here the stress is upon his role as a weaver, coming and going between worlds. As companion of the dead on their crossing to the nether region, the dog is indeed weaving its way in the role of a guide to those who do not know the way. In Hindu myth Indra's dog, Sarama, mothered the Sarameyas, the four-eyed dogs of Yama who run between this world and the nether region, summoning men and women to the other side. Many an Eastern ritual calls for the participation of a dog at the time of death. The Parsees traditionally introduced one to the deathbed and it accompanied the funeral procession. The death of a woman in childbirth required two dogs in order to accommodate two souls. In old Tibet sacred dogs were kept in the monasteries to devour the remains of the dead before the influence of Buddhism encouraged the spread of cremation.

If the dog is a guide to the realm of the dead, it is also a keeper of the boundary between the two worlds. Like the great mastiff of Charon, it guards the entrance way and none can pass without its acquiescence. But on the field of battle the dog throws himself into the fray. He is at once messenger, watcher, combatant and guard. He weaves his way back and forth from the living to the dead or wounded if trained to do so, or he becomes a Hound of Hell fighting along with the boldest soldier on the field. It is said that dogs larger than wolves accompanied the Celts when they attacked Delphi in 273 B.C. Terrifying the Greeks, they raised havoc like Hecate's own hounds of war, against whom regular soldiers had little effect. Often pictured with war-gods and heroes, the dog has been placed in the role of a witness of death as well as its guide. A companion in life, it continues to be such in death and so weaves the two together in a pattern of perpetual coming and going, a continual design of birth, death and rebirth. For this reason the dog is also associated with resurrection and fertility, leaving one to ponder whether Yudhishthira was not motivated by something in addition to compassion when he insisted that his faithful dog accompany him to heaven.

As guide or witness or guardian, the dog seems to exemplify fidelity. Even as harbinger of war and death, it demonstrates a faithful execution of its master's desire. Its faithfulness includes and goes beyond death, and so it is said to be a fidelity surviving death, to be reborn again and again. It was this perception of the death-defying power of faith that caused the Greeks to recognize in the dog the companion of healers like Aesclepius, whose temples were frequented by canines of all sorts. The sick who came to these places for cures believed the dog to have a healing tongue. They thought that if the animals licked their wounds while they observed an "incubation" period (sleeping at the temple), or if the dogs appeared to them in dreams, a cure was heralded and would soon come into effect. Thus, through the transference of the power inherent in the faithfulness of the dog, death was surmounted and life recommenced. Such beliefs demonstrate on a simple thaumaturgic level a profound metaphysical conception of faith and a deep insight into the essential inner qualities of familiar creatures. Northern Buddhists identify this virtue in the lion-dog guardian who is the defender of the Law. Watching, motionless and in complete obedience, the guardian-dog has subjugated all passions through the Law. No bright rag or tasty morsel can divert its attention from the faithful performance of its appointed task.

The diversity of dogs in the world bears witness to the great antiquity of their domestication. Perhaps this is why some people have assumed the animal has been around forever, and it might as well be asserted that in the Beginning even God had one. The physical ancestor of the dog was also parent to the bear and made its contribution to evolving forms forty million years ago. The line from which the Canidae arose flowed through a Pliocene type known as *Cynodictus*, from which developed *Cynodesmus* and *Temnocyon*. From these two archaic animals the *Tomarctus* and the wild hunting dogs of India and Africa respectively arose. The *Tomarctus* was a wolf-like ancestor of the genus *Canis*, which includes wolves, coyotes, foxes, dingoes, jackals and the modern dog (*Canis familiaris*). As to which of these was the direct ancestor of the modern dog there is much dispute. Some feel the dingo is the oldest and closest type, but many believe that the wolf is more directly ancestral, acknowledging that some dogs are much more wolf-like than others. In his interesting meanderings on the subject of dogs, Konrad Lorenz argues that whilst some breeds are descended from the wolf (like samoyeds, huskies and chow chows), most are jackal-blooded, treating their masters as parents rather than pack leaders, as the wolf-blooded dogs do. But the disagreement flourishes with claims variously supported among zoologists, including the interesting assertion that the domesticated canine derives from the pariah-dog of India and southwest Asia, whose present condition exists in stark contrast to that of the pet and work-dogs of other parts of the world.

The word "dog" comes from the Old English *docga*, the etymological origin of which is unknown. But *canis* comes from the Greek *kyon* (κύων), the name Homer and others after him used to identify the Dog Star, the brightest star in heaven. This brilliant orb is known otherwise as Sirius (Σίςοιρ), "the Scorcher", which some believe derives from the Sanskrit *Surya*, "the Shining One". The naming of this star by the ancients in what came to be known as the constellation of Canis Major suggests a notion of the dog which is quite different from that delineated by biological evolution. The word κύνω is etymologically related to κύω, which means "to conceive", pointing to the aspect of symbolism attached to the dog having to do with fertility and rebirth. In *The Secret Doctrine*, H. P. Blavatsky writes that Sirius is the star of Mercury-Budha (Hermes), the greatest instructor of mankind before other Buddhas. She also quotes Isis as saying: "I am the Queen of these regions ... I was the first to reveal to mortals the mysteries of wheat and corn. . . . I am she who rises in the constellation of the dog." This places the idea of fertility and rebirth on an archetypal level wherein one might link the shining face of Surya to its dissemination through the agency of Mercury-Budha, or the Dog Star. Translated into concrete expression, this creative, intelligent force is manifested on multitudinous levels right down to the scorching heat associated with the hottest part of the summer, during the heliacal rising of Sirius. This finds an analogue in the bitch going into heat. It is the time when conception takes place and restraints tend to melt away. The old Greeks explained: "Our ancestors believed that when the Dog Star is in conjunction with the sun, the sea boils, wine ferments and dogs go mad." These are the "dog days", when the brain can cease to work as it dissolves into a oneness with Nature. One imagines "mad dogs and Englishmen" during the British Raj in India wandering about in the torpor of pre-monsoon heat, the latter obstinately attempting to maintain a sense of control while everything about them was falling back into a primordial bake-oven of imminent re-creation.

The idea of "going to the dogs" reflects the negative side of the abandonment of coolness and control. It links up with the pervasive association of the scavenging, lurking and lolling about identified with street dogs who soak up the sun and do not even bother to retire to their own burrow for the purpose of procreation. The Bible is replete with evidence of the low opinion in which the dog was held by Jews and Christians. Muslims too believed the animal unclean, and because of its public sexual displays it became the symbol of promiscuity, and adulterers and sodomites were called "dogs". Even in India the mark of the dog's foot was often the symbol of lasciviousness, and stories tell of those who were branded and forced to bear the mark so all could see. Such condemnation of dogs has been accompanied by the rise of the scavenging pariah-dog who ekes out its miserable life in many an ancient city street. It announces, and doubtless contributes to, a debased condition which inverts the lofty proclamation of Isis and bears little resemblance to the reverence felt for other mother-goddesses of old who were often depicted as whelping bitches.

People's feelings about dogs run the gamut of these extremes because the dog has been close to man for such a long time. It is impossible to consider the condition of dogs, symbolically or physically, without acknowledging that they have been dramatically affected by man. When he despises or abuses or reveres them, it says more about the human condition than about that of the animal. As Professor Lorenz puts it: "There is no domesticated animal which has so radically altered its whole way of living, indeed its whole sphere of interests, that has become domestic in so true a sense as the dog." Many thousands of years ago dogs probably had a loose connection with human groups, being tolerated for their ability to warn and track game. But there is distinct evidence that for well over forty thousand years there has grown a profound symbiotic relationship between man and dog which, from the beginning, involved deep emotional impulses. The excavation of a Cro-Magnon burial revealed the remains of a young girl with the heads of four dogs pointing outward and arranged about her, and dog tooth pendants were widely worn from Aurignacian times. By Neolithic times the link was firmly cemented, and settled communities were breeding dogs possessing specialized characteristics unique to that place and people. Inbreeding within settlements favoured the hereditary transmission of domestic characteristics and the development of distinctive breeds.

Some cultures protected their canine friend. The religious laws of the ancient Iranians decreed that a punishment of five hundred to a thousand stripes with a scourge was to be meted out to the killer of a dog, or fifty to two hundred for giving it bad food. Early English law, however, stated that "It is not fit that a person should die for a dog", causing them to consider the crime of stealing one as less than larcenous (unlike the theft of a falcon, a horse or a cow). Some breeds in the British Isles were bred to hunt, and others, responding to the desires of an oppressed peasantry, became expert poachers. Dogs like the lurcher could silently steal the king's game and, if ever caught, would even disclaim acquaintance with its master, whose very life was on the line if charged. Many an illicit main dish has been enjoyed by the owners of such cunning canines. Among nomadic people the dog has been keenly valued as a guard and hunter and was frequently highly trained by its masters. Before the arrival of the horse, Plains Indians used their dogs as beasts of burden, yoking them to small travois packed with camp goods which had to be transported each time they moved. When not engaged in this work, they watched the camp, guarded the night herds, warned of enemy attack and oversaw the safety of children. The Eskimo peoples of Siberia and the New World always counted their wealth in dogs and depended upon them so completely that part of the education of every child involved a thorough understanding and mastery of the animal. Years of training produced huskies capable of bucking any weather and faithfully working for their master even for days without adequate food. To kill such an animal was, to the Eskimo, tantamount to the murder of a human being – for did not dogs, like humans, have individual souls?

Because of their closeness to man, dogs vary in ability and appearance more than any other species. Selective breeding by humans, together with natural adaptation to vastly different environments all over the globe, have produced astonishingly different breeds: everything from the mouse-like Chihuahua to the great British mastiffs exported by the Romans under Caesar for use as fighters in the Coliseum. With the Imperial Pekingese, the Great Dane (who was bred by Germans), the Afghan and Saluki hounds, one has examples of very deliberately bred dogs whose present form (at least in the case of the latter two) can be traced back several thousand years. Critics of modern breeding for show say that it has involved an overestimation of beauty or style at the expense of intelligence. Breeding to strict standards of physical characteristics is incompatible with breeding for mental capabilities. In the whole of biological evolution on earth, one can see continual evidence that hyperspecialized forms are not destined to be the vehicle for intelligence. When dog breeds become "fashionable" in the eyes of men, they are in danger of becoming highly overspecialized and frozen in terms of developing their greatest canine potential. Just so does man ideologically freeze and delimit the realization of his own broader potential. Surely it is because of a severely externalized and diminished evaluation of himself that man has dedicated so much time and energy to the production of less intelligent, more neurotic and often unhappy dogs for the sake of perpetuating certain physical characteristics.

But if man has enormously affected the dog, so too the dog has affected man. A recognition of this prompted a Seneca chief to remark, "It is true that whenever a person loves a dog, he derives great power from it." The "chemistry" between a dog and man can produce a remarkably high level of mutual feeling, and when it is mismatched, the dog may even suffer a psychosomatic illness, as in some cases where seeing-eye dogs have been paired with masters with whom they could experience no rapport. The fidelity of a faithful dog creates the basis for a deep bond which imposes upon the object of this faithfulness a profound responsibility. In man there are levels of love experienced and expressed, but only in rare cases does one find the depth of pure, disinterested love shown by a dog for his beloved master. When it is given, this love seeks no recompense but flows in a "dogged" faithfulness towards even the least affectionate or worthy of men. Like the pure and universal love held as an ideal by Diotima in Plato's *Symposium*, the dog's love of his chosen master has the power to uplift both lover and beloved and deeply move the hearts of other human beings. One may think back to the dog stories borrowed from the local library when one was a child and recall the tear-stained pages that marked the spot where an act of canine love and nobility ended in the animal's death. But people of all ages and times have felt that, somehow, in the dog's noble fidelity and love, their own highest potential was being echoed, and they have wondered and wept to see its unsullied manifestation in a creature humbler than themselves.

Alexander Pope must have deeply felt this when he wrote these poignant lines describing the homecoming of Ulysses to Ithaca:

> When wise Ulysses . . .
> Arrived at last, poor, old, disguised, alone,
> To ail his friends and even his Queen unknown;. . .
> The faithful dog alone his rightful master knew! . . .
> Him when he saw – he rose and crawled to meet,
> (Twas all he could) and fawned and licked his feet,
> Seized with dumb joy – then falling by his side,
> Owned his returning Lord, looked up, and died!

In his love of an animal a man increases his humanity. If one studies deeply the history of the human race, one will come to the conclusion that becoming truly familiar with animal behaviour enables one to appreciate "the unique and exalted position held by man in the world of living creatures". There is an especially great value in attempting to understand the dog. Bearing so faithfully the menta! and physical impress of man, the dog reflects back to the sensitive observer a great deal about his own inner being as well as animal nature. At a more fundamental level, one can learn that, although dogs do have distinct personalities, their dependence on and loyalty to a master originates in their tie to their mother, which, in the domestic dog, is simply transferred to the master. In wolf-blooded dogs this juvenile behaviour is replaced with an inherent loyalty to the pack leader, which it also transfers to its master. Thus the relationship between a man and his wolf-blooded dog is based more upon a proud "man-to-man" loyalty than upon the child-parent relationship which persists between masters and dogs of other breeds. But both of these inherent traits suggest the biological and instinctual roots for faithfulness and love in a dog.

> Some show that nice sagacity of smell,
> And read with such discernment in the port
> And figure of the man, his secret aim
> That oft we owe our safety to a skill
> We could not teach and must despair to learn.

> William Cowper

The inherited characteristics of different breeds are well known. Sheep dogs without sheep will shepherd children, terriers are aggressive, spaniels are retrievers on command, and hounds are self-hunters. All these are expected instinctual traits of the breed, but it is not instinct that prompts a dog to show its feelings through subtle changes of facial expression or lay its head on its master's knee. These are actions more closely akin to human language than to what wild animals "say" to each other through miming, A dog's expression of feeling may be channelled through a learned behaviour (like giving its paw), but the subtle aptness and timing of its response suggests a capacity to read what lies within human feelings as well as understanding gestures and words or tone of voice. One champion of the animal kingdom observed that "Man is endowed with reason, the infant with instinct; and the young animal shows more of both than the child." With the awakening of the Manasic thinking principle within the growing child, human beings leave lesser creatures far behind. But both man and animals are endowed with a soul and intelligence. An extremely intelligent animal like the dog thinks and seems to know that it thinks "perhaps all the more keenly because it cannot speak". The intelligence in a dog is the same in essence as that of man, if not equal in development or in its level of awareness. Questions concerning intellect, intuition and individuality arise in a serious consideration of dogs. They have learnt to live happily with men and to do useful things which have clearly caused them to feel that they belong with people. They seem to know they are part of human life and, as St. Paul movingly put it, they are "hoping for, and living in the expectation of the same deliverance from the bonds of corruption" as man.

A blind individual who wishes to gain the freedom that can be provided by a seeing-eye dog must have the moral and physical courage to trust completely his dog's independent judgement. These remarkable animals are carefully trained to adhere to all sorts of complex rules in order to usher their masters safely around crowded cities. There are volumes of testimony confirming the intelligence and dependability of these dogs. In their training there comes a point when they must be able to do more than intelligently apply their instinctual powers or adherence to learned patterns. To become a successful guide-dog they must be able to take responsibility in an altered or suddenly dangerous situation, even if this means breaking rules. In Montreal during a bank robbery, when the robbers were attempting to make a getaway, a blind man and his dog were crossing the street at the crosswalk leading to the bank when shots rang out. The dog froze and, blocking her master's path, took a firm lead and jaywalked as fast as she could through the cars to an opposite corner and into a doorway. At the spot where the dog had forced her master's retreat, a policeman was shot and killed only a moment after she broke a whole series of rules in guiding her charge to safety. The independent judgement of such dogs is not possessed by all trainees, and those who may excel in learning all the rules may fail in their ability to go beyond them.

Slow and painstaking observation of generations of carefully bred guide-dogs has revealed that there are critical periods in a dog's life when higher avenues of intelligence can begin to open up. Up to six weeks of age a puppy needs canine socialization. Its later ability to exercise independent judgement is linked up closely with the next period in the puppy's life, where human contact plays an increasingly dominant role. Individual attention during this time establishes the dog's sense of being an individual. It learns to be a co-worker with a human being and takes on many elements of discrimination which exceed the abilities demonstrated in learning by associational memory related to the senses.

In *The Secret Doctrine* a reference to a work by Haeckel includes a description of a double drawing depicting the six-week-old embryo of a human being and of a dog. Except for a slight difference in the larger head of the human embryo, the two are indistinguishable. Passing through the piscine, reptile and mammal phases of evolution, at around six to eight weeks the human embryo most closely takes on the canine form. They share in common five fingers and toes that develop initially in the same way. Their rudimentary links are the same. Even at eight weeks the human embryo with its tail and otherwise animal appearance looks like an embryo dog. At this point of closest resemblance man and dog meet, only to separate with the further and more complex embryonic development of the human. Just as this occurs prior to birth, so when the dog has entered six weeks into life after birth, it is analogously and peculiarly open to the influence of man. If a strong and loving involvement takes place at this time, the natural fidelity, courage and intelligence of the dog can take wings so that the animal can begin to exercise judgement and exhibit higher powers of insight normally ascribed to human beings.

When this happens, the faith inherent within the dog's nature becomes such an intelligent force that humans fortunate enough to have a long-term relationship with such an animal are steadily suffused with a greater degree of this paramount virtue themselves. The faith that is manifest in the dog is the same faith by which men can move mountains. Its power is limitless; only the objects upon which it is fixed enforce any sort of limitation. William Q. Judge once advised a student of Theosophy, "Formulate to yourself certain things to be true that you feel to be true, and then increase your faith in them." The exercise is calculated to bring into conscious focus that which always lies within, for the embodied soul is gifted with faith and each man is of the same nature as that ideal on which his faith is fixed. Men are blinded to true faith (without an object) by the results of false faith, which, based on selfish ideals, provides the very limitations one will have to deal with in lives to come. The dog's faith has as its object his master. He is driven to heights of fidelity by pure and selfless love of that uncrowned king in his life. Like the faithful hound of Ulysses, he lives to demonstrate that love and so seal his life with meaning before his death. For man too, "faith is a series of lessons in love" involving the cultivation of confidence in self, together with an unwavering love of one's Master and trust in Karma.

> Shall damned oblivion ever quench that flame?
> No! that viewless essence shall outlive the world,
> Immortal as the soul of man it served.
>
> Alexander Pope

The faith that is cleansed of false hopes and objects is the gateway to higher intuition. The instinct of a dog can be described as the "direct perception of what is right within its own realm", whilst intuition is the direct cognition of the truth in all things, the memory of the knowledge of one's past existing in one's real nature. The instinct of the dog is universal in Nature and endowed by the Spirit of Deity, a divine spark entering conscious development in the higher animals. This can be guided by the intelligence within or by influences from without. As the dog's instinct is modified by exposure to a sensitive human being, the animal learns to rely increasingly on the "intuitive prompting from within", thus becoming a channel for pure reflected *Buddhi*. It cannot be said that the dog possesses the faculty of reason, nor does it recall its past lives, but through the inherent power of its uplifting nature it can become an acting template for its master's own yet to be consciously understood intuitions. A faithful dog can know, long before the event, of danger threatening the object of his love. A human being who knows of this potential will adjust his approach to the dog so that love, justice, honour and truth will be reflected through their daily relationship. These are qualities of the soul which can spring to life through contact with the soul in man. As a perceptive Lt. Colonel in charge of British war-dogs during the First World War put it, "AH the dog knows about God must come to him through us." One might add to this that man, not fully merged with the Master within, can learn from the dog's yearning love and faithful assimilation of his own master's qualities.

Faith, like the light of Sirius, flows through the world. It exists in the flower, the monkey and the stone, but it is strongly exemplified in the nature of the dog. It is a fiery force which, when flaunted without discrimination or when wrongly focussed, can scorch or drive to madness. But nurtured in its proper season and trained with loving care, it is the fertile key that gives birth to a higher level of insight into the heart of things unseen by the personal man. The homing instinct, so wonderfully manifested in the dog and so much a part of his love and faith in his Master, becomes in man the guide through the intangible realms leading to his spiritual home. Not by sight or smell or hearing but by intense love for a beloved master, the dog is guided home. Man has come on a very long journey, taking him a long way from his spiritual abode. On the way he, like the gods, has been accompanied by the dog. It is fitting, nay poignantly just, that the dog should follow him and sometimes guide him on the long journey home. Weaving back and forth across the boundaries of life and death, guided by a faith that overcomes any uncertainty between the two, the dog unravels the complexities of conditioned existence and pierces to the deathless source of love.

> Hail Sirius, faithful hound of heaven,
> It is along thy blazing leash I would enter
> Into communion with the invisible
> Master I have sensed but never seen.
> O faithful watcher, Hermes' own,
> You teach me how to see the strand
> Of light that courses through the dark
> And shows the way back home.

Hermes, December 1983

THE LABYRINTH

What is this mighty labyrinth – the earth,
But a wild maze the moment of our birth?
Still as we life pursue the maze extends,
Nor find we where each winding purlieu ends;
Crooked and vague each step of life we tread, –
Unseen the danger, we escape the dread!
But with delight we through the labyrinth range,
Confused we turn, and view each artful change –
Bewildered, through each wild meander bend
Our wandering steps, anxious to gain the end;
Unknown and intricate, we still pursue
A certain path uncertain of the clue;
Like hood-winked fools, perplex'd we grope our way
And during life's short course we blindly stray.
Puzzled in mazes and perplex'd with fears;
Unknown alike both heaven and earth appears.
Till at the last, to banish our surprise,
Grim Death unbinds the napkin from our eyes,
Then shall Gay's truth and wisdom stand confest,
And Death will show us Life was but a jest.

Reflection on Walking in the Maze
Hampton Court (c. 1747)

Having penetrated the cave whose small opening was barely visible on the mountain's innocent-looking flanks, he found himself in a deepening cavern whose corridors disappeared into a further more interior gloom. Without thought he gravitated towards one on the right side and began to explore its uneven trench extended in a hollowed curve away from the entrance cavity. The walls grew dimmer but he perceived that they had been marked and hewn with a chisel from the living rock. A few faint pictograms momentarily obtruded themselves in the gloom, to be swallowed up. They nudged his consciousness as he moved along, drawn by an irrepressible sense of curiosity. He accepted the inevitability of his progression without thought or plan and was barely aware of what he was doing until he came to the first branching in the tunnel. Here he devised a simple scheme, deciding to choose the right-hand corridor each time he came to a branch. This served him well until he began to be confronted with multiple branchings and the suspicion that some he had pursued were loops that led back to junctions from a different direction. It was not long before he was lost.

The darkness was complete and corridor walls suddenly gaped beneath his touch where branches ushered in their musty, echoing air. The horror of his dilemma overcame the futility of effort and he groped on in desperation, believing in his ultimate delivery into the entrance chamber and out of the cave. But muffled sounds troubled his ear and the inner sighing of the mountain's breath reminded him that the labyrinthine tunnels must lead to a goal of some kind, a centre not easily found. Even in his despair he wondered what it might be and what might be in it. A distant melancholic moan dampened the small spark of his renewed curiosity and the prospect of a cruel and unwitnessed death delivered by some terrifying monster flooded his brain and caused his body to convulse in fear. Far cry was this from the maze games he had played at fairs as a youth. The ironic comparison briefly interrupted his terror and he remembered the sign that used to be posted at the entrances to the hastily constructed labyrinths. He saw the words very clearly:

Beware the dreadful minotaur
That dwells within the maze.
The monster feasts on human gore
And bones of those he slays.
Then softly through the labyrinth creep
And rouse him not to strife.
Take one short peep, prepare to leap
And run to save your life!

Like a children's jingle, the lines recalled the horror that had been met, for at the end of the tortured course was placed a full-length mirror. Perspicacious though it had been, the joke mocked him now and he was forced by the abyss of sheer terror that yawned before him to take stock, calm himself and begin to think just what it was that he had gotten himself into.

Suiting his dilemma, a classic definition of the labyrinth asserts that it is the structure of a pattern so complex that once inside it is difficult to escape. It can be a series of caverns, a complex building, a design, a closed or open path, a dance, a game or a walk. It is often underground and shrouded in darkness, but the outside and the inside of the labyrinth are sharply distinguished and it must fulfill certain criteria to be worthy of the name. To be properly called a labyrinth, such a patterned structure must entail the work of artifice. Natural caverns may be labyrinthine but a labyrinth is planned. There is a purposefulness of design involving a journey which is really a puzzle, necessitating a certain degree of complexity. The path in the labyrinth must be continuous and there must be an entrance communicating the interior with the exterior.

Basically there are two types of labyrinths: the unicursal or non-puzzle pattern and the multicursal or puzzle pattern. The unicursal type is used by mathematicians to describe a class of problems dealing with the shortest route between two given points involving a method of tracing a figure without covering any part of it more or less than once. It is "once run" or a "single course". Its single route leads into a centre and out again with no choice or puzzle arising. It takes one over the maximum ground, doubling back on itself continually but never crossing itself or branching. In a unicursal labyrinth one is closest to the centre just after entering but then it veers away, and one is forced to journey afar through a tortuous pattern to get back to the centre. In fact, the traveller may be very close to the centre repeatedly but has no way of knowing it. It is always a question of sticking it out to the end.

The multicursal labyrinth is designed with the intention of confusing and puzzling and it contains blind pathways. Its branches may be simple or subdivided and they may or may not rejoin the main path. The goal may be situated at the final extension of what seems to be the main path or it may be located within such a branching loop. To tread this type of labyrinth requires knowledge of a key to solve the problem. Of the most famous labyrinths of the ancient world, the one located at Lake Moeris in Egypt seemed to have combined elements of both types. Herodotus visited it in the fifth century before the Christian era after Egypt had been divided into twelve nomes, whose kings agreed to leave a combined labyrinthine memorial of themselves. "I found it", Herodotus wrote, "greater than words could tell, for, although the temple at Ephesus and that at Samos are celebrated works, yet all the works and buildings of the Greeks put together would certainly be inferior to this labyrinth." He claimed that it surpassed even the pyramids. "It has twelve covered courts, with opposite doors ... all communicating with one another and with one wall surrounding them all. There are two sorts of rooms, one sort above, the other sort below ground, fifteen hundred of each sort, or three thousand in all."

Herodotus was allowed to pass with a guide through the upper rooms only, the lower being strictly prohibited to visitors. Thought to have been built over four thousand years ago, in the time of Herodotus the stone roof and walls were yet beautifully carved and the intricately bewildering pattern of rooms and courts majestically adorned with elegant white columns. Five hundred years later Pliny referred to this same structural wonder as "the most stupendous work on which mankind has expended his labours". He dated its construction at thirty-six hundred years before his time and marvelled that the lapse of centuries had been unable to destroy it. He went on to describe the colossal statues of the gods therein and the great halls reached by steep flights of ninety steps. He stated that some of the enormous doors opened with a terrifying sound "as of thunder" and that most of the halls were shrouded in total darkness.

Beside the careful description of this architectural wonder, the more famous labyrinth at Knossos in which the Minotaur is said to have dwelt appears very sketchy in its outlines. Tradition suggests that it was built by Daedalus, the renowned and clever artificer and engineer at the court of Minos, the Minoan king. It was designed so as to be impossible to discover the exit once inside it, and at its centre was housed the monstrous offspring of Queen Pasiphae, to whom the youth of Attica were supposed to have been regularly sacrificed. Within the framework of this ancient story the myth of Theseus flourished, placing him, the son of the Greek king Aegeus, amongst the youths sent to Crete as sacrificial tribute. Many know the story of Ariadne giving him the sword and thread with which he slew the Minotaur and made his escape out of the labyrinth. But no ones knows the shape of that maze of corridors or where it is actually to be found. The rooms of the elegant palace of Minos at Knossos were so numerous and labyrinthine in design that some came to believe the palace itself to have been the labyrinth. Others have contended that it is to be found in the convoluted passages within the side of Mount Ida at Gortyna.

There, in 1770, an intrepid French explorer described how the dangerous part was near the entrance where, if a man stumbled upon the wrong path, he would soon become so "bewildered among a thousand twistings, twinings, sinuosities, crinkle-crankles and turn-again lanes, that he could scarce ever get out again without the utmost danger of being lost".

As far back as Neolithic times, ground plans, pictographs and various emblematic renditions of the labyrinth appeared predominantly in Europe and Asia. It came to be a popular design on the coins of many Mediterranean people and even appeared as border motifs around temples, houses and at the edges of garments. The famous Greek meander pattern is very like the elements of the swastika labyrinth pattern at Knossos. A rounded version of this simple unicursal pattern became conventionalized and was often portrayed on coins bearing a portrait of the Minotaur. Earlier, Egyptian amulets sported labyrinthine designs with up to five false turns in them, whilst some, like the Minoan swastika, contained a star or moon at their centre, which may have symbolized Paradise regained or death at the end of an illusory journey.

Great mystery and dread surround the centre. Death there may lead to immortal life, or it may be delivered by the hands of the lurking murderer as in an ancient Chinese mystery novel, or by a mindless freak of Nature. The centre may be the springboard into another world of enlightenment, and the path leading to it may be likened to the world which is easy to enter but very difficult to leave. The labyrinth is a knot to be untied rather than cut through, and it is surrounded by an aura of difficulty and danger which, nonetheless, lures as surely as life lures the soul into birth and towards the unknown. One recalls the midnight passage of Damodar Mavalankar who, awakened by his Master, followed him unhesitatingly along a lengthy oceanside pathway which suddenly turned into the sea. There, on a small island, a twisting path and thick bushes concealed the entrance to a hidden building which no one could have found unless the occupant wished it. Damodar's description of the vaulted nature of his instructors and of the secrets imparted to him in that labyrinthine sanctuary offer inspiration to anyone who ardently desires to solve the great puzzle of life, but no one can succeed in this until the power at the centre of the puzzle permits it.

The confusion that one experiences in life's labyrinth is much like that undergone in a mirror maze, where hundreds of distorted reflections compound the difficulty of discovering the passageway that may lead to the goal. The maddening glitter of fragmented thoughts and endlessly changing glimpses of one's own nature coexist like a modern gloss painted over the "tragic gardens, with dark avenues of intertwisted ilexes immeasurably old" that form the buried labyrinths of our collective karma and our unconscious self. The tangled web woven long ago runs like an underground maze beneath the convoluted movements of our busy lives. But if one understood the pattern of the pathway, perhaps one would then possess a key to understanding not only individual or collective twists and turns but what the whole broader pattern is about in the first place. Some have thought that labyrinths were symbolic of the sun's annual or sidereal course in the heavens. The spring maze dances and sacrificial rites may well have originated with man's effort to greet the sun back on its course to the centre of the sky. Or, as H. P. Blavatsky asserts, the progression of Races, sub-races, family-races and various sidereal and sub-sidereal cycles was recorded by the labyrinths, pyramids and zodiacs of old. Thus, the individual as a microcosm treads the pathway of a labyrinth which is both unique to his own perception and reflective of a broad universal pattern to which all levels of life address themselves.

Plato used the term "labyrinth" to depict an elaborate argument, whereas Theocritus used it to designate a fish trap. Lytton Strachey compounded meanings by once writing that the prince consort "attempted to thread his way through the complicated labyrinth of European diplomacy, and was eventually lost in the maze". "Maze", a word of Scandinavian origin, simply means confusion, bewilderment or dreamy aimlessness and could never be given as a name to a gigantic amphibian of the Carboniferous age like the labyrinthodont, though one may concur that it was an apt term to use in connection with the prince consort. "Labyrinth" is a very old term which takes its root, *la*, from a proto-Indo-European source meaning "stone" (as in λαας, *lapis*, λάβρυς or *labris*). Λαβύρινθος or *labyrinthos* means "place of stone". The term λάβρυς; describes a stone axe and, married to *inthos* (a pre-Hellenic word for "place"), means literally "the place (or house) of the Stone (double) axe", the emblem of Minoan culture.

The oldest labyrinths in the world are probably hidden or forgotten, but pictograms of them amongst American Indians as well as ancient stone and pebble constructions in Scandinavia or ground mazes built by the Zulu indicate that the idea is extremely old and very widespread. A fascinating diffusion of ideas in the Old World resulted in the common use of the name Troy to describe earth or turf mazes and labyrinths. In Britain they were (are) called Troy Towns because of the difficulty to be overcome before reaching the centre. The Welsh called them *caerdroia* ("the walls of Troy"), which is related to *Caer y Troiau* ("the City of Windings or Turnings"). Troy Towns were also known in Scandinavia as "Giant's Street", "Troll's Castle", or the "Ruins of Jerusalem". In medieval Greece they were often referred to as "Solomon's Prison", which preserves the central idea that runs through all of these examples, which is the puzzling barrier that must be followed until an entrance leading to the central interior can be found.

In medieval Europe, the labyrinth took on peculiarly Christian meanings. It was sometimes seen as representing the path of ignorance leading to the devil (represented by the Minotaur) in the centre. Its convolutions became, thus, the entanglements of a sinful life. Some church labyrinths, however, may have been designed as symbolic pilgrimages for those who could not (or would not) go to

Jerusalem. Most of these labyrinths were mosaic patterns worked into the forecourts of twelfth century cathedrals and were often called *chemin de Jérusalem*. Others were constructed earlier and sometimes included the motif of Theseus slaying the Minotaur at the centre. Not all were constructed on the ground, and where people wished to avoid the arduous trip to Jerusalem or even the penitential act of walking along the mosaic pattern, they might turn to wall labyrinths wherein their symbolic pilgrimage could be made less arduous still – being performed by the rapid tracing of the index finger. At the cathedral of Poitiers there is a wonderful tree-like labyrinth wherein one exits by the same door one entered and, while encountering no stops on the way to the centre, one may have looped the loop many times before getting there. The intention behind the design is nowhere divulged, but it easily reminds one of the repeated incarnations that seem to be required of the human soul before enlightenment can be achieved.

As the intellectual dreariness of the Middle Ages was replaced gradually by more refreshing and tolerant ideas, imaginative notions intimating the ancient Mysteries resulted in the design of remarkable labyrinthine gardens and hedge mazes. Those fashioned "after the ancient manner" were of very complex patterns planned to bewilder and confuse. A fantastic labyrinth at the palace garden of the prince of Anhalt, Germany, allegorically typified the course of human life. It was composed of hedges, rocks, trees, streams, caverns and tortuous deep-cut paths that were very dark and often covered over. At each turn the visitor was met by some puzzling or terrifying allegory or inscription or, sometimes, by a beautiful statue or flowery dell. Some constructions, like the marvellous Labyrinths de Versailles erected for Louis XIV (destroyed in 1775), exemplified grand flights into the realm of engineering fantasy. There were in this garden thirty-nine groups of hydraulic statuary representing Aesop's fables, each speaking character in the groups emitting a jet-stream of water. Others, like that at Hampton Court, were genuine puzzles which some tried to thread with the help of a formula. These were often called "wildernesses" in which one could manage to lose one's way, a slip of the memory or imperfect transmission of the formula resulting in much confusion. One is reminded of the delightful episodes depicted in "Three Men in a Boat", where the over-confident Harris volunteered to conduct a party through the Hampton Court maze. "Well just go in here", he said, "so that you can say you've been, but it's very simple. It's absurd to call it a maze. You keep on taking the first turn to the right. Well just walk around for ten minutes and then go and get some lunch." Poor Harris!

In 1886 an elderly English gentleman recalled the lively pleasures sixty years earlier of running the turf maze called Julian's Bower, forty feet in diameter. He described how the villagers of Alkborough played May-eve games around it "under an indefinite of something unseen and unknown cooperating with them". Some of the English Troy Towns are indeed associated with ancient earth-works and scenes of magical lore. This, coupled with their similarity to the mosaic pavement labyrinths of early Christendom and the patterns of the most ancient designs, lends to the lowly turf maze the wonder of antiquity and of hoary practices which, though occult in nature, have always been known to humankind. Like the city of Troy itself, they are shrouded in myth and mystery which is scarcely dispersed by an etymological investigation of the name. Many say that 'Troy' comes from the Celtic *tro*, which means "to turn in rapid revolution" or to "dance through a maze", but others push it back further and claim it may come ultimately from the Sanskrit *dru*, meaning "to run". It is significant that the name was not used by the inhabitants of fabled Ilium itself but was popular amongst others in the Mediterranean world at that time. In Northern Europe Troy Town was used over five hundred years ago as a title for the Cretan labyrinth, and much earlier the Etruscans and Romans made the same connection between Troy, Knossos and labyrinths or mazes of other sorts.

> As when in lofty Crete (so fame reports)
> The labyrinth of old, in winding walls
> A mazy way enclosed, a thousand paths
> Ambiguous and perplexed, by which the steps
> Should by error intricate, untrac'd
> Be still deluded.
>
> *Aeneid V*

This description could equally suit the complicated steps of the dance celebrated by Ariadne and Theseus on the island of Delos, where they went through the motions of threading the labyrinth. They were also the motions of the ancient Roman funeral ceremonies and of the myriad Troy Dances and Games that tradition preserved through the centuries. There is much to ponder in Carl Jung's observation that many of his mental patients who were not able to draw a maze were more than happy to dance one for him! An ancient tradition it must be which could well up like deeply etched memories from previous lives. The labyrinthine pattern is more than just fascinating to people; it is familiar. We have at some time been there before: in the spring meadow, the corridor of initiation and the fortified city. The labyrinth permits and prohibits at the same time, and it is a double action we know by heart. We also intuitively understand why the labyrinthine design on temples, houses and clothing borders could keep out evil and permit entrance of that which is in sympathy with the interior. Even the simple villager of an older England or a more timeless India makes tangle-thread chalk designs for such apotropaic reasons, never knowing, perhaps, that he is doing what was done by ancient hierophants long ago.

Just so was Troy surrounded by walls and blinds through which even the persistent Greeks could scarcely penetrate. Tactical labyrinths have comprised walls, moats, trenches, ramparts and blinds of all sorts since the earliest cities. The walls of Jericho were not merely walls but part of a system of blinds constructed to protect the sacred centre of a labyrinthine city. Homer, in referring to Ilium, frequently mentioned the "sacred veil" of the city. Troy was called Troy by many because it was labyrinthine, which is what 'Ilium' means as well. It is certainly significant that in his siege upon the city, Achilles bore a shield on which Oceanus encircled the "dancing floor of Ariadne". It is also meaningful to recall that the walls of Troy were often referred to as Cyclopean, which literally means "Ring Wall". The Ring Wall pierced by the Greeks seems to have been echoed in the piercing of the Cyclop's single eye by Odysseus, thus inviting the intuitive to unravel the occult symbolism veiled in these shifting legends. The Secret Doctrine suggests that the latter act was linked with the loss of the sacred Third Eye, and with the sack of Troy there was surely an analogous loss. For in the crumbled debris of Ilium's walls lay all that was left of the tradition of Mystery Religions and priestly Kings that marked an earlier Eastern era.

Thus was the chapter on a more antique race closed. A circling was made in the labyrinth marking cycles, and a movement towards the West was effected which heralded a less spiritual yet more cerebral phase in human evolution. In the ancient story, Aeneas, son of Ilium (Priam), left the ruined city of the Mysteries to seek a new polis of the gods. His adventures took him finally to the Land of Death (the West) and Rebirth called Cumae. In considering this journey one cannot but think of how the motherland of the East (India) has looked to the West and experienced Death (loss of spirituality) before Rebirth in our own cycle. In the Aeneid the story seems to be referring to a subcyclical reflection of the events affecting a much earlier transition from the Third to the Atlantean Race – events which laid down the pattern for many circlings to come in later races. At Cumae, Aeneas goes to the temple of Apollo (the Sun) on whose gate is depicted the emblem of the Cretan labyrinth and the Minotaur. There he is met by Diana (the Moon) and escorted within the temple labyrinth down into Tartarus, where he learns about the origin of men at their birth and whither they go at death.

The travels of Aeneas to the "death" of the West are almost identical with those of Gilgamesh and even King Arthur's journey to mythical Avalon. In fact, the plot has been told over and again in cultures around the globe and clearly depicts the initiation through death of the mutable into the immortality of spiritual enlightenment. The labyrinth often plays a major role in these stories, for it provides an apprenticeship for the neophyte who must learn to distinguish the correct path. Such practices were intimated by H. P. Blavatsky, who revealed in the last century that "it is a fact, known to the Initiated Brahmins of India and especially to Yogis, that there is not a cave-temple in the country but has its subterranean passages running in every direction, and that those underground caves and endless corridors have in their turn their caves and corridors". This was true also at Epidaurus, where labyrinthine walls concentrically encircled the *tholos* temple of Aesclepius, and it was probably true at Eleusis where a "blind march" was preliminary to full initiation. Shakespeare shows the court party in The Tempest as coming through "forth-rights and meanders", and in the Gospels, Christ went through trials and temptations in the "wilderness" (maze) before fully taking on the mantle of enlightenment.

La means "stone" and the journey into the labyrinth is a descent into Mother Earth. A solar guide shows the entrance place, but a lunar guide or sibyl leads the traveller into the labyrinth itself, just as Ariadne showed Theseus the way. The labyrinth is presided over by a goddess, governed by a god and walked by a man. It is the god who is the Judge of the Dead, whilst the goddess provides the means of reaching judgment. The thread-soul partakes of her very substance and must be followed by man to its solar source. He makes a journey much like that depicted in the Egyptian *Book of Gates,* wherein the solar barque penetrates the first gate in the underworld by magic and so on to the eleventh gate, where the barque is drawn "through the body of the Boat of the Earth". Like Initiates of many other traditions, Aeneas descends into the earth in submission to the sun god (Apollo) and the moon goddess (Diana) in order to realize a true marriage of heaven and earth within himself. Only then can he be fit to establish a new sacred city of the gods and of man. He must fulfill this initiation in the West in order to establish therein the ancient Mysteries of the labyrinth and set the stage for a new mode of consciousness and collective order.

Alone, huddled against the stone fastness of the twisting corridors into which he had stumbled, the lost man sat thinking of all these things. He had calmed himself and taken stock of his situation as well as he could. Thinking about the age-old puzzle of labyrinths and the sacred symbolism attached to them had given him a much needed objectivity and convinced him that nothing ever happened except under karma, and it was therefore significant that he found himself in this predicament. It began to dawn upon him that he had entered into the first stages of initiation and that it was up to him what he made of it and whether he would succeed in passing its trials at all. Having thus decided, he set about trying to think out an actual method of progress that might enable him to locate the goal of this particular labyrinth as well as retrace his steps back to its entrance. He recalled the rather pedantic guidebook he had once casually read which advised visitors to hedge mazes that they should rely upon marks made at nodes (where paths branch off at a juncture). On arrival at a node, the reader was told, "you should mark that path by which you just arrived with three marks. If you see, by marks on other paths, that you have already been to that node, mark the arrival path with one mark only. If each path at this node is already marked, you must retrace your steps. If, however, there are one or more unmarked paths leading from the node, select one of them and mark it with two marks as you enter it. You can now make it a rule that on arrival at a node, one should never take a path with three marks unless there are no paths unmarked or with one mark only. When one enters a one-mark path, one adds the two marks always made on leaving a node – making it a three-mark path at that node."

The details of this approach swam in his head for a moment until he realized that in the complete darkness surrounding him he would not be able to see many marks at all. He thought of carving them so that he might trace them with his fingertips but realized that he could not be sure of marking entrances to new pathways correctly across a node. Stretching out in the darkness, he might put the wrong mark on the wrong entrance and confuse himself further if he looped around and approached it coming from another direction. He realized that those who chiselled out these corridors long ago may well have had a formula outlining successions of turns to the right and left, but it was not available to him and he would have to rely upon something much more fundamental to find his way. Even in the extremity of his situation he was aware that the possible methods that might enable him to thread the labyrinth successfully were strikingly analogous to the mental process he was rapidly having to adopt. In the end he decided that the only solid approach would be the long and painstaking one. He would have to rely on endurance in traversing the long course more than he could upon knowledge of the way. Thus he began inching his way, one hand over the other, feeling every bump and scar in the wall as he went. There was no way he could know whether the overall pattern was a unicursal or multicursal one, and so he could not really know if his persistence would, in fact, take him on a single course to the goal, or if he would endlessly double back through deadends and blinds. He realized the risk but simply decided that there was everything to lose and nothing to gain by not attempting the journey, and he chose to place his faith on the route itself.

It was very important to place his hands closely together, for sudden crannies provided good landmarks if needed, and it was hard to rely upon tiny drafts to signal the nearness of a branch. At certain points the air made itself felt but it was not always constant, and he came more and more to rely upon touch as the means by which to gain some knowledge of the terrain. He consoled himself, recalling that he had once been taught that ninety percent of the thoughts and winds of emotion that pass through us are irrelevant. They merely clutter up our minds and senses to the point where it is almost impossible to become single-pointed enough to hit the mark or find the goal. He resolved that, deprived of sight and a formula providing a key, he would block out all irrelevancies and focus all his intelligence and Buddhic perception through his fingertips. He would rely upon them to give him intimations of the broader plan. Through them the sense of equilibrium maintained in the labyrinths of his inner ears would be expanded, and he would begin to feel the balance of the complex corridors in his aura. As his sense of touch increased, he moved along more rapidly, almost unconscious of fatigue. He did not know how long he had been moving nor did he contemplate how much further he would have to go. Nor was there any way of knowing how many of the possible corridors he had felt his way so painstakingly along when he heard a humming sound and became aware that he was approaching some sort of powerful presence there within the bowels of the earth.

He knew he was approaching the central goal of the labyrinth, and it occurred to him that he might indeed be approaching his death. Rapidly, like shards of previous fears, pictures of the monster, the sinister murderer, the faceless devouring agent, rushed through his consciousness. But he had come too far, schooling his thoughts and nurturing a faith stronger than the chiselled stone around him. The tortured fears were banished and he advanced towards what now appeared to be a dim light reflected off the tunnel wall. Whatever waited for him, even death itself, he would meet it squarely. For he had given over his whole life to this sacred quest, focussing everything in him upon the threading of the labyrinthine path until he had become it. He accepted it completely as himself and with it, whatever the goal had in store.

Slowly he rounded the corner from whence the light emanated and beheld before him a threshold leading through a doorway into a lighted chamber. He stepped forward blindly, unable at first to see clearly in the new-found light and thus stumbled slightly over the threshold and into the room. There, before him with kaleidoscopic effect, a rapid succession of sounds and images accosted his senses. Crashing towards him, a gigantic bull-headed man raised his terrible club, only to break into a million wrinkled fragments which fell limply onto the floor. Immediately behind where he had stood, a mirror reflected back the image of a startled-looking, freckled boy who was quickly whisked aside by the hands of one whose physical beauty was surpassed only by the divine radiance of pure spirituality that shone from his face. The man stared at him and then prostrated before his radiance. He could not see, for his eyes were swimming with tears. He could not tell how long he remained there, but he heard the deep melodious voice that swept over him and said: "I have waited for you a long time,"

> Back into the sanctuary
> of thy fiery heart
> I thread my way.

Hermes, March 1984

THE HEART

For the Lord seeth not as man seeth; for man looketh on the outward appearance, but the Lord looketh on the heart.

I Samuel 16:7

Within the utter darkness of the womb the fertilized egg divides. It divides again and yet again, becoming, in three days' time, a dozen or so cells gathered in a tiny ball. Soon an inequality in their size marks the beginning of differentiation, small planets destined to play their own specialized part in the scheme of things. Within seven days the minuscule mass of multiplying cells has lodged itself onto the wall of the uterus, wherein rapid changes transform its expanding shape to reveal the folds of the spinal cord and the nodal hood that will become the brain. The curving embryo seems to gather itself around the core of its being, which pulsates regularly to a life rhythm which is already its very own. Within the third week of its development the foetus possesses a heart which, by the twenty-seventh day, has four chambers, though it is much smaller than the proverbial eye of the needle through which the pure in heart may enter into heaven.

By the eighth week the heart is a tiny replica of that of the adult. Its cells are replete with genetic data which rapidly cross, converge and weave a seamless structure which takes shape long before any other major organ. By two months, coronary circulation has begun and the now pea-sized organ assumes its mantle of tireless sovereign and distributor of the body's vital river of blood, without which life would quickly cease. All depends upon the faithful pumping of the heart and yet no one is able to identify the precise point in foetal development when it begins. The pulsation of the tiny organ is recognizable at four weeks, but the cells clustered together to form the nucleus of what would become a fully shaped heart carry within them the seed of that pulsation which, even in the earliest stages, is the basis for a unique individual rhythm. Just as mysterious is the question of when the beating of the heart ceases. Disembodied hearts, even the separated individual cells of the heart, can continue to beat. Certain separated heart cells commence beating as they multiply in a nutritive liquid and begin to crowd upon one another. The beating cells impart their rhythm to the others until all the cells form a solid sheet of pulsating tissue. Why these certain cells first begin to beat remains a mystery to exoteric science, one which is basic to the question of what makes the heart beat at all.

From whence comes the first pulsation that ripples unobserved through the growing heart? What is the ancestry of that beat which heralds the beginning of a throbbing, to be repeated in an adult more than one hundred thousand times a day? Those who disclaim all but empirical answers leave the question open and focus instead on the marvel that is the heart itself. They see it as a pump, a machine, a wonderful muscular mass whose layers are composed of strands of individual cells which are the labourers of the whole. Linked end to end and side to side in an intricate network, their individual efforts merge to create the vital contractions of what is the largest involuntary muscle in the body. But they are informed by the heart's own electrical commands as well as those of the autonomic nervous system. In this lies the uniqueness of the heart as a muscle and as a connector and sustainer of life.

Forty-five hundred years ago the medical wisdom of the Yellow Emperor was collected in a work called the *Nei Ching*, which taught that "the heart is the root of life" and the pulse of a healthy heart "flows and connects ... like a string of red jade". Connecting and sustaining life, the heart is necessarily at the centre. If one judges from its encased position in the anatomical scheme of things, Nature does not seem to have intended that it be probed or even easily seen. Unseen, it yet was always believed to be the seat of life and, indeed, the link between lives. The ancient Egyptians believed the heart of one life was linked to that of the next. It was the only organ which the funerary specialists left in mummies or its own canopic jar, the heart being considered indispensable for immortality. Perhaps this was sensed by Cro-Magnon men twenty-five thousand years ago when they painted outsized red ochre hearts in the centre of bison and mammoth figures on the walls of Iberian caves. They wished to possess the life-spirit of so great a beast. They wished to assimilate its power and mystery, not merely ingest its flesh.

From the Aztec sacrifice of the living human heart to the Hindu identification of its essential nature as the Divine Centre, Brahmā, symbolized by the lotus flower emanating the whole of creation, the heart reigns as the indispensable connector to the eternal and the sustainer of the temporal. In its pulsation, in its steady, unfailing flux, it has been thought by many peoples to be the seat of man's immortal soul. But some, like the ancient Hindus, conceived of the heart as the sacred symbol of the One Central Living God. The Mayan tradition poetically speaks of such a Deity in the words of the *Popul Vuh*:

> Alone was the Creator, the Maker, Tepeu, the Lord, and Gucumatz, the Plumed Serpent, those who engender, those who give being, alone upon the waters like a growing light. . . . They are enveloped in green and azure, whence the name Gucumatz, and their being is great wisdom. Lo, how the sky existeth, how the Heart of the Sky existeth – for such is the name of God, as He doth name Himself!

The Quiche Mayan called the Heart of the Sky Hurakan and believed that the lesser gods created the earth through him. Far off in the ancient East theurgists anticipated such inspired notions, referring to the parts of the heart as Brahmā's Hall and Vishnu's Chamber. They asserted that each section corresponded to parts of the brain, whilst "the very atoms of the body (as a whole) are the thirty-three crores (in the Hindu pantheon) of gods". The idea that man is a microcosm of the macrocosm lends special significance to the heart, for surely, some have reasoned, the universe itself must have a heart which throbs and gives it life. In this view, it is most meaningful to identify that Great Heart with God and to express the deepest reverence for it, as did the pharaoh Ikhnaton in his Hymn to the Sun written in the fourteenth century before Christ.

> Thou didst create the earth according to thy heart.

Plato spoke of the valve action of the heart and how it was the fiery origin of human passions. Millennia later Matthew Arnold echoed this widely accepted idea, writing that man could not kindle when he would "the fire that in the heart resides". He poetically suggested that the fire in the heart took its flame from the spirit that comes and goes and that, somehow in this mystery, man's soul abides. Aristotle, offering a somewhat more mechanical explanation, asserted that the soul's vital spirit did indeed rest in the heart, contracting and expanding so as to "pull and thrust from one and the same causes". Most tribal peoples of the globe have also believed that the heart is the seat of the soul and have sometimes put this notion to work in alarming ways. Few engaged in massive human sacrifices like those of the Aztecs, but many people have practised acts of ritual cannibalism wherein the heart was consumed as the organ-seat of the victim's immortal soul or of their potency and courage. To such an end has fallen many a brave warrior, whilst some, like the thirteenth century Danish crusader whose heart was eaten by the Sakkala peasants of Finland, simply blundered into the unexpected role of sacrificial offering.

Throughout the ages hearts have been depicted as "broken", "heavy", "turned to stone", "cold", "warm", "kind", "bleeding", "singing" and "true". Many of these epithets have to do with feelings or dispositions, but a "true heart" is something unchanging, suggesting that Truth is present in an organ capable of reflecting it. The unswerving dependability of the heart is partly responsible for this association, but behind that rests the notion of what lies at the very core of an individual's life, the Truth that explains itself. We try to demonstrate our sincerity by "speaking from the bottom of the heart" and we hope that those who hear us will somehow glean from the tone of our voice and the light of our eyes that it is indeed from that hidden cave of Truth that our utterance springs. This ancient idea has ennobled the thought and speech of many people, inspiring the Egyptians to symbolize the judgement at death in terms of weighing the individual's heart against a feather to measure truth.

> For Mercy has a human heart . . .
>
> William Blake

Not in the busy mind but in the depth of one's heart is sensed the Divine Presence at the centre of one's being. Here, the Buddhists say, is to be found the essential nature of Buddha, which is a reservoir of compassionate wisdom. The purity and indestructibility of this fount gives rise to the term "Diamond Heart", which flames forth in seven streams of sound and light. This heart truly sings – the music of the solar system singing in the cosmic stream. The breadth and depth of the Heart Doctrine speaks to the uncluttered hearts of those who are capable of being profoundly moved by its compassionate message. Thus the Tibetans came to accept Buddhism after the Doctrine of the Heart had been introduced into earlier Buddhist teachings to which they had been exposed. However imperfectly, they intuitively sensed the completion of a sacred design. They realized that only through the wisdom of the heart would the hidden Jewel in the Lotus reveal itself, the Good Law becoming the Heart's Seal on all that came to pass. Through the glimmerings of their hearts men and women may catch glimpses of their connection with the vastitude of the manifest universe.

The Taoists taught that a realized Sage has seven orifices in his heart and they are all open. Such a heart is "the seat of Buddha", wherein all past lives are remembered and where the seven streams flow above the field of synchronized time and bear the essence of the compassionate nature that, through infinite sacrifice and renunciation, ever converts them into manifest rivers of life. According to Gupta Vidya, these are the reflections of the "seven Dhyani-Buddhic rays, which are mirrored by the secondary hierarchies in the complex nervous system". The spiritual heart in man is the link between the heart of the cosmos and the beating physical organ within the breast. One must think and feel through the heart to understand the ideas of ancient Sages and their deep insight into human physiology.

The history of the empirical knowledge of the heart and its workings stretches far back and is strewn with metaphysical concepts. Four thousand years ago the Egyptians understood that the pulse measured the heart and used it to diagnose illnesses, as did the Chinese even earlier. With the Aristotelian emphasis on empirical observation, thought moved from the realm of analogy and correspondence to the concrete possibilities of vivisection. In the second century, Galen, from Pergamon, served as physician to the gladiators for the Romans, during which practice his curiosity about the human body led him to dissect hundreds of animals. A skilled doctor, he was also a shrewd advocate of his methods and became court physician to Marcus Aurelius and chief mentor to medical investigators for several centuries. His influence was felt by such as Andreas Vesalius, who, in the sixteenth century, "determined to dissect everything he could get his hands on" and whose *De humani corporis fabrica libri septem* became the standard reference on human physiology of his time. Even such genius as that possessed by Leonardo da Vinci was inflamed with similar curiosity, causing him to overcome his "fear of living in the night hours in the company of those corpses" (which he had stolen) in his zeal to dissect them and study their innermost parts. He recognized that the heart was a pump with four chambers and believed that the blood in it was warmed through the action of churning in order for the vivifying process to take place – an interesting mixture of alchemical and empirical reasoning.

> There thy Observing Eye first found the Art
> Of all the Wheels and Clock-work of the Heart:
> The mystick causes of its Dark Estate,
> What Pullies Close its Cells, and what Dilate,
> What secret Engines tune the Pulse, whose din
> By Chimes without, Strikes how things fare within.

William Harvey, whose seventeenth century colleagues were responsible for the little *Rhyme of Appreciation* quoted above, was the first to recognize that the human organism contained a fairly constant supply of blood and that it circulated through the whole body as a result of the "function of the heart which it carries out by virtue of its pulsation, and that in sum it constitutes the sole reason for that heart's pulsatile movement". Thus, with a pragmatic stroke, the heart was categorized as a pump which moves more than two thousand gallons of blood through the human body each day, which weighs about eleven ounces and is about the size of a fist. Lying beneath the breastbone like a hollow pear-shaped pouch, it is composed of two upper atria and two lower ventricles. The right atrium receives the dark carbon dioxide-laden blood and releases it through a valve into the right ventricle, from which it travels to the lungs, where it is cleansed and oxygenated so that it takes on its familiar bright red colouration. From the lungs it enters into the left atrium, from which it flows through the mitral valve into the left ventricle, where powerful contractions push it out through a semilunar valve into the aorta, its first step in the long circuit through the blood vessels of the body.

Even to one who merely observes it as a physical phenomenon, the heart is "the very essence and poetry of fantastic precision, perfected motion and endurance". It is composed of muscle fibre whose cells have an abundance of mitochondria which act as power centres, converting food to energy. Electrical currents passing along from fibre to fibre with ease enable the structural lattice-work of separate cells to function like a group that have merged to act as a single cell. As with the separated cells from the disembodied heart, certain cardiac muscle cells of the living heart generate their own electrical current, commanding the rest of the heart's fibres to contract. The valves of the heart open and close with every heartbeat. They are one-way doors whose perfect function is responsible for keeping the blood moving in a fast and endless stream. Their dysfunction can permit a potentially lethal back-up of blood in the veins and arteries. As each chamber fills and contracts, blood presses against the underside of the valve cusps, closing them as part of an endless rhythm of open and close that takes place more than once a second. Their durability and steady response is one of the great wonders of the heart.

Heart attack has probably struck fear into the minds of human beings for as long as a sedentary way of life has tended to prevail. There is no tradition of death through heart disease among the hunters and gatherers of the world, though some are said to have died of a "broken" heart, like Chief Joseph, who was forced to spend his last years as a captive exile from his beloved Walla Walla home. The Chinese who were familiar with heart problems believed that by putting bad ideas into practice, humans damaged their hearts (whereas wrong thoughts themselves were believed to cause lung trouble). Owing to the suddenness of heart attack, people have often identified it with some sort of lightning-stroke retribution, but it is actually the result of disease attacking the heart's muscular essence. At least eighty percent of such attacks are caused by diseased coronary arteries often identified as arteriosclerosis. The heart keeps five percent of the blood it pumps for nourishment. The coronary arteries drain the vital fluid from pockets formed by the cusps of the valves and carry it to all parts of the heart. Small branches of these meet in complex junctions where a blood clot or buildup of fat or cholesterol can cut off the flow to crucial areas of the organ, bringing on heart muscle death.

A weakened heart can result in congestive heart failure, where either or both of the ventricles fail to empty themselves fully during systole. Thus, cardiac output would decrease while pressure builds up simultaneously in the atria and blood is forced back into the lungs or veins. Besides the narrowing or blocking of the arteries supplying blood to the heart, certain other factors can contribute to its failure. Rheumatic fever affects the valves so that with each heartbeat blood leaks backward and a short-circuiting of the heart's electrical system can produce cardiac arrhythmia. In this latter case the electrical impulse is blocked or premature and is actually generated from a site other than the sinoatrial node, the heart's pacemaker. Another electrical circuit problem arises in the form of flutters and fibrillations, sometimes called electrical frenzies. In its "circus movement" the heart's electrical impulses may, as it were, chase and catch themselves. This produces a chain reaction involving the splitting of impulses, and their multiplication can spread out of control, often in the atria.

> The human heart has hidden treasures,
> In secret kept, in silence sealed.
>
> Charlotte Brontë

The systole and diastole of the heart are its contraction and dilation, its great and constant pulsation. In the Greek, ἡ συστόλη (systole) literally means "contraction" or "limitation", whereas the verb διαστέλλω (diastello) means to "put asunder" or "tear open" and comes from the root στέλλω, meaning "to set in order", "to dispatch" or "array". With each rippling wave of contraction, the heart twists a quarter turn and then relaxes. This wonderfully complex process is managed in fine split-second rhythm through the electricity generated by the heart's natural pacemaker. Situated high on the wall of the right atrium, this electrically self-exciting cluster of cells or sinoatrial node has an inherent rhythm of seventy beats per minute. The beat of the heart, along with all the body's circadian rhythms (governing such things as temperature fluctuation, blood sugar level, adrenal activity, RNA and DNA synthesis and cell division), is innate and persistent.

Before birth the human heart rate is constant. This stability or lack of periodicity (relatively speaking) persists even after birth, and it is not until the sixth week after birth that the subtle effects of night and day appear. A clearly defined rhythm takes over only in the latter part of the first year (a similar course being followed by the body temperature, etc.). With growth, the low point of these rhythms moves from the late night hours in the infant to the early morning hours in the adult.

All organisms must adapt to a temporally programmed world. They thus require an endogenous master clock which anticipates external shifts and adapts to them. This process of synchronization or entrainment is carried out by the pineal gland, which translates light into melanin, a substance which has a biochemical impact on the whole regulatory or autonomic nervous system. It maintains the body's rhythms in phase with one another through the hypothalamus. If these rhythms are not coupled to the external environment, dyphasis occurs, causing both biochemical and physiological damage. Dance, music, the noises and actions of machines – all are external rhythms that can become so strong as to "possess" individuals and actually affect the synchronization of the "internal clocks". In more subtle ways the aura of the pineal gland vibrates with every sensation translated into conscious experience. Every perception is registered there. Gupta Vidya teaches that the septenary play of light in the aura of the pineal gland is reflected in the heart's aura, which vibrates and illumines the "seven brains" of the heart, known in the Buddhist tradition as the Saptaparna Cave of the Buddha.

> The blood around men's heart is their thinking.
>
> Empedocles

With these influences from above and from below, the magic of the heart's electrical system asserts itself always towards balance. Holding the heart in a finely poised state, the parasympathetic and sympathetic nerves cast "their electrochemical spells", slowing and quickening as they compete for the "loyalty" of the heart. But they themselves are governed by rhythms monitored by the pineal gland and work in conjunction with the heart's own impulse. The balance to which the heart addresses itself is not merely coordinated with the external physical world nor based only upon the unique qualities of the internal microcosmic world of the human body. It responds to the seven rays reflected in its aura which are themselves reflections of the "hebdomadal Heart of the cosmos and the secret, spiritual heart in man". The light which is translated by the pineal gland and which, in its transformed state, has so much to do with the rhythms of the physical human microcosm is a shadow of the spiritual light that emanates from the Heart of the cosmos. It is an echo of the Dhyani-Buddhic light that "plays" around the pineal gland and fills the cave of man's secret heart.

The pulsation of the physical heart is an echo of that of the Central Spiritual Heart (Sun), and its rate of seventy beats per minute is a precise fractional reflection of an overwhelmingly high rate of vibration which is capable of insinuating its throbbing rhythm into every unseen and seen vessel of the entire universe. Thus planets, stars, species and races all have their rate of pulse which is synchronized with the vaster rhythmic pattern of manifestation. In our solar system there is a regular circulation of vital fluid originating on an invisible plane but percolating through the visible sun to affect the whole of physical Nature. The sun contracts as rhythmically as the human heart, taking "the solar blood ten of its years, and a whole year to pass through its auricles and ventricles before it washes the lungs and passes thence to the great veins and arteries of the system".

The Heart of the Cosmos which is the Central Spiritual Sun self-generates the vital electricity which ever issues forth the regenerating fluid and ever receives back as much as it gives out. During the *sandhyas* the Spiritual Sun emits creative light only passively. But during active periods of being "it gives rise to streams of ceaseless energy, whose vibrating currents acquire more activity and potency with every rung of the hebdomadic ladder of Being they descend". The sacred electric source of life within the Spiritual Sun is triple and concealed, manifesting as Seven Fires (the Dhyani-Buddhic Rays) which are responsible for the seven states of consciousness and the senses which are the causes of the phenomena from which the Self is emancipated. Within the Spiritual Sun lies the "reservoir within which divine radiance, already differentiated at the beginning of every creation, is focussed". In perfect mirroring of this the tiny pulsating heart within the human foetus is the focal point of the descending human monad as it pulsates forth out of the reservoir of its own ancestral potentiality into the growing confines of an earthly form. Just as the visible sun is only a window cut into the real solar presence which reflects the work within, so the physical heart reflects the work of individuated rays of the Dhyanis which continually recharge the macrocosmic and microcosmic systems, breaking down, refining material and washing it clean in the "lungs" of Akashic Space. Weighing in the balance, cleansing and purifying: this is the work of the universal and human heart.

Thus the sun is a heart and the heart is a sun from the most ethereal level to the visible and physical. The Spiritual Sun is the father of the human soul and all divine faculties in man expand with the expansion of its light. Surya-Savitri, Creator and Increaser, "Thou art utterly expressed by the rays of the Sun." This is true if one tunes the whole of one's being to the innermost promptings of the heart and enters fully into the vast pattern of purification which is the great work of all manifested life. The human body is kept alive through a circulatory process which ever cleanses and revitalizes. It is precisely this which human beings need to do in their interactions with one another in order to help unite the separately pulsating cells into a continuous, synchronized whole capable of establishing a harmonious rhythm in which love and truth can become the keynote. To do this in whatever degree is to become attuned to the vibrating pulse of the Spiritual Heart of the universe.

The diseases of the heart are produced by fear, selfishness and the cruel acts of omission that drain the world dry of love and leave human minds parched in a desert of dying hopes and cynicism. The fear which continually short-circuits the electrical flow within distorts one's perspective on everything and encourages the cringing forms of self-protection and indulgence. Fear and such a crippling absorption with one's own interests are the basis for heartless actions of appalling proportions affecting individuals, groups and whole nations and dehumanizing all who are connected with them. To go against the heart is to deny one's humanity and to deny the One Heart of everything that lives. All those who are not utterly without soul know this and intuitively revere the Doctrine of the Heart, which is the Path of the Open and Loving Heart. Enlightened Sages of every age are united consubstantially in the Akashic essence which flows through their hearts and informs their minds. Through compassion they are united in One Truth and their hearts are the links that connect the members of this sacred Fraternity and which overflow as a purifying and vitalizing tonic for humanity. Lesser men are bound together by lesser unities. Their hearts filled with pride, desire, exclusive loyalty and love, they set themselves off against others outside their circles. "The passing sneer, the epithet of revulsion, and their psychic correlations: these are failures of the heart to recognize its own."

As we look "over the head" of the personality of others, into their heart, we can reverse this tendency to draw only contracting circles. One becomes deeply moved by what one sees in another's heart, for the entire history of the human race pulsates there in a unique and ever-poignant cadence. The reality of one's brotherhood with every other human being thus becomes manifest. The open-hearted Sage who does this is as a child among children, a scholar among the learned and a courageous warrior among soldiers. He is at peace with all persons and acts neither in terms of past and future nor loves and aversions, but in terms of the eternal truth which flows freely through his heart.

> O Great Antique Heart
> That beats within the breast of man,
> Never diminished.
> Never failed.
> Never broken,
> Your Divinely Echoed Plan.

Hermes, May 1984

BLOOD

Yea, specially that mortal man hath toiled for service
  of the gods,
Who quickly hath brought near Mitra and Varuna
  to share his sacrificial gifts.
Supreme in sovereign power, far-sighted, chiefs and
  kings, most swift to hear from far away.
Both wondrously, set them in motion as with arms,
  in company with Surya's beams.
The rapid messenger who runs before you, Mitra-Varuna,
  with iron head, swift to the draught.
The true red treasure they have sent, one only son
  born of the three.
They, the immortal ones, never deceived, survey the
  families of mortal man.

Rig Veda, Hymn XC

In the hymns of the most ancient Vedas, Varuna is praised as the most lofty sovereign of the Three Worlds. As he breathed, so breathed forth into being the universe. As he ordained, so the stars and planets took their places in the firmament. It was he who caused the solar orb to shine forth. He opened out the boundless pathways for its radiant fire just as he hollowed out the channels on earth for the rivers that would flow by his command. It was said that no creature in the universe could wink without him, and his messengers beheld all worlds as they sped forth at his bidding. None other than Varuna instructed the Sage Vasishtha in the mysteries, but his secrets were not to be revealed to the foolish, and only those familiar with his realm could tap his hundred thousand remedies for evil and sin. For he was extolled as a barrier against falsehood and as one who seized transgressors with bonds and nooses and restored all who reached him to harmony and balance.

In later times, Varuna's position in the Hindu pantheon of gods was reduced in importance, and his cosmic sovereignty was largely usurped by gods whose names became the focal points of the reverential awe felt by the vast streams of people that meandered and moulded the races of the Indian subcontinent. But the clues of Varuna's former greatness can be found in his continuing association with water, for water is the designation of space and, on earth, of the electric flow of the blood of life. This is why the ancients could claim that "it takes earth and water to create a human soul" and that blood was connected with the initial generative power of the gods. Thus the gods Brahmā, Adam-Jehovah and Mars are the "red" gods who work for the purpose of human procreation. In the Hindu tradition, Mars is Karthikeya, son of Shiva, who is "born of his sweat" (Shiva Gharmaja) and of the earth. He is the god of bloodshed (war) only as a secondary idea which flows out of a primary cause associated with the "shedding of blood in conception for the first time".

Spilt blood is the symbol of sacrifice, the most precious offering of all. Even in earthly battle or human conception there is an element of sacrifice which echoes the greater act of the gods. Among human beings the intuitive understanding of this truth has often been inverted in rituals, wherein men attempt to appease or curry favour with the gods by offering them the blood of living creatures, sacrificing upwards to encourage renewed sacrifice downwards in the form of rain, bountiful crops or material gains. One can recognize in this a persistent attempt to manipulate the laws of Nature for limited ends. Sacrifice by proxy is a grotesquely diluted form of magic. Involuntary death in battle or participation in conception is scarcely capable of mirroring the Divine Will operating through the fiery life-giving streams of the sun. The legendary Red Knight in the Arthurian tales provides a truer reflection of the idea, for his colour expresses the passionate will of one who has mastered both steed and monster. But it is through Perceval that the critical force of the heart comes to play a dominant part in the knight's quest. The very sword which he must find and wield is lodged in a slab of red marble afloat in the watery sea. He must grasp its power from the heart in order to slay the monsters (within) that lie between him and the Grail used by Christ to share with his Apostles his own blood. Faint but haunting traces of the Red Knight can be found in

Thomas Hardy's reddleman, who wanders and watches and silently endures. From the labour of his trade he is red from head to foot and cast outside the circle of common human life. But his heart knows the truth that courses through others' lives and compassion is his guide in defining his part in the revelation of its complexities.

There is a language of the blood of which people speak but it is also held that blood speaks for itself. In its continual coursing through every crook and cranny of the body, the blood contributes to and takes from all parts of the whole. This, together with the fact that men have long conceived of the blood as bearing the essential impress of the conditions of countless ancestors, has caused many to believe that the blood was capable of revealing truth. Thus it was thought that the wounds of a murdered man would bleed afresh in the presence of the murderer. Sir Francis Bacon recorded that when King Richard (the Lion-Hearted) was made to stand before his father's (Henry 11's) corpse, the wounds bled and confirmed the suspicion of many that patricide had been committed. But a deeper and perhaps unconsciously held reason for the belief lies in the analogy, perceived since the most ancient times, between the sun and its rays and the heart and blood in living beings. The penetration into all parts of the living whole is represented in the Rig Veda as Varuna, and in man this is seen as that which will never accept a partial view of things but continually seek the Truth in which all conditions and perspectives can be accommodated. The wise have taught that "so long as man does not attain to the largeness of Varuna's truth, he is bound to the posts of the world sacrifice by the triple bonds of mind, life and body as a victim and is not free as a possessor and enjoyer".

Partial and skewed views of "truth" cause one to be "hot" or "cold" blooded and to act in ways unworthy of human beings. Productive of the "bad blood" which often arises between people, such views can result in a kind of cardiac arrest on the mental plane or in practices even as benighted as blood feuding or drinking the blood of one's fallen enemy. Behind the most abysmal acts of man's inhumanity often lies a superstitious awe of the power of blood. To drink another's is to steal his or her life-essence. To kill a member of an enemy clan is to "get back the blood" and increase the power of one's own family. The term "blood" is mentioned in the Bible more than five hundred times, a testimony to the centrality of its importance to what was initially a tribal religion. It is often spoken of as a covenant and in connection with atonement and sacrifice. In Christian as well as other cultures a sign of blood serves as a pact or seal, like that made between American Indians who cut their thumbs in order to release and mingle their blood and become "blood brothers". The example of the pact between Dr. Faustus and Mephistopheles has proved to be of enduring fascination to writers in the Christian world, where the use of blood in acts of necromancy has been as plentiful as in primitive cultures. The abhorrence and fear of menstrual blood is also universal, causing many people to observe remarkable rituals of avoidance during periods when it was necessary. Pliny referred to this cast-off blood as "a fatal poison, corrupting and decomposing . . . depriving seeds of their fecundity, destroying insects, blasting garden flowers and grasses, causing fruits to fall from branches [and] dulling razors".

The passionate quality of the colour red pervades the symbolism of blood, and the vital character of blood informs the significance of the colour red. Among most people of the earth red symbolizes blood and indicates health, courage, fertility, growth and life itself. Chromatically, the colour red represents the end of a series which begins with sunlight and the colour yellow. The intermediate stage is expressed in the green colour so dominant in vegetable life, and with the movement from yellow an increase of iron marks the progressive involvement of light and electricity in matter. The advent of the colour red, then, symbolically represents the furthest extent of sacrifice from the ethereal to the material realm, and blood itself becomes a pulsating reminder of that profoundly archetypal process. More than one hundred thousand times a day, the human heart (pumping more than two thousand gallons or tens of millions of gallons in a lifetime) reminds us of this. The blood rushes out of the heart, travelling about one foot every second, following the same laws that apply to ground water flowing through the layers of the earth or electricity flowing from the sun through the vastitudes of space. Just as doubling the pressure doubles the flow and doubling the resistance halves the flow of water, so too these factors modify the flow of electricity and blood.

From its entrance into the right ventricle from the veins to its exit from the left ventricle into the arteries, the passage of blood requires two-and-a-half seconds when the body is at rest, and one second or so when it is being exercised. The heart's beating drives it into the narrowest capillaries, forcing the exchange of oxygen for the dead weight of carbon dioxide seventy times a minute. Its passage is swift and powerful despite the fact that only a little more than half of its constitution is liquid. Many of its more solid substances float in a rich sea of hormones, vitamins, enzymes and proteins that are found in the plasma which, composed largely of water, is the blood's solvent. Plasma contains compounds uncannily like those of the ancient Cambrian seas that covered most of the globe over five hundred million years ago. It was from these seas that life forms first emerged. The first single-celled residents had circulatory systems as vast as the ocean itself. Oxygen diffused effortlessly into the cells, and, just as easily, the seas absorbed the wastes. The evolution of forms from more ethereal types involved a collective participation in breath and circulation. The higher sparks of conscious intelligence waited in abeyance while this vast process of generalized physical exchange took place. The forms would evolve for millennia, becoming increasingly complex and inwardly oriented while they waited for a vesture capable of reflecting the individuating mind.

When the correct form evolved, it possessed an individual circulatory system similar to that of other animals, but one whose rhythm and pattern of movement, relative to its centre, reflected a cosmic design. As this microcosmic form evolved, the blood that gave it life developed various specialized factors associated with race and long chains of causation hidden in the forgotten complexities of man's past. Human blood groups with their various factors bear a simple one-to-one correspondence with the genes that are transmitted each generation. These are constant within individuals and not influenced by environment or diet or any other external factor. Two parents both carrying the M factor will unavoidably produce a child having the M factor, whilst one type A blood parent together with another type B blood parent may produce a type A or B or AB child. But there are over sixty different factors and four major blood types known in the world, and the chance of two people being identical in regard to all of them is astronomically improbable. There are what have been called human "blood prints", which are as unique as fingerprints and characterize an aspect of a particular individual, a particular karma which speaks, as the blood can speak, of the history and condition of the indwelling soul whose body it sustains.

Great movements of human beings, unknown to history, can be charted by the geographical increase and decrease of blood factors. The fact that blood type A is frequently found in western Japan (opposite Korea) and diminishes as one moves towards Hokkaido corresponds with a movement of mainland people onto an archipelago once completely populated by another and much older race of people. Some races possess blood factors which others do not possess at all, and some instances of their occurrence seem to be part of a crazy-quilt design that does not readily fit in with broader patterns of migration. Much mystery continues to surround the study of man's physical ancestry and the complexities of all the meanderings and matings that have produced the billions of bodies of the dead and the living. An old English proverb has it that "all blood is alike ancient" and there is much truth in this saying. The blood of our forgotten ancestors is as vast as time extended back along the ages to the shores of the primordial Cambrian seas. The hot and cold blood, the bad blood, the blood of sacrifice, that of the heart's wisdom and that of life's passions flows down along those infinitely tangled courses of animal and human history to circulate in myriad combinations through the bodies of the living. But it is the human ancestors, forgotten and remembered, who have impressed it greatly with the stamp of their lives, for the blood of animals is little marked by hopes or perversions. Man can affect the quality of blood and its circulation through thought and cause it to run as a pure river of sacrifice or as a stream clogged with impurities. Oddly, it is in man's treatment of animals that he has often muddied his nature most foully. This is particularly true in regard to vivisection and blood sports. Oscar Wilde once referred to the institution of fox hunting as "the unspeakable in full pursuit of the uneatable", a witticism which points to the cruelty as well as the absurdity of such a practice. The hostility and fear towards humans that pervade the animal kingdom is a sad result of the actions of human ancestors who lived millennia ago as well as only yesterday. As folk belief would have it, "the blood itself never forgets where it has been".

The primary function of human blood is to supply oxygen daily to the sixty trillion cells in the body. Besides this it transports food, wastes and hormonal messengers. It cools when there is overheating of the system and warms when it is cold, and it destroys alien invaders while at the same time mending and repairing its own vessels. Blood maintains the balance of Nature and homeostasis in man. It is the medium through which the continual re-establishment of this balance takes place and it thus binds the internal nature harmoniously to the world outside. The pressure of the systemic circulation is originated by the heart as the blood is pumped into the large arteries. From there it courses to smaller arteries and arterioles which control the flow to the tissue. From the arterioles it passes through the metarterioles to the sphincter valves, and thence into the capillaries, which radiate out in minutely distinguished dendritic fans resembling great coral fans along some exotic submarine reef. The oxygen and food brought to the capillaries pass through their walls and enter the interstitial fluid that surrounds all of the body's cells and then into the cells themselves. As this occurs, the carbon dioxide and other waste material in the cells leave and cross over into the blood in the capillaries in an exchange which causes the blood, which then makes its return journey through the venules and veins to the heart, to take on a dark purple colouration.

The blood, passing through the heart, then enters into the pulmonary phase of its circulation. It is "breathless" as it comes along the right and left pulmonary arteries leading to the lungs. There it courses along arteries that divide into smaller and smaller vessels, threading for hundreds of miles around and about the millions of tiny air sacs called alveoli which form the respiratory membranes of the lungs. Molecules of oxygen diffuse through the tiny membranes of the alveoli into the blood in a homeostatic response resulting in the equalization of pressure. At any one time the three ounces of blood in the lungs are distributed throughout this network so thinly and evenly that the oxygen/carbon dioxide exchange can take place in a quarter of a second. Air is drawn into the lungs in concert with the blood rising from the heart, and they meet in perfect timing at the tiny membrane stations where diffusion takes place.

Excessive carbon dioxide in the blood causes the breathing and heartbeat to quicken in order to flush it out. Another regulating factor is dictated by the need of tissues and the subsequent signals carried in the blood which cause the arteries and veins of various sizes to contract or dilate. The passageways contain nerves connected to the vaso-motor centre in the brain, which then signals the nerve fibres to secrete a vaso-constrictor or dilating agent. Like the systole and diastole of the heart, the quickness of the breath, the pressure of the blood as it flows and the rate of the exchanges during the phases of circulation, so too, the vessels through which the blood passes reflect a universal centrifugal and centripetal rhythm to which all forms of life, like revolving wheels within wheels, continually adjust themselves.

> The Sun is the heart of the Solar World (System) and its brain
> is hidden behind the (visible) Sun. From thence, sensation
> is radiated into every nerve-centre of the great body . . .

The Secret Doctrine, i 541

If the plasma in blood is its solvent, the red blood cells endow it with its "functional essence", carrying, as they do, ninety-nine percent of the oxygen distributed throughout the body. Constituting only forty-five percent of the blood, the red blood cells are, nonetheless, the most abundant cells in the body. They are sturdy and highly flexible sacs that can squeeze through the narrowest passages without rupturing. Like plasma, they are partly composed of water, but their characteristic constituent (which gives blood its crimson colour) is haemoglobin, which they possess in so highly concentrated a form that it is almost crystallized. In addition to the transport of oxygen, blood has the power to heal. Unlike any other fabric, it can seal rent tissue, magically making its own thread to weave the torn parts together again. The fibrous threads literally "weave themselves into being" at the site of an injury. Tiny platelets rush to a cut or rupture and swell into sticky, irregular shapes to create plugs as backup, and if their abilities to seal the wound are inadequate, they signal for the clotting process to begin. So dependable is the blood's complex electrochemical potential that the signals are continually and faithfully transmitted, releasing the exact chemicals capable of adjusting and mending countless times within a human life. It is only in rare circumstances that the system fails to respond, the most publicized of these being the effects caused by the condition known as haemophilia, which term, in a sort of cruel irony, means "love of blood". One of Queen Victoria's everlasting claims to fame lies in the fact that she transmitted this disease to a good many of the crowned heads of Europe and Russia.

Another important element in blood is composed of a small but active army of white blood cells (leucocytes), whose job it is to engulf, swallow, "explode", break down, digest and neutralize any parasites or viruses that invade the system. Their production in the bone marrow and lymph glands immediately increases upon such an intrusion, and a devouring horde is released to engage "the enemy". They pull themselves along the capillary walls like foot-soldiers, their tiny pseudopods stretching out with each step as they advance along and through the tissue. Billions may perish in an all out battle but, with the assistance of the antibodies which destroy particular antigens they have latched onto, they are usually victorious. But the "army" of leucocytes must always serve the greater function of the blood. If, abnormally swollen with power, they multiply and accumulate unnaturally, they can clog the body's arteries and prevent the bone marrow from producing vital red blood cells. Such an army out of control can result in tragic diseases such as leukaemia or lupus.

> They were going to look at war, the red
> animal – war, the blood-swollen god.
>
> *The Red Badge of Courage*
> Stephen Crane

The god of war reigns in the Iron Age. Forgotten is his primary role associated with ideational sacrifice. His distorted and crippled image is red with lust for conquest and yet can preside over a disease that strips the body of its life-bearing crimson cells. The causes and result of an age whose hallmarks are greed and selfishness are often deceptive in their outward appearances. Iron lies at the very "heart" of the blood's functional essence. It is the "soul" or "jewel" that rests in the centre of haemoglobin molecules responsible for the continual oxidation of the body's cells. As always, the body shows its "wisdom" by producing this vital substance in the protected surrounds of bone marrow (largely that of the skull, ribs and spine). When tissue in the body runs short of oxygen, a messenger hormone called erythropoietin ("one who makes blood") travels to the marrow, where it signals a "primitive" cell to come out of its dormancy and to begin to grow and produce red blood cells. Haemoglobin molecules multiply within them until a saturation point is reached and the nucleus of the cells is released in an act of self-sterilization demonstrative of the blood's sacrificial character. Looking like a pinched disc, the red blood cell will live one hundred and twenty days and then die, forming part of the waste to be transported out of the body. Like the biblical creation of the world, the time required for the production of the cells is six days, but with no rest on the seventh!

Once produced, each red blood cell contains two hundred and seventy million haemoglobin molecules, each of which loads oxygen at the surface of the lungs and unloads it precisely when and where needed. The molecules are made up of four chains of amino acids which form little tangled wheels circling single atoms of iron at their centres. Sheltered in the rings of the chains (made up of hydrogen, nitrogen and carbon), the iron is heavily involved in interacting with them (especially the nitrogen). This dissipates its attraction for the individual oxygen molecules which will attach themselves to the iron, so that the binding is only a temporary one and the oxygen is easily released at its destination.

> And if our blood alone
> Will melt this iron earth,
> Take it. It is well spent
> Easing a saviour's birth.
>
> Cecil Day Lewis

The iron binds only temporarily but it must have the power to do so. The earth may be a magnet, dark as iron, which we must melt away to let the spirit shine forth, but have not those who daily greet the sun called it Great Magnet? Just as the spectrum, passing from yellow through green to red, corresponds with an increase of iron, so too does the sun, passing from its hidden spiritual essence to the manifest orb in our solar system. Therefore, iron, in its physical form, owes its power to magnetize both matter and mind to an essential spiritual magnetism which (along with Fohatic electricity) lies at the heart of the substratum of being. It is a central actor in the centripetal and centrifugal pulsation that takes place in the spiritual, astral and physical realms. This is why the god Varuna, who set in motion Surya's beams and gave the "true red treasure", is called "Iron-Headed" and identified with Hephaestus of the iron forge.

Like little suns in the centres of wheels of planets, the four iron atoms preside over the world of the red blood cell. The elements they work with are the four fundamental building blocks of all manifest life: hydrogen, nitrogen, oxygen and carbon. In occult terms, these provide the basis for the Tetrad, which combines within itself all the materials from which cosmos is produced. From the magnetic point in the centre of the boundless Circle, to the Duad and the Triad, the One is ultimately involved in the Tetrad, whose symbol is the fourth or visible sun as well as the four tiny iron atoms in the haemoglobin molecule. In the macrocosmic process the astral realm lies between the noumenal Tetraktys and the phenomenal Tetrad. At this level it is Akashic, whilst in its lower expression it corresponds with the linga sharira of the phenomenal world and its chemical analogue, nitrogen. One perceives the significance of the iron atom's involvement with nitrogen, which acts to dissipate the binding of oxygen to it. For on the gross material level oxygen represents *prana* and must be free to fly out from the little sun and carry out its vital role in the sacrifice of life.

Someone once asked H. P. Blavatsky if *prana* was produced by the lives of the human body. She responded that the opposite was true, that *prana* was the parent of the lives. She asked the enquirer to imagine the body as a sponge submerged in water. The water inside the sponge would be *prana*, whilst that all around it would be *Jiva*. When the sponge is removed from the water, it dries up (dies) and loses *prana*.

She went on to explain that every principle is a differentiation of *Jiva*, but the life motion in each is *prana*, without which there would be no *kama*. *Prana* wakes the kamic germs to life; it makes all desires vital and living. Thus the Great Breath which breathes out the universes exudes the vital *Jivas* which course through the electrical channels of ethereal space and ultimately bring life to the very air we take into our lungs.

The vessels within the human organism are channels for *prana* as it continually informs the body. *Jiva* becomes *prana* when a child is born and first begins to breathe, enabling the divine life-spark to become an individual spiritual presence. Entering the blood as oxygen, it causes it to become bright red, thus bringing the solar spark to its ultimate expression on the spectrum. A delightful myth in the Puranas explains how this came about through the Sage Vasishtha, who requested the sun to come to *Satya Loka*. Surya said that if he left his place, the whole world would be destroyed. So the Rishi offered to put his red cloth in the place of the sun's disc, and it is this that we now see in the sky. So also, the golden streams of Fohatic electricity which inform ethereal space become red within the body of living creatures. The vast ocean of *Jiva* finds an analogue in the plasma of the blood, which bears in its currents the ghostly remnants of dead cells much like the bhuts that float in the astral realm. Like the ancient Cambrian seas, it is an archaic matrix in which the individuating solar design gradually incarnated.

Man is the pivot where the Great Breath which breathes out is breathed in. The little suns of iron then magnetize it before "breathing it out", so to speak, into the microcosm of the body. At this point, the Red God Karthikeya reigns, for his is the kingdom of the manifest world. Worshipped as Murugan, Subramania or Mars, he is the hope of those who court fertility and the champion of those in whom rajas predominates. But he is born of the "sweat" of his father, Shiva, who, beyond the limits of form, precipitated out watery globules (worlds) much in the fashion that the "primitive" cell within the marrow would come to be activated to produce red blood cells in man. It is these globules which are the realm of the "red sun", the red son and offspring of the Highest Spiritual Will.

In this way, the "interior work" of the Spiritual Sun manifests forth. The "sweat" of Shiva, transmitted by his fleet-footed son, becomes the vital fluid that circulates through our solar system. Every year the blood of the visible sun passes through its auricles and ventricles before washing the lungs and passing into the arteries and veins of the system to complete an eleven-year cycle. This is a reflection in a very limited time of much vaster cycles pertaining to the third and second and most Spiritual Sun. In man the cycle requires a tiny fraction of solar time but it is, in essence, the same cycle of circulation, demonstrating more powerfully than any other physiological pattern man's position as microcosm of the macrocosm. On earth the solar cave of the heart, in which the Buddha of sacrifice resides, lies in the mountain peaks. It is from these heights that the sacrificial streams of blood (water) course forth to bring life to the waiting world. They stream along endless canals and cross over interstitial seas to be returned to the lungs of the atmosphere and recleansed. But it is the heart centres in the world which keep the waters flowing. If it were not for their conscious participation in the whole sacrifice of life, there would not be adequate canals to carry its fruits, and they would sink in the chaos of the great seas long before reaching other shores where the needy wait and hope.

Without the conscious participation of those who make of their existence a heart centre, the "cells" of the world could not be adequately nourished and the global body would begin to dry up like the dying sponge when it is denied its life-giving environment. Living in the world, we are not submerged in the waters of *Jiva*, and we are dependent upon the extension and maintenance of channels capable of spreading the spiritual currents with which man's immortal soul is enlivened and encouraged to incarnate. These rivers of Truth are brought to us by those who act as extensions of the Rays which stream forth as the *Jivas* emanated by their Logoic Solar Source. The Great Lord Shiva is all these *Jivas* combined, and those who attempt to diffuse their spiritual sparks in the world are followers of his example. They sacrifice through their "sweat" that which they have garnered through the innermost penetration of the heart and brain. Those who follow these Rays will eventually move towards their heavenly prototype until they are drawn into the highest Ray of the Sun.

Varuna guides them because he is the Ether of Divine Truth that leads from the fiery Son to the Invisible Father beyond. He strikes down evil and delivers from illusion, like a vast sea in which all is ultimately purified or thrown up. Much like the leucocytes which engulf and destroy invaders into a harmoniously operating system, Varuna ensnares and demolishes the "Sons of Darkness [who] serve self-will and ignorance". But those who seek after Truth through sacrifice are delivered from bondage to sin, like a calf released from the rope or a victim set free from the slaying-post. From within their highest spiritual centres (shielded by the skull, the ribs and the spine), such seekers tune their most sensitive receptors to catch the signal of the erythropoietin, the call of humanity's spiritual needs. They watch and listen and willingly give forth the living blood of Truth on whose vast sea they have set their course.

> Do not pass that long sought cup
> Away from my parched lips.
> Too great the pain that filled it up,
> Too sweet its ruby sips.

Hermes, June 1984

THE SPIRAL

There is a thing confusedly formed.
Born before heaven and earth.
Silent and void.
It stands alone and does not change.
Goes round and does not weary.
It is capable of being the mother of the world.
I know not its name
So I style it "the way".
I give it the makeshift name of "the great".
Being great, it is further described as receding,
Receding, it is described as far away.
Being far away, it is described as turning back.

Tao Te Ching

Sometimes in Nature we stand before a spiralling force which catches us, absorbs us and winds us back beyond the remembrance of beginning to the great yawning vortex of the unknown. The whirling pattern in the heart of a sunflower may carry one's mind along a spiralled curve that spins into the future through the aperture of the past, causing sequential consciousness to dissolve and leaving the force of motion as the sole reality. Few there are who have ever experienced something like this bodily and lived to tell the tale. In the clutches of a sweeping prairie "twister" or the ferocious suction of a whirlpool, the spiralling energy of Nature is too overpowering to permit a mystical journey of the mind while still encased in its earthly form. Charybdis did not, after all, spare the sailors who steered within her whirling clutches. It was with terror that their minds were benumbed as they were swallowed up within her greedy throat. Few there are who have lived to tell of such a mighty power engulfing them and yet sparing them. Edgar Allan Poe's description of the perilous adventure of a Norwegian mariner is a vivid account of one such rare event, but few there are who have ever endorsed its veracity.

The tale was told by the mariner as an old man, who looked back upon the terrifying saga of his youth, still marvelling at his survival and at what he had learnt while caught in the terrible whirlpool called the Maelstrom. Long ago he and his elder brother had been fishing from their smack off the island of Moskoe in the depths of the Maelstrom channel. It was their habit to cross this channel only in fine weather and only at the turn of the ebb and flood. When the flood was full and aggravated by a storm, it was dangerous to be anywhere near the place. Boats, yachts and ships had been sucked into its terrible whirl by sailing too close, and the occasional blowing and bellowing of whales bore testimony to its inexorable power to drag down to its depths anything that ventured into the vicinity. Splintered logs from trees and fragments of torn boats were regularly thrown up by the vortex, strongly indicating that its bottom consisted of jagged rocks upon which they had smashed and been whirled to and fro.

On the day of the terrible event, the brothers, starting back during the calm, were surprised by an unprecedented cross breeze which made it impossible to achieve any headway. As they drifted in the eddies, a storm gathered to break upon them in its full fury, covering the boat with its hurricane force. The mariner grasped the ring-bolt at the foot of the foremast while his elder brother held on to an empty water cask lashed at the stern. "No one", he recalled, "will ever know what my feelings were at that moment. I shook from head to foot as if I had had the most violent fit of ague. . . . With the wind that now drove us on, we were bound for the whirl of the storm and nothing could save us." The boat reached a great swirl of foam and shot off in a new direction like a bolt, and the roaring noise of the water changed to a terrible shriek. Here, strangely, in the very jaws of the gulf, the sailor felt more calm. He even began to speculate upon the magnificence of such a death in the throes, as it were, of such a wondrous manifestation of divine power. They flew around this belt of the whirlpool for an hour or so, moving ever nearer to its horrible inner edge. As they approached its brink, the elder brother, in the agony of his terror, let go the cask and wrested the ring hold away from the younger, who groped astern to the other's former position just before the boat was swept headlong into the abyss.

Thinking they were done for, the young mariner closed his eyes, only to open them and find that their boat was hanging about midway down on the ebony walls of a vast funnel which spun them round with overwhelming velocity. Too confused by this breathtaking situation, it was several moments before he noticed that they were not the only objects whirling about the fury. Fragments of other vessels, masts, furniture and masses of building timber floated in their company. He watched these in fascination, noting that various fragments were descending downwards at different velocities and that while one object would suddenly plunge towards the crashing foam below, others seemed to remain almost at the same level. He recalled that, whilst most of the debris thrown up on the shore by the whirlpool had been splintered and battered to shreds, some objects were thrown up untouched by any violence. It occurred to him that these few articles had never been completely absorbed to the bottom of the whirlpool before the turn of the flood had come and they had been thrust up to the surface. Observing the vortex thus carefully and considering this remembered intelligence, the young sailor ascertained that the larger objects were descending faster and that smaller cylindrical objects were absorbed much more slowly. He saw that the boat had descended some distance below such objects and tried to alert his brother with desperate gestures and signs but to no avail. It was impossible to communicate with the terror-stricken man, and the young sailor sadly abandoned him to his fate, fastened himself to the cask and dove with it away from the boat and into the whirling wall of the funnel.

Within an hour or so the boat descended far below the mariner and his barrel. It made three or four wild gyrations and, bearing his doomed elder brother, plunged headlong into the chaos below. The barrel had descended little further than half the distance, when a great change took place in the character of the whirlpool. Its sloping sides broadened by degrees and its gyrations grew gradually less violent. The bottom of the gulf seemed to rise up slowly and the winds settled down as the sailor found himself on the surface of the ocean in full view of land and above the spot where the grinding depths of the Maelstrom had been. He had survived the terrible ordeal. By calm observation of the vortex into which he had sunk, he had come to understand something about it and to be carried up by the same spiral that had sucked him down. Whether he understood all there is to know of such a phenomenon is not known, for there are many questions left unanswered, many mysteries yet unexplored.

Mathematicians could describe the spiralling force of the whirlpool to the satisfaction of some, but what about the fact that it is a logarithmic spiral whose radius lengthens at the rate of seven percent per turn of thirty-six degrees, or one-tenth of a full circle? Does the ratio of seven to ten have any significance? What is the relationship between such a spiral and the two sets of similar spirals found in the sunflower? What is man's relationship to such a spiral? Is it death-dealing or life-giving? What is the significance of the cylindrical form which remained relatively buoyant in the Maelstrom, and what was it in the younger sailor that gave him the wits to understand this? The vivid description of his awesome ordeal suggests many such questions to one who ever looks for a deeper meaning in all things.

The spiral as a symbol is both ancient and universal. Perhaps the ancients understood some of the mysteries associated with whirlpools or sunflowers and tornadoes. Perhaps they had answers to some of their questions about them and perceived a correspondence between spirals in Nature and in man himself. This would seem likely, for in prehistoric art "no ornamental motif seems to have been more attractive than the spiral". The most common idea associated with the spiral is that it represents a schematic image of the evolving universe. It is a symbol for creation and growth or progressive development, an attribute of power found on the sceptre of the Egyptian pharoah and the crown of the god Thoth, as well as on the *lituus* of Roman augurs. The spiral has always been expressed in art and Nature in three main forms: expanding as in the spiral nebula, contracting as in the whirlpool, and ossified as in the mollusk's shell. Since Paleolithic times it has been portrayed as expanding and contracting, waxing or waning like the moon. The creative aspect of the expanding spiral, which is solar, moves clockwise and was identified by the ancient Greeks with Pallas Athene. The destructive aspect of the spiral can be associated with contraction which, moving counter-clockwise, has been considered an attribute of Poseidon and the moon.

Helical forms in Nature have always accompanied human evolution. In the mollusk, the growing fern's curl, the coiled snake, the human ear, the bull's horns and the rolled-up form of a sleeping animal, prehistoric and historic cultures have identified and celebrated the spiral. Some, like that of the New Zealand Maori, tattooed their faces and bodies with spiralling designs of magical power. Others built temples and even cities in its image. The great minaret of the mosque of Samarra in Iraq is a marvellous spiralling tower reaching towards heaven, and the town of Auroville in South India radiates out in a plan resembling a spiral nebula. The Ionic columns of classical Greece and Rome were capped with double spiral scrolls, and the lintels and thresholds of much older sacred sanctuaries were carved in similar fashion in many parts of the world. The vortical Navajo sand paintings, the Hopi pottery designs, the Aztecan carved gods covered with spirals, the spiral tattoos on the abdomen of tribal women in Africa, the spiral dances of people around the world – all bear witness to the pervasive human awareness of the vital importance of this form of movement. For ages man has been aware that the solar systems, suns and planets are created in a spiralling movement, the inward spiralling of interstellar gas resulting in entire galaxies. There has been a continuing awareness of an omnipresent vortical law which operates throughout the cosmos and can be seen in water as it reveals in its vortical flow the matrix from which forms take their being. It has been said that from the involution of the unformed waters the egg of the world was crystallized "by the turning in on itself of energy, of matter, or of consciousness".

The appearance and disappearance of the Universe are pictured as an outbreathing and inbreathing of "the Great Breath," which is eternal, and which, being Motion, is one of the three aspects of the Absolute — Abstract Space and Duration being the other two. When the "Great Breath" is projected, it is called the Divine Breath, and is regarded as the breathing of the Unknowable Deity — the One Existence — which breathes out a thought, as it were, which becomes the Kosmos.

The Secret Doctrine, i 43

Breathing out, the Great Breath gyrated forth and the Voice in the whirlwind was made manifest. Spiralling forth, the Sacred Word enacted creation. With each outward breath the Divine Principle uncoils, serpent-like, from the *bindhu*, the seed-point of the cosmos, and order is thus wrought out of chaos. With each inward breath it withdraws into its Essence, and Darkness lies upon the unfathomable Deep. Contemplating this never-ending rhythm of expansion and contraction, one seeks for clues that reveal its identification with the spiral. Is it like Ariadne's thread carried round and round into and out of the labyrinth? Is it the labyrinth of the world itself? Is it the gyrating force of Fohat, tying knots or points upon a descending spiral of being? Will these be untied in the unwinding of that spiral? Does the spiral unwind? Where does it go? Clues lie in the words used to describe the spiral. The term "volute" (from the Latin *voluta*, meaning "rolled up") is used in speaking of Ionic or Corinthian columns or gastropods with volutoid shells. But it is also the root of "convolution" ("roll up together") and "revolution", which suggests a wealth of ideas related to casting off allegiance and a great reversal of conditions, as well as the simple process of motion in an orbit.

Whilst these two terms are suggestive of the centrifugal and centripetal nature of the Great Breath, two other terms even more closely pin-point its spiral nature. The word "spiral" comes from the Latin *spira*, which derives from the Greek term σπεῖρα, meaning anything wound or coiled or twisted, like a snake. Some scholars have noticed that the idea in ancient cultures which associated the spiral with breath and spirit is borne out in the etymological similarity between *spira* and *spiro* in Latin and σπεῖρα and σπείρω in the Greek. While *spiro* ("breath") and *spiritus* ("breath of life") can be clearly related to "spirit", the Greek σπείρω means "to sow", "to scatter like a seed", "to disperse and to engender". Its infinitive use (σπείρειν) simply means "to circulate", revealing a close link in Hellenic thought between the expansion of that which gives life and circular motion. The continual breathing out and breathing in can be illustrated in terms of spherical circulation, wherein an unending spiral in a ring joins itself by spiralling through its own centre. Such a spherical vortex demonstrates Nature's perpetual motion, which is ceaselessly expanding and contracting.

One can see these two forces merged in the sigmoid line of the yin and yang symbol and the swastika, which are volutoid in Nature. This sort of double spiral reveals the intercommunication between the principles and can represent two halves of the world egg, the solar and lunar energies coiled within an androgynous whole. But perhaps an even more fundamental attribute of the spiral lies in its demonstration of the relationship between unity and multiplicity. Like the cosmos itself, we begin life at a point and expand out in differentiation, only to contract inward, once again, to the point. Thus our cyclic path ends at the seed-point that contains the potential of the whole. But the point to which we (or the sun or the earth) return is never the same. One could imagine a moving point, circulating in a spiral around a hidden central point, and consider the nature of that moving point. Is it the spark of the One in ceaseless motion through time and space? What is the point of its beginning and ending? Is that a mayavic reflection of a universal seed which expresses itself in the world as necessarily circular motion operating on two, three and four dimensions?

> Thus everything is centre, every centre refers to the circumference, and vice versa. All creatures do not exist only in themselves, in their centre, but in the double undulatory movement by which they receive everything and transmit themselves everywhere.
>
> Georges Poulet

The greater spiral of existence conies from and returns to its Source. It demonstrates cycles of change within its continuum and the alternation of poles with each cycle. It embodies expansion and contraction made manifest through changes in velocity and the potential for simultaneous movement in either direction towards its extremities. Thus centre and periphery on the spherical vortex flow into each other. The One which is omnipresent can be found in the concentrated point in motion. Spheres, belts or layers through which man has to pass in his evolution are really spirals accommodating the dimensions of time and space in manifested existence. The point in motion, so to speak, is a centre in its own right, a centre whose orbit is clearly tied to an invisible noumenal point. The relative beginnings and endings on the spiral course are mayavic increments marked by a consciousness which is enthralled in matter. God is both immanent and transcendent. The movement through the three-dimensional spiral goes towards the Divine without and within. The outward-seeming journey of Perceval or Perseus is the same journey depicted by Dante's inward spiralling mountain or the yogin's meditation upon the seed-point of vision that rests between his eyes.

The journey is that of the immortal soul and it begins, relative to one incarnation, with the downward serpentine spiralling on the tree of life, the involution of spirit into matter. In this sense, man becomes the spiral. The spiral can be said to be comprised of man's awareness. For just as man cannot walk upon the Path until he has become that Path itself, so too he must grow wise in his understanding of the vortical laws in order to move inwardly and outwardly along the spiral. In a sense, the earth itself demonstrates this double motion, for it too illustrates the deepest involution of spirit into matter in the lowest trenches that carve the ocean basins. In almost exact balance to these are the great Himalayan peaks rising up as high as they are deep. The double triangle suggested by this global balance can be translated three-dimensionally into the circular motion of what initially would seem to be a double spiral but which is more accurately illustrated by the form of a spherical vortex.

The journey of the soul involves it initially in successive windings as the individual egoic consciousness crystallizes. The continuum of the spiral becomes objectified with tiny spirals branching off like coiled twigs. In the return to the awareness of the continuum itself, subject and object once more become one and the extremities of the individuating process atrophy or blend back into totality. In attempting to assist this progress, the soul learns from the ubiquitous presence of spiral motion in the world. As a scholar, it may learn of the spiral of Archimedes, wherein the point recedes uniformly from its origin, or of hyperbolic spirals, wherein the radius vector varies inversely to angular displacement. But it is more likely to be arrested by the equiangular spiral revealed in so many growths and shapes in Nature. The equiangular or logarithmic spiral illustrates the principle of growth enabling an increase of size accompanied by an unaltered shape. In this dynamic process each increment of length is balanced by a proportional increase of radius. Observing the glorious sunflower, the soul comes to realize the inner significance of this through noticing the two sets of superimposed equiangular spirals etched out by the pattern of the flower's seeds. One describes a right-handed movement, the other a left. The awakening soul may thus perceive the nature of its own journey and marvel at its echo in physical form. The numbers of spirals represent adjacent Fibonacci numbers: twenty-one clockwise and thirty-four anti-clockwise, demonstrating the arcane Golden Ratio of 1:1.618, which repeats itself in patterns of growth throughout the whole of Nature.

The individual whose ears hear with the sharpened faculty of the awakening soul may discern increments in sound reflective of the expanding and contracting logarithmic spiral. The rate of change of wavelength for each note on a descending musical scale of twelve semi-tones is 1.618 times the semi-tone above it. Plotted as a smooth curve on a polar graph in which the radii, separated by fifteen degrees, are proportional to the wavelengths, one obtains an equiangular spiral. Observing such remarkable demonstrations, one may truly assert that beauty in mathematics is not built upon an artificial basis, but grounded in the beauty of the natural world. For the law of biological growth – of plant or animal or of any part of such – is an exponential law, a vortical law to be understood as analogous to the soul's pilgrimage in and out of the world.

The soul's involvement in matter is marked by the emanation of Shakti from the seed-*bindhu* (Shiva) in a spiralling downward into the body where the creative energy becomes latent. With the unfoldment of the soul, the Shakti-power rises and awakens the chakras so that they readily transmit her energy into progressively finer vibrations. This is what the Buddhists refer to as "untying the knots in inverse order". The spiralled single horn of the unicorn, which appears in so many cultures, represents the same notion of a penetrating spiritual force (connected with the *bindhu*-point of the Third Eye) which is capable of being subdued and directed only by the power of a pure, virginal nature. The journey back to the One point is made possible by the awakening of that pure Buddhic nature which sees the correspondences between the sunflower pattern, the growth of the human body, the whirling forces of lunar and solar consciousness within the mind and the macrocosmic spiral which unifies all these. Only with pure Buddhic perception can the seeming opposites be transcended and analogous points along the spiral provide one with recollections of patterns already mastered in the past. One can then begin to acquire conscious understanding of the vortical laws governing spiritual evolution.

The whirling dervish begins his dance with arms folded over his breast. Moving his right foot out, he begins to turn like a planet on his own axis, his arms gradually expanding outward as he gathers speed. Faster and faster he spins, bringing the spiritual down to the earth while his own spirit soars up through the still centre within him. He becomes the spherical vortex in which the forces of expansion and contraction are translated into a perpetual continuum between unity and multiplicity. Without spinning thus with the outward physical body, the serious disciple must pass through analogous stages in his meditative efforts to align and merge himself with the *bindhu*-seed of spiritual awareness. As he approaches a point within him where the vortex of awakening potential power begins to exert its pull, he may well experience a great gyration similar to that undergone by the mariner, who shook so violently when he perceived the Maelstrom before him. The higher mind must take care to preserve calm at this point and rely upon the knowledge it has accumulated through many windings of its spiralled incarnations. Informed by the immortal soul, it can recognize the Path it has followed to reach the same point on another winding and master the forces in the light of things learnt in a former life. The more this is done, the steeper the gradient that measures its growth. Such points of awareness provide glimpses of the deeper recurring pattern. They can serve as keynotes of initiation whereby the decisions made critically affect the subsequent cycling.

From narrow, obscure knowledge the mind passes to larger understanding. It gropes and fumbles about and suddenly, at the passing of a certain point, it sees. Poe conveyed this as the replacement of the horror of ignorance by an even greater horror of knowing. The mind now knows. It is stripped of nagging doubts and vain hopes and clearly perceives the cycles of inexorable causes and effects that encircle it. Whirling dizzily in the vortex of these, without a ghost of a chance of escaping their terrible and most logical concatenation, the soul as pilgrim and mariner faints and the mind is plunged in blackest despair. But if a point of awareness is grasped firmly, even in the wildest gyrations where one feels utterly overwhelmed by forces swirling within and about him, the saving memory of the immortal soul can operate. The point in line with points on another winding reveals the presence of the past in the present and the immediacy of both in what we call the future. True memory brings foreknowledge, the foreknowledge of the becalmed sailor who, while spinning down within the funnel of the Maelstrom, remembered that some objects escaped the vortex unscathed, whereas others were smashed to pulp. Even in the jaws of that terrible oblivion he calmly remembered and observed. His desire to understand and his awareness of the ultimately divine nature of all power in the cosmos outstripped his fears and the maniacal desire for physical survival exemplified in the action of his elder brother, who blindly wrested the iron ring from his grasp. Becalmed by remembered wisdom, he saw what it was that he had to do.

> Alcemon, pupil of Pythagoras, thought that men died
> because they could not join their beginning to their end.

William Butler Yeats

The pilgrim and mariner and hero – all must find the way to travel back along the same spiral that involved them in the first place. He who would know the origin of things must also understand their dissolution. The wild chaotic spirals of the snakes on Medusa's head must become the ordered spirals of the Buddha's curls if one is to understand and avoid the deadly extremes of the whirlpool of self. The great spiral force of the outbreathed world cannot be avoided or negated. One is in the whirling stream of its all-informing energy as surely as one is in a bodily vesture. To go backward against this is to go against the order of things. One must learn, instead, to trust the vortical forces and lighten one's load in order to move wisely with them. Letting go of the extremities of individuation is like the mariner letting go of the ring instead of grappling with his brother for it. Letting go of identification with name and form is like letting go of the doomed ship and trusting to the knowledge that has arisen from within. The cylinder-shaped barrel to which the surviving mariner lashed himself is symbolic of the zero to which one can reduce the angularities of the persona. By mirroring the greater circle of vortical power itself, one can avoid being sucked down into the destructive depths of egotistic identity where, hugging and clutching one's little boat of self, one is smashed life after fear-ridden life.

> Going on means going far,
> Going far means returning.

Tao Te Ching

Like the dervish, spinning faster and faster, one can move with assured fleetness through the maelstrom of life. Expanding outwardly the cleansing aura of spiralling spiritual energy, the mind contracted in calm meditation upon the seed of spirit can merge with the soul and soar up in conscious understanding to its divine origin. Life involves the many spiral windings made by oneself as one plodded along. Going on does mean going far, but not in the same circle over and over again. Through compulsive desire and careless wonder one falls along the windings of one's involving spiral. But by marking the recurring points, by remembering and trusting one's Buddhic awareness of the connections between these points, one may return.

Going far requires great courage and calm, and he who hugs the shore may perish yet out of fear of the journey. Far out there on the great deep lies the testing of our fears. Opening up its terrible jaws as some unexpected wind rushes onward, the whirlpool of personal destruction threatens to obliterate the very purpose of the journey undertaken. Going so far, the pilgrim who would return to the other shore knows that its ferocity can be endured and conquered, that with the calmly spiralling wisdom within him he can rise up through the still centre of the vortex to the Divine Source of his own Beginning.

> For this is the Path we have followed before,
> The spiralling trail which borders the chasm;
> That leads aloft past the dragon's lair,
> And returns us whole to the other shore.

Hermes, September 1984

THE SHIP

There go the ships: there is that leviathan, whom thou hast made to play therein.

Psalms 104:26

White arching wings rose slowly over the curving edge of the world. With majesty they rose, billowing upon tall masts, driven by easterly winds fresh out of an endless sea. Those whose eyes watched from an undiscovered land trembled and believed that the gods approached. Closer they came, bearing down upon them from greater and greater height, splitting the waves and bristling with airy power. At the time of his voyage to the New World, Christopher Columbus attempted to describe the wonder that seized the Caribbean natives with the arrival of his fleet. He wrote that "they know neither sect nor idolatry, with the exception that all believe that the source of all power and goodness is in the sky, and they believe very firmly that I, with these ships and people, came from the sky, and in this belief they everywhere received me, after they had overcome their fear".

The gods of many an ancient religion were believed to sail the skies in heavenly ships. Inspired by this almost universally shared notion, the Indians imagined the Spanish ships to be portable shrines in which the immortal ones navigated the celestial seas. Had Columbus's men shown equal recourse to sacred themes, they might well have recalled the biblical passage which speaks of the Lord as one "who layeth the beams of his chambers in the waters".

Even as they made anchor and lowered their sails in the island bay, a few may have recalled near-forgotten childhood stories of the Egyptian Barque of a Million Years, in which the sun-god Ra traversed the heavens, or the tale of ivy-crowned Dionysus reclining in his dolphin ship with its Tree of Life mast. A few may have remembered such things when confronted with the expressions of awe and reverence in the faces of their island hosts.

There is an old saying, whose origin nobody knows, which states that "the three most beautiful things in the world are a full-rigged ship, a woman with child and a full moon". Surely the windblown sails of a graceful ship seem to expand with generational promise. Her hull is like a sheltering womb carrying seed across the vaster womb of chaos to a promised land. The Egyptians envisioned the ship of the sun making its voyage through daily adventures with various adversaries. But sailing the subterranean abyss of the ocean at night, its perils increased. They believed there were two ships to complete the journey: Me'enzet by day and Semektet by night, when the spirits of the dead were awakened by the solar light and arose to draw the barque on its course. Thus, the full cycle of the journey involved two aspects of the solar barque. The daytime voyage was self-propelled, but the subterranean voyage entered the lunar realm of mortality, where it had to be helped on by the souls of men. Centuries later the Vikings would build ships that had an uncanny resemblance to the solar barque of Ra, but they did not always sail with the promise of a woman with child or the full moon. They themselves were not fearful of death, and their black sails bore for them only a sense of daring as they hunkered on board beneath them. But many a stranger stood on the shore and dreaded their coming. For them it was no solar light that neared but the perils of the long, dark night.

> Oh build your ship of death. Oh build it!
> For you will need it.
> For the voyage of oblivion awaits you.
>
> D. H. Lawrence

Ships carry the seed of promise but they also bear the dead across the unknown waters to the world beyond. They leave far behind the known and the ordinary. They go beyond all recognized landmarks in an uncharted course and thus become a powerful symbol of transcendence. They are like the raft in Buddhist teachings which enables the disciple to cross the ocean of experience to the shores of enlightenment. Many of the prow-shaped curves on temples and houses in various parts of the world artistically assert this longing for transcendence, whilst some more primitive people simply place small ships in their entirety atop their roofs. The old idea of the ship of fools inverts the symbolism by suggesting sailing as an end in itself instead of the notion of sailing in order to transcend.

> Our life is closed – our life begins,
> The long, long anchorage we leave,
> The ship is clear at last – she leaps!
> She swiftly courses from the shore,
> Joy! shipmate – joy.
> Walt Whitman

Sailing off across the flood, what is the ship that travels on when ordinary life is done? Is it the barque that bears the seed of life's next play upon the boards? Is it Aguirre's ship of death topping Amazonian trees, or the ark that Ravan saw in his haunting ancient dream? As the demon king watched from lofty Lankan towers, he discerned an object looming through the darkness. He felt at first relief to see what appeared to be a barque coming towards him, but there was "something supernatural. . . in this dim phantasmal ship. Its outline is nowhere sharp and firm, but wavy and ragged, like a swaying cloud; it has neither helm nor sails, and appears to move and to stop at will. There are human figures on board; but they appear shadowy, and almost transparent; they neither speak nor move, but seem wrapped in *Samadhi*." Pulled by Matsya's strength, this was the ark in which the germ of Nature floats upon *pralaya*'s abyss. It was the *argha*, the crescent-shaped moon of Diana, whose wake is the umbilicus connecting the old with the embryos of the new race. It was the vessel of rebirth, the sarcophagus afloat in the king's chamber, from which the novice rises up initiated into the arcane mysteries. And those who ride in it, in shadowy transparency, are the Rishis who never sleep.

On the distant horizon, on a lowering day, Viking ships may also have seemed outlined in clouds. But no phantom would they be, nor would those robust adventurers have been wrapped in meditative silence. Theirs were the "longships", whose prows rose to a high spiral, ending in a serpent's head. The top of their stern-post was their tail, the whole ship looking like a fabulous monster breasting the waves, its head and tail glistening, its body filled with men. The biggest vessels of Knut the Great were nearly two hundred feet long, and so fearsome was their mien that in A.D. 930 Ulfljots laws decreed that sailors must not approach land with the figureheads on their ships. It was ordered that they be taken off so that the land-vaettir would not be frightened by their yawning jaws and grimly gaping heads.

Such ships were the Vikings' supreme achievement, the pinnacle of their cultural expression, their delight and most treasured possession. The unearthing of the Gokstad ship revealed a vessel with a mast forty feet high, which was rigged with a square sail in its day. Its stern and stern-posts being composed of a single piece of timber, it possessed a true keel and its rows of planking overlapped each other in a clinker-built design. When built, its strakes were caulked with tarred rope and lashed to the ribs by withes passing through cleats cut from the strakes. Sixteen pairs of nineteen-foot oars were used to propel this ship, and an eleven-foot-long rudder fastened to the starboard quarter by stout riveted cleats was used to steer it. This was done by means of a thick rope that ran through the ship's side, the cleat and the rudder itself. When Captain Magnus Andersen sailed a facsimile of the Gokstad ship to America in 1893, he claimed that the rudder was a work of genius and that a man could steer with such a tiller in all kinds of weather without the least discomfort.

What the temple was to the Greeks the ship was to the Vikings, and at places like Gokstad, Tune or Oseberg great mounds concealed the nautical tombs of chiefs and kings. Ship burials followed the example set by the myth of Haider's funeral, in which it was said the god's corpse was brought to the sea and placed on a pyre in Hringhorni, the greatest of all ships. The boat was thrust upon the water by the giantess Hyrrokin and the pyre was kindled as it floated out. Nanna, his wife who had died of grief, was placed beside him in the blaze, a Nordic version of suttee oft repeated by the Vikings. Of those ships that burnt while floating out to sea, there remains no trace. Only from evidence found in those buried on land and from the remarkable description of a tenth century Arab scholar who witnessed a ship's burial do we learn about the practice and come to realize more deeply how central a part the ship played in the life and death of these barbarous people.

When the Vikings spread south, they came as seamen so deeply inbred with the spirit of their ships that they seemed a new kind of people. Theirs were certainly not the first vessels to open up new worlds of trade or conquest, but never before had ocean craft embodied the very essence of a culture. The ancients of the Mediterranean tended to feel only a guarded enthusiasm for ships which were treadmills for oarsmen and torture chambers for passengers. By contrast, the Vikings took to their ships for the gay pursuit of perilous conquest and rolled down the water in vessels sporting glorious carvings and heroic lines expressive of their loftiest aspirations and deepest feelings. They entered a world wherein the splendid barques of gods and pharaohs had long retreated into the mists along with the earliest Red Sea trading ships and galleys rigged for war. The development of the great Phoenician art of seamanship had already taken place more than two thousand years before, when, led by a "canny, unimperial intent upon profit", they had constructed superior cargo carriers in which they sailed the East African coast.

The earliest vessels were fashioned of hollowed trees and paddled along rivers and the edges of lakes. They were followed by the skin boats (the coracles) of the Stone Age Norsemen, who fished twenty or thirty miles offshore to ninety fathoms. Rudderless and paddled on the rough and unpredictable seas, they scurried over the hills and valleys of Atlantic-born rollers from the northwest coast of Norway to the outer Skerries. Several thousand years later, in calmer seas, the Egyptians were carrying three-ton cargoes in thirty-five-foot papyrus reed boats. They paddled and steered with an oar in the relative calm of the Mediterranean and eventually developed acacia-planked vessels in the same shape. Trading with India, East Africa and Persia, they evolved true oars that proved efficient enough to inspire the notion that superimposed rows of oarsmen could double and triple the ship's power. Thus were born the multibanked galleys, the biremes and triremes of the Levant and the Greek isles. Those were the days when the fortunes of galley slaves depended desperately on the fleetness of their ship and chances of war. The ram on such warships was their chief weapon, and slim indeed were the chances of men chained to their oars in the bottom tiers if the side of the vessel was breached. A typical Greek trireme ran a narrow length of one hundred and thirty feet and carried one hundred and seventy oarsmen, working oars of three different lengths on three levels. Slim and flexible, they cut through the bright sea with their crowded, disciplined oars, simultaneously lifting and dipping in time to the metronomic notes of a flute. They could achieve up to eight knots in speed and must have provided an awesome study in motion.

During the reign of King Sahure (2480 B.C.), the passage up the Syrian coast, into the eye of the northerly wind, required much rowing. But on the way back the masts were hauled up, and with square sail set they ran before the Westerlies. Such palm or matted-leaf sails had been around for centuries, and their invention set the stage for the essential story of ships and seamanship, having at its heart the struggle with the wind as a major mode of propulsion. The Mediterranean galley was highly specialized and confined to coasts, owing to its size and the provisional needs of the many men aboard. Such a vessel could never have won the freedom of the oceans available only to a craft that could move quickly enough and carry enough stores to survive a long absence from land. But with sails the need for steering arose, rudimentarily accomplished by sweeping oars towards or away from the ship's sides. From this, side rudders evolved, necessitating the team-work of helmsmen controlled by a master, who guided them as though conducting an orchestra through the waters. The Roman corn ships, one hundred and eighty feet long, possessed twin quarter rudders, which evolved into the larger, deeper rudders in the classical Mediterranean form of one per quarter. To hold against the wind and ocean currents, anchors of stone or of bags of shingle with a trip-line were developed, and masts both collapsible and stationary were raised to fifty feet or more.

Believed to act as a magical axis between heaven and the sea, masts were identified with the Tree of Life and often given special treatment at the time of their construction. Even in later medieval times German shipbuilders held that Klabautermann (the helpful spirit of the ship) dwelt in the mast made from a tree which, as a sapling, was split in order to pass a sickly child through and then joined together again. If the child died, they believed its soul passed into the growing tree, which then took on a peculiar form and was eventually cut for a mast. When the mast was fully rigged, they referred to its beauty as a living spirit, which was raised in spring and lowered in winter in the stormy northern seas.

Sailing ships sail with the wind and the tide. The wind commands. It gives the power and creates the limit, but men have learnt that, within the parameters of obedience they can win a subtle victory. Like a study in the operation of the free within the framework of the cosmic will, the sailing ship courses the ocean span. Of all creations made to move man where he will, they are the most noble and bravely poised on the fine line which separates the divine from human design. Driving ocean-going ships along this line, the square rig was well adapted to gather the great steady belts known as the trade winds. Square riggers, as they came to be called in the fifteenth century, sported from two to four masts and six basic sails: the mainsail, main topsail, foresail, fore topsail, a lateen on the mizzen-mast and a small sail under the bowsprit. Various modes of rigging came to be identified with vessels ranging from ships proper to barques, brigs, schooners, ketches, cutters and yawls. They could be used on different hulls for varying purposes and sometimes made a significant difference in speed or maneuverability. This was often lacking in early square riggers whose fo'c'sle (forecastle) and aft'c'sle (aftcastle) were very high and cumbersome affairs, built as floating fortresses for the cannon's advantage in warfare. Such vessels had lost the elegance of the Viking ship's sleek lines or the gracefulness of early Greek galleys. They sported figures of impressive monsters or angels on their bows but often resembled heavily bustled ladies lumbering over the swells.

> The image of a beautiful woman is the proper ending to a sailing ship's bow. . . . A windship should have an amazon or a valkyrie.

Bow ornaments were very important to sailors as charms and as that to which they entrusted their lives. They thought the figure, like the ship's name, conveyed the life of the vessel, its unique individuality. Joseph Conrad once described a gathering of tall ships at a South China Sea quay. "It was", he wrote, "a noble gathering of the fairest and the swiftest, each bearing at the bow the carved emblem of her name as in a gallery of plaster casts; figures of women with mural crowns, women with flowing robes, with gold fillets on their hair or blue scarves round their waists, stretching out rounded arms as if to point the way; heads of men helmeted or bare; full lengths of warriors, of kings, of statesmen, of lords and princesses, all white from top to toe; with here and there a dusky turbaned figure, bedizened in many colours of some Eastern Sultan or hero." Whatever gender the ornament, sailors everywhere address a ship as being feminine and would agree with a famous navigator who once said that ships were all a "wayward she" and needed handling accordingly. Certainly, a sailing ship is an exceedingly complex, sensitive and capricious creation, borne up by an equally unpredictable mother sea. Her close association with the wind gives her a masculine aspect, but her hull and rigging are constantly giving and swelling and creaking and displaying all the changeability and moods of the moon and of all that is feminine. But does she carry a solar cargo? Will she bring onto that foreign shore all the promise that her winged sails and bow ornament suggest?

> Without the sail real ships would not have been evolved; without real ships the continents and their people would have remained separate entities.

> Elis Karlsson

The people of the New World, and later of the Pacific, must have thought the European ships that rose over the horizon before them were like envoys of the solar deity they all worshipped. Like the natives that greeted Columbus, they welcomed the white-winged vessels to their shores and believed that a divine wind had wafted them hence. Painful though the fruits of these encounters would prove to be, they were the first lines cast out upon the deep that would eventually knit together races that had lived in largely separate worlds. The wind, *Pravaha* (the mystical force that gives the impulse to and regulates the course of stars and planets) had guided ships through the ocean, like tiny islands brought into contact with spheres revolving in the waters of space. The business of connecting the seven seas and the seven continents and races had begun. Like spiders blown by the wind from one tree to another, the ships connected the subtle magnetic webs which had been traced ages prior by the instrument of karma.

> O keep us from the Sailing Gods
> That they bring not death and disease among us.

> *Old Samoan Prayer*

By the end of the sixteenth century English and Dutch ships were in a position to challenge the Portuguese domination of the Far East. The Red Dragon Fleet of the East India Company had set about the business of war and trade, and the Dutch, in spite of having no trees in their homeland, had rounded the Cape of Good Hope in their lightly built East Indiamen in large numbers. By 1610 there were sixteen thousand Dutch ships trading wherever there were ports. To navigate they used rutters, cross-staffs, and compasses eventually fixed with an adjustable double card so that the needle could be turned at will to offset variation. From the Cape they often passed inside Madagascar, before sailing east with the monsoon, along the Maldines and finally up to Goa. The British came from east and west, rounding Africa or braving the murderous one-hundred-and-twenty-foot waves that rolled unchecked below Cape Horn. They plied their trade, fought their competitors and divided the spoils won from the treasures that flanked the Celebes, the Sulu and the South China Seas. Along Sumatra's jungled cliffs they sailed the Strait of Malacca to Kuala Lumpur and Singapore and Sarawak's rivered shores. Their ornamented prows rounded each isle of the Philippines and penetrated the harbours of China and Japan. The connecting lines were thus drawn down the winds, and the booty of the East, in rolling storm-chased holds, was shifted, sail by sail, to the opposite side of the globe.

> Home is the sailor, home from the sea;
> His far-borne canvas furled.
> The ship pours shining on the quay
> The plunder of the world.

The names of captains are remembered along with their ships. Who does not link the fame of Drake with the Golden Hind, Bligh with the Bounty, Anson with the Centurion, Cook with the Endeavour or Columbus with the Santa Maria? Amongst the sailing men of clipper ship days the reputations of captains and ships likewise conveyed a quality of fortune both good and evil. To such men the name of a vessel conveyed its aura. It defined, somehow, the nature of its *mana*, its elemental force, which then became augmented by years of marine talk, gossip and tales amongst those who gave the better part of their lives to the sea. Conrad once said that "all that talk makes up her name", which could never quite be divorced from that of her commander. The Marco Polo, a very famous Canadian-built ship, lost her reputation for speed after a change of captains, and it was said of the English captain de Cloux that "if he had had the sluggard Mozart, he still would have won the grain race" (from Australia to England). Such captains had a reputation for recklessness, and others more authoritarian were sometimes called brutal. The beautifully built Bluenoses and Downeasters from Nova Scotia and the northeastern states were notoriously captained by "drivers" who maintained discipline with "belaying pins, knuckle-dusters and six-shooters". Typically, American merchant captains enforced their authority by sheer power of character and will against overwhelming odds of brute force and often among cutthroats and desperadoes. Strong-armed tactics sometimes bred calamitous results, and it was wisely said that captains who could maintain morale without them were more important than sound rigging or sturdy masts.

Lucky and unlucky captains and ships tended to be like self-fulfilling prophecies. Firmly associated with Conrad was the lucky clipper Torrens, whose outstandingly successful passages featured even such flukes as finding a barrel of lamp oil afloat at sea when her own supply was running low. In contrast to this, Commander Byron of Dolphin fame never shook the sobriquet of "Foulweather Jack", and seamen firmly believed that, on whatever ship, his presence ensured gales, and it did! Still, quite aside from these more subtle examples of superstitious anticipation, clipper captains like "Bully" Forbes plowed the seas, making up to twenty-one knots. On masts one hundred and sixty-five feet tall they kept their sails unfurled even in the worst gales, resulting in record clips of ninety-two days from New York to San Francisco around the Horn. But neither superstition nor danger nor bully captains kept the seamen from shipping out again. They had been seduced by the endlessly receding horizon curving over a plunging bow, the wind moaning in the mainmasts and the promise of paradise that lay ahead. They were bitten with sea fever and many, if they could, would have echoed Melville when he prayed, "Forbid it, sea gods! intercede for me with Neptune, O sweet Amphitrite, that no dull clod may fall on my coffin! Be mine the tomb that swallowed up Pharaoh and all his hosts; let me lie down with Drake where he sleeps in the sea."

I must down to the seas again, to the lonely sea
   and the sky,
And all I ask is a tall ship and a star to steer her by,
And the wheel's kick and the wind's song
   and the white sail's shaking,
And the gray mist on the sea's face and a gray dawn breaking.

John Masefield

The haunting beauty and majesty of the great China tea clippers racing under the British flag was matched by names like Black Prince, Ariel, Yang-tze, Thermopylae, Sir Lancelot and Cutty Sark. American clippers sported names of equal power, such as the famous Witch of the Wave, Romance of the Seas, Neptune's Car, Phantom, Alert and Flying Cloud. The clippers and the windjammers were the "tall ships" bearing as many as twenty-nine sails and captains who had a reputation for keeping them on. During a Cape Horn passage one observer recorded with awe this sight: "Bearing down on us, with the wind on her quarter, was a huge square-sailed vessel bearing full topsails and, like a gesture of defiance, above them a close-reefed topgallant on the main. . . . By her snowry white cloths and her glistening black hull – for she lifted with the speed of an express – we knew her an American."

The American clippers were built of soft wood. They were fast, light and of short life, which, it has been said, is true of all that is beautiful. Because they leaked, they tended to become waterlogged, and much longer hours were required at their pumps than in the oak and teak ships of the English. A clipper like the two-hundred-and-twelve-foot Cutty Sark was called a "wet" ship, having a "long snaky hull", over which the water would sweep from end to end in a high wind and sea. Her handsomely raked masts carried a "skysail", and at her prow sailed a beautiful witch, with her long hair and cutty sark (short chemise) flowing in the wind. She was a British "composite" type built of wooden planks over an iron frame, with copper sheathing on her bottom to discourage ship worms and reduce friction with the water. Like her sister Thermopylae, she was beautiful and swift, representing a rare flowering of shipbuilding as an art. The windjammers that followed were less elegant, deriving their speed from length and strength rather than shape. They received their name from the fact that they habitually sailed with their yards jammed into the wind. Built of steel with light, strong steel masts and rigging, they were in their element in a powerful gale. Carrying sails when lesser ships had long furled theirs, vessels like the Herzogin Cecilie, with her fifty-nine thousand square feet of sail and eighteen and three-quarters miles of running rigging, set records of twenty-three knots and more.

With the sailing ship the primordial power of the wind and sea exhilarated and inspired sailors to accomplish feats perhaps impossible under ordinary conditions. Those who struggled together in a storm felt the fury of the gods in their faces and shared with each other the life-or-death trials of the long voyage home. Ships tossed and floating on the ocean's swell are communities isolated from the world. Melville spoke of a whaling ship as his Yale College and Harvard. But it is more than that. For the gathered crew that mans the rigging is faced with the inescapable immediacy of working mightily with one another in the face of overwhelming forces from which none of them can walk away. Surrounded by endless-seeming sea, a strange spell descends upon ship-goers. A sense of reason and proportion familiar on land is lost, and is replaced with an urgency and reckless potential well suited to meet some of the exigencies of a stormy passage but often absurdly played out in modern steamship antics. Ordinary life, with its endless capacity for dodging issues and avoiding the unpleasant or difficult, is left behind, and all one's stark hopes and fears and foibles surface and pour out in unforeseeable mixtures with those of the others on board.

The ships of old, crossing and connecting the continents and races of men, were each embarked upon a voyage mirroring that of the ark whose shrouded shape approached Ravan's isle. They reflected the passage of stars and planets moving as little worlds across the uncharted depths of space. They carried seeds blown by the Breath of Life across the astral thresholds of becoming. Few perhaps of the rough sailors among the Vikings or the "Cape Homers" would have been conscious of such a mission. Their idea of treasure was usually both tangible and capable of worldly conversion. But dreamers sailed among them and some of the world's most haunting and beautiful imagery has come from the experience of men who toiled upon the sea. Men of nondescript backgrounds, with unformulated hopes, have been thrown together on a ship, where they saw and heard, as though with a shared soul, the mysteries revealed on a long ocean voyage. Conrad described the wonder shared by the whole crew of the Marco Polo in 1861 when their ship passed a floating iceberg in which lay, as if asleep, a fully clothed man. Unable to reach him and certain that he was dead, they left him to ride the berg mysteriously until he and it became part of the sea. A hush enveloped the ship and all felt as one with this silent passenger. They too voyaged as in a dream, facing dangers as a matter of course, sailing to a safe harbour but never fully arriving home. They were aware, each in his own unspoken way, that they were closer to truth on the voyage and that their real home would always lie beyond the world's busy quays.

I have seen old ships sail like swans asleep . . .

James Elroy Flecker

Phantom ships carry dead men's dreams. They sail the astral oceans of our consciousness and we quake with foreboding as they loom over the edge of our minds. Ghostly barques, filled with the dregs of human passions and fears silently looming, are blown by evil winds. Even painted up and jauntily rigged, such ships bring corrupting fancies and dread disease. These are the fallen sisters of the ark, wombs that have gathered the astral flotsam that drifts upon the sea. Theirs is not the godly cargo descendant from the sky, nor is their mast the Tree of Life borne out in sacrifice upon the waters of the world. Among all the ships that have sailed the seas, they have carried over to other minds and other lands the failure of mankind to grasp the essential meaning of its voyage in the world. They have drawn out the lines of karma into an ever-entangling web of causes and effects and collected around them the great night that imperils the solar barque as it descends into the worldly subterranean sea.

But there have been gallant ships whose majestic beauty was matched by courageous sailors who pooled their energies time and time again in an enterprise far greater than they consciously understood. Skipping down the waves like the crescent moon on

Shiva's flowing locks, the pure arching lines of such noble ships have lit up and awakened men's spirits even as they inspired the deepest poetry within their souls. Windjammers, rising over the tide with the speed of an express, stir up dreams of transcendent voyages in men who have never even watched them. The soul is aroused and rises buoyantly with their sails, sight unseen. We long for the voyage and we revere the pure-crafted vessel that can make it. Afloat on the greater cosmic sea, such a blessed vessel knows the perils of the deep yet sails above them, skimming the swells and tacking round the rocks and floating bergs. She is not stilled in the doldrums nor sluggish in the seaways, but has the strength and resilience to carry her canvas even in the heaviest storms. Only a fearless sailor can sail this ship, for she is built to cross the uncharted deep and she carries only the distilled cargo of the soul. She is a pure womb that transports the seed beyond the horizon of death and on to an unknown shore. Those who man her do so in humility even as she bears them faithfully on the long voyage home.

> Pinnacled masts that pierce the sky.
> Sails leaping in the wind.
> We take the sea upon our faces,
> Our anchor we rescind.
> Tossed and merging with the stars
> On the track of gods we sail.
> Our ship a gallant clipper,
> Our life a seaman's tale.

Hermes, January 1985

THE WIND

O the Wind's chariot, O its power and glory! Crashing it goes and
hath a voice of thunder.
It makes the regions red and touches heaven, and as it moves the
dust of the earth is scattered.
Along the traces of the wind they hurry, they come to him as dames
to an assembly.
Borne on his car with these for his attendants, the God speeds forth,
the Universe's Monarch.
Travelling on the path of air's mid-region, no single day doth he take
rest or slumber.
Holy and earliest-born. Friend of the waters, where did he spring
and from what region came he?
Germ of the world, the Deity's vital spirit, this God moves ever as
his will inclines him.
His voice is heard, his shape is ever viewless. Let us adore this Wind
with our oblations.

Rig Veda CLXVIII, *Hymn to Vayu*

From what lung, out of what bellows, comes this wind? Where lies
that aperture in the heavens that blasts its current into our universe?
What god's lips purse its stream? One may as well ask where is the
source of motion, where the source of breath? And if it is breathed out,
must it first be breathed in? Into what? Into that which is perfectly still?
Into motion itself, which knows itself not? Standing upon the cliffs at
the end of land, at the edge of the known world, one receives the wind
full upon one's soul and quivers with the awareness of communion
with all it has touched. Its wildness invades and obliterates the defence
of the small self standing there. It batters and whips and cleanses.
It overwhelms and yet awakens the heart to a forgotten promise
eddying through endless corridors of space. Dreams of childhoods
lived long ago and of mythic flight to vision's lofty peaks momentarily
appear. Written on the wind, the vision swirls and is blasted across
the universe, carried away and yet never erased.

163

Some have called the wind the primary element by virtue of its connection with the creative breath in its exhalation. Others have claimed it is merely air in its active and violent aspect. But the languages of people spread widely through the world indicate a persistent connection between wind and breath and spirit. Often 'breath' and 'spirit' share the same identifying terms, as with the Arabic *ruh* and the Greek πνευμα (*pneuma*), or the will of God is identified with the voice of a howling gale or whirlwind. To many the wind has seemed to be the spiritual and vital breath of the universe. Its power to sustain life and hold it together has caused it to be associated with cords, threads and ropes. "The rope of the wind" and "the thread (which) is the same as the wind" are spoken of in the Upanishads. It links all together as the invisible chain and bears within its twists and coils the intangible, transient-seeming, insubstantial and elusive presence of Deity. On the cliffs, the presence storms and makes sails of the senses, which are filled to bursting with its power. Standing there, the body clings like a feeble root to the rock of earth and the soul leaps up to fly in the soaring stream.

> Wild Spirit, which art moving everywhere;
> Destroyer and preserver; hear, oh, hear!

> Percy Bysshe Shelley

Destroyer or preserver? Is the wind possessed of evil powers as the ancient Egyptians thought? Is it the might of a horrible Pazuzu, the raging and wrathful Semitic "Lord of wind-demons" called "the Destroyer of the beautiful hills" and believed to spread fever and disease even while commanding the four directional regions? Even the Greeks, who possessed a more subtly shaded view of natural forces, believed there was evil in the winds, until the fleet of Xerxes was destroyed by a tempest as he sought to attack their coast. Perhaps its unpredictability, its suddenness and lack of discrimination make the wind seem so blindly devastating. At times its relentlessness wears down the mind just as it erodes the beautiful hills. William Butler Yeats wrote of "the levelling wind", and one pictures such erosion through days and years and centuries, displacing, devouring and spewing away. But it is equally true that the wind separates the wheat from the chaff and carries the rain cloud over the parched earth. In the words of Thomas Tusser,

Except wind stands as never it stood,
It is an ill wind turns none to good.

To the ancient Hindus the winds were the Four Maharajas, the Regents of the Four Cardinal Points. Like others of the classical world, they associated them with corresponding signs of the zodiac and notions of qualities to be assigned to the various directions. The Vedic god of wind, Vayu, played a central role in the magnificent conception of cosmogenesis outlined in the profoundly suggestive hymns of the *Rig Veda*. The Greeks also recognized a powerful god of wind, who controlled all winds from all directions. Hesiod wrote that they were all the sons of Typhoeus (derived from τυφωεύς), kept chained or unchained to the rocks at the will of Aeolus. He was their master and the lord of all musical instruments, producing sound by his power. By his leave, Boreas (the cold and stormy north wind) wrecked the four hundred ships of the Persian fleet, and Zephyrus breathed the mild western breeze that refreshed the sun-drenched land of Hellas. The name Aeolus (from Αἴολος) reveals much about the nature of this god, suggesting quick movement, nimbleness and a rapid shifting of wiles and forms, the attributes proper to some sort of *Demiurge*. If one traces the etymological roots of the term "wind", one finds that one is led to the *vindr* of the Old Norse, the *ventus* of the Latin, and *vatas* of the Sanskrit, whose root, *va*, lies in the name Vayu and means "to blow".

The Egyptian word *bai*, found in the names of all the four winds, was the term used by them to describe both "soul" and "breath". One can trace a similar connection between the Latin *animare* (quicken), *anima* (air, breath, life, soul), *animus* (spirit), the Greek ἄνεμος (*anemos* or wind) and the Sanskrit *aviti* (breathe). More specialized names like Boreas (Βορέας or devouring) indicate the nature and effects of a particular wind or a type such as "tornado", which derives from the Spanish *tornar* (turn), or "storm", which can be traced to the old Germanic *sturm*, meaning "to stir". The Greek τύφειν (*tuphein*) describes a smoking up caused by a terrific wind and suggests a remarkable link with the Chinese *tai fung* – "typhoon", from *tai* (big), *fung* (wind). The notion that spirit has no form, no tangible permanence, is suggested by "smoke" in various cultures. Perhaps this is because it takes on some of the substance and coloration of the earth while yet remaining ethereal. A big wind stirring up the dust and the loose ends of the world seems to exhibit a similar power while carrying them aloft and grinding them into an ever smaller common denominator.

> If we may trust to language, it was the movement of the air that provided the image of spirituality, since the spirit borrows its name from the breath of wind.
>
> Sigmund Freud

Plato taught that the Four Elements were that "which composes and decomposes the compound bodies". What we see are only their visible garbs, the "symbols of the informing invisible Souls or Spirits". These phenomenal expressions of noumenal Elements are then informed by elementals, or the nature-spirits of the lower planes of manifest existence, through which the shaman attempts to control the wind or rain. Ancient man experienced a close communion with these potencies and recognized in them a hierarchy of expression. The Greek word for the elements (στοιχεῖα) points to rows of potencies, ranked one above the other in causation, from gods to physical expressions of force. In the Hebrew tradition the first Sephiroth wrapped himself in the garment of Elements which was the world to be. "He maketh the wind His messengers, flaming Fire His servants." Theosophically, the wind as messenger is equated with ether and described as the agent of transmission by which the solar and lunar influences are carried down and diffused on earth. As such, it is a "nurse" acting to quicken and nurture new generations of life. In the hurricane is found the synthesis and conjunction of all the Four Elements. The wind, at the height of its activity, is credited with the power of fecundation and regeneration. Some dim awareness of this might lie behind the folk sayings found among Mediterranean peasants who credit the formidable Boreas with the many conceptions accomplished during its shivering blast. At Ithaca there is a cave whose northern gate is guarded by Boreas, and it is said that through this gate souls are ushered into mortal life.

The Gnostics, like the ancient Pythagoreans and students of Plato before them, recognized a hierarchy of Beings or Elements. They spoke of the Aeons, who created the world and were, in their various branches and levels, the Tree of Life. With the Creative Fire of the manifest Logos at their summit, the first six Aeons answered to what is described as the Seven Winds or Priests of the *Anugita*. They are the Dhyan Chohans through whom Divine Ideation passes into action. As indicated by Simon Magus, they perform this lofty function in pairs or syzygies: the occult expression of the solar Father manifesting as Spirit, voice and reason, and the active expression of the lunar Mother as thought, name and reflection. From their union, the second generation of Aeons is brought forth to express Divine Ideation on a slightly grosser plane (the astral). Thence, their progeny in turn will usher in more and more diversified and concretized worlds of being. They are the offspring of the Priests, the Winds, who take on an increasingly material garb and who sometimes manifest in a whirlwind of communication, spanning the generations from a higher realm. Thus we have the example of God admonishing poor Job through the voices of the whirlwind to gird up his loins and act like a man.

> There appeared a chariot of fire, and horses of fire, and parted them both asunder; and Elijah went up by a whirlwind into heaven.
>
> 2 *Kings* 2:11

In the arcane treasure-house of the Puranas the *Pravaha* wind is described as the mystic and concealed Force that gives impulse to and regulates the course of the stars and planets. Its septenary nature is discussed in the *Kurma* and *Linga Puranas* in terms of seven principal winds, which are the basis of cosmic space and connected with Dhruva (the Pole Star), which, in turn, is connected with the production of phenomena through cosmic forces. Similarly, the Orphic hymns sing of *Eros-Phanes* evolving from the spiritual egg impregnated by the Aethereal winds. This idea corresponds to the description of the "Spirit of God moving in Ether" (brooding over the waters) as well as the electrifying nature of His coiling movement. The Kabalistic cosmogony places the wind in an equally lofty position, indicating how the Divine Substance emits the manifest Spirit, the Fiery Word, from whose triple nature emanate Air or Wind (the Father or Creative Element), followed by Water (the Mother), which proceeds from Air. The primary importance of wind in cosmogenesis is further underlined by the fact that in the first *Mandala* of the *Rig Veda*, of the first two hymns (ascribed to Rishi Madhucchandus Vishvamitra), the first is to Agni and the second to Vayu, who is asked to come to the ritual where soma has been prepared for him.

In vivid prose, the *Puranas* describe how waters flood the globe and the world becomes enveloped in darkness during a solar *pralaya*. When the waters reach the realm of the Seven Rishis, the breath of Vishnu becomes a strong wind which blows until the clouds are dispersed and reabsorbed, leaving Hari to sleep upon the Oceans of Space. At the time of the greater elemental *pralaya* the waters again swallow the earth but are, in turn, swallowed by fire, until the whole of space is one flame. Then the wind seizes upon the rudimentary property of fire (which is the cause of light) and extinguishes it. Air, accompanied by Sound, is then extended everywhere, until Ether seizes upon its cohesion, which is its rudimentary property (experienced by man through the sense of touch) and brings about its destruction. Now *Akasha* pervades the whole of Space, having only the rudiments of Sound (the Word), which is finally devoured by the Origin of the Elements, causing the Host of Dhyan Chohans and Consciousness itself to be absorbed into *Mahat*, whose characteristic property is *Buddhi*. Beyond this threshold of reabsorption, *Prakriti* is pervaded by and merged with *Purusha*. As such, it seizes upon *Mahat*, which disappears, leaving both to be resolved back into the Supreme Oneness of *Mahapralaya*. This breathtaking metaphysic, perhaps more than any other description, suggests the qualities one might attribute to wind, from its most mundane to its most abstract level of being.

With further consideration of this process, several questions arise concerning cosmological order. The Divine Spirit is universally symbolized by the sun or fire, and yet the description of *Mahapralaya* suggests that it is extinguished by the wind. *The Secret Doctrine* speaks of Spirit as the sun or fire, the Divine Soul as the moon or water, and claims that symbolically, both are parents of the human soul or mind (*pneuma*), represented by the wind or breath. This accords with many ancient systems of thought. But H. P. Blavatsky warns against confusing the "Breath of Life" with the immortal Spirit. She says that they are as distinct from one another as *prana* and *jiva* are from *Atman*. Similarly, spirit and soul are not to be confused, for the latter emerges out of the substance-aspect of the former, as does "Breath" itself, which awakens and informs the soul. Here 'Breath' is certainly the dynamic energy called *prana*. In the *Vedas*, Vayu is called the Master of Life and Inspirer of Breath (*prana*), represented in man by the vital and nervous energies that support the mental energies governed by Indra. In attempting to clarify the cosmological order, one may readily assume that the fire extinguished by the wind during the elemental *pralaya* is on a lower hierarchical level than the Divine Spirit. Less evident are the subtle relationships between Agni (the solar), Soma (the lunar), Vayu (whose active nature seems to suggest aspects of Fohat) and Indra (who is symbolically expressive of *Mahat*, brought down into the world through *kama*).

> The Father of THAT ONE ONLY THING is the Sun; its Mother the Moon; the Wind carries it in his bosom, and its nurse is the Spirituous Earth.
>
> *The Secret Doctrine*, ii 109

According to the wisdom of the *Vedas*, the chief gods (Agni, Vayu and Surya) are three occult degrees of fire. Invisible Fire manifests through the most ethereal substance by way of the cohesive linking power supplied by the fluidic fire of Vayu (air). The liquid fire of chaos (water), when permeated by the Father's fire, is the soma of which Vayu is invited to partake. In this Vayu is both the bearer and imbiber of the electrical spark of life. He is the disinterested force that blows and brings together and mixes, gradually separating the aspects of manifest life. Unlike Fohat, Vayu brings things together but does not give his name to the knots of formation that provide the basis for life on its many levels. Rather, he moves and eddies and circles. He brings endless shifts, recombinations and changes. He is like a blind force of adjustment, a steady breeze of karma flowing and howling around the world. He is often associated with Indra, the supporter of Mahatic energies in the world. The relationship is very close, and in some places the principle of *Manas* in man is actually related to the wind. But whereas Indra's career is powerfully linked with the Fall of Spirit into matter involving man, Vayu's character remains unscathed by the sacrificial results that plague Indra. As the wind, he may worry and torture, but he himself is not worried or tortured. He disseminates the seeds of intelligence in the world and blows away the useless chaff, but he does not tarry, even in the ghosts of their forms.

> Hither and thither spins
> The windborne, mirroring soul;
> A thousand glimpses wins,
> And never sees the whole.

> Matthew Arnold

Ever on the move, the wind carries upon itself doctrines and doubt, frolic and fear. Within the angles of its curved passage the world appears at each point differently, but the curve itself soon disappears and no point along its course will ever be the same. As this is so in the macrocosm, so it is within man. At every level of his being the motion of the wind acts together with the other elements in what were known in ancient and medieval times as the humours. Even in contemporary times Tibetan medicine recognizes that the humours (or winds) in the body must function in harmonious mix with each other. On the physical level wind (as a humour) predominates in the pelvic area and is said to move through the skeleton. In youth the elements of bile and phlegm reign supreme, but with old age the wind prevails and eventually overwhelms the organism. The Buddhist *Tantras* teach that there are as many as eighty-four thousand recognized diseases that can occur from imbalances in the humours. Many of them result from the superseding of the light, oily and hot characteristics of the bile and the sticky, cool, heavy and gentle characteristics of phlegm, by the rough, hard, cold, subtle and motile nature of the wind. To the Elizabethans, tempering one's temperament had to do with bringing the humours into harmony by controlling or moderating one of them. Thus, the wind in man ultimately dissolves life and impels the soul to a higher state. When properly understood, one can work with this process, let go of ideas and passing forms when a change is needed, and realize that in the world there are no eternally safe havens, no permanent solutions.

Who fails to comprehend the enormous, two-fold power of Fortune for weal or woe? When we enjoy her favouring breeze, we are wafted over to the wished for haven; when she blows against us we are dashed to destruction.

De Officiis, Cicero

In the *Old Testament*, there is frequent mention of the wind in connection with the idea of karma. "They have sown the wind, and they shall reap the whirlwind", says the book of *Hosea*. "The ungodly. . . are like the chaff which the wind driveth away", say the *Psalms*. Scripture and literature are replete with metaphors concerning breezes, gales, storms and winds of every sort. In Shakespeare, adversity is often associated with tempests and happiness with calm seas and the "gentle breath of loving winds". Ariel's music allays the fury and passion of the wind with its "sweet air", and Gonzalo speaks of the "foul weather in us all". In his *Metamorphosis*, Ovid illustrates the common tendency to refer to the wind when speaking of situations possibly affecting one's fortune. He muses: "I should first have found out his feelings, by talking to him in a way that committed me to nothing: I should have tested the wind, with close-reefed sail, in case it should prove unfavourable, and then have voyaged safely over the sea, instead of allowing winds still untried to fill my canvas, as I have done now, with the result that I am being carried onto the rocks." Such sayings as "spitting against the wind" and going "into the teeth of the wind" have to do with standing up to adverse opinion or circumstances, whilst "getting wind of something", finding out "what's in the wind" or "casting prudence to the wind" suggest the element of chance and one's willingness to take advantage of it (hoping for a "windfall") or to trust its outcome. This trust may be nothing more than the passive acceptance of results following imprudent action, or it may spring from a transcendent burst of willingness to accept all that may come in order to be carried aloft on the wind-borne wing of Spirit. Shelley's exuberant "*Ode to the West Wind*" celebrates this divine carelessness with the plea

Oh, lift me as a wave, a leaf, a cloud!
I fall upon the thorns of life! I bleed!

To control the wind is an art which few possess. Fewer still can control the fortunes of their lives. But there have always persisted stories about the special power certain Brahmins have had over the wind, and to this day Hindu priests perform rituals to bring on the monsoons with their blessings of rain. Jesus was said to have rebuked the wind and the raging water and to have made them calm. Emperor Constantine sentenced the philosopher Sopatrus to death for unchaining the winds and thus preventing grain ships from arriving in time to end a famine. In Homer's epic, Odysseus was given a bag of wind by Aeolus to speed him on his way home. His companions, suspecting treasure, opened the bag and released it while he was asleep under sail. Thus, they were beaten back by adverse breezes to the wind god's isle, only to learn that Aeolus would not favour them a second time but merely send them ruefully on their way. As a result of this missed chance, many years would pass before Odysseus could see the shores of Ithaca. From very ancient times the Greeks believed the wind could be controlled by playing a wind instrument. The god Pan marshalled and dispersed at will such great elemental hosts as to cause panic and pandemonium among observers, conditions which thus bore the label of his name.

Over the centuries man has learnt to harness the wind with ship sails and windmills of many different sorts. Wind power has driven myriad machines that pump, grind, drain and sail. The more primitive, like the *aeromilos* in southern Greece, were simple circular stone towers with apertures to catch the wind so that it would cycle around inside the structure with such speed as to lift the grain off the floor and whip it round the rough walls. The more complex bore sails whose rotating motion ran the gears within that pumped the water or ground the grain. At sea, when ships sported sails, the rule was that when the wind arrived, it was time to embark. Sir Francis Drake, in his direct Elizabethan English, expressed it succinctly to his queen: "The wind commands me away." To a square-rigged ship, usable winds mattered far more than mere distance. The longest way around often proved to be the shortest way home, for speed usually depended on scudding before these winds rather than moving in a direct route. With such winds the world's greatest trade routes were opened up and the continents were gradually knitted together. But winds like these have also changed the course of history, as in the case of the Persian fleet or when Kublai Khan's ships were swamped in A.D. 1281.

> The relationship between superiors and inferiors is like that between the wind and the grass. The grass must bend when the wind blows across it.
>
> *Confucian Analects*

What the wind does not blow away, it steadily erodes. Pitted ruins and statues in the desert, bereft of recognizable shape, stand mute and humbled before its blast. Great crescent dunes inch their way along the wasteland: sand in flux, eddying and flowing like a living thing. Where the grass can grow, it wisely bends before the wind and clings to the shifting earth. In the heavens, wind currents flow unimpeded by such lowly things. Around the globe, jet streams course five to eleven miles up at as much as two hundred miles per hour. Carrying heat and energy, they drastically affect the weather and climate of the world and are a major influence upon atmospheric circulation. Curving in bands sixty miles wide, they do not start at any specific place, but are endless rivers of air, meandering, accelerating and slowing as they flow along in the upper troposphere or stratosphere. Around and beneath them, general winds stretch thousands of miles and follow semi-permanent directional patterns largely determined by the unequal heating of the atmosphere at different latitudes and altitudes and by the earth's rotation. Their distribution is closely related to atmospheric pressure.

In the Northern Hemisphere during summer the land is warmer (low pressure) than the sea (high-pressure cyclonic). In winter this is reversed, causing anti-cyclonic circulation over land masses, with low pressure predominating over the oceans. Generally, winds tend to blow parallel to "contour lines", clockwise around "mountains" of high pressure and counter-clockwise around "valleys" of low pressure. In the Southern Hemisphere this entire pattern occurs in reverse, the Coriolis effect working in the opposite direction to that which it takes in the North. In both hemispheres where the contour lines are close together, a steep "slope" from high to low pressure is indicated. It is there that the winds are stronger. In the middle latitudes, where the two great contour patterns approach one another along the low pressure belt of the doldrums, the pressure gradient is at its steepest. But here the Coriolis force deflects the wind vector from the gradient vector so that it does not merely fall with the pressure gradient but surges forward in the great jet streams that rush around the globe.

All of the earth's energy and heat comes from the fire of Surya, our sun. Warmed and enlivened by it, the earth gives off heat in convective bubbles which rise into the lower pressure aloft. As the pressure of the rising air decreases, the air cools with expansion and, if moisture is present, produces clouds reaching up to the troposphere. Thus, convective currents from the earth continually affect the fluctuating pressure and temperature of the air close to the earth, tempering and moulding the contour patterns of the winds. But in the stratosphere the temperature is not much affected by convection. It is controlled mainly by radiation, which fills the stratosphere with short-wave components of the solar energy that drives its gigantic circulation system. Stratospheric winds obey patterns of great mystery when viewed from the perspective of the earth. Layers of west winds are sandwiched between east winds flowing faster than the earth's rotation at the equator. To further deepen the puzzle, it has been discovered that the layers of equatorial stratosphere which show east winds one year experience west winds the following year. This strange cycle repeats itself over a period of twenty-six months. Further observation has shown that the easterly or westerly layers appear first at a very great height. Gradually, as the cycle continues, they work themselves downward, finally losing themselves near the tropical tropopause. Though the mystery of this pattern remains, one wonders whether the twenty-six-month cycle is linked with the activity of great sidereal winds, whose patterns shift in decimal units instead of divisions of twelve.

I have forgot much, Cynara! gone with the wind . . .

Ernest Dowson

With winds so lofty, howling unheard in greater space and endlessly shifting around the earth, a fragment blown is indeed lost. In that sense, we live in a wind-swept world where the air fills us and blows through our minds continuously. New thoughts come, snippets from cast-off thoughts, and they fly away, unloosed from their pathetic moorings by forgetfulness. We loll in the phlegmatic breezes of the doldrums, only to be swept up in a local Boreas, a minor mistral, or to be spun off into the cyclonic tumult of a westerly blast.

> Hither and thither spins
> The windborne, mirroring soul.

How poignantly true are Matthew Arnold's lines for the majority of mankind. One can see that the bodily winds (humours) are mere reflections of greater currents affecting the mind and heart. Taking the analogy further, the types of global winds provide interesting contrasts. The trade winds are steady in direction and speed, whilst the migrating cyclones of winter Westerlies cause an unsteadiness in winds, further affected by the interruption of land masses. When the wind direction alters seasonally as much as one hundred and eighty degrees, monsoon (from the Arabic word for "season") cycles prevail like those affecting the east coast of Asia and India to the Arabian Sea. In the summer, air flows from southwest subtropical high-pressure areas towards the low-pressure zone over Asia, bringing the trade winds with them and the prayed-for rain. From the equatorial belt towards the two poles there are bands of easterly trades, bordered to the north and south by westerly winds. Around the poles easterlies prevail, complicated at the North Pole by the fact that the largest glaciated land mass on earth is not centered by the pole.

The promontory of the Himalayas and the Tibetan plateau acts as a great thermal, a dynamic pivot affecting the entire monsoon pattern of the Northern Hemisphere throughout the year. The Tibetan plateau is almost snow-free in autumn, winter and spring, and so acts as a high-level radiational heat source. Pressure surfaces are raised there, diminishing the north-south temperature gradient and the strength of the subtropical jet stream to the south, all of which dramatically affect the weather over China, central Asia and the Middle East, while acting as a constant buffer to the Indian subcontinent below. If one imagines oneself as the earthly globe, surely the Himalayas and the Tibetan plateau would be the place of one's heart. Storing the heat of divine solar Fire, the heart pours forth warming, ever rising air, which modifies the distributions of vital winds in lands all round it. The steepest gradient lies in the middle latitudes, where the opposing Coriolis forces of the Northern and Southern Hemispheres approach one another. This provides a dramatic analogue to the often turbulent relationship between the immortal man and his earthly vesture. Trade winds streaming along smoothly in one hemisphere may cross over this "equator" and head off in exactly the opposite direction. The steep gradient itself encourages powerful winds, even jet streams, which may be impossible to beat against and may carry one down a fierce tunnel of varying passions. In these areas the "head" gets embroiled in the concerns of the animal nature and the body obtrudes itself upon the thoughts and feelings, making one vulnerable to these cyclonic and often unpredictable currents. But like a good pilot, the wise man or woman can learn where the jet streams are. Keeping their ultimate destination firmly in mind, they can take advantage of the great speed of the jet streams. In *Kali Yuga* turbulence rules the world, but one can use that quickened movement to one's benefit and extend the breadth of awareness to incorporate greater and more inclusive patterns within one's moral and mental framework.

One could imagine moral, mental and emotional counterparts to every alteration of atmospheric pressure, every updraft and "contour" fall of wind. Seasonal shifts and variations caused by land and sea provide rich analogies to the fluctuating conditions experienced by the human soul in a body. But the real secret, the vital lesson to be learnt, is concealed in the wind itself. If one wishes to understand the wind, one should listen to it and try to pick up the message it carries. The old idea that "something is in the wind" is based upon a deeper truth, for its breeze comes from a distance far outstripping the petty gossip and cares of the world. One feels the wind and senses a greater communion. One soars with its voice and glimpses the world astride its wing. One begins to feel the pulse, intuit the Breath of Brahma coursing in its numberless fluctuations. Its sighing voice speaks of other worlds, lifting the mind to new and aerating currents of thought. Though it choke the lower man with the dust of tribulation, the Inner Man rises with its song and flows out to embrace space. Along "the rope of the wind" he experiences the disinterested power of karma and, looking down towards the earth, feels compassion for those who twist and strive in its eddies and whirls. To soar like this, to touch the feet of the Aeons and glide to the very threshold of *pralaya*, is to fulfil the *raison d'être* of the human odyssey on earth. The key to its mystery in all its myriad conditions is indeed written in the wind.

> Hearken to its voice,
> Its compelling melody.
> Are you merely a leaf
> To be tossed and blown?
> Listen to the Sigh
> Borne upon its breath,
> The whispered word
> From Brahma blown.

Hermes, April 1985

THE VOYAGE

They that go down to the sea in ships, that do business in great
waters; these see the works of the Lord, and his wonders in the deep.
For he commandeth, and raiseth the stormy wind, which lifteth
up the waves thereof. They mount up to the heaven, they go down
again to the depths: their soul is melted because of trouble. They reel
to and fro, and stagger like a drunken man, and are at their wit's
end. Then they cry unto the Lord in their trouble, and he bringeth
them out of their distresses. He maketh the storm a calm, so that the
waves thereof are still. Then are they glad because they be quiet; so
he bringeth them unto their desired haven.

Psalms 107: 23–30

So you want to take to the sea, lad, ship out before the mast?"
The old salt's gaze curved out over the youth's bowed head to the
swells gently rocking the vessels in the bay. "It isn't an easy task,
you know. It isn't something you do out of curiosity or just because
you're at loose ends." He noticed the tenacious bob of the boy's head
and continued, "It's dangerous out there and very heavy work and
you might not find what you're looking for." The silence of the lad
conveyed his determination louder than words, and the old man,
sensing it, shifted his tack and demanded: "Before you make up your
mind, I want you to look deeply into my eyes and tell me what you
see there." The young man gazed at the old, seeing the weathered face
that had endured many a gale and the furrowed patterns of lines that
etched out a life hard lived on the sea. He looked at the tangled brows
curving over hooded eyes which shone from his aged map like lights
reflected from a far-off shore. The boy looked deeply into them and
knew that they were gazing through him, beyond him, to things he
could not see and maybe never would. He shivered, for he recognized
in the gaze a meditation on the unknown – a native inclination to
leave behind all that was familiar and predictable. He saw in the old
man's eyes the passion of a quest unfulfilled and the long years of
plumbing the horizon's void. "Would you do business in great waters,

lad? Does not what you see cause you pause?" But the boy's eyes had seen the sketch of an uncharted shore and he shipped out on the Argo that very night.

Thus did Jason ages ago sail in search of the Golden Fleece. From Iolchos in Thessaly he sailed to find the remains of the sacred ram given by Hermes to the mother of Helle and Phrixus. He did this in order to obtain his rightful kingdom from the usurper Pelias, a theme that is echoed in the sagas of Odysseus and later Aeneas. "The wondered Argo which . . . first through the Euxine Seas bore all the flower of Greece" takes its name from the crescent-shaped *argha*, *arca* or "ark" that bears the sacred germ over the abyss to a new world. The voyage of the Argo witnessed a successful garnering of the Golden Fleece and return to Iolchos, but it did not result in Jason regaining his rightful crown. The fact that the boat was built with Athene's help and the bow contained a piece of oak from the oracle of Zeus at Dadona contributed to its safe return. But the dire magical powers of Medea which had enabled Jason to capture the Golden Fleece became, in the end, his curse, robbing him of all he held dear and dooming him to die alone and in anguish. It was said that he met his end while resting under the Argo as it lay propped up on dry land. In a twist of irony, he was struck on the head and killed by a piece of timber that fell from its stern.

> With a taut sail she forged ahead all day, till the sun went down
> and left her to pick her way through the darkness.

> Thus she brought us to the deep-flowing River of Ocean
> and the frontiers of the world, where the fog-bound
> Cimmerians live in the City of Perpetual Mist.
>
> *Odyssey*

Pompey the Great once said that "living is not necessary, but navigation is". This would mark the distinction between living for oneself and living in order to transcend. In terms of this notion of transcendence, the *Odyssey* is an archetypal navigation myth. It is a triumph over the perils of the unconscious, as represented by the ocean, and over regression and stagnation. One can trace in it the involution of the soul into matter and its evolution back to its spiritual home. One can also see in it the age-old story of the masculine mind, the child of Spirit, striving to win its way back to its Buddhic home. From Ilium, Odysseus and his fleet sailed to the Thracian city of Ismarus, sacking it and sparing only the priest of Apollo, who, in return for his life, solicited for them the help of that god. But storms off Cape Taenaron blew them back to Cythera and the land of the Lotus-Eaters, wherein anything eaten induced forgetfulness. From thence they came to the island of the Cyclopes and the adventure which was to bring the wrath of Poseidon upon them. After this, even with the gift of winds given them by Aeolus, they failed to make a clear sail, for the men fell asleep and let the winds escape willy-nilly. Thus, once again almost in sight of their goal, they were swept back to the land of the Laestrygonian cannibals, who ate many of the men and sank most of their ships. From there the survivors reached the isle of Aeaea, where Circe turned several of them into the pitiable state of swine with human minds, and Odysseus was told he must go to the land of the Cimmerians at the fog-bound western limit of the world. There, in that sunless place at the entrance to Hades, he was instructed to call up the spirits of the dead and learn from Tiresias the way to complete his voyage home.

Fulfilling the *nekuia* rite at that shadowy place, Odysseus found himself surrounded with the souls of the dead. His mother, partaking of the sacrifice, said to him: "My son, how have you descended, while still alive, to this gloomy realm which is difficult for the living to behold? Great rivers and terrible waters lie between; first Oceanus which, if one does not have a sturdy ship, he cannot in any way cross on foot." Indeed, it was only Circe's instructions that had enabled them to find it, just as the prophetic warnings of Tiresias would guide them in their further travels. Nonetheless, despite the wise counsel which got them safely past the dangers of the Sirens and of Scylla and Charybdis, some of the men could not resist killing one or two of the sacred cattle of Helios when they landed on the isle of Thrinacie. As a result, a storm sank the ships and all but Odysseus were drowned. Clutching the mast and part of the keel, he floated, eventually arriving at the island home of Calypso, in whose fragrant bower he remained entangled for seven long years. Only the order of Zeus, brought by Hermes, finally forced the enamoured daughter of

Atlas to help Odysseus build a raft and send him on his way. But even then Poseidon did not relent and, as the raft neared the island of the Phaeacians, he sent a storm that destroyed it and left the struggling voyager adrift in the water for two days and nights. On the third day he was washed ashore and found by the noble Nausicaa, who took him to the palace of her parents, Alcinous and Arete, who ruled a nation of magnificently skilled seamen. It was in their good care that, sunk in a deep sleep, Odysseus was finally able to return at last to the shores of his Ithacan home.

> O God! thou mayest save me if thou wilt,
> and if thou wilt, thou mayest destroy me; but
> whether or no, I will steer my rudder true.
>
> Michel De Montaigne

Nausicaa bears a name of central importance to the theme of the voyage. Stemming from the Greek root ναῦς, (ship), it is linked with ναύτης (*nauta* or sailor) and, ultimately, with the Latin *naves* and such derivatives as "nave" (of the church), "navel", "naval", "navy" and "navigation". There is a wealth of Greek terms evolved from this root and reflective of a people much involved with the sea. This includes now obscure terms such as ναῦβιον and ναῦον, which define Egyptian measurements and suggest that the Greeks derived much of their basis for measuring from their marine experiences. The trackless character of the ocean would seem to defy measurement. One can readily grasp how its depths might have been plumbed, but how did the ancients measure their passage over it and how did they, or even later seamen, know where they were upon its surface? To the landlubber the question is merely academic and, in recent times, seems to have been answered. Taking for granted instruments that have evolved over centuries of seamanship, modern man tends to entertain a casual or utilitarian view of the world's great oceans, shrinking them to suit a world-view largely devoid of wonder.

> Where lies the land to which the ship would go?
> Far, far ahead, is all her seamen know.
>
> Arthur Hugh Clough

After his long voyage on the Beagle, Charles Darwin felt moved to express the awe that he had come to feel for the sea. He wrote that it was necessary to sail it in order to begin to comprehend its immensity. Flying over it, we arrive at a destination, never knowing what lies between where we started and where we have come. In a very deep sense, we do not know where we have come because we have not found our own way there. We have not struggled and dreamt and overcome all the risks while charting each phase of the journey. This is in marked contrast to the few master navigators who have charted their own courses from shore to shore over many seas and do not suffer from a delusive sense of time and distance or the limits of the passage. To one who simply follows a course or is hurtled from one position to another without grasping the nature or significance of what has intervened, the whole world is likely to become shrivelled and stuffed into tidy socio-political categories that provide a false sense of order and understanding. This condition is so common that it appears to be normal, and one experiences a slight jolt to consciousness when confronted with the arbitrary and superficial nature of one's sense of direction, distance and time.

Arguing that ancient people experienced a deeper and richer involvement in these dimensions, one naval historian observed that it is we who have had our conception of distance destroyed. The men of the Stone and Bronze Ages knew no frontiers nor did they need any passports, identity papers or tickets. The earth was free, the oceans lay open, and they wandered across them, acquainting themselves with their myriad dangers and havens. Thus they came to know the seas and lands as well as themselves, never separating themselves from them or from the journey they had made across them. It is for this reason that in their myths and religious ceremonies, all the ancient cultures merged into one the path of migration and the voyage of self-discovery. One might argue that the same experience can be garnered by one who runs the obstacle course of growing up in a ghetto or simply survives the psychological odyssey of modern life. But one intuitively realizes that there was a greater collective depth in the ancient experience, that the continual and progressive checking and counter-checking between man's nature and greater Nature surrounding him had resulted in a truer sense of his place in the universal scheme of things. In attempting to understand the nature of the spiritual voyage, one comes to realize the same necessity of confronting every phase of the journey oneself. As with the seamen of old, the goal is unknown, and the need for a means of establishing location, distance and direction is equally pressing. The example of early seamen and their struggle to evolve the art and science of navigation provides rich clues for those who would venture upon the great ocean of the Self.

Much of the earliest knowledge of seamanship involved what is known as piloting: going from point to point along a coast and relying upon a highly developed memorization of numerous variables operating in any one locale at various times of the year. Navigation relies upon the same use of the senses, but the reference point shifts from the coastline to celestial bearings observable on the open sea. As with the cyclic motion of the evolving soul, the ancient navigator had to act upon a spherical world. The flat mental map of a local coastline no longer provided him with accurate calculations of location. Long centuries were to elapse before the logarithmic tables that eventually made spherical calculations a simple matter would have been so painstakingly evolved. The errors and disasters wrought by plane sailing (sailing according to flat-earth charts, where meridians were parallel to one another) persisted among Europeans until the end of the sixteenth century, when the Mercator chart was developed and plane sailing became a term used to describe what appeared to be the uncomplicated business of sailing in a straight line from one point to another.

The discovery of a means of steering a ship with some degree of certainty was a mechanical problem whose complexity appeared originally to be no less than that of discovering how a sense of direction could be maintained when out of sight of land. If one is sailing north before a southwest wind and finds oneself further east than estimated, there must be a current moving the ship eastward, and in the future one must tack a little more to the west rather than straight to one's destination. To do this, navigators must know where they are. They learn that ships may have to sail a greater distance to avoid being pushed to the lee shore (on the lee of the ship is the shore onto which the wind is blowing). In later centuries, during the great voyages around South America, it was essential that they beat hard to westward in order to clear the Horn when going from west to east.

The eight Mediterranean winds were named after the countries from which they blew and were charted in a circle of directional points called a wind-rose. Their relative seasonal regularity enabled early seamen to sail by them with some confidence, just as navigators elsewhere voyaged with the various monsoons and trade winds. Where the winds were less reliable, however, checks were made by observing sunrise and sunset during the day and the pole-star during the night. In the Far North, if the winds changed and the sky was obscured, the Vikings released ravens, whose flight would indicate the direction of land. They also used sun-stones, which were crystals believed to indicate the direction of the sun even through a cloud.

In his initial voyage Columbus relied upon dead reckoning, which involves a continuous record of speeds maintained over known periods of time by a log-line (a rope run out from the stern until the log at its end had drawn it taut). This sort of method had been used by earlier seamen, and it would later be sophisticated by the English, who tied the line in knots every forty-two feet. This was set in conjunction with a fixed interval of time (usually half a minute) so that one length of forty-two feet measured one mile (or knot) per hour. While using this mode of reckoning as well as the pole-star to determine latitude, Columbus found that his compass was unreliable. In earlier times a lodestone was floated in a vessel of water and navigators attempted to ascertain when it was freely and truly pointing to the north. By the twelfth century the lodestone was fixed in its own container but generally kept out of sight by the navigator, who wished to preserve his reputation for skill and avoid being accused of witchcraft. This latter threat was due to ideas associated with the mysterious property of magnetism, for, as Brunetto Latini wrote in the thirteenth century, "No master mariner dares to use it, lest he should fall under the supposition of being a magician; nor would even the sailors venture themselves to sea under his command if he took with him an instrument which carries so great an appearance of being constructed under the influence of some infernal spirit."

In addition to the unreliability of his compass, the sailors with Columbus steered badly. In one night they covered one hundred and twenty miles and found themselves twenty-two and one-half degrees off by dawn. The fact that they could calculate their error was a result of being able to establish their latitude. This could be ascertained by measuring the angle between a line from the eye to the horizon and a line from the eye to the North Star (the smaller the angle, the further south one was), or by measuring the altitude of the sun at noon, allowing each day for the difference caused by the sun's apparent movement between the tropics as the seasons changed. Quadrants, cross staffs, back staffs, sextants and astrolabes were gradually developed to facilitate these measurements. The compass too was improved and, overcoming superstitions about witchcraft, was openly fixed on the ship. Its magnetized needle was fixed to a wind-rose card so that, as the ship altered its course and the needle and card remained pointed to the north, the direction in which the ship was moving (in line with the central axis of the vessel) could be read off the card. Thus it was that fairly early on in the great voyages, speed, direction and latitude could be measured with some degree of confidence. There were still the currents, fluctuations of wind and weather, reefs, icebergs, rogue waves and many other uncontrollable factors to concern these sailors, but, leaving aside bad steering, enough navigational knowledge had been garnered to make possible the extraordinary circumnavigations of the sixteenth and seventeenth centuries.

The great problem that remained was establishing accurate longitude. It had long been known that the earth revolves at a rate of fifteen degrees per hour relative to the sun. Thus longitude could be got from accurately measuring time. The problem lay in the inaccuracy of the means that had been traditionally used to measure it. On Chinese junks intervals of time were measured with incense sticks. Sand-glasses were used on European ships and noon readings were obtained each day, enabling the exact division of the watches (from which we take the name for our portable timepieces). The extent of the problem can be appreciated when one learns that a thirty-degree error in longitude is equal to eighteen hundred sea miles at the equator. Captain Edwards of the Pandora, who tried to find the mutineers of the Bounty, used a chart which marked Pitcairn Island far to the west of its real position, due to such a thirty-degree error. The distance between the moon and certain fixed stars (called a lunar distance) proved somewhat helpful in establishing longitude, but it was difficult to rely upon in obscure weather or when the ship was rolling in a heavy sea. It was the development of chronometers which eventually solved the problem and provided a major advancement in the science of navigation. Invented by the British, they were extremely well made clocks which were set on London time before the journey began. This time had to be checked against the time calculated with an astrolabe at sea, the difference between them giving the longitude. The astronomer and first lieutenant aboard each of the sloops Resolution and Adventure (commanded by Cook) kept the keys to the boxes containing the chronometers and were always present when they were wound up. Greater and greater precision thus marked the subtle transition of navigation from an art to a science. But there were still the imponderables – the unexpected changes of sea and weather and the weaknesses, strengths and sometimes purely capricious behaviour of the ships themselves.

> The sea has ever been more conservative than the land, for the simple reason that at sea every attempt to step forward has to be paid for in human life rather than the coin of the realm.
>
> Basil Lubbock

Ships are living vessels possessing temperaments and hidden potentials. This is how sailors have always seen them, and indeed the complex interrelationship between strengths, strains, stresses and supports in their makeup results in constant adjustment. One especially thinks of the creaking and groaning of a wooden ship in heavy seas, but a metal ship equally adjusts, flexing its entire body as it breasts rolling swells and dips down again into the troughs. A good navigator comes to know his ship intimately and ever charts his course with her capabilities in mind. He is like the mind striving to win its way back home, and he must act in total consonance with the vessel's captain, who orders from the bridge and could be seen to represent the higher mind which is already linked to the Buddhic goal. Among captains in the world there have been few who could be said to have fully incarnated this lofty condition, but there have been some notables who, helped by the gods or by their own wisdom and breadth of soul, have inspired generations. Good captains always know the worth of discipline and morale, but captains like Cook have that indefinable "something more". To sailors, service under such a one is an honour as well as a benefit. Along with supreme confidence, Cook possessed a sense of presence, movingly affirmed by a Maori boy who once said in reference to him, "A noble man cannot be lost in a crowd."

Good seamanship can save a vessel even in violent storms or when run aground. The leadsman of the Endeavour had just called out seventeen fathoms (off the east coast of Australia), and before he could heave another cast, "the ship struck and stuck fast". Under Cook's command they downed the sails so she would not press forward, put the anchor out at a distance to haul against and tossed all their extra weight overboard. With a little help from the gods, perhaps, the coral from the reef on which they had run remained in the hole and acted as a plug as she was eased back into deeper water. In contrast to this there is nothing sadder than the wreck of a majestic and spirited ship through the inadequacies or lack of skill of a captain and navigator. Many a noble ship has been lost at sea or dashed upon rocks by uncontrollable natural forces, but many another has been doomed by foolhardiness or by lamentable errors in judgement. The long list of ships which have disappeared with all hands lost at sea is a melancholy roll that reads like an ancient lamentation for vanquished hopes and dreams of discovery. The voyages of men upon the sea have, indeed, been paid for in human life and the spiritual journey on the ocean within has been no less hazardous. Many are the wrecks that hang broken upon the astral reefs ringing its continents and many more have been lost in unknown seas.

> Alone, alone, all, all alone;
> Alone on a wide, wide sea.
>
> Samuel Taylor Coleridge

Deep within the individual where one's higher sense of self arises, the desire to make this lonely voyage awaits. As Pompey recognized, the navigational quest is more essential than life, and the voyage, sooner or later, must be made. Thus one follows the journeys of Odysseus or Jason or Aeneas, sensing the immediacy of their trials in one's own inner life. Every human being must reach his true home and regain his rightful crown and queen. Until the mind is fully united to Buddhi, the vessel of the personality will drift helplessly with the tides and cross-currents of the worldly sea. The voyage must be made and the individual, as his own captain and navigator, must confront every phase of its vicissitudes. One cannot reach and realize the goal by simply boarding another's ship, for such a passenger crawls ashore and never understands where he has arrived. But the inner ocean is as trackless as an unexplored astral wasteland wherein no landmarks present themselves. The lone sailor on that sea cautiously feels his way through the mists and is startled to come upon suddenly the wreckage of failed voyages and the ominous presence of great reefs and bergs looming in the whirling currents. The journey takes him to the very entrance of Hades, or even through its realms, and his astral eyes and ears are accosted by the horrors and woes that reside there. But it is only by journeying through death and back into the realm of the living while alive and still in a body that one may learn how to navigate one's craft through the dangers and trials that abound along the way.

One learns true navigation when one gains the courage to sail away from the shore where mere piloting suffices and enter the open sea, to the River of Ocean beyond. As the reference point shifts from the land to the celestial bodies, one slowly learns to place more and more trust in the inner lights that rise upon the night sky of one's deepest meditations. Voiding the mind of all known landmarks, one learns to rest upon the great Ocean of Being and await with alert confidence the appearance of that fixed guiding star. Thus gradually is the door of the mind opened to divine breezes which, like the gift of Aeolus (so pathetically squandered by the men of Odysseus), will reverberate through one's instrument and melodiously waft one towards the destination.

> Yes, as everyone knows, meditation and water are wedded forever.
>
> Herman Melville

Odysseus learnt from divine guidance. He, unlike his men, used his native intelligence in its service. Thus, even the sorceress Circe, who destroyed others, aided him, and Calypso too ultimately helped him on his way. Nymphs of the sea and aspects of the astral matrix that can either ensnare or help, they, in their turn, served him. In the case of Jason this was not so, for he neither understood nor did he ultimately control the powerful sorceress who played such a dominant role in his quest. Taking her love and her malevolent magical practices equally for granted, he was unprepared for her violent revenge and her curse when thwarted. Thus do foolhardy seamen challenge a stormy sea with all sails set but without knowledge of the jagged rocks that lie ahead. In contrast to Jason, brave adventurer though he was, Odysseus demonstrated the heightened powers of memory and observation required of those who know very well the nature of what they experience during the course of their journey and come to realize fully what lies at its conclusion.

The ship in which the journey is made is a living vesture, the ark that will give one birth. The compass needed within is one's conscience, the small voice of one's soul which always points to the unchanging Truth and which comes into conscious development (just as it was invented and slowly improved in worldly navigation) as one hushes extraneous directives and learns to listen to its faithful instruction. One's chronometer can be found in the steady pulsation emanating from the cave of the inner spiritual heart. This is the true basis for all measurement while moving around the inner and outer world. When its beat has been consciously charted, the voyager can discover how its rhythm complements and blends with the fixed point of Truth. Just as the invention of the chronometer solved the problem of establishing longitude, so too the discovery of one's spiritual heart facilitates any real progress towards the goal. Compassion possesses a pulsation which can be consciously experienced and is the motor force of true navigation. Hearkening to this inner beating, and with meditative eyes fixed on the star of Truth, the sailor upon the inner sea can navigate wisely, latitudinally and longitudinally, moving at ease around its shoals and doldrums and myriad dangers. Such a voyager thus recapitulates the navigational myth of Odysseus and comes to triumph over the astral abyss of the unconscious. Skirting the trap of forgetfulness presented by the Lotus Lands and Calypso's cloying affection, the sailor-disciple can avoid the fate of the men of Odysseus who were turned into animal-men or drowned in the mother sea. Even if others fail around him and are carried away on the mindless tide, the resourceful and devoted navigator presses on. Even if the ship itself is lost, he can, like Odysseus, hold fast to the *axis mundi* of the mast and the balancing power of the keel while drifting towards a temporary haven.

Each of the arduously garnered rules of worldly navigation provides profound analogies for the inner voyager. Captain Cook was wise to act swiftly and decisively when the Endeavour ran aground. Just so must the sailor-disciple respond when confronted with a challenge to his further passage. He should be ready and willing to throw overboard all his excess baggage. It will have to be done at some point in any case. And he would be foolish to keep on sail when the winds of adversity would only drive him further towards destruction. It is unwise to jeopardize one's vessel before the other shore is reached or until, like Odysseus, one is assured of divine guidance. Even when the shore is sighted, resorting to plane sailing is not wise. Winds of unexpected change may force one to temporarily tack away from the goal in order to circle around towards it at a later point. Thus, even in sight of the goal, one may be blown back and forced to assimilate the lesson that the soul's evolution, like all real growth, takes place in cycles. Thus the spiritual navigator circumnavigates the globe many times over, circling back over the same track but never meeting the identical seas. Always the trials are varied and of an ever more subtle nature.

The old salt, who requested the youth to look deeply into his eyes before taking to the sea, had, in this way, voyaged many times around. His far-gazing orbs were filled with mirrorings of the struggles and wonders he had experienced. On many a night he had followed his fixed star and sensed the beating of his spiritual heart, but he had not yet wedded the two and made of his mind a pellucid and eager servant to the divine within him. It may be that in this life he had become too old to make the voyage again, and yet his concern for the boy revealed his hope that the lad, in taking precautions, might succeed in realizing the goal. He recognized that quality in the boy which would rise up incontestably within himself in subsequent lives, namely, the longing to "go down to the sea in ships" and "do business in great waters". The voyage for such souls is undeniable. It must be made whatever the dangers. For a haunting though misty sketch of an uncharted shore has been glimpsed by them and it can never again be forgotten.

> West of these out to seas colder than Hebrides
> I must go
> Where the fleet of stars is anchored and the young star-captains glow.
>
> James Elroy Flecker

Hermes, February 1985

THE DODECAHEDRON

From man or angel the great Architect
Did wisely to conceal and not divulge
His secrets to be scann'd by them who ought
Rather admire; or, if they list not to try
Conjecture, he his fabric of the heavens
Hath left to their disputes, perhaps to move
His laughter at their quaint opinions wide
Hereafter; when they come to model heaven
And calculate the stars, how they will wield
The mighty frame; how build, unbuild, contrive
To save appearances; how gird the sphere
With centric and eccentric scribbled o'er,
Cycle and epicycle, orb in orb.

Paradise Lost, John Milton

The ancient Greeks honoured the twelve signs of the zodiac in the sacred host of the *Dodecatheoi,* the twelve gods whose temples were placed in the twelve equally divided sections which radiated out from the centre of the city of Athens. Their popular worship shrouded the secret correspondences of sets of twelves observed in a multitude of natural and cultural phenomena. There were twelve hours of the day and night, twelve months in the year, twelve units in various measurements and weights, twelve labours, columns of sacred temples, and the twelve days between the winter solstice and the first day of the new year which marked a return to chaos and the subsequent rebirth of order. The many derivatives of the basic term *dodecatheoi* in the Greek suggest a fundamental twelve-part division discernible in many facets of human life. The number twelve itself was seen as symbolic of cosmic order, archetypally represented for much of the ancient world by the twelve points through which the zodiac revolves.

Such correspondences were based upon arcane philosophical tenets as well as upon actual observations of natural cycles. Plato spoke of the twelve signs (gods or *theoi*) of the zodiac as modes of manifestation of the single creative force which governs the universe, calling them the Gates of Heaven. The zodiac itself was associated with the Demiurge and the primordial Eros or the will to create. This is rather similar to the theme found in many cultures of the twelve fruits borne on the Tree of Life or the twelve tribal progenitors. Metaphysically, the twelve divisions through which the sun seems to orbit have been seen for millennia as corresponding to the twelve degrees or stages in the continuous action of the active principle upon the passive. This cosmic creation, within the division of twelve, involves vital combinations of numbers such as twice five plus two and three times four. It also involves depth and breadth of action on three and more dimensions, yielding the fifth and final of Plato's regular solids, the dodecahedron. Just as the symbolism of each sign in the zodiac springs from the number it bears in the series, so the twelve pentagonal faces of the dodecahedron express the point, the line, the plane and, in their totality, all the geometric solids. Thus the dodecahedron, which Plato called the supreme spiritual metaphor for the One and the many, is a paradigmatic model to serve as the archetypal framework for every possible manifestation.

> The Highest and most Good Creator in the creations of this mobile world and the arrangement of the heavens had his eye on those five regular bodies, which have been most celebrated from the time of Pythagoras and Plato right down to our own day, and that to this nature he accommodated the number of heavenly spheres, their proportions, and the system of their motions.
>
> Johann Kepler

Confined by the theocentric language of his time, the bold statement of Kepler showed a vision which extended far beyond the truncated notions associated with the unique creation of an anthropomorphic god that persisted in the seventeenth century. The Platonic concept that the manifest cosmos was gestated through Divine Ideation is clearly traceable in Kepler, as it is now in the few daring contemporary physicists like Fritjof Capra, who invokes "metabolic mentation" from cells to the higher levels of conscious intelligence, culminating in the

Cosmic Mind. He suggests that "both life and mind are manifestations of the same set of systemic properties", thus arriving, despite the limitations of the language of systems theory, at the threshold of Pythagorean-Platonic cosmology. In conveying the majestic grandeur of cosmic manifestation, the lofty prose of *The Secret Doctrine* enables us to explore the subtle correspondences and textures of meaning lying in and around words capable of intimating that which lies beyond and also precedes the visible cosmos. H. P. Blavatsky declared that the visible universe "was built on the model of the first DIVINE IDEA", which existed from eternity in a latent state. Reiterating the teachings of the initiated Plato, she taught that, just as the animating soul of the invisible universe is the Central Spiritual Sun, so also the sun is the soul of the visible which is built by the first-begotten of the One, who constructed it "on the geometrical figure of the dodecahedron". This first-born is the aggregate of the Host of Builders or first constructive forces, the Tetragrammaton at the head of the seven lower Sephiroth and the triad at the top of the Pythagorean decad.

> That there are distinct orders of Angels, assuredly I believe; but what they are, I cannot tell; Dicant qui possunt; si tamen probare possum quod dicunt, saies that Father, Let them tell you that can, so they be able to prove, that they tell you true. They are Creatures, that have not so much of a Body as flesh is, as froth is, as a vapour is, as a sigh is, and yet with a touch they shall moulder a rock into lesse Atomes, then the sand that it stands upon; and a milstone in smaller flower, then it grinds.
>
> John Donne

In the magical unfolding of cosmogenesis a vast hierarchy of spirits is involved, led by the Divine Fire of *Daiviprakriti*, given direction and force by the mysterious magical potency of *Fohat*. From this primordial motion the Fire and Aether, which constitute the Atma-Buddhic prototype of incarnating monads, come into being and give life to the Triads (the Atma-Buddhi-Manasic prototypes) who work through the sacred matrix of human consciousness (the *Rupa* Angels), in which lies the vital germ that will fall into incarnation. From this springs the fifth group of Dhyanis connected with the microcosm expressed in the pentagon and the five-pointed figure of man. In arcane philosophy the hierarchy of creative powers is divided into seven, whose components four and three, when multiplied, equal twelve:

the four bodies and three faculties of Brahma (the four elements and three *gunas*), thus yielding the twelve orders of the zodiac expressed three-dimensionally in the dodecahedron.

Each descending level of this hierarchy is marked by increased differentiation which unfolds according to law. At the beginning of a period of activity this law, resting in a latent state of concealed wisdom (*Chitshakti*), awakens and begins to act in the pre-cosmic Mind. Fohat then commences to form the universe "in accordance with the conceptions generated in the universal mind out of the differentiated principle of Cosmic matter". Cosmic ideation continues ceaselessly as long as there exists a manifest world. If it ceased, even for a fraction of a moment in time, the process of differentiation would stop and the night of pralaya begin. Owing to a deep and lasting comprehension of this fact, especially as it is expressed through sound vibrations, the tradition persists that to utter the sacred Word is to join one's voice with a vibratory current that can be traced back to the very genesis of Being. In the mundane language of systems theory, this idea can be traced in terms of interdependent, living organisms which are always at work, renewing themselves within their stable patterns of organization and dying only when the continuous exchange of energy and matter with their environment ceases.

> The latent design exists in the one unborn eternal atom, the centre which exists everywhere and nowhere.
>
> T. Subba Row

Conceptions of latency and of primordial beginnings evoke questions about whether the universe is infinite or bounded in time. Is it closed or open? Is it evolving or in a steady state of equilibrium? Does the creative and destructive dance of Shiva Nataraj continue endlessly or does it too have periods of rest? Is it contained within the twelve faces of the dodecahedron or is it beginningless and without limit or order? Contemporary cosmological theories engaging the minds of astrophysicists tend to swing between the notion of the universe as a steady state and the so-called Big Bang theory. Proponents of the steady-state theory envision the universe as endlessly expanding, evolving new radiation in compensation for that lost through expansion, whilst those focussed upon beginnings assume that an exceedingly simple matter exploded out of a super-dense kernel. Followers of the latter theory believe that this matter was initially composed of photons, protons, electrons and neutrons, and that after only seconds the universe cooled enough to permit their aggregation into larger units from deuterons to heavier elements. In the early aeons of its expansion, light-energy predominated, subjugating, so to speak, the expanding matter in a sort of "reign of radiation". When the temperature dropped (as a result of expansion) below the threshold of thermonuclear reactions producing photons, the "density" of radiant matter decreased more rapidly than that of dark matter, until the density of the latter exceeded that of the former, ushering in the "reign of matter". According to this model, during the predominance of light-energy, matter spread uniformly as a "thin" gas until, with its increased density, it broke up into gas balls which slowly drifted apart to become eventually the galaxies of our universe.

The problem with this model lies in its slavish acceptance of a dualistic reality wherein the term "matter" is muddled and pushed around to accommodate everything that is acted upon by something. In addressing itself to primeval beginnings, it places the same mechanically conceived muddle at the threshold of the infinite. The steady-state theory has the merit of leaving the question of causation alone. As a few modern thinkers (often borrowing freely from the ideas inherent in Taoist, Buddhist and Hindu metaphysics) have pointed out, mass is not matter (substance) necessarily, but a form of energy. What we call objects are really patterns in a unified cosmic process. Things are events or happenings and only secondarily "things". The teaching of Nagarjuna that "things derive their being and nature by mutual dependence and are nothing in themselves" is echoed by the atomic physicist Henry Stapp when he asserts that "an elementary particle is not an independently existing unanalyzable entity. It is, in essence, a set of relationships that reach outward to other things."

The energy patterns of the subatomic world build up stable atomic and molecular structures whose aggregation presents the "solid" appearance we call "matter". At the macrocosmic level this translates usefully into the idea of substance, but at the atomic level the idea loses its meaning. The dynamic relationships of the sub-organic world describe patterns (rather than substance) like a dance of energy, and the answer to the question whether the creation and destruction in the cosmic dance endure in a steady state is contingent upon the relationship between the existence of patterns in the manifest cosmos and the pre-cosmic Mind. Considering these ideas from the standpoint of relative cycles within cycles, it becomes apparent that the steady state and Big Bang theories are alike partially correct and inadequate. Hampered in their expression by mechanistic language and the intellectual polarization of spirit and matter that has crippled the thinking of philosophers and scientists for the past two thousand years, they do, nonetheless, as theories manage to touch the garment hem of a greater cosmological truth. The interesting idea here involves the notion of relationship within the whole manifested as a pattern, a noumenal basis for seeing form in terms of archetypal designs rather than simply aggregations of matter. In considering the process of the coming into being of form or morphogenesis, modern physics is coming to realize that DNA alone does not suffice as an explanation. This realization led, as early as the 1930s, to a consideration of morphogenetic fields which are spatial dispositions rather than material structures. In them is preserved a design body that is causal and guides the development of form, remaining associated with it and restoring it if necessary. Some investigators point to the regenerative capability of certain plants and animals as indicating the presence of such a purposeful form-fulfilling potential. Such fields are physical in the sense that physics can explain them but they are not material structures. They cannot normally be seen or touched, but any member of a species of any of the kingdoms of life taps into such a field and is thus affected (even prior to birth) by developments and adjustments experienced by that species throughout its history. The DNA code is thus necessary merely for tuning to the right frequency and participating in patterns contained timelessly in the right field.

Such a reaffirmation of arcane metaphysics opens doors through which the fresh air of archetypal ideation can flow and begin to sweep away the creaking structure of Cartesian thought, which itself has become an imprisoning design in the collective "morphogenetic" field of the human mind. It has been suggested that hierarchies of morphogenetic fields work upon each other, the more archetypal ordering and designing the lesser: some responsible for the forms of chemical systems, others for organisms or crystals, etc. New compounds, lacking a morphogenetic field, are not strongly influenced (for example in the case of a crystal) to assume a particular form. But once they are crystallized a first time, each subsequent crystallization becomes more automatic. Precisely in this way learned behaviour amongst members of higher species spreads without any physical communication. It would seem to follow that the more generalized and universal the form, the greater its ability to tap into the higher archetypal morphogenetic fields and express their designs through form, behaviour and even thought. Here, the Theosophical teachings concerning the levels of the astral light related to the *sthula*, *linga* and *karana shariras*, as well as *Akasha*, are needed in order to carry the discussion further. The main point in the concept of a morphogenetic field is that it indicates a continuous medium in which causation can work through archetypal forms.

Another central fact about the universe, revealing something fundamental concerning the geometrical form upon which it was constructed, is that it maintains an isotropic state. There is an isotropic uniformity with respect to the direction of arrival of radiant energy, and cosmic expansion as a whole takes place isotropically. No matter where a galaxy is found, its recessional velocity is related to distance by the same proportionality. This means that the universe is remarkably symmetrical, and it would seem from these observations that we happen to be at the very centre of it. But this is deceptive, as the same would be true if we were observing and measuring from the standpoint of any other galaxy. In such an expansion every point is its own centre and there is no preferred centre. One could say that our galaxy is indeed at the centre of the universe – but so is every other galaxy.

The form that best accommodates such an isotropic condition is a sphere whose centre and surface constantly shift according to the perspective taken. But as Pythagoras and Plato indicated, the point and the circle (including the three-dimensional sphere) cannot in and of themselves perform the work of manifestation. Lines of connection must enter the picture. In ancient cosmogenesis the labour must fall upon the fiery triangles and pentagons. That the dodecahedron with its pentagonal faces is the ideal form to express this can be shown in terms of a vast working of necessity which operates universally and lies at the basis of all manifestation and growth. The dodecahedron answers closely to the sphere and expresses the isotropic tendency which transcends ordinary experiences of time and space, but it also represents order and interconnected macrocosmic and microcosmic relationships capable of generation.

> The creation of the world is the combined work of necessity and mind. Mind, the ruling power, persuaded necessity to bring the greater part of created things to perfection, and thus after this manner in the beginning, through necessity made subject to reason, this universe was created.
>
> *Timaeus*, Plato

In the orderly development of forms, a criterion of spatial and structural economy involving the least expenditure of energy or movement to accomplish ends is always observed. If the universe is symmetrically constructed and its faces are indeed pentagonal, then they will be regular pentagons and the figure of the universe will necessarily be a dodecahedron. Put differently, the dodecahedron is the necessary representative or expansion of the pentagon in three-dimensional space. As a projection of the pentagon, Plato considered the dodecahedron to be the culmination of the hierarchy of five solids, alluding to a growth or development associated with the four elements plus *aether*. Thus the dodecahedron contains all the other elements, framing, as Timaeus described, "one visible animal comprehending within itself all other animals" while remaining more fiery than anything else. The ancient Kabbalists put it in terms of "the Dodecahedron [which] lies concealed in the perfect Cube", suggesting that the earthy body of the world contains within itself the archetypal cosmic design which reveals itself, however, only to the eyes of one who understands the mysterious process whereby the One becomes the many through divine geometry.

In the development of solid forms, the icosahedron precedes the dodecahedron and symbolizes the realm of the astral light. Thus, despite its fiery triangular faces, it is a form associated with water and carries within it the seed of the design yet to be born. In terms of the hierarchy of spirits, the icosahedron would correspond with the Rupa Angels who follow the Triads and represent the matrix of human consciousness, in which lies the germ that will fall into incarnation. Thus the Atma-Buddhi-Manasic prototype (of the Triads) passes into that subtle and watery pre-cosmic realm of anticipated form before manifesting as the fifth group of Dhyanis, the Pentagons or Kumaras who sacrifice themselves in the "fall" of spirit into a gathering density of matter. In the physicist's description of the shift from the "reign of light" to the "reign of matter", one can recognize an echo of this conversion. One can also illustrate it by describing a sphere around the icosahedron, from the centre of which perpendiculars are drawn through its faces to meet the surface of the sphere. If the points of these intersections are joined together, the pentagonal faces of the dodecahedron will be formed. Thus, points become lines and lines define the perimeters of the next level of geometrical complexity, leading ultimately once again back to the sphere, the circle and the point.

The pentagon is the shape of supreme sacrifice. This is symbolized by the fact that it is the only face of a regular solid having angles wider than a right angle. Its outspread arms at each corner seem to illustrate an open acceptance and willingness to accommodate. Its five sides answer to the Sanskrit *ma-karam*, the name of the twice five or tenth sign of the zodiac and an anagram for the sons of Rudra-Shiva, the Kumaras. The number five itself signifies this willingness to uplift matter by bringing the fiery triad of spirit to bear upon the duad of the Mother substance in the embodiment of the Manasic principle. As a figure, five is comprised of the two Greek accents over vowels which indicate whether they are aspirated or not. The higher, aspirated mark signifies the "strong spirit" of God, whereas the lower, unaspirated mark is that of the secondary "Spirit of Love" reflected in the world. Together these describe the five mystic vowels uttered by Brahma at creation and are expressed in the spiritual and terrestrial human compound.

Following the criterion of numerical and structural economy inherent in intelligent Nature, the logical elegance and beauty of the dodecahedron presents itself as a perfect expression of the twelve transformations of spirit into matter that are said to have taken place during the four great ages of the first *Maha Yuga*. Thus the three of spiritual fire and the four of the earth gave depth and breadth to that which is represented in the ten points of the Pythagorean decad. One can imagine the perfect economy of growth involved in this in terms of sphere-points describing the Platonic solids ultimately contained within the dodecahedron. Four equal spheres are the greatest number that can be in simultaneous contact. They represent the first regular pattern, which is the tetrahedron. Six equal spheres form the next regular pattern, with each sphere touching four neighbours in the cube, which is the "dual" of the octahedron. Twelve equal spheres may surround and touch, not one another, but a nucleus of equal size. When this occurs, the form contracts so that each sphere touches its five neighbours, completing a threefold transformation referred to as the "twelve degrees of freedom". The linear and turning movements required in this process thereby draw together the tetrahedron (fire), the octahedron (air), the icosahedron (water) and the cube (earth) into the dodecahedron containing all, plus the aether of the heavens.

This numerical and structural economy is further demonstrated by the golden ratio which presents itself diagonally on each of the pentagonal faces of this cosmic form. Within it the centroids of the twelve faces are divisible into three coplanar groups of four, which quadrads lie at the corners of three mutually perpendicular and symmetrically placed golden rectangles, their one common point being the centroid of the dodecahedron itself. This perfect structural economy results from a gnomic growth, from inside outward, as opposed to an agglutinative growth involving a simple addition from the outside of identical elements. It is a more basic, subtle, internal growth which begins on the unseen planes of the Cosmic Mind and slowly takes on the logically unfolded expression of fully manifested life. It is an ideational growth involving archetypal relationships that yield patterns capable of echoing the One in the many. The beauty of the dodecahedron swells in the mind with the growing understanding of this idea. It combines so perfectly the wholeness and oneness of the sphere (which is its constant reference point) with the great sacrificial presence of the Triads in the quaternary (represented in each of its pentagonal faces) that its form could easily become the focus of one's deepest reverence and gratitude.

In the dodecahedron one can see the outline of the unmanifested ideal, the manifesting cosmic ideal fathered by sacrifice, and the human microcosm capable of centering itself and focussing – like one of the twelve disciples – upon the central nucleus which isotropically informs the whole. Thus each human soul can fulfil the potential symbolized by the pentagon and become a Gate of Heaven through whose five-limbed vehicle the undimmed Light of the fiery Triads streams. Each can do this by taking the perspective of the whole made up of galactic centres everywhere, realizing that each true disciple of Krishna experiences himself or herself as one with the Lord at the centre of the universe. There can be no exclusivist element in this experience. Every pentagonal face worships and has its being in that centre, and each must come to know that in this centre lies its indivisible unity with all the other faces. Only thus is the macrocosm made manifest in the microcosm and the disciple made worthy of entering the perfect cosmic symmetry reflected in the twelve-gated city of the Lord.

> The cosmic dance is fiery,
> Yet it moves within a sphere;
> Pulsating with the drum of time
> Around the centre there.
> The radiant flames encircle
> The moon on Shiva's brow,
> And the mixtured glow intones
> The sacrificial vow.
> "I, Shiv, bring forth my sons,
> A youthful virgin race,
> That all creatures yet to be
> May come to see their face."
> And so saying, the Fiery Lord
> From point and sphere produced
> The Triads and the Pentagons,
> Their forms with light infused.
> Thus did the Cosmic Plan unfold
> In twelvefold symmetry,
> And thus did man obtain the form
> To match Divinity.

Hermes, August 1985

THE MIRROR

For mind is like a mirror; it gathers dust while it reflects. It needs the gentle breezes of Soul-wisdom to brush away the dust of our illusions. Seek, O Beginner, to blend thy Mind and Soul.

The Voice of the Silence

"Last night I had a very strange dream, perhaps a dream within a dream. I found myself, I know not how, gliding down a long hallway. Mirrors lined its walls – or were they windows? – I am not sure, but it scarcely seemed to matter, for the effect was one of myriad moonlit corridors ramifying out, each as inviting yet baffling as the next. As I turned towards any one of them, I confronted a surprising variation of my own reflected image, as though each stood at the entrance of a gallery belonging to a different life. And yet I easily recognized them as myself and was strangely moved to see them facing me, reflecting forgotten masks or even visages yet to be. One after another of these I passed, silently moving along the hallway towards a door at its end that stood partially open. Or was it a reflection of a door, for surely there was a figure approaching me from its moonlit portal and surely that figure resembled me. Was it a reflection of the door through which I had entered the hall? Or was the door through which I had entered merely a reflection of the one ahead? Even as this possibility crossed my dreaming mind I shuddered, for the more urgent question of whether I myself had entered the hallway in a reflected form presented itself. Or was the form in which I found myself indeed the original, whose reflection now approached so precisely in step and rhythm with the movement I was making towards it? Was the ' I ' that observed ail these forms, these corridors of mirrored vistas, aloof from all this coming and going, or was it too a reflection of something else?"

Seeming to have come to the end of his narrative, the speaker turned to examine its effect upon the face of his listener. While describing the dream, he had been gazing off intently in an abstracted way, almost oblivious to the presence of his comrade, but now he saw that the latter had listened well and followed him in his imagination along the haunting corridor of mirrors. The listener might have initially dismissed the dream, treating it like a sort of poetic funhouse excursion, where one is confronted with a series of distorted self images and rooms with mirrored walls leading nowhere, but the serious manner in which his friend had conveyed its details to him caused him to pause. Still, he tried to tease him into a lighter mood, reminding him of the mirrored stagecraft practised by trick artists and carnival hucksters with their ghostly apparitions and magic cabinets. He spoke of the time they saw the half-woman, whose normal upper body ended abruptly at a waist resting upon a table, under whose thin unembellished top one could plainly see only four simple table legs, the carpet and the drape at the back of the stage. It had taken them a considerable length of time to figure out how the trick had been done entirely with mirrors. But the light-hearted reminiscence did not succeed in diverting the dreamer, and so his friend launched into an earnest discussion about the use of *glaces à répétitions* in architecture, hoping thereby to engage his intellectual curiosity. Perhaps an academic consideration of the wonderful mirrored halls at Versailles or the Amalienburg Pavilion in Munich would coax his mind away from the somehow disturbing images of his strange dream.

Launching into an enthusiastic description of mirrors opposite mirrors, creating oblique views of windows and doors leading the eye out along foliaged parkways or into rooms with other mirrors, the listener sought to capture the imagination of the dreamer. He tried to drag him out of the shadow realm into what he fancied to be waking reality, like a director leading the audience out of a play which takes place within a play. But he made the mistake of speaking of architectural decoys and disguises and of rounding off his point with an allusion to ghosts that haunt the hallways of mirrors, while far in the distance a true reflection looms of something real which is very close at hand. As soon as the words escaped his lips, he saw the shadow of abstraction eclipse the dreamer's face and was forced to admit defeat. Narcissus-like, his friend had become once again absorbed in the mirror of his dream. Something fundamental concerning the problem of individual identity and levels of reality had been touched in him, and the listener perceived at last that either he would have to withdraw altogether or join his friend in a meandering and probing reflection upon the subject of mirrors.

> The mind, that ocean where each kind
> Does straight to its own resemblance find;
> Yet it creates transcending these,
> For other worlds and other seas,
> Annihilating all that's made
> To a green thought in a green shade.
>
> Andrew Marvell

The mirror is the symbol par excellence of consciousness, of thought as an instrument of self-contemplation. In the mirror is reflected the formal reality of the visible world from which the imagination soars to mirror yet loftier possibilities in itself. In the mirror appearances find their champion, reflections of discontinuities, changes and substitutions, everything that is ephemeral and of the world. It is a reminder that all images and forms are mere reflections, contrivances of thought, effects of karma. Nature herself is an apparition, deceiving and charming and filling one with dreams of longing for the things of the senses. The deceptions can be very subtle and need not be limited to such things as the magic box trick or the wiles of Nature. Plato pointed out how the Sophists, with their use of reason, created "semblances", like images in mirrors which duped people into deceptively false lines of reflected thought. For the mirror of the mind can be likened to the capacity to think, making it all important that one use noetic discrimination in selecting the ideas to be reflected upon. The mind reflects the ideas and images which are before it and which originate at many different levels within and without the individual, each level itself a reflection of something else. The dust gathered on the mirror of the mind dims the ability to discriminate and refracts further reflections that join the semblances and fragmented images gathered from outside, combining to create a collage of misleading impressions.

The physical mirror into which mankind routinely gazes is usually a shiny surface of flat glass with a metallic backing. The bright silvery backing is really the essence of the mirror, and the main function of the glass is simply to protect and stabilize it. Early mirrors did not possess this glass cover but were made of the highly polished metal itself, competing successfully in clarity of reflection with water mirrors. Beautiful hand-mirrors fashioned by the Etruscans were carved with the motifs of gods and goddesses and given as highly valued gifts at times marking major rites of passage. Metallic mirrors of ancient China were likewise coveted, their presumed ability to reflect the image of deities of all sorts causing them to be used in many magical practices as well as for toiletry. With the invention of Venetian glass, European mirrors became increasingly large. The simple mixture of sand, soda and lime was refined in a highly guarded secret process, enabling craftsmen to press large flat sheets upon mercury and silver backings. The Hall of Mirrors at Versailles was designed to accommodate three hundred such mirrors, setting a fashion which promoted the manufacturing of plate glass in 1687.

The stunning amplification of light and the opening up of reflected vistas by the use of mirrors led to remarkable architectural innovations which must have had a profound psychological effect upon people enjoying such surroundings. A whole language of mirrors came into being when individuals spoke to each other's image in mirrors and watched each other's as well as their own behaviour in reflecting panes, providing many simultaneous dimensions to every movement or gesture. The illusion of individuals meeting themselves walking into rooms, the déjà vu effect of things recapitulating themselves over and over again, of people coming when they are going, of walls seeming to be windows and doors – all this became part of a reflected reality accepted as normal and, somehow, real. Perhaps because Voltaire sensed the importance of this in terms of its effect upon the collective human experience, he considered the mirror (together with printing, the telescope, gunpowder and the compass) to be one of the truly great discoveries of mankind.

A regular or specific reflection such as one sees in a mirror requires a very smooth surface on which all irregularities have been rendered smaller than a wavelength of reflected light. The surface must be very bright in order to absorb as little and reflect as much light as possible. According to the laws of reflection, the incident ray from an object strikes the mirror and bounces off its surface at an equal angle in the opposite direction. Owing to the highly reflective nature of the surface, the reflected light-energy bouncing off it can be said to contain the same message as the incident ray. Nothing has been absorbed so as to "restructure" the energy flow, and the observer sees the image of the original in precise detail, right down to the necessary "reversal" that has taken place. The image of an object seen in a plane mirror is as far "behind" the mirror as the object is in front of it. This behind-the-mirror image or virtual image is actually at a vanishing point, existing only as a theoretical vertex of the reflection angle. Whilst the plane mirror gives an image that is the reversal of an object, two plane mirrors at right angles can eliminate this reversal. With two such mirrors set at a ninety-degree angle to one another, three images are seen; set at a sixty-degree angle, five images present themselves. One can see that, whether in terms of conjuring tricks, architectural illusions or semblances of the mind, the ramifying possibilities represented by the physical and symbolic mirror are infinite.

Yet within that plane, the illusion of infinity can be contained.

Pamela Heyne

What might be called mirroring power is in essence the ability to make things appear similar on or within something which is quite dissimilar. Thus the mirror is an excellent symbol for analogies and the evocative poetry of correspondences. In the face of a great astronomical mirror one sees the heavenly bodies captured, as it were, their enormous light-energy reflected upon a few inches of glass. Thus observatory telescopes, like that containing the seventeen-foot concave disc at Mount Palomar, are not lenses but reflecting paraboloids which can bring the far-travelled light-rays of outer space into a single focus. Despite this awesome capability, however, the mirror, with its silvery backing, is symbolically associated with the moon, which receives light and passively reflects it. Having no image of its own, its ability to reflect depends upon the presence of an object to be reflected. There is no selective process involved nor does it seem to possess a power in and of itself. And yet the moon does exert an independent influence upon the earth, which is far from passive, and one may wonder if this capability might also in some mysterious way be true of the mirror. One may question whether its proverbial reputation for revealing truth or exposing evil is based only upon some material sense of reflected revelation, the observed glint in the eye or shadow across the face.

The Japanese kagami (mirror of accusation) is said to reveal both truth and evil, but the fact that it is also believed capable of being entered into by a deity would suggest that what was revealed was something more than just a physical phenomenon reflected in a glass. More fundamental to the question of whether the mirror is in itself powerful is the assumption made by magicians and conjurors of widely diverse cultures that the mirror serves to invoke apparitions, reflecting images which it has received in the past. The Etruscans considered that once a mirror had held an individual's double, it would be imprudent to leave it lying around after his death, and so it was entombed in the sarcophagus with the remains.

The implications of such an idea are vast and potentially alarming. If one believed that every act that one had engaged in before a mirror, even unwittingly, was permanently contained in it and capable of being invoked by some conjuror, no doubt one would become extremely self-conscious of everything one did and very careful to act in a manner creditable to oneself. Though few individuals are haunted with this concern in the modern world, it was not long ago that most people turned mirrors to the wall or covered them up when someone had died so that the soul of the deceased would not be drawn to and linger within the mirror. They were concerned to assist in a clean separation between the immortal being and the vestures left behind, and they also feared that their own well being could be affected by a failure in this process. One may not care to believe that the mirror into which one gazes becomes permanently stamped with one's image or some aspect of one's inner being, but for the apprentice in spiritual alchemy the similarity between this and the great astral tablet of Nature is most striking. It might strike a thoughtful individual that the mirror, like the astral light, is not reflecting upon an image in an active or contemplative sense, but simply receiving it, containing it and reflecting it back. Thus mirrors "entered" by gods are reflecting surfaces off which a reflected aspect of that being can reveal itself, the projector of the image remaining invisible. But mirrors from which "stored" images are conjured "contain" the subtle impresses of innumerable "photo negatives" which are invisible to the physical eye but capable of being "developed" with the assistance of the magician.

> Oh Kitty, how nice it would be if we could only get through into the Looking Glass House! I'm sure it's got, oh! such beautiful things in it! Let's pretend there's a way of getting through into it, somehow, Kitty. Let's pretend the glass has got all soft like gauze, so we can get through.

> Lewis Carroll

Some have seen the mirror as a symbol of a door through which the soul may free itself by "passing" to the other side, whilst others have seen it as the gateway to the realm of inversion. The anticipated inversion can be accounted for much like the interpreters of dreams do when they say that left means right and black means white. The dream, like the mirror, is still important as a reflection of something which eludes the sense-oriented waking eye. Again, the mirror presents two aspects of itself: one leading through to another world, the other capturing and reflecting back. The ritual of interring mirrors with the dead as practised by the ancient Egyptians and Etruscans combines both of these ideas in a meaningful way, for they believed that the mirror could contain the soul and carry it to a new birth. Thus they thought that the mirror, during the life of an individual, could reflect the condition of the soul (exposing both truth and evil), and at death it could act as a sort of doorway through which the soul was liberated, while at the same time storing the impress of its residual elements. This idea easily lent itself to grosser interpretations and practices, but one can see in it a dim reflection of subtler metaphysical teachings regarding states of after-life and skandaic residues impressed on the timeless astral light,

Amidst quickly flashing mirrors and reflections, past, present and future collide and interpose themselves on one another. It is often said that time is the mirror of passing events, but it is also the progeny of the mirror of Nature itself. Thus Merlin, gazing into his mirror which reflected the whole world, could see into the past and future alike. A clairvoyant gazing into a mirror sees a smaller world, perhaps, but one which is still less grounded in sequential physical events and therefore capable of reflecting things that have happened in the past or are yet to be. Perhaps this is what the dreamer glimpsed when he saw visages of himself in different lives gazing at him along the mirrored hallway of his dream. He saw them out of the corner of his eye, as it were, which is how signs and visions in the astral might present themselves. His dream had that oblique or indirect quality as though afforded by the angled mirrors of the mind that permit, for a flashing instant, a penetrating glimpse of a reflected truth. He was left with an afterglow, a haunting and dreamlike sense of having come into incontrovertible confrontation with some great, potentially all-embracing, revelation about himself and the selves of others.

> God is the mirror in which thou seest thyself as thou art his mirror.
>
> Ibn Al-'Arabi

> The universe is the mirror of God. . . . Man is the mirror of the universe.
>
> Ibn Al-Nasafi

Like Plato and the great poet-mystics of the Islamic tradition, many have seen the world in terms of a series of reflections of the ideal. In our time Vladimir Nabokov has characterized this in terms of a sort of "thievery", wherein everything in the world had "captured" its nature by mirroring something which existed on a less phenomenal plane. One of his characters speaks of himself as "the shadow of the waxwing slain by the false azure of the window pane". He is like the persona regarding the reflection of the persona in the mirror and somewhere suspecting that the persona itself is but a reflection of something else. If God is a mirror, as the Islamic poet says, then who is man, the thinker, to say that he is more than a reflection? And yet man can reflect upon God as a mirror and thus see himself as the mirror of God. If the whole of manifest existence is a hierarchy of reflections which man is capable of reflecting upon, then he is like the dreamer who enters a vast hall of mirrors and gazes along them, trying to see what is at the end of the hall. It is this Platonic notion of hierarchical reflections which lays the basis for all sympathetic magic and lends such a penetrating force to thought based upon analogy and correspondence and the consideration of symbols. In these terms the whole cosmos could be considered as a composite Narcissus in the act of contemplating its own reflection, and man, the microcosm, as truly capable of reflecting deeply upon the cosmic re-enactment.

The dreamer reflects upon a dream wherein a reflection of reflected aspects of reality is mirrored. The wholeness of his multi-level existence is broken into refracted images and yet wholeness is somehow suggested, insofar as a sequence of superimposed pictures can reflect a whole which has no limit or beginning or end. The reflector reflecting upon the reflection of himself does so in coadunition with matter suitable to such a detached and liberated state. Thus such insights are experienced in dreams or in visions wherein the mind is freed from identification with the body and its senses. Even so, the reflector must beware of the flattering or distorting mirrors of many such states. For in trances and psychic dreams reflections may be magnified, reduced or fragmented by dust gathered on the mind's mirror, which itself may be tarnished, clouded or cracked. Perseus may have been protected from the curse of Medusa by gazing at her only in a mirror, but mirrors can be very tricky, and instead of removing the danger by one notch, they may actually deceive the observer and lead him into endless corridors of delusion. One has to be calmly assured that the mind is continually cleansed with "the gentle breezes of Soul-wisdom" so that one will know if the reflection one sees reflects a deeper truth or merely deceives. As in the case of the physical mirror, one must take care that all irregularities are removed and a very fine and smooth surface maintained in order to produce a clear, specific reflection.

> There is within
> A glass, they say, that has strange qualities in it;
> That shall resolve me. I will into see,
> Whether or no I man or monster be.
>
> Thomas Randolph

One may come to learn to what extent the outer body may reflect the soul within. An animal which sees its image in a mirror thinks that it is looking at another animal. Man, looking at his own image, knows that it is a reflection of himself but cannot necessarily tell if his reflection faithfully mirrors his inner condition. The experiments of John Dee showed that any evil intent would reveal itself in mirrors. Many human beings brush shoulders with evil daily and even look into its face but do not always sense that there is something amiss. It is not surprising then that many look into the mirror and fail to perceive the true inward condition of their incarnated soul. Socrates taught that it was an excellent practice to regard oneself regularly in a looking-glass in order to gain self-knowledge. Parents can often be startled by penetrating glimpses of their own inner nature when looking at the mirror of self represented by their children. Sometimes these revelations may happen in the most unexpected and fleeting ways. One may be walking down a busy street and suddenly catch one's own image amidst the crowd as it is reflected in a shop mirror. This can be a strangely moving experience, jolting one into seeing one's own form as merely typical of the human condition: one small human being cast by karma into the vast sea of humanity at a particular time and place. One thus experiences afresh a vividly distinctive glimpse of the collective psychological effect wrought by mirrors.

> Ill read enough,
> When I do see the very book indeed
> Where all my sins are writ, and that's myself.
> Give me the glass, and therein will I read.
>
> William Shakespeare

Unlike Richard II, who was dismayed to find that he could not discover a congruence between his inner and outer condition, one can gradually learn to identify clues revealed by one's eyes reflected back in a mirror. Eyes which are said to be the windows of the soul are also its mirrors. Just as people contemplate themselves reflected in the mirror of another's eyes, so the individual seeks to find what lies behind the reflected light by considering the mirror image of these mirrors. If this is done each day, one may come to notice subtle changes in the quality of light emitted by the eyes as well as in the colour and clarity of focus. Checking this with one's state of thoughts, emotional and physical condition and the quality of meditative efforts will slowly reveal a portrait of an inner condition. Just as another's folly can act as a mirroring of one's own, so too one's own reflected stance, one's image caught unawares or the eyes studied over a period of time can teach volumes about one's condition and what one should do to modify it.

All too often individuals act from the basis of a grossly limiting idea of Nature and the Self. On such a basis they conclude that they are great, good, bad, happy, miserable, beautiful, etc. The truth is that they are actually none of these but simply involved in combinations of qualities that take on certain appearances. These appearances involve the effects of the three gunas impressed variously upon elementals, which then become living mirrors in which man views and experiences himself on levels below the plane of the fourth principle. Peering into the mirror of the tamasic world, an individual perceives an image of himself which is dark and sluggish. That of the rajasic realm reflects back myriad desires and urges to action which he will assuredly identify as springing from the innermost core of his being. So native to his inner self will these urgent desires seem that he will deem it unnatural and soul-killing to deny their fulfilment. So also, upon gazing into the mirror of sattvic elementals, ordinary men or women will see themselves as happy, content and blissfully wise. They will be filled with a glowing satisfaction with themselves and with things as they are, until the wind shifts and the tamasic or rajasic mirror rises uppermost into view. As has rightly been pointed out, "the ordinary man is so negative and passive in his attitude that the mere vicissitudes of circumstances, or the praise and blame of others, is sufficient to change his polarity in relation to any given state and totally alter his idea of self".

To overcome this slavish condition, one needs to develop the positive mirroring power which exists within the mind. In the development of an inner dialectic process, one can sift through experiences and thoughts, the thesis reflected in one mirror, re-reflected as antithesis in another, and transcended as synthesis at a higher level of self-reflection. A Master of Wisdom once said that one has to acquire *Paramartha* – true Self-consciousness – if one is to understand the origin of delusion. *Paramartha* is *Svasamvedana*, "the reflection which analyzes itself. In the *Stanzas of Dzyan*, the pre-manifest state when the *Alaya* of the universe was in *Paramartha* is spoken of. *Paramartha* is enigmatically described as Absolute Being and Consciousness, which are Absolute Non-Being and Unconsciousness. But if one examines the etymology of the term (*parama* meaning "above everything" and *artha* meaning "comprehension"), together with the meaning of its synonym, Svasamvedana, one can begin to perceive the outlines of an archetypal mirroring process. *Alaya* which was "in *Paramartha*" is the "Soul of the World". It is identical with *Akasha* in its mystical sense and with *Mulaprakriti* in its essence. Eternal and changeless in its pre-manifested essence, Alaya alters during manifestation with respect to the lower planes, where it reflects itself in every object of Nature. Thus it is not Nirvana but the condition nearest to it. It is both the universal Soul and the Self of a progressed Adept. According to the Yogacharya school, *Paramartha* is reflective and therefore dependent upon that which is noumenal to it. It is not *Parinishpanna*, which is emptiness, but that which reflects and analyses its own reflection. *Parinishpanna* without *Paramartha* is described as extinction for seven eternities, implying that *Paramartha* is the first expression of the self-conscious potential, the glimmering reflection of the mirror of mind at the dawn of manifestation. Alaya is merely the *upadhi* of this self-analysing capability, the lofty universally present Soul which will contain the flashing spark of the reflected light of pure Spirit.

The journey of one who would reach the threshold of spiritual self-knowledge may begin with a dream of mirrored hallways. In waking life such an aspirant can gradually come to see every experience as a mirror in which something critical about his own inner nature is reflected. Slowly he can establish a distance between himself as a spectator and the reflected aspects of his thinking processes, his personality and other outward expressions. Wisely he comes to understand that the great astral tablet of Nature has surrounded him continually along his journey with its reflections of impressed photo negatives, and he has learnt to discriminate between them and the reflections of the highest truth which analyses only itself. Knowing that the mirror of his mind must be blended with the soul of Truth, he ever keeps before his gaze the loftiest reflected idea of the Master within. Walking down the hallway of mirrors, gathering oblique glimpses of his history as a soul and of his future potential, the aspirant approaches the image walking towards him which is himself. Not by any external characteristic does he know this, nor by likeness to his own form, but by a recognition of the Master who has guided him in secret and who now reaches out to him and merges with his own Higher Self. The concave mirror of his own heart focusses clearly the dazzling light of that solar Serf and he becomes a perfect mediator of Divine Will, his mind and heart reflecting the cosmic harmony of its design.

> Amidst flashing glass
> The soul is glimpsed,
> And mirrors its
> Discovered Joy.

Hermes, October 1985

THE DRUM

O my Lord, Thy hand holding the sacred drum has made and ordered the heavens and earth and other worlds and innumerable souls. Thy lifted hand protects both the conscious and unconscious order of Thy creation.

Chidambara Mummani Kovai

In the emerald forest which has known little change since the beginning of the world, a traveller, wishing to penetrate the leafen veil of the past, sat in a dug-out canoe. On jaguar skins he sat, together with the chief, while two native men operated the paddles. In another canoe men armed with bows and blow-guns sat together with a drummer, who awaited an order that would engage his critical skills. Two upright forked sticks rose from either side of the canoe in front of him, near the centre where he sat. From these sticks a frame was secured, angling towards him and fixed to a horizontal bar which crossed the width of the canoe bottom at his feet. Across this frame were lashed four vertical pieces of capipari wood of varying thickness, each hollowed out with a longitudinal slit and decorated with finely carved designs. The traveller noticed the chief give a signal, and the drummer, seizing skin-covered mallets in both hands, commenced to beat out a complex rhythm of four notes on the drum slats. The sound was awesome and the still forest around the small party resounded with its echo. He repeated the message several times, but receiving no answer from upstream, the canoes advanced another mile before stopping to try again.

Very faintly came a reply from some invisible source. The traveller leaned forward eagerly from his jaguar seat. He knew that the village towards which they were headed was at least five miles upstream, and he was deeply anxious to catch the gist of the message conveyed by the distant rumbling of the rhythmic beats. The message that had been sent by the drummer in the canoe was: "A white man is coming with us; he seems to have a good heart and to be of good character."

216

The answer that came back along the waters of the river and through the darkly overgrown jungle was: "You are all welcome provided you place your arms in the bottom of the canoe." With this, the small party paddled briskly ahead, and at the end of an hour's work, made a sharp turn in the river. Before them in a large open space on the opposite bank, perhaps five hundred Indians had assembled to await their first glimpse of the fabled and feared "white" man. Their chief, a large man adorned with squirrel tails around his waist and the brilliant scarlet and blue feathers of the arara parrot upon his handsome head, stood in front with folded arms. The traveller sat in stunned silence while the canoes glided towards the bank and were secured at its edge. The two chiefs greeted one another and a dozen brown arms reached out to assist the pale khaki-garbed visitor. As his feet touched the soil of the shore, the first thunderous rolls of the drum, whose muted pulse they had heard at a distance five miles downstream, formally announced their arrival. Looking over the sea of faces confronting him to the source of the sound, the traveller saw a powerfully armed drummer absorbed in complete concentration as he beat his unerring mallets against an enormous tree drum resting on a raised platform at the edge of the village clearing.

If the traveller could possibly have possessed any doubt as to whether he had lifted the leafy veil of the past, it was engulfed by the enormity of sound that emanated from the drum. Like others who had dared to attempt to penetrate the primordial, he was confronted with its power in the form of omnipresent and insistent sound. Contained for a moment within the shape of the instrument, it seemed to have emanated from everywhere and nowhere. It seemed as though it had always been and was now merely bursting forth in a fresh wave of expression. The drum is the archetypal symbol for this sound, no more eloquently depicted than in the hour-glass drum which Lord Shiva holds aloft in his right hand whilst dancing at the centre of the world. Buddhists look upon the drum as sounding the Voice of the Law and hearken to the Drum of Dharma, whose beating awakens the ignorant and slothful. Primordial sound exists as a timeless potential in such drums and need not necessarily be confined to the archives of modern iconography or the untrammelled and "primitive" reaches of a lost world. The resplendent intonation of creation might be heard in the cultured environs of a native village just as surely as in the barbaric night clubs of modern cities or in the temple sanctuaries of dying religious faiths. One cannot be certain where in the world or under what conditions one might hear its haunting voice.

> We treat the Drum as a person. That's the way we Menominee were taught by the Ojibwa. . . . They even make special beds for the Drum. Keep it as a person. We Indians do that for the sake of God; appreciate, take care of that Drum well, because that's His power. That's why we decorate the Drum, make it look pretty, clean, because it's from God.

The Plains and Woodland Indians revered their drums and took great care of those which they believed to contain the Voice of the Great Spirit. Drums with thunderbirds depicted upon them were treated as sacred communicators of His word, and various ceremonial drums received enormous respect during their use as well as when they were resting or being transported. Among many tribes the Grass Dance drum was treated as a representation of the world. Members who surrounded it and played it during a ceremony were thought to be "standing in" for spirits that hover around and guard the earth. The old legends tell that it was first given by the Great Spirit to a Mdewakanton Dakota from the "mystic lake" area called Tailfeather Woman. Because such a lake does not exist in the physical world, people think that it must have been the place of a great spiritual vision through which the drum emerged into the world. Tailfeather Woman's revelation taught that the drum was to be passed on from tribe to tribe in accordance with the will of the Great Spirit. It was to travel clockwise and to be kept no longer than four years at each tribal gathering place, during which time the Drum Dance ritual was to be learnt and a replica drum constructed. Thus, the drum passed to the Mandan, the Hidatsa, the Ojibwa, the Menominee, the Fox, Potawatomi and Shawnee, among others. In every case, peace was established and the circle of brotherhood affirmed. Even today Drum Dance members believe they are "sitting in" for the various spirit helpers of the Great Spirit, a belief which causes them to enact their roles with great seriousness. Their leader watches the ritual and corrects it on behalf of the holy drum, whilst the leading female dancer re-enacts the vision received by Tailfeather Woman when the Great Spirit drew her forth out of her hiding place in the lake.

Shaped on a wooden barrel, the frame of the drum is covered with a skirt decorated with dream symbols received in visions. Being a representation of the world, it is feminine, but women are forbidden to touch it at any stage of its construction. When played, it is only by men, who place the legs at the four cardinal points like the pillars often depicted holding up the universe in Buddhist traditions. As in the cultures of Africa, Oceania and Asia, the wood used for the drum is that of a sacred tree, a "world tree", whose trunk conducts the sap of life from the unseen to the visible world. Beating upon the skin which once covered the heart of a consecrated animal, the native drummers begin the slow, dignified pulse-beat which marks the antique throbbing of the Great Spirit within and upon the fertile sphere of His own making. Thus, it is believed, the Mother Earth will sympathetically bring forth life, and the women of the tribe, like Tailfeather Woman before them, assist in its birth and propagation but not in its design.

> O my Lord, Thy hand holding the sacred drum has made and ordered the heavens and earth and other worlds and innumerable souls.
>
> *Chidambara Mummani Kovai*

Looking at the evidence presented by the ancient Indus Valley script, scholars have noticed that the origins of the great god Shiva can be found in the guise of a pre-Aryan shamanistic ascetic. This is in accord with the rich ideas associated with the Maha Yogin who acts as the supreme mediator between heaven and earth. Shamans of all levels and degrees of knowledge echo this function in their attempts to act as mediators between human beings and the invisible realm. Using the drum as a means of translating their own power into rhythm and sound capable of summoning supporting spirits, shamans go into a trance state and are transported to the spirit world. Drummers smeared with specially prepared paste are thought to be able to drum diseases down-river, away from those they are afflicting, and medicine men try to call forth "allies" capable of diagnosing the cause of illness or guiding them to medicinal herbs.

O Great Ones of the Sky World,
Hear my drum!
Lend me thy vision
That I may bring harmony.
Hear me! O my chiefs.

Potawatomi Chant

In the *damaru* (drum) of Shiva one can perceive the interlacing triangles of the two worlds between which the Great Lord acts as the archetypal bridge. The downward-pointing triangle represents the watery realm of the *yoni*, the upward-pointing triangle the *lingam*. Where they overlap at the centre, creation begins, and when they separate, dissolution commences. With their coming together in the hour-glass-shaped drum, the primordial causal sound (*nada*) comes into being, inspiring the epithets bestowed upon Shiva in his Nataraja aspect such as *Da* (meaning, simply, "sound") and *Nadatanu* ("consisting of sound"). From this sound comes the Word which is the Law, the pulse-beat of the hidden spiritual heart of the cosmos from which all forms of life derive their vitality. From this voice made melodious by the substance principle of the manifesting world (drum), all speech finds its source and all communication its energy. It is because they have glimpsed something of the implications of this that so many people have cherished the drum as sacred and surrounded it with great ceremony and celebration. For in its voice lies the vibratory timbre and potential rhythm which is the basis of all magic and spiritual transformation.

I already dwell in thee, O, my world,
Thy dream of me – 'twas I coming into existence.

Alexander Scriabin

Having a voice, drums can talk. The whole world has heard of African "talking" drums. And yet most people, if one asked them, would venture an assumption that this "talking" was really communication by some sort of Morse code. "Not so!" say those who know. Tympanophony observes the precise pitches and tones of syllables existing in a given language. As the famous H. M. Stanley noted while passing through the drum language area along the Congo, "Their huge drums being struck in different parts convey language as clear to the initiated as vocal speech." Another early visitor to the Congo described how the particulars concerning the wreck of a mail steamer seventy miles away from the mouth of the river were communicated by relay drums within an hour's time. He claimed that "a good operator with his drum sticks can say anything he likes upon the drum in his dialect. .. . The drum language, so called, is not limited to a few sentences but, given a good operator, and a good listener, comprehends all a man can say." The linguistic elements capable of conveying the morphological properties of such tongues are: accent on a particular syllable, stress or emphasis on a particular word in a phrase, pauses, stops, punctuation, duration of phrases and speed of utterance. In most African languages syllables maintain a fixed tone wherever they arise in a phrase. Thus a listener in the Kele language can distinguish the difference between *lisaka* (a marsh), *lisaká* (a promise) and *lisáká* (a poison), as well as, one would hope, between *liála* (fiancee) and *liala* (rubbish pit). So also the Lya Ilu (Mother of Drums) of the Yoruba, which has an octave range and can produce the glides so characteristic of their language, beautifully intones the subtle distinctions between *oko* (husband), *okó* (hoe), *oko* (spear) and *óko* (canoe) in the hands of an able drummer.

Many of these talking drums are similar to the Lakele slit drum design. They are fashioned from large camwood trees which are ritually cut, sectioned and hewn out through a long slot left on the side to be played. One side of the lips of this slot is rendered thinner than the other, producing a deeper, male voice. The thicker side produces the female voice, which is higher and often called "small". The Ashanti, however, use skin-covered, barrel-like drums for the purpose of talking. One high note and one low note drum are used in pairs and partially suspended from a frame so that they sit upright at a slight angle, awaiting the impact of elegant adze-shaped sticks held in the hands of one who has inherited the privilege and skill necessary to bring them to life. For they are living beings, these drums, and great care is taken not to desecrate them in any way or fail to observe proper ritual in their use.

If the traveller who visited the emerald forest of the Amazon had been paddling up a coastal river of one of the isles of the New Hebrides instead, he would have been startled to see great ten-foot-tall slit drums set up in "groves" outside each village that he visited. Like ghostly giant sentinels they stand, each having a mournful face etched upon it, each linked with a dead ancestor and capable of being brought to life in a thundering orchestra of atavistic power during important religious ceremonies and sacrifices. Some, weighing well over eight hundred pounds, lean in huddled gatherings as though they possess certain affinities for one another. Others stand in a dignified solitude, slightly to the side, scowling down at anyone who would be so foolish as to go there without having proper business. To communicate between closer islands in the South Seas, the Lali, or slit drum which lies on its side, is used. These are not talking drums but part of a telegraph system which best communicates in the early morning or late evening when the air currents are settled, their sound being carried over water considerably further than over land. The messages they convey are not dissimilar in essence from those one might hear along the Amazon or the Congo. They announce a trading expedition, perhaps, or send out a warning, one of the most common being that related to war. One only need recall the war drums of North America or the drummer boys enlisted by military forces going back to the time of Xenophon to realize how frequently the drum has been associated with war. The ancestral drums of the Hebrides, the Grass Dance drums, the talking drums – all these that are imbued with spirit and kept for other purposes have heard and been witness to the aggressive beat upon war drums. Even the Vedic hymn to the sacred drum of Indra uses the language of war:

> Send forth thy voice aloud through earth and heaven, and let the world in all its breadth regard thee;
>
> O Drum, accordant with the Gods and Indra, drive thou afar, yea, very far, our foeman.
>
> Thunder out strength and fill us full of vigour: yea, thunder forth and drive away all dangers.

Drive hence, O War-drum, drive away misfortune: thou art the
Fist of Indra: show thy firmness.

Drive hither those, and these again bring hither: the War-drum
speaks aloud as the battle's signal..

Rig Veda XLVII, 29–31

Europe had been largely bereft of drums until the thirteenth
century, when the Arabian kettledrum was brought back from the
Crusades. It was not long before it became an instrument used to
announce weddings and festivals and, more often than not, the alarms
of war. The military importance of the drum became so marked that if
the enemy's kettledrum was captured, the battle was considered won,
for there no longer existed the means of signalling the troops. The
reply to the entreaty of a captured drummer who begged for his life
on the ground that he carried no weapon conveys the critical role the
drum had come to play in war. For he was told that, though he did not
carry a weapon, his drumming had enabled scores of his fellows to
use theirs with deadly effect, and for this he must forfeit his life. Even
the word "drum" is connected with military life through the office of
what came to be known in the sixteenth century as the drum major.
The origin of the term seems to come from the Old German (*trom,
drom*), which was closely connected with the word slag, meaning "to
beat or strike". In the English army this relationship between "drum"
and "beat" took on a more concrete expression, for the drum major
was not only responsible for the drummers and their maintenance of
the drums, but had to superintend the flogging of soldiers and courts
martial which were held at the drumhead. The sound of the beating
upon the skin of the drum, synchronized with the terrible thud of
the whip across the skin on the back of some poor conscriptee of the
Crown, was a harsh use of the drum's voice, a terrible expression of
the law it symbolized.

The idea of primordial sound and its manifestation through
universal Law found a strange and almost unrecognizable parody in
such practices. Though few would associate it primarily with corporeal
discipline, for many in the world the drum became firmly linked in
their minds with uniforms, marching and aggressive displays of

ethnic or national assertiveness. One may wonder if the compelling beating of enormous parade drums pounded along the pavements of Pasadena contain anything of the power and cadence of universal Law. Is this what makes the hair on one's neck stand on end when one hears it? Is there something sacred in that booming sound, even on the streets of California? Among the Ashanti the question would not arise, for there are clear rules as to what is a secular context and what is a sacred context and when indeed it is appropriate to awaken the spirit of the drum. It is well known that a husband does not talk of his wife on the drums at his home (one can imagine the relief!). But it is quite appropriate that he praise her on the drum in the dance arena. A drummer of the talking drums cannot criticize his chief, but while drumming he is the Creator Drummer or the Divine Drummer and can say what he likes, being protected by the Sacred Person's Law. Every Ashanti knows of these ancient edicts and responds accordingly. They know that the drum of a god or a chief cannot be used to announce the affairs of commoners and that the formal drum language of a collective ceremony has four parts, beginning with the Awakening and ending with the Proverbs of the Drum.

Sacred drums are often painted for the purpose of divination as well as evocation. In Lapp mythology constant references to magic drum oracles describe large disc-shaped drums with figures of gods and denizens of the underworld painted on the skins. Shamans, placing a brass ring on the skin as they drummed, routinely succeeded in inducing a trance, during which they would travel to the spirit or god upon whom the ring had settled. It is perhaps in this sense more than any other that the drum is connected with religious ritual. Supplication, evocation and divination are all aspects of religious practice, often accompanied by drumming, but it is the ecstatic experience of the shaman, dervish, voodoo cultist or Ghost Dancer which is directly affected by the drum. The key to trance and ecstasy is forged in great part by the steady rhythm of some kind of drum, and in this fact lies one of the most powerful aspects of the drum as a symbol of primordial sound.

In the night of Brahmā, Nature is inert, and cannot dance until Shiva wills it: He rises from His rapture, and dancing sends through inert matter pulsing waves of awakening sound, and lo! matter also dances appearing as a glory round Him.

Ananda K. Coomaraswamy

The drum held aloft in Lord Shiva's hand at Chidambaram marks the first beat of the cosmic heart. "Thy dream of me –'twas I coming into existence", I, the pure sound of the antique heart setting the rhythm, the very unfolding cadence of the world to be. Through His *damaru*, the rhythmic pulsation of life thus begins, and as he dances to its beat, it is sustained. In His form of Nataraja, Shiva holds creation, destruction, hope and release. The world goes on like the unending beat of time, but the ecstatic release of rhythm is always potentially there. While it is Shiva's foot held aloft that gives release, it is the pause that precisely provides the essential element producing rhythm. If the rhythmic dance of the Lord is the source of all motion, then motion itself is some sort of mighty cosmic pulsation perpetuating itself throughout a *Mahamanvantara*. Against this background, it is easy to see why human beings find release in rhythm, why they drum and whirl themselves into trances and rock themselves into mental oblivion. For vast masses of humanity, the only release from the oppression of materialized minds is through abandonment to some sort of hypnotic recurring rhythm.

If a man does not keep pace with his companions, perhaps it is because he hears a different drummer. Let him step to the music which he hears, however measured or far away.

Henry David Thoreau

Some rhythms, beaten out loudly and indefatigably, can release powerful floods of joy, passion or anger. The gates to unexamined primordial desires are opened, and the body begins to twitch in its unconscious efforts to express what is welling up in the astral nature. The passions and desires registered in the broader astral world can be thus focalized in an orgiastic dance circling around drummers hunched over their instruments. Or the steady beat may be more like that envisioned by Thoreau, who tried to live his life according to the deeper rhythmic pulsation he sensed in natural cycles and within the longings of his own soul. The beat which one hearkens to may be quite complicated; there are those who effortlessly operate in a polyrhythmic mode. In a collective context, an outstanding example of this expresses itself in African drumming, where two or even five rhythmic patterns are played simultaneously and synthesized by a fundamental underlying beat. As long as all patterns coincide on the first beat of the fundamental cycle as it repeats, the whole intricate system expresses overall harmony.

Probably the most complicated and difficult to master of all rhythmic systems is that produced on the Indian *tabla* or *mridangam*. Whilst the *mridangam* is a two-headed drum played with electric rapidity and complexity of rhythm in accompaniment to the traditional Carnatic music of South India, the *tabla* is actually a pair of drums played side by side with the right and left hands. Called respectively the *daina* and the *banya*, they both have dark "eyes" in their centre which produce a dampening effect. Different areas of their surface have different sounds, yielding a combination of at least five fundamental tones which can be struck with different parts of the ball of the hand and the fingers. The strokes of the right and left hands are all defined and named, and the combinations and variations of these are unlimited in scope. It is small wonder that even rhythmically gifted individuals spend long years in order to master many but not all of its possibilities. Without attempting to go into the whole theory of rhythm in Indian music, one can appreciate something of its mathematical potential by listening to certain *ragas* which seem to depict the gradual descent of spirit into matter at the dawn of cosmic manifestation. The great process percolates through the highest levels of inaudible sound, wherein dwells the loftiest and subtlest pulse-beat of the invisible spiritual heart. As the entire unfoldment rushes downward towards the waiting stage of the manifest world, the drum begins its staccato marking of event and sequence in time. Gathering strength and power, the drum ushers in wave upon wave of energies, gods and elemental beings. Buffeted and marshalled by the drum's insistent pace, they rush about and interrelate in what comes to be seen as a whole, delicately interconnected design.

As with African polyrhythmic patterns, the *talas* (distinctive groupings of fixed numbers of beats) act as the fundamental patterns with which all rhythmical variations must coincide to sustain this wholeness. They act as a basis, a ground against which the intervals of the *sruti* and the sequence of notes of the *svaras* define themselves and express their meaning. Back and forth, back and forth, the masculine and feminine heads of the *mridangam* as well as the *tabla* "speak" to one another, roll forth their fecund beat in intertwined sequences as the basis for each new stage of evolution reveals itself. If one imagines this great process in terms of Shiva's *damaru*, the male and female drumheads can be seen as the bases of two triangles barely touching at their apexes. Softly, the inaudible drumming on each of them moves them into slightly overlapping conjunction with one another, which increases as the beat becomes stronger and the process of manifestation unfolds. At the meeting point between them, creation begins, and as they overlap to form the hour-glass, time comes into existence with the still point of eternity captured in the exact centre of the diamond-shaped area of their interpenetration. No more perfect expression of the essential energy that lies behind all phenomena exists than in the sublime form of Shiva Nataraja. Those who envisioned it millennia ago must have soared onto the highest Akashic heights at the centre of the cosmos, wherein its ideal form resides. No earthly condition or experience could suffice to explain its transcendent truth and beauty. Time and Eternity are reconciled in every line and epitomized in the alternating phases suggested by the *damaru* in Shiva's hand. Extending out over vast reaches of space, its pulsating rhythm sets the key pattern of arcane mathematics in a primordial and universal *tala*.

Gathered around the sublime *Maha Yogin*, who appears in the guise of enlightened Sages and great Teachers in the world, the fortunate ones perceive within their hearts an echo of that fundamental beat. It is not just that they would try to become drums upon which this rhythm is struck, but rather that they can seize the opportunity to discover their own unique rhythm and learn how to bring it to its fullest expression while synchronizing it with the universal *tala* manifested through their Guru. Through meditation one can come gradually closer to understanding the nature of this archetypal rhythm, how its cycles repeat and what sorts of complex combinations of pauses, sequences, emphases, phrasings and flurries are involved. One can come to glimpse something of the pattern, but one cannot nor should one try to imitate it. For it is a unique reflection in the world of that design in sound that establishes the perimeters and possibilities for a particular phase in soul evolution. Its inspiration conies from the still point at Chidambaram and pours like a flood of notes drummed in rapid succession through the hands and fingers of the Teacher.

Those who are intuitive may sense in this the language of the constellations, the stars and planets brought into a rhythmic code for the sake of anyone who desires with all their heart to bring their own unique rhythm into synchronization with it. Thus, just as the heart beat of every human being is characteristic of his or her vast journey as a soul, so too the complexities of that journey find a unique metabolic expression in the rhythm which is native to them. In each of these rhythmic patterns there is the truth of sound and the truth of the pause or still point which interrupts it and breaks it up into a pattern. By meditating upon the purest tone, the tonic note which expresses the timbre of one's true individuality, and upon the still, silent points wherein one's highest spiritual potential rests in anticipation, intuitive seekers can recognize and bring into play the finest fruits of soul evolution which they have to offer. If this is truly done and the rhythm they rediscover in themselves is unadulterated with unwonted glides and slurs or asymmetrical accretions, it will certainly synchronize with the beat at each beginning of the fundamental rhythmic cycle of the great Teacher of the age.

In this subtle sense, each human being is like the drum of the world which can be played with their own hands to produce their own unique expression of primordial sound. But there is one cosmic rhythm, one inaudible pattern, which beats behind all these and which gives them all their reflected validity and power. Those who hear the beat of this distant and silent drumming at any point in human history are few, and those who have the wit and intuition to recognize who they are, are fortunate indeed to have found them. Such rare beings move in unexpected places in the world. Just as the sounding of the primordial note of creation might be heard at any time or place, so also the Great

Teachers of Mankind, whose rhythmic thoughts continually refer to that unchanging keynote, may be found where least anticipated. Wherever such a one may be, disguised in the trappings of the modern world or seated on a jaguar skin before the barrel of a sacred drum, the beat which decides the metrical movement of their life will be silent. One might imagine oneself toiling long and hard through the jungle of life and finally breaking out into a clearing. There one may encounter a solitary drummer seated in stillness with his sticks in his hands. In front of him rests a great drum. It is difficult to know whether it is a talking drum, a telegraph drum or a war drum, for it has all the characteristics belonging to these types and yet seems limited by none of their specialized functions. One could imagine that drum representing the world and being passed clockwise as an emblem of peace. One could also imagine it coming alive and calling down the gods in heaven or the elemental beings hovering around the world. But the drum in the clearing rests silently, and the Master Drummer makes no move to strike it.

One might then sit at the edge of the clearing, waiting and watching, with one's ears straining to catch a sound. The Drummer makes no move, the drum's skin does not vibrate, and yet, slowly, one begins to hear a light but penetrating pulsation which fills the clearing and dances through the trees and vines around. Subtle accents and pauses reverberate in complex cycles, coming in waves across the clearing and doubling back in polyrhythmic designs. Soon others appear at the edge of the jungle, breaking free of the trees, at first not hearing the rhythm but drawn towards the form of the Silent Drummer. Many begin to arrive, struggling through to the clearing, each bringing with them their own small drum. They all look and strain their ears and settle down, at last, to wait and understand. Some of them begin to hear the dancing rhythm of the Silent Drummer, some do not. Others begin to take up their drums and express their own tempos, beating with their hands or sticks in a cacophony of varied rhythms. The silence and the waiting have made them restless and they do not know how to harmonize their beats. Some who have heard the silent rhythm take up their drums and try to imitate its cadence, stopping and starting and attempting to move their arms and hands in a way that they think will produce the rippling cadence that they hear. But they lag and strike false notes and fail to pause in the right places. They end up contributing to the cacophony of disharmonious rhythms filling the clearing.

Wise seekers who have toiled long and hard to arrive at the feet of a true spiritual Teacher will intuitively realize that they cannot imitate the cosmic rhythm as it pours through their being. They will remain silent and listen until they understand the fundamental underlying message of his beat and grasp something of the pattern of its repetition. Then they will strive to bring their own drum into tune and use the tonic note, the initial beat of the master pattern, as the unchanging reference point for their own rhythm. Time after time they will cycle through their own pattern of beats, but they will never fail to bring it continually back into synchronization with the great *tala* given forth by the Teacher. Thus in polyrhythmic textures, greater numbers of drummers can come together and express a beauteous and harmonious correlation of the parts of one whole. Gathered together around the silent, still and yet thunderously dancing form of Lord Shiva as Nataraja, as Nadatanu and as their embodied Guru in the world, such privileged ones can come to reverberate, in every aspect of their being, with the pulsating rhythmic will of the great cosmic heart.

> On the pure white head
>   of my dancing drum,
> O let me find thy
> Divine Beat!

Hermes, November 1985

THE LYRE

Number, fitting all things into the soul through sense-perception,
makes them recognizable and comparable with one another. . . . You
may see the nature of Number and its power at work not only in
supernatural and divine existences but also in all human activities
and words everywhere, both throughout all technical production and
also in music.

Philolaus of Tarentum

Their paths converging at the entrance to a gently sloping ravine, two men together began the descent to the undulating plain below. Their strides were steady and they moved abreast and behind one another as the rocky terrain would allow. There seemed to be an urgency in their steps answering to something which drew them forward, which even now could be heard floating up the sides of the hills. "Friend," the elder addressed the younger, "my soul's own melody bids my feet to fly into its presence, and I can see by the rapture stamped upon thy face that thou art likewise called." "Yes," answered the other, "I too hear this divine strain. Its first notes reached my ears up yonder in the olive grove, erasing from my mind all thoughts of why I was there and filling me with the desire to find its sweet source." The older man noted the youth's intent expression with sympathy and urged that they should press on until they located the fount from which such celestial song had sprung. "It is not many who hear the music of the spheres, whose ears are thus blest and whose hearts are filled with the promise of encountering a divine presence. Let us hurry to what must be a veritable god of melody that we may resonate more closely with the strings of his heavenly lyre."

The two men emerged from the ravine onto a curving meadow festooned with a line of aged oak trees and became witnesses of an extraordinary scene. Upon a granite outcrop surrounded by a sea of waving grass sat a man so beautiful of mien and so gracefully postured that in his shape the sculptured lines of Nature's growth seemed to exult. Cradled in his perfectly formed arms, a lyre bowed and scintillated as he lightly strummed its silver strings. His voice rose with sweetly mournful power, perfectly tuned to the instrument's pristine tones and cadence. It filled the dancing meadow and coaxed the very trees into swaying and dipping their ancient boughs in empathetic rhythm. The men stood rooted to the spot at the edge of the meadow where they had paused, their souls suffused with the divine melody. That they were in the presence of Orpheus, son of Apollo, they knew, for no other being, god or mortal, could wield such musical magic as that which they saw enacted before them. So poignantly vibrated the strains of his melody, and his face seemed to register all the wild beauty of love barely shadowed by its not quite apprehended loss, that the older and more learned of the two men marked this near-tragic expression and was moved to tell his companion of its cause.

In seasons previous, it seemed, this fair son of the muse Calliope and the great god Apollo had wooed and won the lovely dryad Eurydice by the charm of his heavenly lyre. As fate would have it, the new bride, wandering in a meadow, was killed by the bite of a poisonous serpent. The bard wept forth his lament to the breezes of the upper world and dared to descend to the cave at Taenaron, where the river Styx marks the passage into the underworld. In search of his beloved, he ventured past ghostly throngs of the dead and approached Persephone and her lord where they ruled their shadowed realm. Before them he bowed and, plucking his melodious lyre, made his impassioned plea. His eloquent words floated about them in purest tones. Even the shades quivered with their power and the bloodless spirits wept. The cheeks of the Eumenides were moist with tears as they were overcome by his song, and Hades himself could not refuse his pleas. "Then it was", the story-teller continued, his tone deepening with feeling, "that the tragedy occurred. Orpheus was given permission to lead Eurydice out of the underworld to a new life but was warned not to look back at her before they were both safely in the upper world." The old man sadly shook his head. "It was love that turned his head when she stumbled along the path and love that looked upon her face as she was drawn inexorably back into the realm of death. He heard her utter a farewell as she disappeared, leaving him stunned with grief and stricken dumb for days. Then he began to roam the mountains and valleys of our Thracian countryside, wailing his wild songs of love and shunning all women attracted by the irresistible strains. It is thus, my friend, that we are privileged to hear his music now."

After the tale had been told, the two men stood in reverential silence, listening and feeling themselves transported to a realm of immortal longing and beauty. It was only gradually that they became aware of the encroachment upon this idyllic scene of a band of rough-clothed women brandishing their sense of rebuffed passion for the glorious bard in the form of menacing gestures and snarling epithets. With disgust and dread, the onlookers watched while the wild-haired band approached the musician and began to hurl stones and branches and rough implements of the field. At first the hurtled weapons were overcome by the magical harmony of his lyre and voice. They fell at his feet like suppliants begging for forgiveness. But the clamour grew, the shrieks, the horns and drums and hateful chanting of the angry maenads drowned out the sound of Orpheus' lyre, and the stones and other weapons, unhearing, grew red with the poet's blood. The men, who moments before had basked in the enchantment of his song, now watched in horror as he was pounded and torn apart. They saw his lyre fall away from his crippled grasp, as his soul streamed forth to meet the winds on the breath of his silenced voice.

> For you, O Orpheus, for you the trees let fall their leaves and shorn of foliage made lament. They say, too, that rivers swelled with their own tears, and the Naiads and Dryads changed their robes to black and wore their hair dishevelled. His limbs He scattered in various places; his head and lyre you got, O river Hebrus; and – O wonder – while they floated in midstream, the lyre made some plaintive lamentation, I know not what; the lifeless tongue murmured laments too, and the banks lamented in reply. And they left his native Thracian river and were carried out to sea. , . . The shade of Orpheus went down below the earth and recognized all the places he had seen before; he looked amidst the fields of the pious and found Eurydice, and clasped her in his eager arms.
>
> Ovid

The magical power of Orpheus' instrument was shared by other members of the Hellenic theogony. It was considered an attribute of Apollo, Erato, Aeolus and Harmonia, and believed to have been invented by Apollo's enigmatic and divinely creative brother, Hermes, who was inspired with the idea one day as he happened upon an obliging tortoise. Using the willing animal's carapace, Hermes ingeniously stretched across its underside the hide of an ox, and fixed to its sides two horns that curved upward to support a bridge from which seven strings were stretched. When struck, the lyre produced the sweetest of tones, delighting its creator and making him loath to hand it over to Apollo under the instructions of their father, Zeus. But Hermes had mischievously stolen his brother's cows and was forced by a powerfully ruling parent to compensate with the gift of his heavenly creation. Apollo made the lyre his own. He mastered it and made it his attribute. Through it he expressed all the powers of divine reason and the rhythm of discipline of instinctual animal life.

Apollo's lyre, so majestically immortalized in marble by Praxiteles, had seven strings, each tuned separately upon its own roller. On each roller a small peg projected, around which the string was looped. By turning the roller, one could raise the pitch, and it was fixed by slipping the end of the notched roller onto a fastened piece of wood of corresponding shape. This represented certain sophistications over the creation of Hermes, but even later designs continued to suggest the shape of a tortoise's carapace. Choric song, so prominently discussed by Plato in *Laws*, required an instrument with stronger tonal carrying power, encouraging the adoption of the *kithara* form of lyre, said to have been introduced by Terpander, a seventh-century poet from Lesbos. Though of Oriental origin, the *kithara*, as well as Hermes' lyre, was firmly fixed in Apollo's province, unlike the four-stringed Asiatic *phorminx* referred to by Homer, or the *barbitos* associated with Dionysus. In general, the Oriental influence emphasized unreason and ecstasy, and the *aulos* (or flute) came to be regarded as its chief musical expression. Thus, in its pristine usage, the lyre was seen as an instrument of refinement, intellectual triumph and harmonic purity.

The lyre is the symbol *par excellence* of the harmonious union of cosmic forces. It represents, with its basic seven strings, an underlying numerical harmony of the universe echoed by the seven planetary spheres. Pythagoras taught that at the centre of all Unity was the source of harmony, the *Logos* which is no number. But the world was called forth by sound or harmony and constructed according to musical proportion. He believed that the distance between the moon and the earth was one tone; between the moon and Mercury, one-half tone; thence to Venus, one-half tone; Venus to the sun, one and one-half tones; the sun to Mars, one tone; thence to Jupiter, one-half tone; Jupiter to Saturn, one-half tone; and thence one tone to the zodiac. Philolaus of Tarentum, speaking of this later, pointed out the evidence for these harmonic relationships in what the soul could recognize through the senses in human activities, technical productions and especially through music.

Both cosmic and microcosmic aspects of harmony are suggested by the etymological roots of the word. According to the oldest evidence in Greek, ἡ ἁρμονία (*harmonia*) referred to a joining, a fastening together (of a ship's planks, for instance), a covenant, agreement, settled governmental order or, simply, a concord of sounds. Originally, it is said, Harmonia was a mythical personage. According to Boeotian tradition, she was the daughter of Ares (War) and Aphrodite (Love), a duality which could be said to be blended in harmony. From her lineage sprang the royal founders of the city of Thebes, whose walls were built with stones moved by the magical harmony of Amphion's lyre. That harmonic order could be supremely demonstrated with the lyre was a very old belief among the peoples of the Mediterranean world. In teaching of cosmogony and cosmology based upon harmonic relationships, Pythagoras used the lyre. If numbers were the constituents of reality, then string lengths arranged in a pattern of twelve, nine, eight and six gave the intervals of the fourth, fifth and octave, with consonants as the framework of scale derived from arithmetic and harmonic means between two quantities in the ratio of two to one. The strings of the lyre were thus the audible and visible manifestation of numbers as lengths as well as differences in tension and so forth. Tone or pitch was thus an expression of number, and consonance of multiple and super-particular ratios, all of which were related to and demonstrated by the tuning and playing of the lyre.

Such abstract and fundamental concepts of *harmonia* lent themselves well to cosmic as well as political and musical interpretations. The idea of a certain order expressive of the correct *harmonia* was discussed by Plato (*Laws*) in terms of cultic song as well as political order, both of which he referred to as *nomos*. Governance believed to reflect a higher divine order had been symbolized by the mastery of the lyre among the Sumerians, who placed the instrument in the tombs of their kings long before the time of Pythagoras and Plato. But it was the Greeks who gave the idea the most explicit philosophical expression and raised the lyre to the level of divine symbolism.

> Grant me, sound of body and of mind, to pass an old age lacking neither honour nor the lyre.
>
> *Odes*, Horace

The *kitharodos* or lyre player took his or her inspiration from the example of Apollo. The frenzied music and dance of the orgiastic Mysteries associated with the flute of Asia (Thrace and Phrygia) contrasted dramatically with the calmness and control of the musical expression of the lyre. The paean associated with Apollo was based upon decorous stamping of feet and measured chants and exclamations. It was exemplified in the dignified seated position of the *kitharodos* or the slow, symmetrical and militaristic dance of the ancient Dorians. Dionysian music was dithyrambic, expressed most usually by the aulos in a Phrygian mode calculated to inspire powerful emotions and trance states. Comparing the two instruments, one notices that, while the lyre's tones cannot project the melody with great carrying power, those of the aulos can. The notes of the lyre are individually distinct, offering a precise rhythmic punctuation of poetic metre or dance, while those of the aulos are necessarily slurred. The instrument can merely accompany rhythm, not dictate it. It is this distinction which caused the Greeks to value the lyre rather than the aulos in a paedeutic role. In the *Republic*, Plato advocated the banning of the aulos from Kallipolis. He wished (especially in *Laws*) to make music wholly hieratic, utilizing the lyre, and, like other serious thinkers, found any theory of modality dependent upon the aulos to be suspect. They believed that true learning depended upon freeing oneself of moral and conceptual slurring, and grasping instead the underlying mathematics of reality through the pure and distinct notes of reason.

It is idle to play the lyre for an ass.

Greek Proverb

Up to the fifth century, Greek music embraced many styles differing markedly in emotional character. The notes required for each necessitated a *harmonia*, or tuning of the lyre. These diverse modes (Dorian, Phrygian, Lydian, Aeolian, etc.) expressed not merely a particular scale pattern but a distinctive musical idiom or dialect, similar to the ragas of Indian music. It could be said that each tribe had evolved a characteristic *harmonia* which expressed its cultural values, its sense of reality. Rhythm, playing a role in this expression, was seen by Pythagoras, Plato and others as a refinement of innate impulses appearing in bodily movements, cultivated movements revealing the character of individuals separately and collectively. *Tropos* (manner expressed through mode) dealt with vertical relationships of pitch between successive notes, while rhythm was seen to express horizontal relationships over time. Members of various tribes then, as of various cultures now, shared thus a complex, subtle and highly developed ethos which they brought to bear in an evaluation of the ethical worthiness of a musical piece. To people of such highly integrated musical awareness, aesthetic or ethical blunders committed by a player would be immediately apparent.

The development and refinement of this awareness was closely related to the usages of the spoken word in magic, religion, poetry and song. It is of great significance that words cannot be chanted or sung while playing the aulos. Language represents a conscious expression of cosmic and human numerical relationships. Uttered in the proper pitch and rhythm, it was believed to have immense potential occult power. In its original forms, Greek poetry was musical and always sung to the accompaniment of the lyre. The oracles at Delphi were sung in hexametric form to the lyre's clear note and beat. These songs were called θεσπαοίδη (*thespaoide*), related to θέσπις (*thespis*, thespian), meaning to have words from or be inspired by God. Thus, though the lyre was less able to project a powerful melody than was the aulos, it was more valued because it could accompany with precision a usage of sound deemed to be of higher spiritual value than melodic strain. The *harmonia* expressed by the lyre had its direct root in the mathematical precision of universal order rather than in a secondary or tertiary expression of it.

When the Ideal Forms spoken of by Plato became aesthetic, they rendered Truth, Beauty and Virtue perceptible to embodied consciousness. When music thus became perceptible, it became ethical through rhythm. The rhythm of language, metre, tempo, mode and dance expressed by the lyre delivered all these qualities to the threshold of a conscious human order based upon a perceived order in Nature. Natural philosophy could not alone contain this expression, and it was inevitable that it would flow into every aspect of society and art among the Hellenes, just as it had done in more ancient cultures. In bringing these ideals into the human sphere, a reciprocal exchange took place in human consciousness infusing ethical, religious and aesthetic values into Nature which sometimes reflected faithfully a deeper truth, but at other times coloured the manifest world in highly emotional hues.

Harmony in human affairs, based upon a knowledge of the true nature of things rather than upon feelings of like and dislike, was believed by Plato to be of primary importance in education. He taught that fundamental notions of justice and moral action could be developed through musical instruction on the lyre because the harmony of the soul was capable of being awakened through the ear, and the properties of the human body could be likened to the lyre, which does not itself furnish the elements of harmony but can express them. The body could be brought, he asserted, into harmony with the soul by fine tuning its strings and learning the correct modes and rhythms suited to its bonding.

> In singing and playing the lyre, a boy ought properly to reveal not only courage and moderation but also justice.
>
> Damon of Athens

Education in ancient Greece revolved around aristocratic values and courtly accomplishments, and included training in song and dance and lyre playing as prominent features. As with other ancient peoples, models of greatness were enshrined in song, and the chief mark of a cultivated man was his ability to transmit them with grace and precision. Plato advised that a compulsory education of both boys and girls be universal and include three years of lyre study begun at age thirteen. In *Laws* he said that for the sake of good melodic mimesis (representative of the soul of a good man under the stress of events), the lyre must be used so that its notes will be clear. Playing it in unison with the voice, no heterophony or ornamentation should be encouraged, nor should closely spaced notes contrasted with wide, or fast tempos with slow, or high range with low, be permitted. The stately and clear expression of one note only for each single word was the ancient ideal. In one of his parodies, Aristophanes even criticized Euripides for setting a word to more than one note in his lyric dramatic choruses. Aristophanes contrasted him with Aeschylus, whom he acknowledged as making a deliberate effort to represent the older order when the tragic poet was *poietes*, "maker", never borrowing from other *nomes* but remaining faithful to the one-word/one-note standard. When Plato proposed to achieve his paedeutic ideal by chants which would have the power to "en-chant", he fully realized that all music enchants. Because of this, he urged that the rhythms and modes played on the lyre should be subordinate to the words of the text in order to observe their rightful place. He believed that musical material ought to be used no longer than necessary, for the object of its instruction was not to achieve virtuosity on the lyre, but to recognize moral excellence in melody and rhythm. To Pythagoras, Plato and other upholders of the ancient standard, the virtuoso was merely a workman who sold his art, not to be compared with the free citizen using it as a means to rise above the pleasures of the senses to a higher moral bliss.

Numerous tales in Greek literature attest to the belief in the irresistible moral powers of music. Empedocles is said to have prevented a murder by his lyre playing, and Homer recorded the manner in which such music could calm the most tortured heart.

This sort of inspirational effect shades almost imperceptibly into the enchanting potentials of the lyre as a magical instrument, as demonstrated by Orpheus and Amphion. But this was quite distinct and immeasurably more lofty an art than that which had begun to develop in Plato's day. The great philosopher believed that a poet-singer could be a useful member of a community by performing appropriate social and political activity. He did not, however, envision that this would include virtuosi skilled mainly in self-aggrandizement. When freeborn amateur lyre players began to be replaced with professionals pandering to mass tastes with stock devices and calculated gimmicks, he must have been deeply saddened. For thus his standards of self-education in order to harmonize the lower nature with the soul were inverted and transformed into external standards dictated by crowds. The two Platonic goals of music – "to take pleasure rightly and to discern what is excellent" – were thus stood on their heads, with the result that a slave mentality increasingly replaced the liberated self-determination of the true autodidact.

Plato claimed that musical consciousness was a gift from the Muses as well as from Apollo and Dionysus. That he included Dionysus, yet advised exclusion of the aulos from Kallipolis, does not necessarily represent a contradiction. In sifting through his dialogues one comes to the conclusion that the Orphic influence is very strong in Platonic thought, as it had been in the Pythagorean school, an influence profoundly stamped with both Dionysian and Apollonian characteristics. In *Laches*, Plato showed that the true musician is in tune with a higher harmony than that capable of production on the lyre itself, for he has arranged in his life a harmony of words and deeds. This would reflect a harmony between the tripartite aspects of the soul, adjusted in such a way as to produce a perfect harmony between it and the perfectly tuned vehicles. The correct mode, rhythm, pitch and *tropos* would be unique to each individual and reflect in distinctively varying balances the soaring potentials of mystical ecstasy associated with the Asian god and the clear powers of pure reason and illumination related to Apollo. That the instrument of that former deity could be used for less than worthy purposes has been shown. It is not the instrument itself which is immune to corruption, no more than the human body. Rather, it is a question of the potential production of the spiritually unadulterated sound which does not ensnare the listener in lower psychic realms. One could readily imagine that a Krishna in the Hindu tradition breathed the pure breath of God into his flute and enchanted many on behalf of the spiritual emancipation of mankind. But on the lips of the satyr, the wandering shepherd of the hill or the frenzied Bacchae, the flute could easily slur the sensibilities into a non-discriminative dream of sensual beauty and psychic escape. The clear intervals of silence, so critical to understanding sounds, ideas and the order of manifestation and so wonderfully producible upon the lyre, are missing.

It is significant, therefore, that Orpheus, who charmed and enchanted even while addressing the soul, should have played the lyre. In his profoundly mysterious magic, words played a major part. He moved the lords of the underworld with his words as well as with the intonation and rhythm of his accompanying instrument. In sixth century B.C. Greece, the Orphic religious movement paid allegiance to Dionysus but also incorporated the Apollonian cult, especially at Delphi. Thus the mystical emphasis on purification through ecstasy was wedded to clear perception and a knowledge of Platonic Ideas. Orpheus, its prophet, was, after all, considered to have been at once a mortal spiritual teacher and the son of Apollo. As the movement spread, doctrine was added to ritual and mythical thought moved closer to philosophy. What had been a Dionysian cult was thus elaborated into a monastic code of life. The science of harmonics took precedence over the wild outpouring of emotion which had so dismayed Pythagoras as a young boy growing up in Samos. His teachings as well as Plato's were strongly influenced by Orphic concepts, blending ritual purification and catharsis with the affirmation of the immortality of the soul and providing a disciplined control over the ecstatic passion of the Mysteries.

The very sorts of contraries which, when "fitted together", "adjusted" and brought into a new "order", produce a harmony were blended in the Orphic movement. Just as Harmonia had been the daughter of the seemingly opposing forces of War (Ares) and Love (Aphrodite), so too the new philosophical Mysteries were the progeny of reason and vision, a transcendental blend of the mind and the heart. The very concept of harmony rests upon the inevitability of a relation between opposites. It presumes a universe of constant flow and change, a process revolving around a balance of measure and proportion rooted in wholeness, which is the central connection between permanence and change. If the Logos is the source of harmony, harmony itself is the child of arcane duality. The contraries over which she, as the goddess Harmonia, reigns are both her cause and her effect. From the very beginning this idea was connected with music, for though the harmony for the world remains an abstraction that must be intuited, in the tuning of the lyre there was discerned a simultaneity of mutual adjustment which could be immediately heard and experienced in its playing. All the spatial, vertical and horizontal, sequential and simultaneous elements of karmic adjustment could be sensed by the awakening soul. This is why Plato so strongly advocated its use in education and why he was so concerned not to let the instrument become an end in itself. He understood that a polarity of spirit and matter, rooted in the Absolute, mixed and blended in human nature to produce good and evil qualities. He also fully realized that these contraries were necessary to embodied life and that they were mutually interdependent aspects of what could be potentially a harmonious whole. In the continual balancing of the contraries, "if one is arrested, the action of the other will become immediately self-destructive". A recapitulation of the cosmic War in Heaven takes place.

Looked at in a more negative sense, karma can be said to be the effect of an act which cannot but be harmful lo others because it is produced egotistically, whereas the law of harmony depends on altruism. Looked at in a broader way, karma is the eternal action itself. It creates nothing nor does it design anything, for it is man who creates and designs while karma simply adjusts the effects. It is universal harmony tending ever to resume its original order, its mode reflective of wholeness in the cosmic realm. Thus, the contraries of karmic law can be gathered in an adjusted harmony within the human heart and mind as upon the strings of the lyre. Eternal action, like sound, cannot cease nor can the effects of human ignorance disappear immediately from the realm of manifest existence. But an individual can learn to separate the pure notes of trust and love from the clutter of extraneous noises and embellishments. He or she can practise those notes upon the lyre strings of the inner being until one discovers gradually the correct mode, the timely intervals, the pitch, the rhythm and the overall melody of the soul. Finding thus the harmony within, one can bless with the uttered word, make of one's relations with others a song, and, like Orpheus with his golden lyre, move to sway in ecstasy the very rocks and trees. But one must learn the strength of reason and wed it to the heart so that the two in harmony walk as one, never doubting, never looking back, out of the jaws of death into immortal life.

> Along the coasts of Arcady
> Thy melody yet lingers,
> Thy strings mount up into the clouds,
> The winds caress thy fingers.
> Thy chanting circles round the globe
> Mournful yet endearing.
> Each note a pluck upon my soul,
> Each word a boon to hearing.

Hermes, October 1986

THE CROSS

The philosophical cross, the two lines running in opposite directions, the horizontal and the perpendicular, the height and breadth, which the geometrizing Deity divides at the intersecting point, and which forms the magical as well as the scientific quaternary, when it is inscribed within the perfect square, is the basis of the occultist. Within its mystical precinct lies the master-key which opens the door of every science, physical as well as spiritual, ft symbolizes our human existence, for the circle of life circumscribes the four points of the cross, which represent in succession birth, life, death and IMMORTALITY.

Isis Unveiled, i 508

Like many people who have blundered out into the world without knowing what they might expect to find, the Europeans who came to the New World were surprised and gratified to find objects and symbols among the natives similar to many of their own. When they saw crosses decorating faces, clothing, baskets, tools and religious paraphernalia, they presumed these had a meaning akin to that held by Christians and were puzzled that the symbol could be so widely cherished by such primitive and "un-Christian-like" people. Where explorers or missionaries tarried long enough to learn the varied myths that told of a great deluge or the coming to earth of an arcane spiritual teacher, they often leapt to the conclusion that hitherto unknown contacts with Christians or even the Apostles themselves were responsible. Some of them, ironically, experienced no doubts whatever in claiming antique visitations by the peripatetic St. Thomas. To this day, sites where he is believed to have taught or performed miracles are trustingly pointed out in Yucatan, Mexico and Peru. The possibility that the cross might have symbolized philosophical and cosmological concepts gestated out of the spiritual and cultural experience of the natives themselves occurred to very few. Fewer still of these ethnocentrics perceived in its ubiquitous presence proof of the fundamentally universal nature of the cross. Centuries would pass before the world would realize how late in the day the Christian rood had joined a long parade of crosses displayed and venerated by human beings for countless millennia.

According to the Sia Pueblo Indians, the initial act of Spider Woman, the First Being, was to draw a cross in the amorphous womb of the causal world. Focussing upon its eastern and western points, she brought forth Utset and Nowutset, mothers of the Indian people and of other races. Eventually Utset led her people through a reed to emerge through a *sipapu* into the physical world. Wandering for ages, they finally found their way to the middle place of the world where, circling around on the arms of a swastika pattern, they arrived at the centre of the cross, which was the sacred heartland of the physical Mother Earth. Marking the emergence of order out of chaos as it does, the Sia cross stands at one end of a spectrum of meanings associated with manifestation, the cardinal directions and the conjunction of heaven and earth. At the other end of this spectrum lie beliefs linking the cross with human beings, serpents and stars. Many Plains tribes, perpetuating variations of a beautiful myth, told their children of a mortal maiden who was taken as a wife by a solar being who lived as a brilliant star in the celestial world. Abiding with her husband in that astral realm, this greatly honoured lady gave birth to a child who was of heaven and earth combined. With joy the young mother watched him grow and taught him the laws of the sky world as she knew them. She had tried to adapt herself fully to her husband's realm and had taken care to observe its teachings and taboos. In her heart, however, she had never been able to subdue an intense curiosity, and so it was that she came to uproot a plant she had been explicitly forbidden to touch. Beneath its root, instead of greater depths of astral mists yawned a gaping hole opening out onto the physical world far below.

She had opened a door from which she could not retreat and was forced to descend to the earth, leaving her husband and child behind. The North American tribes envisioned stars in the shape of equilateral crosses which, in the case of this sadly fallen mother, beamed over her during many lonely nights as reminders of her loss. The Kiowa version of the tale continues, telling of how Little Star (the son of this lonely mother) descended to earth, took on human form and killed a great serpent, which then lodged in his head. Though his body disintegrated, he lived on in the shape of a cross until, after fervent prayers, the serpent came forth from what would have been his mouth. In this way he was restored and, using the serpent's skin as his weapon, he became Venus, the morning star.

The mysteries suggested in these provocative myths are complex and reveal so many similarities with universal occult teachings concerning the fall of spirit into matter and the sacrificial role of Venus-Lucifer that one cannot avoid being reminded of Plato's notion of archetypes. In the realm of symbols and myths such as these there can be found abundant evidence of the global "borrowing" from the rich collective storehouse of highly refined and synthesized ideation that has existed for as long as thinking man. Out of this tapping and culling the cross has emerged with a frequency that suggests something both essential and universal, not only at the level of cosmic prototypes but buried deep within the individual and collective human mind. Plato alluded to the more cosmological aspect of this when he described the creator "splitting the whole world along its entire length into two parts and joining them together across one another". As with the activity of Spider Woman, the perpendicular and horizontal of the cross here express in the most fundamental manner height and breadth: the geometrizing deity dividing from its intersecting point the above and below, the right and left, the before and after – in short, all dualities expressed in a manifesting world.

The cross expresses division and conjunction and epitomizes the paradoxical melding of unifying and opposing forces that typify human nature and the world of which it is a microcosm. Thus, the very structure of the garden of Paradise in myth is decussated by crossing rivers, at the intersection of which grows the *axis mundi* or Tree of Life upon whose cross-branches sprout the fruits of good and evil. Looked at from one point of view, the design of the garden is the symbol of and symbolized by crucified man. It also shadows forth the perimeters of law, justice and evolution. Eating from the Tree of Life, man is crucified on it, and it comes to represent the history of his evolution. But it also represents an order which sustains and balances a conjunction of higher and lower forces whose complex interrelation must necessarily be marshalled. One sees a clear grasp of this at some level in the belief of the ancient Sumerians, who heralded the cross as the emblem of the god Shamash, who gave to King Hammurabi his famous laws.

The identification of the cross with the idea of order is echoed in the axis of the Buddhist wheel of the Good Law, whose spokes delineate a multiple of its basic four arms. For many peoples the law exerts its effect through the lords or genii of the four quarters. The circling swastika of the American Indians, the ancient Aryans or the Tibetans conveys the same notion, while the still centre of the cross, like the heartland of the Sia, is the place of the rosy flame of transcendence. It is the sacrificial fire burning where the wood pieces cross in the Inipi Lodge of the Dakota, which, like the fire sticks of Agni, bring together in conjunction the opposite forces of life. In the mundane world of daily coming and going this opposition is met every time one arrives at a crossroads. It is at such a point that choices are made and law comes into operation. One is confronted with choices that may lead one onward, to the right or the left. They may lead into enlightenment or confusion, white or black magic, life or death. The antiquity of this idea is responsible for the many beliefs about demons and witches who hover and perform their dark rites there. In cultures all over the world people have gone to the crossroads on a full moon or new moon night to enlist the forces waiting there in their magical efforts. The road that is crossed may be full of possibilities, or the greatest loss in one's life may have been avoided by not turning into it. Or the crossed road may have led to endless night, a darkness of missed opportunity, a lamentation of shrinking hopes.

> But man must light for man
> The fires no other can,
> And find in his own eye
> Where the strange crossroads lie.

> David McCord

The conjunction of opposing forces or possibilities can be traced in common English slang where to "double cross", "play the cross" or do anything "on the cross" implies dishonesty and deception in the face of certain concepts of law or morality. To "cross-examine" someone is to question them from opposite sides of an issue in an effort to discover the truth, while to be "cross" is simply to be in opposition to or out of harmony with someone or some particular set of circumstances. The emphasis shifts subtly when considering the various types of crosses that have been carved into stone, stitched into silk or buckskin or shaped out of a living tree. The cross in the form of an P signifies the upper and lower worlds, the + orientation, the ⊹ centrifugal force, the ⊹ or ⊹ centripetal force, the ⊹ peripheral force. The cross as a bridge or ladder to God is like Jacob's ladder or the great tree laid down as part of the entrance leading into Solomon's temple. Here the main idea has shifted away from conjoining forces to the link connecting heaven and earth. The Siberian Voguls thus kept a fir-wood "pillar" with cross-pieces bearing sacrificial offerings, at the base of which they said the son of God tied his steed while visiting his father. Sacred poles with cross-pieces readily function as meeting points between God and man in rituals like the great Sun Dance of the Plains Indians. There the central pole is the emblem of life and cosmic organization and the link between the solar god and the warriors who, by attaching themselves to its top with rawhide lines and dancing about it while gazing at the sun, sacrificed of their stamina and flesh to their deity. The tree chosen for this important rite represented the world Tree of Life similar to that symbolized by the *tau* cross among the ancient Maya of Yucatan which was, along with their equilateral cross, mistaken by the Spaniards as proof of an earlier Christian influence.

When the link between heaven and earth and the notion of communicating spiritual power is thus emphasized, the cross can clearly be seen as related to the Tree of Life and Knowledge around which a serpent is coiled. One can identify this form and meaning in the caduceus, wherein the outstretched wings appear as the horizontal bar and the dark and light serpents embody the opposing forces of good and evil. In Mexico the cross was the emblem of Quetzalcoatl who, like the Sumerian Shamash, gave to the people their laws and all their arts while being identified as the plumed serpent. Crosses are associated with his shrines and powerfully dramatic serpentine representations. As a man, Quetzalcoatl was believed to be pale of skin, having a long white beard and robes. In his struggles with the forces of darkness in the world there came a time when he was forced to abandon mankind and cross the Eastern Sea to Tlillan Tlapallan, the resting place of the gods. When the white-skinned Spaniards came, with robed priests carrying crosses upon ships sporting tall masts and cross-spars, the Maya along the Caribbean coast believed that their god had returned to them and they unwittingly embraced their future conquerors. Taking full advantage of this mistake, the meagre forces of the Spaniards were soon able to subjugate far vaster numbers of the relatively peaceful native people.

> Onward, Christian soldiers,
> Marching as to war,
> With the Cross of Jesus
> Going on before!

The common factor lay in the frequent identification of some form of the cross with a divine messenger. Whether it be Thor's *fylfot*, Hermes' caduceus, the *tau* and cross pattée (✠) of Quetzalcoatl, the ansated cross of Venus-Lucifer or the *ankh* associated with Osiris, it is an emblem of life and of all the sacrifice attendant upon the manifestation in the world of a spiritually enlightened being. As the inheritor of such great archetypal sacrifices, man himself can be likened to the cross. If he is imbibed with the desire to embrace this sacrificial spirit, he stands straight with his head thrown back and his arms outstretched, looking for all the world like a cross. The Chinese believed this stance symbolized man's divine potential, and because they believed certain criminals had profaned this, they crucified them on crosses. In willing the fullest manifestation of his potential, man stands at the crossroads of evolution, his nature the meeting-place of all opposites. With his arms extended and his body erect, he is the figure of humanness at full stretch, the potential bridge between heaven and earth. Looked at in this way, man joins the ranks of the great Teachers and spiritual sacrificers spoken of in myth and religious tradition, and the cross takes on a much broader association, its arms extending in cyclic time to include the whole of humanity, not merely one central being.

In the Christian tradition the P stands for χρίστος (Christos) as well as for "cross". Coming to the world through the Greek language, the basic concepts and symbols in Christianity were stamped with the meanings associated with the Hellenic alphabet and words. P stands for "chaos" and "chasm", but it also yields χρίω (*chrio*), "to be rubbed on", and χρίεν (*chrien*), "to anoint". Thus Christ, associated with the cross that emerges out of chaos, was known as the Anointed One. We have seen that this P cross symbolizes a conjunction of the upper and lower worlds, and it is interesting to note the opposite meanings attached to its popular usage, where the X of the Vikings' runic alphabet meaning "bad luck" is balanced off by the X of the Romans, meaning "a kiss". Though the crossbones X beneath a skull signified pirates in earlier times and poison to us now, X is equally associated with number and increase as well as unknown factors. Identified with man, it contains all these opposites and has been for ages his signature mark. In the shape of the X the Christian cross was borne up the tortured path to Calvary, and Emperor Julian waged warfare with it emblazoned on his banner, believing that the elongated vertical of the Latin cross abused the original symbolic association with the occult meaning of the crucifixion. But the more abstract ideas represented by the equilateral cross gave way over time, and the emphasis in the Christian tradition came to rest ever more exclusively upon the material cross of crucifixion echoed in the physical form and passion of Christ. There grew an increasing confusion wherein aspects of the Tree of Life, the ansated cross, the P of Christos and the rod or staff linking heaven and earth were all mixed and moulded to suit a particular event.

Ironically, the legend of the Holy Rood (the cross of Christ) provides clues of greater symbolic latitude concerning the cross than does the dogma of Christian theology. Beginning with the Garden of Eden, the legend makes the connection between the tree at its centre and the later cross supposed to have been used for the crucifixion. The imagery is rich, describing how Seth, the third son to Adam and Eve, attempted to locate the fruit of Paradise. Arriving at the Garden of Eden, he saw through its closed gate four streams coursing out from a central well where stood an aged tree. The top of this tree bore at its highest heavenly point an unborn babe, while its roots reached to the nether realms of hell. From its branches an angel gave him three pips which Seth planted on earth and watched grow into a cedar, a cypress and a pine. These, it is said, were later used as rods of divination and curing by Moses, after which King David brought them to Jerusalem where he planted them once again. They grew into one marvelous tri-branched tree which King Solomon used as a bridge leading to his temple. The legend meanders on through these remarkable generations to tell how the Queen of Sheba, visiting Solomon, advised him to bury the tree reverentially at a place where subsequently sprang up a deep well capable of miraculous healing. The tale then describes how, when Jesus was born, the tree began to float on the well water's surface, where those who prepared to crucify him later found it. The cross was made of two-thirds of the great beam, with eight cubits standing above ground and three on each side.

> O tree, thou art only made for traitors,
> Yet virtue is slain along with vice.
> Truth now united to treason.
> With a thief my son is hanged.

> *Mary Disputes with the Cross*

After the Crucifixion, the legend relates, the Holy Rood was buried with the crosses of the two thieves and Adrian built a Roman temple over the spot. Years later, during the reign of Constantine, his mother Helena went to Jerusalem to find it. The Jews there tried to keep its whereabouts secret but she threatened them with severe consequences and, interestingly, a man called Judas finally told her where it lay. It is said by some that four equally divided parts of the cross were sent to the four quarters of the earth, but the more popular notion is that Helena sent part of it to Constantinople and enshrined the rest at Mount Calvary. Its extraordinary odyssey did not seem to rest even there, for it is recorded that in A.D. 615 the Persian king Khosrau stole the Holy Rood and that it was captured by the emperor Heraclitus and brought back to Jerusalem, where, it is suggested, its presence filled the air with a sweet aroma. One comes to the conclusion of this saga impressed with the numerous elements that have been woven together to create a sort of living tree capable of extending its branches, as it were, from the beginning of the Old Testament to the end of the New. That this is artfully done cannot be disputed and yet, behind it lies a continuing focus upon the terrible agony suffered by Christ on this Cross.

> ... pain's almost the God
> Of doubtful men, who tremble expecting to
> Endure it, their cruelty sublimed. And I
> Think the brute cross itself
> Hewn down to a gibbet now, has been worshipped;
> It stands yet for an idol of life and
> Power in the dreaming world.

Robinson Jeffers

Miguel de Unamuno made a profound distinction between the utterly killed and dead Christ portrayed in the painting *The Recumbent Christ of Palencia* and the eternally agonizing, living Christ of Velazquez. As for Pascal, to whom Christ would "continue to be in agony until the end of the world", so too for Unamuno, the Christ of Velazquez symbolized endless struggle. This view focusses upon the cross and the condition it represents as an ongoing fact about the world and humanity rather than as a specific historical event. The implication is that the agony leads to a redemption which is also ongoing. If one reads the Gospels with a deeper intuitive awareness of the cosmological and universally human symbolism involved in the Crucifixion, one will readily see that Christ is not depicted as a martyr. Instead, one will see that the Cross plays a fundamental role in what is a divine transaction transcending time and space and individual suffering. But for centuries much of Christendom has been mesmerized by the blood and agony marking one particular highly dramatized event. In popular and serious religious art as well as in poetry and plays, the tortured bloodiness of the Crucifixion has undoubtedly affected the collective psyche of vast numbers of people.

Reacting strongly to this in his inimitable way, George Bernard Shaw asserted that in Europe "the instruments of his (Jesus') torture were made symbols of the faith . .. and the crucifixion thus became to the churches what the chamber of horrors is to a wax work". While this may be an oversimplified exaggeration of the problem, it does provoke questions about the deep-seated morbid tendencies which have caused so many to enjoy surrendering themselves in waves of transferred self-pity and supplication before the most harrowing statues of Christ, depicted in bleeding agony upon the Cross. There is little doubt that elements of this lugubrious identification would tend to flow into irrational expressions of doleful righteousness giving vent, from time to time, to bigotry and even violence towards those of other faiths.

Odour of blood when Christ was slain
Made all Platonic tolerance vain
And vain all Doric discipline.

William Butler Yeats

In the catacombs of Rome the early Christians focussed upon the Resurrection instead of the Crucifixion. But it was not long before a sort of religiocentric righteousness, partly motivated by a vague sense of justifiable reparation for the martyrdom suffered by Jesus in the hands of non-believers, led to a stronger and more aggressive identification with the emblem of his terrible passion. The emperor Constantine saw the cross in a dream during a battle at the Danube. He fixed its image to a banner, so they say, and drove his heathen foe before him as they panicked with its display. Increasingly such banners were carried aloft in war, contributing to a more intense and militant consolidation of messianic fervour focussed upon the cross. With the eclipse of the classical world and the conversion of many within the Roman fold to the new religion, it was perhaps inevitable that the cross would become a central symbol of the waxing Christian era. It was worn as an emblem, traced in a ritual sign across the breast and carried forth by pilgrims or settlers as they entered a new land. More and more, as the centuries passed, this shape of suffering and hoped for salvation dotted the landscape of the Old World and embedded itself into the architecture, the minds and emotional associations of countless generations of people. By the thirteenth century it would seem perfectly reasonable for Thomas Aquinas to teach that the cross itself should be adored with supreme worship.

The majority of Christian crosses carved in the earliest centuries during which the new religion spread were wheel-shaped. Those in Ireland and places like Cornwall were exceedingly simple designs having flat, circular heads of stone with Maltese (cross pattée) crosses carved on each face. Some of these, smoothed by winds and snow, still bear dates placing their origins in the sixth and seventh centuries. As in other northern countries, they far outnumbered Latin crosses, the old pre-Christian associations with the Nordic and Celtic equilateral cross prevailing, even in the recognition paid to the increasingly dominant new religion. Many centuries would pass before the elongated cross so emblematic of the actual Crucifixion would become the most clearly recognized symbol of organized Christianity. The slow shift of favour away from the cross within the circle to the cross with the circle about its centre and, finally, the Latin cross with no circle at all occupied several centuries. Modestly adorned with the lamb of God or some other non-anthropomorphic symbol, all of these styles remained relatively simple and abstract until the Quinisext Council of Constantinople in 692 decided that it was permissible to depict the figure of Christ in human form instead of the lamb. It was this decision which lent an edge to the Latin cross, whose shape so closely echoes that of man and which quickly began to be seen, supporting in wood or stone or on canvas, the emaciated and bleeding body of the Prince of Peace.

This shift from the circled cross to one outside a circle is a reflection, writ small in a few centuries, of a far greater shift that can truly be related to a vast and antique process of spiritual involution. According to the symbolism depicting this greater process, the cross first appeared as part of an occult sequence beginning with a boundless circle. Within the unformed space of this circle a Logoic point emerged, to be followed by a horizontal line symbolizing "a divine immaculate Mother-Nature within the all-embracing absolute Infinitude". A vertical line dropping down from this forms the sacred *tau* cross, the "Alpha and the Omega of secret divine Wisdom" and glyph of the androgynous Third Root Race up to the point where the separation of the sexes took place, symbolized by the crossing of the horizontal line in the circle with an equal vertical. As long as the cross remained within the circle it symbolized a state wherein, though the cause of all manifestation may not have been presumed knowable, there persisted a refusal to worship an external god of physical generation. The circled cross affirms the universal presence of vast and recurring cycles of space and time typified by the Hindu *chakra* or Plato's decussated circle. From the fully encircled cross evolved the *crux ansata* of the ancient Egyptians, the *ankh* or key to life held by the goddess of truth, Maat. This symbol, identical in essence to that associated with Venus, still clung to the expanded sphere of the Logoic point and continued to assert man's fundamentally spiritual ancestry. Suspended below the sphere, the *crux ansata* indicated that mankind and all animal life had "stepped out of the spiritual circle and fallen into physical male and female generation". From the end of the Third Race this sign took on a phallic meaning which came to be fully expressed in the cross having no circle at all.

The evolutionary history of the cross is as complex as that of man himself. The *crux ansata* marks a step in a line of development moving from a relatively subjective oneness of consciousness and being to a separative objectivized condition manifested at its greatest extreme in man. Parallel with this, the simple ideas of the four cardinal points and their presiding powers, the axis of the wheel of the Law in Buddhist or American Indian belief, and the idea of the *tau* as the Tree of Life flow and become blended. Many glyphs and legends trace the development of the intertwined characteristics of these various crosses.

Astrologically, Taurus was said to have "pushed off the dragon" with the ansated cross on his horns. The ancients believed that this celestial event was reflected on earth in terrestrial generation involving the cross as the "framework of all construction". To them Taurus represented the lower physical world that eclipsed the realm of intuitive wisdom by means of the cross. Such notions might seem to be arrived at over the millennia through man's observations of the constellations and their shifts relative to this globe. But the double glyph that underlies the idea of the cross is not of human invention. "Cosmic ideation and the Spiritual representation of the divine Ego-man are at its basis." This is alluded to in the Hindu idea of man crucified in space and identified as "the Second God who impressed himself on the Universe in the form of Cross". It is described in terms of the Universal Soul which, as a material reflection of the Ideal, is the sevenfold source of life represented by the cross, whose branches are light, heat, electricity, terrestrial magnetism, astral radiation, motion and intelligence.

The dragon eclipsed by the cross of Taurus is echoed in the serpent so frequently associated with the cross. The dragons of Wisdom are, however, to be distinguished from Nidhogg gnawing at the base of the Yggdrasil tree, just as are the white and dark serpents wound round the caduceus. Behind this duality presides a necessity based upon the fact of manifestation itself and relentlessly expressed through its basic cross-shaped framework. The transcendent source of this necessity cannot be arrived at in one leap but requires many steps along the arms of its doubled dualistic expression. Beautifully expressing this, the powerful stone-carved pyramids of the ancient Maya slope up to a sacred capstone where man and the gods were believed to meet. Each of their four sides is centered by a tapered band of steep steps leading up to the shrine on this platform. Looked at from an aerial view, the steps resemble the arms of a cross pattée extending out from a square centre, while the corners of the pyramid describe an X or St. Andrew's cross. An illustration of this cross in the Codex Ferjervary-Mayer reveals a *tau* cross or Tree of Life in each of the larger cross-arms symbolic of the four seasons of cycles great and small. The cross-bar of these *tau* trees rests at the wide outer extremities of the arms, while the trunks extend towards the centre, from which flows the life-giving spirit of the mother and father of the gods.

Looked at from above, the tree crosses extend from the central heavenly source upside down into the world. Like those of the sacred Ashwatha tree of Hinduism, their branches bear the leaves and creatures of phenomenal existence whilst their roots disappear at the top of the steps, merging into the realm of the noumenal. The divine king whose death scene is so powerfully and elaborately carved on the sarcophagus at Palenque sits tilted backwards in front of an upright Tree of Life cross. He appears to be about to fall backwards into the underworld of the dead. Turning this around and assuming that the ancient priest-artists understood that everything in the world is an inversion, the king is actually falling into the realm of the divine, whilst the tree can be seen to be growing downward into the world.

Growing down into the world, as it were, the four arms of the Mayan cross pattée containing the trees also represent the four elements. Extending out, the separate elements are bound to perish, but if united by the central platform of the fifth principle, the central sun, they will merge in creative life. This centre is the heart, archetypal to that around which the Sia cross of migration circled. It is the precious jewel where opposites meet and transcendence occurs, the symbol of the solar messenger, Venus-Quetzalcoatl. Through this heart animal man and divine man merge, inaugurating a force capable of freeing the world from inertia whilst preserving the sacred fire of spiritual awakening. In this heart lie the seeds of both crucifixion and redemption accepted and pursued through the sacrificial compassion of initiated Adepts. This was initially understood by the ancient Maya, whose later degraded sacrificial practice of cutting out and offering to God a living human heart simply represented a loss of spirituality reflected in a gross concretization of the idea. Just so, the crucifixion upon the arms of that great heart can be understood at many levels. The poignancy and profundity of human consciousness can either be suffused with a realization of the ongoing, omnipresent nature of sacrifice in the entire manifest universe, or it can be shrunk to the focus of one agony, one sacrificial passion crucified on the cross of time and place.

If the heart of the cross, the still, central solar point, is ever held foremost in consciousness, these degradations would never occur. Only with the loss of the circle extending to encompass all space can the cross be shrunk to a piece of wood or a physically anthropomorphized theme. The Tree of Life grows out of No-thing and extends endlessly into manifested existence, inevitably yielding the cross upon which the great compassionators of mankind will deliberately and willingly suffer. The cross was always there, for it is the unfolded cube through which the solar unity of all lays itself out, stretches itself to the full in the plurality of manifested life. As with the tree in paradise, there is nothing intrinsically good or evil about the cross. Only man's mental exaggeration of the fall of oneness into manyness, his concretization of its nature and fixation upon physical separation, has blinded him to its cosmic nature and rendered him incapable of seeing in it the simple necessity of its character.

The way to bliss lies not on beds of down,
And he that has no cross deserves no crown.

Francis Quarles

The cross, like the Tree of Life, is unavoidable. There is no manifestation without the circle having become pointed with the Logoic seed, crossed and crossed again in the union of the father and mother from whose embrace extend the limbs of the world. Having arms and legs like branches from the trunk, the cosmic man is thus crucified in space so that divine intelligence may percolate out through his ethereal substance into the world. Inheritors of his intelligence are also inheritors of the burden of this cross. Human beings carry its weight from morn to night through much of their lives. Only those who locate its centre within the depth of their own heart can free the cross from its rigid Latin stance and turn it into a moving wheel within an all-encompassing circle. The terrible weight of doubt, anxiety, fear and hatred born of prolonged identification with one life, one body, one event in time, crucify lesser mortals over and over again. Only the wonderfully bold and great-hearted have the vision and strength to discard this and use the cross as a means for emancipation.

Those few who have succeeded in doing this free their own souls into the hands of their higher immortal selves and thus arrive fully in consciousness at the intersection where heaven and earth meet. Of these only a few will turn back and attempt to gather up the rest of mankind to share in their enlightenment. Only a few will take up the cross – not because they must any longer, but on behalf of the human race. In their crucifixion lies not an event with beginning or end, but a willingness to shoulder and lighten the inescapable suffering of worldly existence. That part of Christ which cried out "My God, my God, why hast thou forsaken me?" was his link with the mind and consciousness of the fallen humanity he sought to uplift. In seeking to lead it towards the truth, he had to join and take on its fear-ridden characteristics. This is the agony willingly assumed by great redeemers. It is their cross of suffering which may weigh so heavily at times upon their hearts that they cry out in a momentarily bewildered sense of loss.

The poignancy of this would touch any human heart capable of trying to imagine the trials of such great souls. It would be a great mistake, however, to imagine that any such being's sacrifice could do the job for others. Its merit lies in that it can inspire and arouse a deep compassion and desire to emulate, a desire to accept the cross of existence, even as it is weighted down and distorted with human ignorance, and bear its burden as bravely and lightly as possible. Struggling along with this worldly weight, a patient and courageous pilgrim will eventually reach the hill of Calvary, the place of Odin's tree, the platform of the Mayan pyramid. There his terrible burden will fall from him and he will see before him the great cross of initiation upon whose arms he will be bound into the mysteries of the immortal fire burning in the central Spiritual Sun. This is his destiny and the ultimate destiny of all human souls. The cross is always there, it ever awaits. It is up to mankind to shed the crippling moral and psychological shape of its splintered and morbidly limiting shadow in order to embrace the joyously liberating truth that lies at the crossroads of its heart.

Mounting the steps of its arms
The pilgrim pauses.
He looks out over the familiar world.
The pyramid looms above.
Mounting higher he
Pauses again.
And the world appears less real
A dizzying distance below.
Weary beyond measure,
He closes his eyes and
Trudges on,
Step by step and narrow step.
His feet are like lead,
His breath in short rasps,
His mind fixed
On the summit above.
He does not know what is there.
He does not look up or down.
He raises his aching limb.
And suddenly, he is there.

Hermes, December 1985

THE FOOL

Foole Upon Foole, or Six Sortes of Sottes: A flatt foole and a fall foole, A leans foole and a cleans foole, A merry foole and a verry foole: Shewing their lives, humours and behaviours, with their want of witte in their shew of wisdome. Not so strange as true.

The Nest of Ninnies

On his Olympian heights Zeus yawned with boredom, for there was not a fool among the gods with wit enough to keep the divine assembly diverted. Complaining in the midst of such celestial ennui, the king of gods frowned with displeasure and sent a ripple of anxiety through the heavenly halls. Hermes, ever quick to mediate in times of need, directed his attention to a large field on earth below. "Great god," he said, "look at that broad tract of land near Aliakmon. It is all alive with mortals in their holiday dress. See how they are eating sweet melons, singing till they are hoarse and dancing until they drop. Can we not find in their revelry the entertainment we lack here?" Observing them for a moment, Zeus chuckled. "I do believe that with a few improvements this rustic festivity will indeed provide us with a laugh. By my decree, let that priest, who is fast asleep by his deserted shrine below, announce that a shower is about to descend but that it shall wet none but fools."

With a muffled sound of thunder, the aroused servant of the gods stood up and made the requisite announcement to the people. Upon hearing it, a philosopher standing nearby hastily covered his head and retreated into his modest habitation. None of the others who were gathered around prepared to avoid the tempest, and each, waiting to see the drenching of the fools, was, in two minutes, wet to the skin. When the sun reappeared, the philosopher walked out into the field. The thoroughly soaked idiots, observing his comfortable condition, hailed him with the epithet of "fool" and pelted him with stones. Bruised and staggering, the philosopher nevertheless contrived to keep his wits. "O sagacious asses!" said he to the roaring crowd, which at once sank into silence at the compliment paid to their wisdom, "have patience for a moment and I will prove to you that I am not such a fool as I look." Bending back his head and turning the palms of his hands upwards to the sky, he cried, "O wise father of the witty and the witless, vouchsafe to send down a deluge for my individual benefit. Wet me to the skin even as these fools are wetted. Constitute me, thereby, as great a fool as my neighbours; and enable me, in consequence, a fool, to live in peace among fools."

At these words the idiots below and the Olympians above shook with laughter. Down came the shower of rain prayed for, with the peculiar effect that the philosopher rose drippingly from his knees ten times wittier than he was before. Hera, leaning close to the ear of Zeus, whispered, "We have spoilt that good fellow's robe but also made his fortune, for I have put in the mind of the local ruler the wish to take the philosopher home with him as instructor for diversion." That night all Olympus looked down into the court of the prince where the wise fool lay, pouring forth witty truths as fast as his lips could utter them. "That fellow", cried Zeus, "shall be the founder of a race. Henceforth, every court shall have its fool and fools shall be, for many a day, preachers and admonishers of kings. Let us drink to the health of the first fool!"

Had the gods communed in Latin, they may have looked down upon the revellers and remarked along with Seneca, "*Tanta stultitia mortalium est. . .*" What fools these mortals be! But in isolating the wise fool and making him the admonisher of kings, they established a relationship on earth which broke all the rules of order they themselves held dear. For the fool is the symbol of chaos; he inverts the order of things and his penetrating criticisms would have found a less than welcome reception from the gods. Perhaps the institution of his race was merely an unkind joke played upon mortals who were held, it often seemed, in low esteem by the Olympians. Or perhaps the introduction of an agent of chaos into the pathos of world order was considered by them to be a just and fitting antidote to the conceits of strutting empire-builders and self-created lawmakers. Whatever the reasons may have been, the court fool would find himself in a position at the bottom of a scale of temporal power at whose top a ruler of castle and kingdom could be found. Sometimes less than wise, the fool was often at the total mercy of those above him and may not even have known from whence he came or where he was going, His only freedom lay in his lack of place, his powerlessness within the social scheme of things. Being always an outsider, an oddity, a force unfettered by reason or cultural grace, he represented the unexpected and irrational, the upsetting and absurd. Being a fool, he could say what he pleased and caustically unleash a drenching dam of truth upon the free play of sophistry and manners.

Well might one ask, if such caustic critics they could be, why would anyone wish for the company of a fool? Why would anyone seek out his company and even come to love and cherish such a one? The court fool was often mentally or physically abnormal. Many were dwarfs, some monstrous in form, others quite definitely insane. Deprived of both human rights and responsibilities, they could become either pathetic recipients of abuse or impossibly lazy barnacles cluttering up the halls of royalty. Why would people of wealth and power wish to surround themselves with abnormal outcasts who sometimes possessed neither wit nor will?

The earliest trace of such beings is revealed in the accounts of the mysterious little pygmies called Dangas, who held positions of some privilege at the court of Dadkeri-Assi, a Pharaoh of the Fifth Dynasty. Some of these were apparently his confidants and one, Knumhotpu, was even made superintendent of the Royal Linen until his death, when his dwarfed form was immortalized in a statue at Giza. The Egyptians were awed by the Dangas because they were from the mysterious South, the country "ten leagues beyond man's life", the region of ghosts and talking serpents. The pygmies, big-headed and clothed in leopard skins, could dance like the god Bisu from Puanit, thus diverting the court and rejoicing the heart of the king. But there was more to it than auspicious diversion. Forty years after the time of Assi, a magical invocation was carved into the pyramid of Papi I. Addressed to the pilot of the boat bearing the king's soul to the Blessed Isle of Osiris, it reminded the gods that Osiris eagerly awaited Papi "because he is the Danga who dances the god". What this meant was that the Pharaoh hoped, rather touchingly, to come as a "fool" and thus be welcomed in the celestial court of Osiris. The several things suggested here include the notion that the Dangas could cross over the boundary between mortals and gods and that, as fools, they possessed a magical power related to this ability that could somehow be transferred to men, Pharaohs included. The fool, even the insane fool, or perhaps especially the insane fool, was believed to be in touch with the world of spirits and gods. To keep such people close and in one's care was deemed an act of wisdom rather than charity.

The magical power associated with the fool derived also from his role as scapegoat. Though it is true that sometimes this role thrust the fool right onto the sacrificial altar, in most cases it manifested in his acting as a decoy capable of drawing away evil from his master. Whilst certain Romans became notorious because of keeping morons or deformed slaves for entertainment, most of their wealthy countrymen, like Persians and Egyptians before them, kept such people only because they genuinely believed that their immunity to the evil eye would protect them from the arrows of envy and malice. This is based on the notion that the malign power of the evil eye is not only concentrated in some people but suffused in a vague and undefined way throughout the universe. Therefore, the self-mockery and verbal abuse so characteristic of the fool could act as a deflecting screen against evil capable of surrounding the person of a rich and enviable man. The king who is mocked before witnesses not only supports the only role given to one who is himself immune to envy, but he also deflects the potential grudge which his unassailed superiority might inspire. As a slight variation on this theme, the fool was often treated as a sort of spiritual whipping-boy, for when bad luck threatened it was thought wise to transfer it by provoking someone and getting his or her abuse. In our own time some people do this with only a partially conscious purpose, having a sort of instinctive tendency to stir up someone else's antagonism and thereby shift the burden of attachment through dislike onto the other's shoulders for a while. Using a fool for this sort of arcane manipulation could easily have been made permanent by employing a perpetual scapegoat who abused his owner as an official duty. On the other hand, the tie between king and fool might have become so complex and strong that the latter would willingly substitute for his master in ritual or even actual performances of regicide. Or he might do it out of love. The Irish fool Dodera was so loyal that he changed clothes willingly with his master, Prince Maccon, and died in his place in battle. Maccon used to say, "Since Dodera is departed, no laughter is produced; for after Dairine's merry jester there is desolation."

In a letter written early in the sixteenth century, Desiderius Erasmus expressed the opinion that "the sorts of fools which princes of former times introduced into their courts were there for the express purpose of exposing and thereby correcting certain minor faults through their frank speech". This identification of the fool as truth teller is brilliantly illustrated in Shakespeare's *King Lear*, whose tragic protagonist reiterates the theme by enigmatically crying out at the discovery of his daughter Cordelia's death, "And my poor fool is hang'd", thus recognizing in her the truth teller. Being but a truthful innocent, Cordelia could not speak the truth during her lifetime with impunity. Only the fool could do that and, with his absurd rhymes and ridiculous antics, get away with it. From outside the ordered world of self-serious reason, he could dash in and out with his parries, make his caustic point and leap away into undignified self-mockery. A magical decoy, a scapegoat and a teller of truth in the face of powerful authority, the fool added to his role the sometimes unconscious, sometimes conscious, element of comedy. Clever fools played the fool with a marvellous sense of timing and circumstance. Others were simply laughably foolish by nature despite their sudden ability to penetrate to the heart of some matter or other.

The ability for which the fool was forgiven all his defects was that which enabled him to render everyday life comic at the moment, on the spot. Man's appetite for comic relief has flourished for a very long time. One wonders if it acts upon the spirit as a sort of vitamin, or could it be more aptly described as a narcotic? Does the enjoyment of it engender a deeper insight into human nature, a keener critical faculty, or does it merely encourage an evasion of reality? Perhaps one can answer such questions only in terms of many subtle combinations of elements, but the fact remains that societies of fools which carefully recorded jests have existed since ancient times. Philip of Macedonia paid a talent in gold for the mere loan of the jest book kept by the club of wits in Athens known as "The Sixty". Culled from the quaint lunacies of fools, both natural and assumed, these laugh-provoking sketches quickly became stereotyped so that their appearance in the borrowed jesting of a would-be fool could easily elicit the dampening observation, "Ah, that comes from the Sixty." Much adapted foolery did, however, find a ready patronage, if for no other reason than the persistent belief that having a joker at the table was good for the digestion.

In later centuries the Romans and their descendants encouraged a host of buffoons whose antics astounded and amused and were partially recorded for posterity by Boccaccio, Sacchetti and Bandello. With the development of such characters as Punch, the entertainment provided by fools too often reflected a sensual and heartless appetite for low comedy, sustained by certain patrons as well as the public at large. A note of pathos, however, was introduced into the picture through the foolish character of Pierrot, whose pantomimed sketches threaded their way between the tragic and the hilarious. The wistfully absurd figure of a Deburau or a Chaplin has memorably exemplified this more touching aspect of the fool. Their comic appeal engages the sympathy of the audience even while they reveal absurd truths about the human condition. They are foolish but so clever as to cause one to laugh with them at oneself. Being the outsider or the underdog, they do not threaten directly the worldly personality, the puffed up sense of dignity men struggle to protect. Rather, they seem to have popped in from the moon, with their wildly unconventional point of view.

> Nobody can describe a fool to the life without much patient self-inspection.
>
> F. Moore Colby

Outsider though he was, the fool was the inversion of the king and therefore, in a sort of negative way, integral to the structure which was believed to reflect a divinely ordained society. Close to the king as spiritual adviser was the priest or cardinal who hoped to sway the temporal ruler in the direction of the ecclesiastical concept of God's plan for humankind. But the burden of rulership has often been tedious to kings and many of them frequently turned for relief to their fools. If this resulted in merely a passing hour or two of frivolous gaiety, naught would have come of it, but the fool had a knack for bluntly speaking the truth about matters dear to the church as well as to the king and a good deal of enmity was stirred up. It was well known that Will Sommers, fool to Henry VII, was a much despised enemy of Cardinal Wolsey, and there was a continual feud between Louis XIII's favourite fool, Marais, and Cardinal Richelieu. The very nature of their roles ensured that this sort of enmity was typical, despite the fact that a good many of the fools favoured by monarchs were extremely simple-minded. In his role as inverter, the fool would naturally be at odds with the pious establishment of the church, for he was the king, not of the socially accepted rule, but of misrule. His license to turn the grim realities of life into a farce flew in the face of sober-minded and penitent sinners as well as those who merely used the respectability and influence of the church for their own worldly ends. Thus, though all fools did not inspire universal affection or sympathy in the courts, their real enemies were usually the priests. Historically, this seems odd if one considers the Vatican patronage which exalted certain fools to heights of enormous privilege. Pope Leo X's *valet de chambre* had the authority to admit them at any time to his apartments to the exclusion of anyone else. Descriptions of Fra Mariano Felt, *capo di mati* ("chief of fools"), jumping up on the supper table and running from one end to the other, slapping cardinals and bishops all the way, do not prepare one for the more cool and critical differences of interest to be found later between fool and priest.

Suddenly, it was as if the world began to take itself more seriously. Divine madness receded more into a past regarded with suspicion and distrust. Inversions began to be seen as perversions and not dialectical broadsides capable of clearing the air and opening up a more critical perspective. Organized religion began to lose its ability to laugh at itself and a broader wedge was driven between the sacred and secular realms. It is difficult to overestimate the effect this had on human society. One wonders if people remotely realized that they were losing a critical check which worked to forestall the tendency to concretize the spiritual and shrink it down to ego size. As difficult as it may seem to understand at first glance, ancient wisdom had hitherto prevailed when the "Lord of Misrule" and the "Abbot of Unreason" played their mocking role even in connection with such arcane mysteries as those which took place at Eleusis. It still pervades such celebrations as that of the rural Indian Holi Festival, where the King of Holi rides backwards on a donkey amidst a joyful chaos of social reversals and inversions of every sort. He is the chief fool among fools, kept busy with the task of turning the caste system upside down and reversing roles of age and sex which otherwise tend to become so inflexibly set and grimly adhered to. Whether in a communal situation like this or on his own, the fool strips away the facades and exposes human weaknesses for what they are. Quite naturally he would have had a role to play in preparing a candidate for initiation or in tearing aside the veil of worldly identity so that villagers might see beyond appearances and greet Lord Krishna in their midst.

> Seest thou a man wise in his own conceit? There is more hope of a fool than of him.
>
> *Proverbs* 26:12

If the fool can perform such valuable functions for humanity, his extremely marginal position in society can only be understood in terms of humanity's ignorance about the whys and wherefores of its own traditions. It is as if the role of fool really did come by way of a whim of Zeus and mankind never possessed an intelligent understanding of his true nature. At any rate, the fortune of the fool has always been chancy, with very little assurance that he would be able to avoid living and dying as an underfed beggar or worse. In ancient Greece certain types of γελωτοποιοί called Parasites used to take part in banquets by special invitation in association with priests and magistrates. Gradually these became degraded and began to show up at symposia without invitation, brazening their way in with impudent repartee in order to garner a free meal. The Parasites were usually free-lance and lived by their wits, having names like Lark, Pod or Mackerel. They seem to have been more wily than mad, and they abounded in the rich courts of Philip of Macedonia and his son, Alexander. To pursue consciously the life of a fool entailed a willing and open acknowledgement of one's failure to attain the normal standard of human dignity either in bodily or mental tendencies. Such a one would then set about exploiting his own weaknesses to the advantage of his security and comfort. In order to have succeeded in such a tricky profession, these fools must have possessed a great ability to adapt themselves to whichever way the wind happened to be blowing from moment to moment. Placed in an inferior position at table, Aristippus, fool to the tyrant Dionysius, managed to maintain his audacity in the face of ridicule. When asked if he liked his new seat, he boldly replied, "Ay truly, for the place I held yesterday, I despise today, since I hold it no longer." Trickier still was the test of Nasr-ed-Din, who would have lost his head when he first presented himself to the conqueror Timur-leng (Tamerlane) had he not wittily been able to answer the questions put to him by the Mongol. That he succeeded in pleasing his new master was borne out in a story describing how Timur-leng once wept to see lines of ageing in his face when he looked into a mirror. His entire court wept in sympathy along with him for two hours, but the fool continued to sob even longer. Finally, asked by the conqueror why he still wept, he replied: "If you saw yourself in the glass for a short moment and wept for two hours, is it surprising that I weep longer since I see you the whole day?" How nervously relieved the onlookers must have been to see Timur-leng collapse in uncontrollable laughter!

Other fools evidently pushed it too far, risking life and limb for their antics. Charles Chester, fool to Elizabeth I, irked Sir Walter Raleigh and other noblemen until they bricked him up to his neck in a corner and he shrieked repeatedly for mercy. Some of the natural fools had trainers or prompters and reached remarkable levels of inspired madness. Around the turn of the fifteenth century, one Haincelin Coq wore out an inordinate quantity of shoes and on one occasion tore his clothes into shreds while wildly leaping and dancing before Charles VI. More poignantly, an order form written up for the seat of the Duke of Burgundy in 1494 requested a fool's dress patterned with the arms of the city of Lille for a lad described as "mad and out of his senses". It is doubtful that such fools were wise, but they were sometimes visited with the remarkable insights and even prophetic visions associated with the fey or the insane. Fools less natural and more shrewd were often capable of a good deal of wisdom in handling awkward situations. Some of these were actually entrusted with the business of arbitration, as in the case of a quarrel that broke out between a street porter and the keeper of a cook-shop in Paris. The porter had sat down near the shop door in order that his fare of plain bread might be made more savoury by the smell of roasted meat. The avaricious shopkeeper wished to charge him for this privilege and a fight between the two ensued. Seigni Johan (court fool to King John), who was called in to conciliate the brawlers, effortlessly pronounced that the porter should pay for the *smell* of the roast with the *sound* of his money. Such cleverness would have, no doubt, been beyond the dancing fool to Charles VI, but in many other cases it was not always so easy to discriminate between the wise fool and the cunning fool, let alone the mad, the mystical or the merely malapert.

> The fool doth think he is wise, but the wise man knows himself to be a fool.
>
> William Shakespeare

The fool's relationship to the philosopher seems to have been closer than to the priest, with a good deal of overlap on both sides. Xenophon described how the fool Philip presented himself uninvited at the famous supper party of Callias, where he provided welcome diversion from the serious moral discussions led by Socrates. He parodied and badinaged, indulging in impertinent comparisons and personal remarks directed at the guests. Socrates rebuked him for his impudence but was unable to subdue the fool's self-satisfaction. This is on its own somewhat misleading, as Socrates himself was given to childish play and extravagant dancing when the mood seized him. Indeed, Zeno called him the "Athenian buffoon" and Alcibiades claimed that he resembled the image of Silenus, chief of the satyrs, who rides as a fat, drunken man upon the back of an ass. Doubtless there were times when such a superior mind, flooded with the unworldly elation of noetic perception, would break the bounds of its earthly vessel and release the nymph, the Puck and the inspired fool in the body of a very plain, ageing man. How wonderful to imagine, for surely only a natural fool or a truly wise man could give himself so effortlessly to an unself-conscious divine madness. But while a philosopher may act the fool, are fools potential philosophers? Does their "gyring" and "gimbling" disguise a sort of special access to disinterested truth? Certainly, many a dim-witted fool would seem to be further from this than even a puffed-up doctrinaire. But history has shown a peculiar propensity to confuse the two and a recurrent tendency to bring them together. It pleased patrons in Germany to watch professors from the universities augmenting their incomes by playing the fool at court in the eighteenth century, and much earlier a favourite sport at Roman banquets was to pitch rival philosophers against one another, egged on by a fool. No doubt some found it gratifying to their own feeble intellects to witness learned men being made fools of by a fool or making fools out of themselves. But one suspects, at least in the former cases, that the learned men needed little assistance. Their egos did the job for them nicely, proving once again how hypocrisy and pedantry could be punctured by that prime dissolver of formalization, foolishness.

> Let a fool hold his tongue and he will pass for a sage.
>
> Publilius Syrus

Acting as an aggressive agent of dissolution, the fool breaks down the distinctions between folly and wisdom, life and art. When he is really successful, he breaks this barrier for us, his observers, as well, so that we too can inhabit for a moment a no man's land between the worlds of what is and what might be. He draws out our latent folly and, by our recognition of it, we are freed to follow the fool into a chaos of possible new beginnings. The genius of the fool, his ability to make us believe that he can divert the evil eye, draw us away from pain and outwit the intolerable tyranny of worldly circumstances is contingent upon his continual tendency to invert, dissolve and ever play the wild card. Like the final enigma of the tarot, he plays the part of the zero that can become any number at all. He is unnumbered and unplaced, his many-coloured costume symbolizing the multiple and incoherent influences to which he is subject. But he walks in the mountainous heights where one may not know what is going on in the world below yet receive glimpses of visions glittering beyond ordinary men's dreams.

The fool as a prophet or seer is a soothsayer without a temple, a lunatic or, perhaps, an oracle. In the ancient Semitic and Celtic traditions they were often considered possessed men who used verbal arrows to do war against established and complacent forms. The Shā 'ir of Islam, the *kāhin 'ar arrāf*, all were believed inspired by *jinns* in ways similar to the Irish *fill* or the Teutonic *thul*. They were fauns who spoke as mouthpieces of the spirits and often appeared bumbling in their varying conditions, as did Parsifal, who was called the Pure Fool. During the Christian era mystics continued to speak and behave in ways often outside the understanding of society. As "fools of god" they pursued their own peculiar path after the fashion of St. Paul before them. Inspired by the intense abandonment of worldly reason demonstrated by Francis of Assisi, Franciscans liked to call themselves Fools of the World (*Mundi Moriones*) and deliberately wore the pointed cap of the fool. Russian holy fools walked with heavy chains about their naked bodies from village to village, railing against every injustice. They sometimes froze and starved and often ridiculed the church but no one doubted that they were on fire with a love of God. In fact, the God-intoxicated individual has often been thought a fool by ordinary people because he does nothing to protect himself or further his own interests. Thus Prince Myshkin, Dostoievski's Idiot, was taken to be a fool by those around him simply because he was incapable of understanding their mixed motives. With the mystic fool, the higher mind can take possession precisely because the lower mind is inactive. With the psychic fool, glimpses of truth may often be revealed as he reacts to the changing forces whirling around him. But he is an erratic seer, a pawn capable of being possessed by any sort of entity as he revolves in his desperately madcap dance through life.

The aura of mysticism adhered to even the psychic fool, however, and it is significant that only when belief in the divinity associated with kings began to break down did the fool cease to have a deeper *raison d'être* in society. As men increasingly sought dignity and respectability in worldly contexts instead of a place in cosmic law, the fool became lost in the comedian, the harlequin of the stage and the clown of folk fairs and circuses. This was a great loss to the world, for together the king and the fool had represented solar and lunar dynasties or races among men. However imperfectly, the king had ruled as the sun rules the solar system and the fool had acted as his fluctuating check against over-concretization. Like the tarot Fool whose tunic bears the crescent moon, the king's idiot ever moved towards the edge of chaos, dragging with him a court otherwise too complacent, too prone to blind and self-serving rationalizations. The solar king symbolizing *Manas* in the world had, from the time of Rama, fallen from the heights of manasic righteousness into increasingly lower manasic blindness, but the true and natural fool never possessed such worldly reason. Informed either by mystical visions, madness or possessing spirits, he looked on the machinations of the lower mind as though through a window from the outside. He leavened the lump of man-made order, which always threatened to get too hard, and acted as a living link between men and gods.

In Shakespeare's *King Lear,* the fool's role seems to exist to emphasize one strange and tragic instance where the positions of the fool and the king are reversed. The king, in his foolishness, acts to dissolve the order of things by turning over his kingdom to his daughters and placing himself in the position of their childlike dependant. This act of folly unleashes powerful forces of good and evil which pour forth in exaggerated form through the important characters in the play. Lear's fool, being a man devoid of worldly wisdom, has the wisdom to see how the worldly are fools. In response to his master's ill-conceived action, he jokes and sings his silly songs and tries, in his grief, to expose the nature of the folly. The great evil expressed through two of the king's daughters results from the inversion whereby they both embrace the adage "Evil be thou my Good." Embracing this, reason cannot reach them. It cannot prove them wrong in itself. This perverse assertion that love and fellow feeling are foolish can only be reinverted by the fool, who says, "Folly (love) be thou my wisdom." The breaking of blood ties and the denial of love are so abnormal as to suggest a great convulsion of the natural order of things, and when Lear finally becomes aware of the inhumanness of Goneril's heart, his wits begin to lose their bearings. As his madness sets in, his sympathy and vision expand, inspiring his fool to comment, "Thou woulds't make a good fool." And, indeed, having hit the bottom, having lost his place in society as well as everything else, he has become the fool. He comes to see clearly that "When we are born, we cry that we are come to this great stage of fools."

The fool is the unbinder of man's slavery to the lower mind and the creator of freedom, but it is unwise to try prematurely to play his part. Lear seems to have indulged a whimsical but also egotistical fancy in thinking that he understood the consequences he was about to reap from his grandiose gesture. Far from understanding the true character of those around him, he had equally little understanding of himself or his responsibility in the world. By playing the fool, he was catapulted into madness rather than into a state of visionary wisdom. In dissolving his kingship, he cut away the raft of manasic control which could have seen him safely to the other side of chaos and onto the shore of true spiritual perception. He had plunged himself into the state of the most pathetic and witlessly dependent of fools. In a similar manner, the disciple who struggles along the path towards spiritual enlightenment encounters the same dangerous possible miscalculation. Though in essence a king possessing the germ of divinely endowed intelligence, such a seeker may fail to realize the importance of engendering within himself the rule of the true philosopher. He may free himself from the limitations of worldly identity and position only to cast himself into a turbulent psychic sea. The old myth of Zeus and the philosopher can, if properly interpreted, assist an aspirant to avoid such a pitfall. For the philosopher who had wished to be made a fool among fools was a truly wise man and had the wits to realize that he could shed his wisdom upon his fellow mortals best disguised as a fool.

Who knows how many wise men there are amongst us who pass thus disguised! How many souls have chosen in this or in past lives to forfeit respectability and position in order to work out some line of deeper truth while appearing the simpleton to others? Can we distinguish them from the witless fools whose appearance they share? Along the sidewalks and country lanes of the world walk legions of fools lacking in divine madness. Dull, with confusion swamping their minds, they are prey to cunning spirits or the grief of uncomprehended loss. Perhaps lives ago, perhaps even more recently, they abdicated their crown of manasic responsibility and tried to play the child, the freebooter, the unwise fool. These are not the truth tellers nor do they have the ability to deflect or neutralize the evil eye. The only dissolution they accomplish is wreaked upon the feeble order of their own minds, which skitter and threaten to break away entirely from their souls. The mystic Fool of God sees them upon the stage of life and knows them for what they are. He sees too the other fools, the buffoon playing at playing the fool, the priest playing at truth, the king playing at God. He sees, and yet he too is a fool, self-chosen in some life. For he knows his foolishness and is willing to abandon all concern for the opinions of men in order to become a better vehicle of his higher vision, his divine madness. He is a fool but also a philosopher-king. He is in control and yet pierces and dissolves the facades of control imprisoning the lower mind. He is chaos threatening the lower orders and sweeping like a peal of compassionate laughter through the hearts of weary humanity. Oh welcome him, the seer, the unexpected visionary with matted locks or fool's cap! Welcome him when he comes!

> The dullness of the sun
> Is eclipsed by the moon
> > on a foggy day.
> But the moon truly shines
> Only by the blessings
> > of the sun.
> Therefore, wed thou the moon
> To the solar orb;
> And let them in tandem
> > rule the way.

Hermes, April 1986

THE DWARF

Oh Son of Virochana! This dwarf is no other than the eternal divine Lord Vishnu, who is born of Kashyapa and Aditi, with the object of accomplishing the will of the gods.

Bhagavata Purana

Weaving richly embellished tales into a tapestry abounding with gods, giants, heroes and dwarfs, the old Norse Eddas trace back to events occurring before the creation of the cosmos. In the boundlessness of space they describe how, on opposite sides, there arose fire and ice. Between them was a great emptiness, a void in which huge clouds of vapour billowed out from the ice, called forth by the warming flickering of the fiery realm. The clouds churned and thickened as flame and ice merged more closely, producing heavy droplets that reflected light around them. Swelling in response to a growing heat of life within, the crystalline drops of melting ice joined together to form a rudimentary shape of gigantic proportions whom the ancients identified as Ymir. Exhausted by his titanic struggle into manifestation, Ymir slept. From the sweat that gathered in the hollows of his colossal armpits, a giant man and woman were formed who quickly spawned a race of their kind. These were the frost giants of chaos, who ruled the void before the world was ordered.

While they multiplied, an enormous cow took shape out of the melt-water of the ice. From her udder flowed their nourishment, while she took sustenance from the ice itself. As she steadily licked its frozen surface with her tongue, she uncovered the beauteous figure of an entombed god who sprang to life with his first breath of the warm air. From his single being he bore a race of gods who grew in vitality and power and came to feel themselves the rightful masters of the anticipating world around them. *En masse* they fell upon Ymir's vastness, bit into his flesh and tore away his arteries, releasing a gushing tide of blood which drowned almost all his kind even as he himself died. Thus, the old Norse said, from the parts of

Ymir's body was fashioned the world over which the gods would reign. Within its soil, life began to quicken; squirming movement like that of earthworms working through rich loam began to show itself. It bubbled and seethed across the fallen carcass of the future world, until it erupted in a vast army of dwarfs, children of the earth, who would be endowed by the gods with wit and speech and a physical form that was a squat parody of their own. Four of these the gods set at the corners of the world that they might support the sky for as long as creation endured. The rest they left to the clefts and grottoes of the earth.

Those who remained in the hidden places of the world were earth-coloured and shunned the daylight, which could turn them to stone. They moved through underground passes with as much ease as a fish moves through water or a bird flies through the air. The earth was their element and they understood intimately its structure and possible transformations. Like their four brethren who upheld the sky, they too in their fashion were agents and upholders of order. Being first in the world, their appearance ushered in its manifest possibility and they closely associated themselves with the material out of which it would take its shape. Thus, many races of dwarfs were known for their marvellous powers of metallurgy. They could fashion the sharpest, most exquisite, most magically potent tools and weapons for which later human mortals would pay dearly. One writer, comparing the dwarf and the giant, aligned the former with the arts and quoted Jonathan Swift, who noted that "they [the Lilliputians] see with exactness but not at a great distance". This is interesting when viewed in the light of Carl Jung's assertion that dwarfs stand as guardians of the threshold separating the unconscious realm (chaotic void of Ymir) from the conscious. In their artistic powers they act as agents of a vast and powerful order coming into being.

But they are not consciously aware of exactly what its source is, nor do they seem to be able to sustain control over its manifestations.

Possessing wit and speech and magical skills, the dwarf yet remains just outside or at the doorway of consciousness. Symbolized by his hidden life within the earth and his shunning of daylight, the dwarfs existence embodies mischievous, childlike and amoral forces which become tempered and sometimes exaggerated in his dealings with humans. But he is a guardian and a protector as well. In the archetypally meaningful story of Snow White, the Seven Dwarfs immediately took it upon themselves to guard their lovely house-guest night and day when she fell into the swoon induced by the wicked queen. Even so, to most mortals, dwarfs are a race apart, a "second" race now seldom seen. In earlier times they had mingled with heroic mortals as equals, and earlier still, before the coming of humans, they had known unequalled power and glory. Slowly they became a race in decline. Old as the rocks, they still possessed the mundane knowledge and power of the earth's mysteries, but before mankind's heavy-footed march they began a retreat.

A retreat, yes, but they did not remain entirely unseen, at least if one is to give due recognition to the stories about dwarfs passed down for millennia among almost every group of people that has lived on this globe. From *The Secret Doctrine* one can learn that the old Turanian races were typified by dwarfs and that there were Atlantean dwarfs as well. The ancients of the Mediterranean world identified οι πυγμαιοι (pygmies) as descended from Pygmaeus, a son of Dorus who founded a race believed to live in India where, it was thought, they lived under the earth on the east bank of the Ganges. Others wrote of the Pechinians of Ethiopia who sustained an annual attack by Scythian cranes who eventually exterminated the tiny militia. The word "pygmy" describes a fist and was recognized by the ancients as an increment of measure (from fist to elbow). The term "dwarf" comes from the Old Norse *dvergr*, whereas Viruli, Virunculi, and Montani find their etymological roots in Eastern Europe. The Germans passed down tales about Erdleute and Stillevolk, the Britons of goblins, knockers and leprechauns, and the Scandinavians added to their family of dwarfs, trolls, bergfolk and huldrefolk. Russians, Africans and Asians all have names in their folklore for dwarfs who, not content with populating every continent, followed the Polynesians out onto the many islands they made home and became known as Menehune, Patupaiarehe, Chokalai, Malavui, Luveniwai and Ponape, to name a few.

> High in the midst the chieftain-dwarf was seen,
> Of giant stature and imperial mien;

Full twenty inches tall, he strode along.

James Beattie

It is interesting to wonder if such beliefs could persist for the great length of time that they have without evidence of the actual presence of dwarfs in the world. Are they twenty inches tall? Are the tiny dwarfs of myth and lore being confused with dwarfed races of human beings? Can the dwarfs of the Eddas and other traditions be seen by the physical eye of man? It is said that humans have come upon the telltale signs of their industry: tiny forges in rock falls and caves, the sweepings of minute smithies. Some have believed that certain hollow trees in the forest have lodged them, noting the remains of small fires. Children often quite naturally assign them such domiciles, having reverentially identified the homes of the Seven Dwarfs in many far-flung places, including the redwood trees along the wild and rocky coast of Big Sur. A description of an actual encounter passed down among Nordic folk living on the Faeroe Islands is revealing. The tale refers to long ago when a peat gatherer, inching his way along a mountainous cliff overlooking the sea, stumbled upon a cave containing activity which so astonished him that he dropped his peat knife down on the rocks below. Upon the noise, the dwarfed occupants of the cave froze and the fire they tended at their forge died down. Straining their eyes, unaccustomed to daylight, towards the mouth of the cave, the tiny smithies waited. Their dumbfounded observer moved not a muscle and watched with breath held as one of the dwarfs bent over a pile of completed tools and selected a knife as long as a mortal man's forearm. The observer drew back in fear until he noticed that the dwarf held the knife by its blade as he, "bandy-legged and hunch backed ... scuttled quick as a spider across the rubbled cavern floor. With a glance that mingled shyness and a hint of warning, he thrust the knife into the man's grasp." The observer marvelled at the fineness of the blade and the beauty of the workmanship, but when he looked up to thank the tiny workers, his eyes were met with naught but a yawning stone wall. The dwarfs were closed in the living rock once more.

The dwarfs magical power over lifeless-seeming metal is evidence of their effortless acquaintance with the subtle structures composing the substances of the earth. They work easily with fire because it is the earthly manifestation of light which in its other expressions they shun. They understand perfectly how things grow and change and can be altered on the subtle plane of material becoming. Thus they provided the gods, who functioned to effect things in the manifesting world, with wondrous weapons whose fame was so great that heroes among emerging mortals eagerly sought out the little craftsmen for their counterparts. Even the gods who acted as celestial smiths were sometimes depicted in dwarf form. The Egyptian Ptah and the Greek Hephaestos are two such examples believed to have given structure and shape to the elemental forces of creation while hunched in diminutive stature over their forges. Mortal heroes found it easier to strike bargains with earthly dwarfs than with such lofty craftsmen and sometimes took great risks to acquire riches or magical weapons from them. For his assistance to the Nibelungs, the hero Siegfried was awarded the fabled sword Balmung, which he then was forced to use against its givers who subsequently attacked him. Though he had aided the dwarfs in settling a quarrel amongst themselves, they could not contain their avarice and perfidy and treacherously turned against Siegfried, causing him to vanquish them and take away the cloak of invisibility and their treasure.

Though many stories tell of the generous and often unsought assistance the dwarfish races have offered to man, a frequent theme in other tales points to the fact that dwarfs tend to be prey to lust and pride and resort to cunning when things do not go their way. This may be traced to the fact that their links with the earth necessarily involve a close involvement with the death and decay inherent in Ymir's corpse. Avarice, lust and pride are all qualities sprung from blind identification with material forms, and it is not surprising, perhaps, that dwarfs should be uncontrollably seized by these forces from time to time, especially in their relations with men who bring to the contest an extra focus of conscious vice or virtue. The strange theme of dwarfs lusting after mortal women or vice versa, which can be found even in some of the characters of the Arthurian legends, suggests a confusion of longing born out of a sense of inferiority and of atavistic perversion. In the story of Snow White the dwarfs do not participate in such futile and envious longings. They simply love her purity and beauty of soul and wish to protect it. They are tiny and deformed and cannot play the role of the prince who will awaken her, but it never occurs to them to lament this fact. No more does Snow White see in the dwarfs anything other than guardians who flourish under her grateful and wise care. Her love for them is born of gratitude but she does not intrude herself backward into their place in evolution. Instead, an interaction delicately based upon respect and open-hearted wonder is preserved between them.

Dwarfish smallness is often interpreted by man as deformity, abnormality or inferiority. After all, the dwarf under Shiva Nataraj's foot is unhesitatingly identified as symbolic of the blindness of life and the ignorance of man. Perhaps it is something about this blindness that explains why human physical dwarfs have so fascinated people in the past. This is not to say that even the more perverse of these mistook a human dwarfs size as an indication of lack of intelligence, but that the size of such an individual conveyed a childlike and unthreatening quality. To individuals whose lives embodied some degree of the wilful pursuance of atavistic decadence, small, ungrown people offered a pleasantly gratifying diversion away from the difficult business of manasic development and responsibility. It is significant that rulers like the emperor Augustus of Rome, who adored tiny, well formed dwarfs, had them sent to him from all over the world so that he could immerse himself with them in play and childish prattle and forget, for a time, the cares of the world. In this indulgence the emperor joined the ranks of many wealthy and aristocratic persons of full stature who have taken enjoyment in surrounding themselves with dwarfs who marched conspicuously in their retinues, sat for portraiture with their families and often wore extravagantly tailored clothes designed to draw attention to their diminutive physiques. Such owners were often fixated upon the size and possible deformity of their hapless chattle to the extent that they placed them, consciously or unconsciously, in the position of legendary dwarfs. Thus, an appreciation for their talents and intelligence was frequently obscured by childish or crudely insensitive interaction, treatment bearing the imprint of attitudes reserved for an inferior, less than human, race apart. It is a telling fact that the longest career enjoyed by the dwarf in human art forms is that of the small, deformed hunchback rendered in plaster or stone for the garden. He is a perfect caricature of certain chondrosystrophic dwarfs whose antics delighted the jaded eye of courts from time immemorial.

The human physical dwarf is most commonly the result of a genetic mutation. In the seventeenth century one of their patrons, the Empress of Austria, caused all known dwarfs and giants of the land to be assembled in Vienna for study. Amusingly, she placed guards to protect the dwarfs from the giants, only to find that the latter were mercilessly preyed upon by the former, who teased and insulted and robbed them repeatedly. The guards' instructions were altered but the incident gave credence to the old folk saying, "Long and lazy, little and loud." After attempting it, Isabella d'Este conceded that "you cannot raise a race of dwarfs". What she and others gradually came to realize was that most of the one out of ten thousand births producing a dwarf involve normally sized parents. In the case of a dwarf like the gifted painter to King Charles I who married another dwarf and fathered nine children, the surviving offspring were all normal size. Other dwarf genealogies more recently traced show that dwarfs can indeed produce dwarfs but that the majority of offspring will revert back to normal size. This is particularly interesting, as the factor favouring dwarfism involves a dominant gene with complete or high penetrance. A Danish study of one hundred and eight dwarfed individuals revealed that out of twenty-seven offspring, ten were chondrodystrophic dwarfs, the type of dwarfism where the extremities are disproportionately short relative to the trunk of the body. This condition as well as that of dyschondroplasia (disturbance of skeletal growth) are both due to genetic mutation affecting the endocrine or pituitary glands (also thought to lie at the root of racial dwarfism such as that exemplified by the pygmy people of Africa, India and Oceania). Metabolic disturbances caused by disease and certain environmental forces are far less typical causes. The discovery that fathers of mutant dwarfs are often disproportionately older than mothers reveals that older sperms have a greater chance of containing mutant alleles and suggests that spontaneous mutation of this kind is due to errors in genetic replication.

The smallest human physical dwarfs are those possessing normal proportions. Of these, some are primordial dwarfs from birth, others undergo retardation in growth after their first couple of years. Such dwarfs (or midgets) remain sexually immature and are sometimes quite attractive, as in the case of Charles S. Stratton, known to the world as General Tom Thumb. Born in Connecticut to normal parents in 1832, he grew to a height of little more than two feet, his head barely reaching above the knees of a normal individual. With the famous P. T. Barnum, he travelled to England and began a series of tours that made him the toast of the crowned heads and *hoi polloi* of Europe. In England "this little, great small man" had an elegant carriage made and furnished in the richest style. Its body was twenty inches high and it was drawn by a fine pair of tiny Shetland ponies, with two small boys acting as footman and coachman. Certainly, with all his triumphs and resultant wealth, the tiny General remained unintimidated by the biblical warning (*Leviticus* 21:20) which brands dwarfs as blighted and decrees that their presence shall not be suffered at the altar. Nor was he embarrassed by the frank fascination others showed him. Unlike some dwarfs who have been forced to make a living from their deformity, he thoroughly enjoyed his fame and waxed proudly in its glow. Others, like Jeffrey Hudson, who was knighted at Hampton Court in the early seventeenth century, so overwhelmingly waxed in their self-perceived glory that they repeatedly had to be put in their place. The many recorded instances of this sort of uncontrolled swaggering or lust after something or other tend to strengthen the comparison between mortal dwarfs and their less admirable counterparts in myth. The fact that they arrived at their condition through a genetic mutation instead of through a natural and necessary step in cosmic evolution stands in contradistinction to such similarities, and it is probable that human expectations eliciting this sort of behaviour are at least partially responsible.

> What vast perfection cannot Nature crowd
> Into a puny point.
>
> Attributed to Sisyphus, two-foot-high
> dwarf of Marcus Antonius

In the great and richly symbolic Hindu tradition the most famous and illustrious dwarf is Vamana, the fifth avataric incarnation of Lord

Vishnu. The story goes that in the Second Age, called *Treta Yuga*, the Daitya king Mahabali performed such sacrifices and austerities that the gods were rendered helpless to deal with his growing control over the world. They feared he might gain ascendancy even over the heavens through his powers, and so they implored Vishnu as the embodiment of the perception of cosmic law pervading the three worlds to put things aright. In the form of a dwarfed Brahmin (whose name, Vamana, etymologically suggests that which tends to the left, is perverse or turns things around), Vishnu appeared before the king. Though exceedingly small, he was comely to look upon and, as a Brahmin, he was treated with great respect and courtesy by the ethically minded ruler who requested him to ask for a gift. Modestly, the tiny guest asked only for as much ground as he could step over in three strides, and the king, smiling to himself, readily granted that he should have it. Of course, as soon as this had been granted, Vishnu grew into gigantic proportions and took three mighty strides across the universe. He took as his own the earth and the heaven of the gods, leaving to the generous king the realm of *Patala*.

> That dwarf form of that infinite Hari, comprised as it is of three gunas, miraculously expanded to such an extent as to include that earth, the heaven, the cardinal points, the space between the heaven and the earth, cavities and hells, oceans, the subhuman beings, human beings, gods and sages and everything else.
>
> *Bhagavata Purana*

King Mahabali was the grandson of Prahlad, that archetypal devotee of Lord Vishnu who had lived during the time of the latter's *Narasinhavatara*. Being a Daitya, he was the Hindu equivalent of a Titan or a giant who ruled before the gods who subsequently presided over the orderly manifestation of the worlds. Here there is a striking parallel with the Eddaic Ymir and the frost giants, for the Daityas and Titans were similarly defeated and put in their place, their substance (chaos) becoming the stuff marshalled by the gods in accordance with their materializing design. While the dwarfs in the Eddaic myth emerged from the matter of the fallen Ymir as earthly ushers of anticipating order, the dwarf Vamana acted as the vehicle of the establishment of that same law, Vishnu deliberately assuming that form to wrest command of the energies and powers of creation from the Daitya race. Another parallel lies in the identification of Lord Vishnu as an Aditya, one of the children of Aditi, the Infinite Light, the pure consciousness of infinite existence, one and self-luminous. As daughter of Daksha (one of her offspring) Aditi becomes the thought of this divine consciousness in the symbolic guise of a cow whose udder feeds all the worlds and who, like the cow in the Eddaic myth, gives rise to the gods. "Aditi is the infinite consciousness in the cosmos espoused and held by the lower creative power which works through the limited mind and body, but [which is] delivered from this subjection by the force of the divine or illumined Mind born of her in the mentality of man." Thus, she is the source of all cosmic forms of consciousness from the physical upwards, including that which enables man to realize his true divine nature.

It is said of the Adityas that they have a twofold birth: one, above in Divine Truth as creators of the worlds and guardians of Divine Law and, two, here in this world and in man as cosmic and human powers of the Divine. In the visible world they are male and female powers associated with the elements just as the dwarf is associated with the earth. In his three steps Lord Vishnu moved like the Light of the highest Sun of Truth, on earth expressed as fire, in space expressed as lightning and in heaven expressed as spiritual, omnipresent sunlight. Reversing this, Lord Vishnu, heeding the entreaties of the gods, strode down from his heavenly state like lightning flashing through the sky and presented himself on earth in the guise of a fiery dwarf, who proceeded to act as the agent extending the gods' rule and banishing (for the *manvantara*) to the lower regions the kings of chaos and untimely dissolution.

Vamana is identified with Brihaspati or the planet Jupiter. Called in the *Rig Veda* Brahmanaspati, "the deity in whom the action of the worshipped upon the gods is personified", Brihaspati represents the materialization of divine grace through means of ritual worship. In the occult hierarchy of the manifested cosmos, the *Cosmocratores* who fashioned our solar system are said to be prior to the gods and the spirits of the earth. As each of the seven great races of this globe evolves, it receives its light and life from one of the seven planetary Dhyanis who radiate (in conjunction with a planetary body) the pure spiritual rays of the Invisible Sun. The first race received such through the sun, the second through Jupiter, the third through Venus, the fourth through the moon and earth, the fifth through Mercury. Thus, the Second Age or *Treta Yuga* is linked up with the Second Race which, in the scheme of manifesting forms, possessed relatively unformed ethereal bodies, forerunners of the conscious human entities that would emerge in the Third Race. The dwarf is then an agent of the Second Age, a partially conscious usher functioning to prepare the soil for a fully blooming self-consciousness to follow.

When the tiny dwarf smithy gave the peat-gatherer a wondrous knife, he also gave him a shy but warning glance. His glance held a world of meaning, for he must have known that it was dangerous for the mortal standing at the entrance to his cave to even contemplate following him back into his world. With a delicate observance of unspoken law, he acknowledged the superior potential of the human being by presenting him with a gift while clearly discouraging any further exchange. He did not wish the mortal intruder to look back on him and his kind, seeming to know that this was unwise for all concerned. It is interesting that the human in the story was unaware of this etiquette and quite consumed with his own curiosity. But whereas the dwarf can know what the proper order is and how to work with its elements as they present themselves to him, a man (albeit ignorant of many things) has the potential ability to consciously grasp the meaning of this order and join the smithy's fire to the spiritual light of understanding by the lightning of intuitive thought. Whether of dwarfed or normal stature, the human being has passed the threshold guarded by the dwarf and must not look back or perversely interfere in matters pertaining to a previous stage in evolution.

> Thrice Vishnu paced and set his step uplifted out of the primal dust; three steps he has paced, the Guardian, the Invincible, and from beyond he upholds their laws. Scan the workings of Vishnu and see from whence he has manifested their laws. That is his highest pace which is seen ever by the seer like an eye extended in heaven, that the illumined, the awakened, kindle into a blaze, even Vishnu's step supreme.

> *Rig Veda* 1.22:17–21

No doubt the mutation responsible for physical dwarfism has often been the karmic result of an ego looking backward in evolution, getting caught in some sort of atavistic fixation. But there have been remarkable souls born in dwarfed bodies who seem to have lived out their lives as witnesses of a hidden truth about evolution or even as guardians and reminders of the precious gift of self-consciousness which man possesses yet so constantly squanders. One need only recall the sage-like dwarf in *The Ship of Fools* to realize the danger of attempting crudely to understand the history of a human ego in terms of externals. The highest pace of Vishnu may be seen by a seer in a dwarfed form who, like Doc in the Snow White story, acts as a wise leader, marshalling the Sleepy, Dopey, Sneezy and Grumpy forces of his less evolved brethren.

In becoming a self-conscious child of Aditi, an individual steps through space in such a way as to marshal the dwarfs, sylphs, salamanders, undines and all their powers within his or her own being. This is accomplished not by focussing upon these beings or trying to bargain for their energies, but by raising one's inner sight to the source of power that lies beyond them which they, themselves, in their obedient natures serve. When man has purified the soil of his lower nature and rendered its most rock-like and resistant parts into instruments of a truly refined nature, capable of responding to every desire of the higher Divine Will, he will command a devoted army of dwarfs eager to assist him in every way. But unless his spiritual nature rules, he would be wise to leave them in the land of myth and legend, for, disturbed while yet undominated by Divine Will, dwarfs may easily fly out of control and repay ignorant curiosity or desire for powers with treachery. To the pure soul of Snow White the dwarfs were devoted friends, and blessed are they who would seek to match this purity. Before their gaze the stony wall of the whole universe will open wide to reveal hidden treasures, powers and races unseen.

> Within the cavern of the mind,
> Inside the crevasse of the heart,
> A golden sword of Truth consign
> The members of a race apart.

Hermes, June 1986

THE DESERT

A science that could comprehend and describe the phenomenon of
deserts would possess the key to the past and future of our planet.

Uwe George

Out in the Pinto Basin, far beyond the last trace of California sprawl, an eroded washboard track bumps along the alluvial skirts of a low desert range. Very little vegetation breaks the ochre stretch of the hills, leaving only the igneous outcrops and the occasional arroyo to relieve the eye. Sounds travel for miles there and, in spite of an engine grinding under the floorboard, the creaking moan of loose timbers from the deserted Virginia Dale Mine can capture one's attention long before its spindly derrick reveals itself around a curve of the slope. There it stands, all worked out like other wrecks left behind: the desert's claim to man's squandered dreams. But over the range the road winds to another vista where the hills curve down around the pebbled floor of what was once a vast inland sea. Circling around its edges, the Coxcomb and Eagle mountains offer jagged profiles to the relentless sun and collect long vertical shadows as the afternoon wears on. The eyes of few have watched this drama day after lonely day, and since the Indians left centuries ago, only those of one old miner had learnt it all by heart.

He was an immigrant who, as a young man, had somehow made his way across the world to end up mucking out in the hard-rock mining operations that had survived the turn of the century in this area. And when the companies folded and the prospectors drifted away, he stayed on to follow his own vein of gold and life. He lived alone all those years and worked six shafts in as many days of the week. Thus he was able to grubstake himself and sit in the evenings watching the shadows curl up the arroyos in the basin and set off the flames lit by the dying sun on the hills. He was a man of contemplation. When he looked at a person he seemed to be looking way beyond them, and yet he knew exactly what was on their mind. Once a young greenhorn dropped by to visit him and enthused about the great romance of life alone in the desert and how he would like to pursue its challenge. Old Carl gazed at him and through him with eyes that measured by the increments of mountain ranges and advised him, in so many words, to put up or shut up. The desert has that effect upon people who are drawn to it and stay in it. It destroys the embroidery work of the mind and leaves behind only the glaring contours of truth perceived at a distance. There is no room for fuzzy thinking in the desert. And the mysteries it reveals in the evening stillness cannot be expressed by mere words.

If one tries it, one will find that the experience of tramping through desert wastes, trusting only in one's own abilities, has a way of throwing a person back upon who one really is. In a landscape whose very starkness prompts the spirit to exult, one returns to the most deeply buried dreams of childhood. A French Saharan explorer once said that the desert might be the most intensely loved environment on earth. But it is also frightening in its boundlessness and lack of obvious landmarks. In many languages the very word "desert" is used to mean the opposite of shelter, safety, order or the familiar. It symbolizes instead that which is empty, lost, without bearings and yielding seemingly nothing. Within the great Sahara there are areas as flat as a table, stretching without feature, to the equivalent in size of the state of New York. Called "serir", such places support only the life of micro-organisms, and a camp tent pitched at random would be the only visible (if artificial) landmark. Leaving his small party in their tent one morning, one geologist walked out upon the serir with his eyes fastened on the "desert pavement" looking for tiny forms of life. So intent in his study was he that he had covered some distance before he stopped to look around. To his horror he could see nothing. In all directions miles of flat, featureless terrain stretched with no camp in sight. He had walked more than the five miles which, on the sea or on perfectly flat land, results in the disappearance of such things as ships or tents due to the curvature of the earth. An indescribable sense of loneliness and desolation clutched at his heart. He experienced a loss of a sense of relationship to anything, of measure, of time or place. There was no sound aside from the throbbing of his pulse, and his eyes frantically sought out the faint outline of his own footprints leading back to camp. Though an old desert-hand, having spent years of geological exploration in such places, he panicked and ran wildly along that track until he could see the tent over the horizon, with the Land Rover parked nearby. One wonders what he would have done in his fright if there had been no footprints at all. Standing there, as we say, in the middle of nowhere, he might as well have dropped down out of the sky, possessing no beginning or relationship to things in this world.

As a symbol, the desert represents desolation, abandonment and contemplation of that which lies beyond the familiar. It is the most propitious place for divine revelation, being, in its starkness, the realm of abstraction, where the non-essential is stripped away. It is the domain of the sun, not in terms of fertility on the physical plane (which involves water), but as pure celestial radiance, blinding in its manifestation and capable of consuming the body for the salvation of the soul. The vegetation, the overwhelming variety of life forms thriving cheek by jowl in other types of environments, endlessly divert the senses and create a structure of compelling reality which directs and moulds the desires and efforts of men. The desert is bereft of such props. In the words of the fabled poet of the desert:

> The Worldly Hope men set their Hearts upon
> Turns Ashes – or it prospers; and anon,
> Like Snow upon the Desert's dusty Face,
> Lighting a little hour or two – is gone.

> Omar Khayyam

It was in the desert of Sinai that Moses saw God, who, manifesting on the Mount there, gave to him the Commandments by which his people should live. It was also in the desert that the ancestors of Christ's disciples received manna from heaven and Jesus himself advised them to "come ye yourselves apart, into a desert place". The desert was regarded as a place of abstraction, revelation and sacrifice by the tribes of the ancient Middle East, but it was filled with mystery and danger as well. In its desolate places the Jews forgot the teachings of Moses and "tempted God", and Jesus underwent severe trials of temptation. A tricky place where one can lose one's way and forget, the desert is believed by many to be haunted by djinns and evil spirits of various kinds. To the Egyptians it was the region of the dead ruled over by Osiris, and people of Central Asia believed that the tormented souls of unmarried or barren women wandered there. Keeping company with spirits attracted to the earth, they became evil over time and were much feared by the Yakuts, Buriats and Altaic Tatars who believed they used the deserts of Turan and Gobi as centres from which to set out on their destructive excursions. Awesome and desolate, the spiritual rejuvenation offered by the desert could be matched by unexpected forces of trickery and death.

> But a desert stretched and stricken left and right, left and right,
> Where the piled mirages thicken under white, hot light;
> A skull beneath a sandhill and a viper coiled inside –
> And a red wind out of Libya roaring "Run and hide."
>
> Byron Khun de Prorok

On the edge of the Gobi, the remains of gigantic statues lie partially buried in the wind-driven sand. They are said to have been shaped by the Lemurians long before the cycle of floods which left the Central Asian plateau high and dry. Transformed into a sea twelve thousand years ago, at its centre there remained an island of great beauty inhabited by the last remnants of this Third Race. The Chinese records also mention these "immortal men" who found refuge in the Gobi Desert, where "they still reside invisible to all, and defended from approach by hosts of Spirits". Their dwelling place is Shamballa, which has fascinated so many and lured them into the wilderness in vain. Covered now by the sands of an enormous wasteland, there is little hint of what lies hidden. Nor do we know much about the traces of past greatness concealed in other deserts. Occultism, however, teaches man to be patient and contemplate the nature of the spiritual impulses which utilize matter in ever-shifting cycles. Of the seven continents and races of this *manvantara*, Sakka and Pushkara will be the last into which will enter portions of desert lands now existing in America, Africa and Central Asia. Thus, drawing upon concealed resources whose effects in the world at present are difficult to trace, the stage for further human evolution will be set. If one considers how the knowledge of the phenomenon of deserts could provide the key to the past and future of our planet in this light, one adds a greater breadth and depth to Uwe George's proposition.

The distribution of deserts on our globe is also linked with its spherical shape, the inclination of its axis and the rate of its spin at the equator. Most deserts of the world lie within the horse latitudes, or the belts known as the Tropics of Cancer and Capricorn. In the Northern hemisphere this is expressed in the Sahara, Arabian, Iranian or Mexican deserts, while in the Southern lie the Kalahari, Patagonian and Great Victoria. The reason for this is largely due to the angle at which the earth spins around the sun, exposing these areas to its rays, each for half of the year. It is the angle of the sun's rays that determines the temperature, which acts as the most powerful agent of desert formation. In addition to this, the turning of the equatorial belt at one thousand miles per hour heats up air masses which rise, causing low atmospheric pressure and rain. The dry air descends on either side of this, creating high pressure areas where the warm air absorbs the moisture of the lower atmosphere, leaving the land dry. Other deserts are encouraged by cold ocean currents moving from the poles towards the equator along the western sides of continents, whilst relief deserts like the Gobi lie beyond high mountain ranges that stop the rain.

The lack of rain and high temperatures are closely connected. In such an area clouds form rarely and the moisture content in the air is very low (two to five percent), so that the sun's rays strike the ground almost unhindered. In a temperate climate clouds, plants, rivers, lakes and general humidity absorb around forty percent of the sun's rays. In some tropical rain forests as little as one percent of its light reaches the actual floor, while the desert can easily receive as much as ninety-five percent. In the Sahara the exposed igneous rock areas reach a temperature of 185 degrees Fahrenheit, with rapid cooling at night to 50 degrees Fahrenheit, resulting from the same lack of atmospheric obstruction. Such dramatic temperature changes boldly express the unembellished starkness of the desert as it lies exposed and unprotected beneath the celestial forces acting upon it. Over some areas of the vast four million and more square miles of desert in Africa there may fall as little as two inches of rain in a year.

During some years there is no rain at all and then a whole year's rain falls at once, creating flash floods, carving out wadis and arroyos like scars across the baked land. The water races over the desert pavement, soaks the dunes and, in a few hours, disappears without a trace. It is a dramatic action, fast and seemingly unprepared for, like the floods of a revelatory vision – flashing through the mind, filling the cavity of the heart and then evaporating.

Aided and shaped by the wind, deserts can grow and spread. If a small clearing is created in a forest, the trees there are less resistant to Aeolian forces than on its fringes and so others will be toppled. Left unreplanted, the clearing will spread, animals will feed upon the grasses which take the place of trees, and overgrazing can lead to erosion and the increase of windblown dust and sand. Man has come to play an increasingly powerful role in this process over the last few thousand years. With his shift away from the hunting and gathering of wild animals and plants, he began to exert a radical influence upon the globe's fragile ecosystems, joining his impact with the fundamental forces of temperature, rainfall and geological upheaval that cause the formation of deserts. This complicates the picture considerably, especially from a symbolic point of view, for man-made deserts are the result of ignorant mismanagement of resources sustained largely through lack of humility and increasingly materialized motives and goals. It is one thing for human beings to go into a desert seeking that which is capable of being revealed. It is quite another for man to create deserts in which subsequent generations are forced to live. In the longer curve, however, the cause and effect relationship between man and the conditions of the earth is far more generalized; race and national karma operate in a very broad sense where cycles exist within cycles and one man's desert revelation is another man's poverty and despair.

> The 'orse 'e knows above a bit, the bullock's but a fool,
> The elephant's a gentleman, the battery-mule's a mule;
> But the commissariat cam-u-el, when all is said 'an done,
> 'E's a devil an' a ostrich an' a orphan-child in one.
> O the oont, O the oont, O the Gawd-forsaken oont!
> The lumpy-'umpy 'ummin-bird a-singin' where 'e lies,

'E's blocked the whole division from the rear-guard to the front,
An' when we get him up again – the beggar goes an' dies!

Rudyard Kipling

To the Taureq, the Bedouin or the Berber, the question of whether anyone can love a camel is academic. Without the wondrous beast, they surely would never have been able to navigate the awesome sea of sand and rock that stretches five thousand miles from Mauritania to Arabia. As with the Gobi, there was a time when the Sahara was a sea, then a fertile continent, only to become, after temporary resubmergence, a vast desert. In the course of this fluctuating history it had been part of a vast land stretching from its present eastern boundary across the Atlantic to the Caribbean. Thus, it bears within its shifting dunes the imprint of an Atlantean age with all its creative powers and abuses. Now a vast and growing desert, it is well named by the Arabs a "sea without water" (*bahr belà mà*), upon which they have traditionally embarked as though upon a voyage to another shore. The great dunes are like frozen waves of the ocean blown into ridges sometimes a thousand feet high. Across these ergs or great dune areas skilful navigators aboard their superbly trained camels have made their way along well known routes for thousands of years. It would seem impossible to imagine how a route could be established in wind-blown sand, but the surface of the desert changes only very gradually and old maps show the same great ranges and *gassis* (corridors) for centuries at a time. The natives of the Sahara have never been known for their peaceful ways but they have shown a wise humility before the desert, learning gradually its secrets and coming to feel a great love for its stark and uncompromising ways. Many a European testing its desolation has failed to understand the need for that humility and has come to grief. Kipling's picture of a stalled army division is amusing to imagine, but it hides a history of intrusion and ambition come to naught through ignorance and misplaced dreams.

Far hence he lies,
Near some lone desert town,
And on his grave, with shining eyes,
The Southern stars look down.

Matthew Arnold

More recent in the making is the Thar Desert of Rajasthan, which is thought to be a mere two thousand or so years old, at least in its present state. Its beginnings are probably much older, traceable to Miocene times, thirty-five million years ago, when the Himalayas thrust themselves up to initiate the monsoon cycle and the sea retreated, leaving behind it the sedimentary deposits of the desert floor. Parts of the region were evidently well wooded and capable of supporting extensive human settlements at the time of Alexander's visit. People in civilizations on the Indus and Saraswati Rivers flourished and scarce would have believed that a thousand years hence their descendants would be nomads eking out a slender living from the arid land. The monsoons would shift to the east, and deforestation for fuel resulting in erosion and salination of the river systems would bring destruction more surely than any invaders from the north or west. Man would add to the workings of Nature to create a vast and ever-growing desert.

On our globe the desert areas are growing at the rate of forty miles daily, killing directly or indirectly about two hundred people in the same amount of time. Crop-smothering sandstorms, the choking of springs, the loss of trees capable of attracting the rain, all contribute to drought, death and famine. There are some who believe that the terrible famines in Africa are merely a prelude to a world-wide process of desertization that will mark the decades to come. Within the framework of karmic geological effects, man seems to be intent upon creating these deserts far in excess of what Nature would have provided. An overwhelming greed, matched by a loss of an intuitive sense of cyclic balance, seems to be driving the human race in its wasteful attack upon the life forms of this planet. In contrast to this, wise men would husband the rain forests, the savannahs, the timberlands and the valleys with care, taking only what they needed to live a simple, introspective life. They would respect and work with the balance Nature revealed and they would realize that the deserts of our globe represented laya points, not to be created through ignorance, but natural places of withdrawal and rest where the maya of the world is peeled away to reveal a realm of potential beginnings and endings.

Moses begged Pharoah to let Aaron and him go into the desert in order to "sacrifice unto the Lord our God". They, like others of old, associated the burning drought of the desert with spirituality and asceticism. It was the natural place to make sacrifices. The biblical prophets and the Muslims to come considered their "desert religion" to be pure and undefiled as compared to the fertility rites which formed the exoteric basis of the religions of agrarian people living in lusher climes. The starkness and cleanliness of the desert represents not only abstraction and revelation but direct exposure to God without the ameliorating buffer of His seasonally aspected manifestations. Thus monotheism (in the Judaeo-Christian and Islamic sense) is born of the desert and casts man down onto a barren soil where he truly experiences himself as separated from his Maker and consumed with longing to meet Him face to face. The extremes of heat and cold, barren sky and barren earth heighten this sense of separation and longing. The sun coming up without warning and the absence of twilight in the evening accentuate an atmosphere of extremes and instantaneousness. The setting itself suggests revelation, even a flash flood of sudden enlightenment. It also suggests the unyielding, uncompromising spirit of fanaticism, an element often apparent in monotheistic traditions.

> And thou did'st shine, thou desert moon upon
> All this, and cast a wide and tender light,
> Which softened down the hoar austerity
> Of rugged desolation, and fill'd up,
> As 'twere anew, the gaps of centuries;
> Leaving that beautiful which still was so,
> And making that which was not, till the place
> Became religion, and the heart ran o'er
> With silent worship of the great of old –
> The dead but sceptered sovereigns, who still rule
> Our spirits from their urns.
>
> George Gordon, Lord Byron

Like the Essenes of the Dead Sea or the Sufis who have wandered in barren places unseen except by the all-seeing Eye of Spirit, others from time immemorial have sought the desert in order to commune with God. When John the Baptist was born it was prophesied that he would perform the mercy promised to the fathers, that he would "go before the face of the Lord to prepare his ways". And so John grew, waxing strong in spirit and remained "in the deserts" until he came forth unto Israel to teach. He, like prophets before him, pursued the time-honoured way of withdrawing into the place of meditation and preparation before coming forth to share the fruits of his spiritual awakening with the world. For prophets the desert was the lay a place of incubation, of inner growth and realization. It was also the place of trial and temptation. If man hoped to confront the god within himself there, he could also expect to confront the devil. The *Gospel According to Matthew* describes how Jesus was led by the spirit out onto the desert to be tempted by the devil. After fasting for forty days and nights the tempter rose up and challenged Jesus to prove himself the Son of God by performing lower magic and to accept the rulership of the whole world in exchange for his worship. Like John before him, Jesus began to teach in the world after his instruction and initiation among the Essenes and his trials in the desert were completed. First the desert, then the *Sermon on the Mount*.

The desert holds within its hot sand surviving seeds that burst into bloom with the slightest rain. Like a revelation, this quick flush of vegetation waxes and dries away. Those who know how to cross the desert know where to find its hidden nourishment. Alone, out there beneath the naked elements, they are witness to the flashing bloom, the process of birth, growth and decay, quickened to such a degree that it is possible to grasp the illusory nature of time and see the end in the beginning, the beginning in the end. One who travels thus can sense the dormant progeny of past civilizations buried for a time but alive and exerting a hidden force upon the world. What once was the Holy Isle is now a desert and rightly so. For in the element of earth there is no greater likeness to the sea than the waving sands of the desert, and both bear Manu's seed from one cycle of worldly efflorescence to the next. Among those who spend their lives on the desert, few indeed conquer the fearful abyss of loneliness and come to fathom the antique mystery presented in its vast starkness. When their eyes, like those of old Carl, become permanently focussed upon a timeless condition, they become as initiates in a desert brotherhood, linking them with the wise men and prophets of old.

Old creaking mine the work of men
Who hoped to find your treasure.
And sun-bleached bones the mark of them
Who failed to take your measure.
I see within your wind-blown face,
your dried arroyo basin,
The dreams that men have dared to dream
And leave their spirit's trace in.

Hermes, July 1986

THE LAKE

Thou art to know that what thou beholdest yonder as a wide lake is, in truth, a plain like unto this, all bedight with flowers. And likewise thou art to know that in the midst of that plain there standeth a castle of white marble and of ultramarine illuminated with gold. But, lest mortal eyes should behold our dwelling place, my sisters and I have caused it to be that this appearance as of a lake should extend all over the castle so that it is entirely hidden from sight.

The Story of King Arthur and His Knights

Being mortally wounded, the noble Sir Pellias sank with pain and much lamentation to the very threshold of death. Gone to the world was he in consciousness, but before his spirit had passed over, he was approached by a pale lady all dressed in emerald green, with dark hair swaying around eyes as deep as the lake from whence she had come. She gave to him an *elixir vitae* which, when he drank it, made his body feel as light as air. His immortal soul dilated with pure joy and he rose from his couch with the desire to remain with his benefactress, who assured him, "It shall be as thou dost ask, for it was to that end that I have suffered thee nearly to die and have brought thee back unto life again."

In his renewed state Sir Pellias had become half-fey and half-human, having partly entered into another world. Readily accepting this, he proclaimed to the lady, "Thou hast given life unto me again. Now do I give that life unto thee forever." Thus it was that, after having followed a pale silver light in the forest which led to the plain of the fairy lake, Sir Gawain came upon him. There at its mist-bound shore Sir Pellias stood with the Lady of the Lake, and as he approached, the fearful Gawain trembled to see the face of his former adversary. It shone with a strange light and its expression was that of no ordinary man, but was fixed instead with a kindly though eerily remote smile. "Touch me not," Sir Pellias said, "for I am not as I was aforetime, being not all human but part fey." Whereupon he turned and disappeared into the lake, leaving the younger knight to marvel and recall that to just such a place had King Arthur come years before. Seeking the magical sword which rose from its swirling waters, the king had been warned by the same emerald-clad lady that no mortal man could cross the lake "saving in one way. Otherwise, he shall perish therein."

Shrouded in such enchanted mists, the lake has ever evoked a deep sense of awe in men. To the ancient Egyptians its hieroglyph symbolized the occult and mysterious. Even artificially constructed lakes, like that at the Temple of Amon at Karnak, were considered to represent the waters of Chaos over which the sun god proceeded in his eternal boat. For many people water has always suggested a connection between the superficial and the profound, a transparent, fluidic mass which conceals and yet reveals the way to another world. The lake embodies this in its fearful depths as well as on its glittering surface. It is profoundly feminine, being the humid spawning place of monsters and magical female powers, and yet the image of self-contemplation, consciousness and revelation. Sitting beside a lake, one is calmed and led inexorably into a reflective state. But upon entering its waters, one slips into a bottomless realm where cold draughts rise up from unseen depths to curl like cloying tendrils around one's exposed and pathetically vulnerable body. In this fearful guise, the lake is a fatal abyss symbolizing and sometimes becoming the means of transition between life and oblivion, form and formlessness, solidity and fluidity. Lying, as it often does, far below the pure air of mountain heights, the lake can represent a low spirituality, a watery quagmire filled with death-giving life. One is not at all confident that such soggy depths could enshrine the soul's immortal castle or that one would wish to enter its fairy world. But Sir Pellias was a gentle and pure knight, and the lady to whom he gave his life also provided the sword of Arthur's spiritual victory. To enter into the domain of such a one would seem to represent more than merely becoming bewitched or floating in some limboed half-life between worlds. Perhaps there are lakes of clear vision as well as those that open into oblivion.

Certainly, there are many sorts of genii believed to dwell in and govern lakes. People everywhere have had traditions of "water masters", maidens or "lake mothers". And whilst tales of hapless youths drawn to watery graves by lacustrine nymphs can be found in many parts of the world, equally widespread is the notion that lakes are the source or resting place of gods. Goddesses of Norse myth often return to secret lakes, just as the Aztec god Quetzalcoatl is said to have ended a cycle of his manifestation by submerging into a sacred lake. The Indians of ancient Peru believed that the divine Inca came to them through the waters of Lake Titicaca, driven forth by an aquatic serpent from their other world. In considering this, one is reminded of the dragon pools of Chinese tradition or of the serpent Sesha Ananta, coiled in cyclic curves around the resting form of Vishnu-Narayana. One may think of Lake Superior (which the Algonquian Indians called Gitche Gumee) with its great thirteen-hundred-foot high Thunder Cape held to be the recumbent form of the Great Spirit, whose voice reverberated from its heights during storms.

> By the shore of Gitche Gumee,
> By the shining Big-Sea-Water,
> Stood the wigwam of Nokomis,
> Daughter of the Moon, Nokomis.
>
> Henry Wadsworth Longfellow

Hiawatha embarked upon a great vision quest at this lake and endured many trials and dangers to achieve his goal. Each in his own way, Arthur and Sir Pellias encountered the mystery of the lake: Arthur reached the sword in a boat with swan's wings, and Sir Pellias rode into the lake on his horse. In considering these examples one may imagine gliding across the astral wastes upon the wings of Kalahansa or directing back into dissolution the vital energy represented by the horse. Celtic lore taught that "those who want to return to the divine land must not dismount from their horses", a warning similar to the one related to the admonition against prematurely abandoning the raft in Buddhist tradition. It is significant that, had Sir Pellias pursued his adventures in a Greek context, he would, as a knight, have been called (*hippotis*) from ἵππος, or "horse". Perhaps in becoming the knight of the Lady of the Lake, he had become identified with that vital force which surges forth out of chaos from time to time and gives impelling energy to the great work of the world. But was the lake merely chaos or was it the divine land? Are some lakes capable of divulging their watery secrets to those on the threshold of greater understanding? In search of the answer, some intrepid souls have travelled great distances and endured enormous hardships to reach a lake reputed to have sublime and truly magical powers. Of all such sacred lakes in the world, perhaps the most fabled and revered is Lake Manasarova, whose name itself reveals something of the deeper reflective power attributed to it.

> There are no mountains like the Himalaya, for in them are Kailas and Manasarova.
>
> *Skanda Purana*

Around the turn of the century the Japanese monk Ekai Kawaguchi wandered the length of the Himalayas, having as one of his prime goals the most sacred of mountains and lakes. After months of difficult adventures, he sighted the holy Mount Kailas and soon after was looking down upon the clear, placid waters of Lake Manasarova, which appeared to him as a marvellously symmetrical *mandala*. In his diary he wrote that "the hunger and thirst, the perils of dashing stream and freezing blizzard, the pain of writhing under heavy burdens, the anxiety of wandering over trackless wilds, the exhaustion and the lacerations, all the troubles, and sufferings I had just come through, seemed like dust, which was washed away and purified by the spiritual waters of the lake; and thus I attained to the spiritual plane of Non-Ego, together with this scenery showing Its-Own-Reality".

According to the Puranas, Lake Manasarova was "formed in the mind of God". The story goes that the sons of Brahmā had performed austerities at Mount Kailas for twelve years with very little rain or water. In their distress they requested Brahmā to create for them a place to bathe while engaged in these devotions. In response, by a mental effort, Brahmā formed the holy lake of Manasa and the Rishis resumed their worship. The lake lying thus at the foot of Lord Shiva's abode, its sacred powers have been extolled since the days of the *Ramayana* and the *Mahabharata*.

The poet Kalidasa wrote that "when the earth of Manasarova touches anyone's body or when anyone bathes therein, he shall go to the paradise of Brahma, and he who drinks its waters shall go to the heaven of Shiva and shall be released from the sins of a hundred births". The pilgrim who succeeded in enduring the hardships of crossing the Himalayas was expected to follow the religious precepts laid down in the Puranas, namely that such a one should bathe there, pour libations to his ancestors, worship Mahadeva in the form of a royal swan, make *parikrama* of (circumambulate) the holy lake while gazing at Kailas, and bathe in all the neighbouring rivers.

Whilst only the Sutlej River now takes its actual source from Lake Manasarova, the Indus, Ravi, Ganga and Brahmaputra have all been believed, at one time or another, to have originated there, and even in modern times they arise in the general area, lending added sanctity to the lake itself. With the Gurla Mandhata Range rising beyond, a small stone lamasery at its turquoise shore, the lake has inspired even the secular visitor with reverence. In 1864 Thomas Webber described Manasarova as he beheld it from atop the Sutlej and Brahmaputra watershed as a "most brilliantly beautiful blue sea", and Sven Hedin later noted that the lake and sky shared the same ethereal value. In the light of such observations it is wonderful to reflect upon the fact that twenty million years ago the whole of the fifteen-hundred-mile Himalayan chain, including the great plateau of Tibet, lay at the bottom of the sea. Great long, parallel folds were then thrust up as the land mass that would become the Indian subcontinent pushed northward into the underside of Central Asia. The depressions between them were filled with alluvial silt, and rifts or pockets became the basins of lakes like Koko Nor, Baikal or Manasarova, all high and very clear reflectors of equally clear and depthless heavens.

Let them dream life just as the lake dreams the sky.

Miguel de Unamuno

Whatever the term used for it – the Latin *lacus*, the African *nyanza*, the Mongol *nor*, the English 'tarn' or the Celtic 'lough' – the critical factor distinguishing a lake is that it is completely surrounded by land, with no direct communication with the sea. It has been rather jocularly said that in their development, as with the serving of soup, two things were necessary: the bowl and its contents. Nor are the two invariably found together. Several different sorts of geophysical factors have produced the world's lakes. Tectonic action resulting in vast inland seas such as the Caspian and Aral can also produce crustal sags or rifts that become deep lakes like that of Baikal or Victoria. Volcanic activity can result in crater lakes, whilst extreme continental folding may yield pockets like that at Geneva. In the case of Titicaca, the whole lake basin was thrust bodily skyward by the upsurging Andes to its present elevation of 12,507 feet. Fluvial and glacial movement have, in places, carved out large depressions, such as the Canadian or Scandinavian shields, where lakes abound, including some as enormous as the Slave and Great Lakes. Of all of these, the largest by far is the Caspian Sea at 169,300 square miles, Lake Superior at 31,820 square miles being second in size. Next to these, Lake Baikal's 13,300 square miles seems small, but it is the size of Switzerland and five times deeper than Lake Superior. Called by the Tibetan and Mongol people Dalai Nor, or Holy Lake, it is beautiful, clear and cold. Over a mile deep, this appalling gulf is the most abysmal to be found on the land surface of the globe, and unlike most lakes, Baikal is tens of millions of years old, a vast aquarium (5,785 cubic miles of water) of archaic forms of life.

Very few lakes have mirrored the passing clouds for so many millions of years. Most date back to the glacial age or are more recent still, whilst the majority are dying; many thousands are already dead. Symbolically associating lakes with the mirror of the mind, one could see their relative duration as representing cycles of consciousness: some great, the majority smaller. Each does this in a unique way, for every lake has, as it were, a dramatic personality of its own. Some are sublime, others simply alluring, whilst still others fill the sensitive observer with foreboding and even at times a distinct impression of evil. Few things in Nature have the capacity to embody such qualities so forcefully. On the physical plane alone, each breathes air which circulates through its entire volume, causing highly distinctive pulsations, oscillations and tides. Over time, each lake models its own outline out of the surrounding basin, creating a subtle boundary giving shape to a miniature world. A wide variation in colours reflects their individual characters. Ranging from an almost colourless hue to yellow, pink, red, green, black, turquoise and deep blue, the several hundred thousand lakes of the world display a kaleidoscope of nutritive and reflective potential. Some, like the shallow green lakes of Kashmir, contain feeble currents in which grassy weeds unfurl in long, sinuous arabesques. Those of the Tibetan plateau take far less nutritive substance from their cold and awesomely barren environment and are often clear and deep blue. Among the tens of thousands of lakes in North America and Europe, these and every other sort of condition can be found mirrored within the individually unique microcosm of each limno-system.

Being individual entities, every lake responds slightly differently to the external environment. Because of this, a lake can be considered a climatic recording instrument. Depth, fetch, basin shape and exposure to the wind are internal factors, whilst air temperature, humidity and stability of air and wind are external. All of these variables come into play in the continual transfer of radiant energy within the system. Changes in the lake's heat content are determined by the algebraic sum of these radiation processes, evaporation and conduction into the atmosphere affecting the temperature of the lake in layers from the surface to its deepest depth. Except in cases where there is an extreme angle of incidence, water is easily penetrated by the shorter wave-lengths of solar radiation to a considerable depth, depending on its clarity. In return, only the very top layer of the lake emits long-wave radiation into the atmosphere. Being nearly opaque, any clouds above the lake are strongly absorbent of this long-wave radiation, which, as it increases with the water's temperature, augments the back-radiation from the clouds to the lake.

Evaporation from the lake's surface is the major means of heat loss, its rate depending upon the vapour pressure gradient across the skin of the air/water boundary. When water is colder than air, it cools the air, stabilizes it and reduces the wind action on the surface. One can more readily grasp the nature of how the limno-system works by observing its seasonable mode of exchange throughout an annual cycle. In a deep, temperate lake, spring witnesses the disappearance of ice, and the water, at about four degrees centigrade, is isothermal from surface to bottom. Incoming radiation from the sun mixes evenly at first, until surface temperature increases to a point where there is sufficient buoyancy to resist vertical mixing. As summer approaches, most of the heat is stored in the epilimnion layer, from whence evaporation and heat transference with the atmosphere take place, whilst below it the cooler water of the hypolimnion stabilizes. With autumn, the last evaporation begins to exceed radiation input, the lake cools and the thermocline separating the epilimnion from the hypolimnion begins to descend. Winds arise and mix the two layers, so that the lake tends to rebecome isothermal but with a higher temperature than in the spring. Cooling continues, with evaporation and increased unstable conditions of cool air overlying relatively warm water until, at about four degrees centigrade, the lake approaches an isothermal state. A winter drop to freezing temperatures produces a protective ice sheet which then shields the water from the wind and minimizes further loss of heat energy. The sedimentary basin returns to the water some of the heat it has absorbed during the summer and, together with a very limited solar radiation, gradually warms the water. With the breaking of the ice and the coming of spring, the whole cycle begins again.

In a balanced lacustrine ecosystem, a near equilibrium between production and destruction of organic matter as well as production and consumption of oxygen is maintained. Compared to a terrestrial ecosystem, that of a lake has a small biomass and a more complicated food web. It is more sensitive to change, and pollution of any kind results in a reduction in the diversity of trophic levels and a narrowing of the food chain, accompanied by unpredictable increases of bacterial and animal growth. In every lake solar energy is extracted by the phytoplankton and used to support a biological community. In this sense above all, it is a little world. But it is also a mirror of its environment, its system of energy flowing through interlocking cycles being profoundly affected by chemical and physical perturbations. Every stressful change increases the ratio of biotic energy flux to biomass. Nature responds by simplifying its ecostructure, by impairing negative feedback mechanisms and by accelerating nutrient cycles. Thus, a randomness of the system increases as its organization decreases.

Proliferation and changes in the composition of phytoplankton (despite corresponding increases in zooplankton density) cause a significant part of it to settle into the deeper water layers, where uncounterbalanced oxygen consumption and ultimate anaerobiosis drastically alter the fauna at the water-sediment interface, triggering an overall imbalance. In contrast to this, a natural lake comprising a non-perturbed ecosystem exposed to solar radiation can maintain a macroscopically constant composition, in which steady state an optimum in metabolic efficiency is attained.

> It is upon the serene and placid surface of the unruffled mind that visions gathered from the invisible find a representation in the visible world.
>
> Mahatma K. H.

Man has always possessed what may be called a limnetic drive. Some, whilst suggesting that this was prompted by something deeper than economic needs or a desire for recreation, have tried to explain it in terms of aesthetic attractions. But the effect of a lake on the human mind and soul is much greater than can be described by that feeble word. The desire to have a body of water nearby has prompted wonderful works, resulting in such beautiful man-made lakes as those in Rajasthan, in some of which float fairy-tale palaces to rival that described by the Lady of the Lake. If one sits at evening beneath an arabesque cupola suspended over the darkening flow, one's mind melts and becomes merged with the lake, reflecting the scattered rays of the setting sun. The soul's knowledge of the relationship between man and all of Nature is released, and a great peace surpassing the grasp of intellect settles within one's heart. The higher and clearer the lake, the greater its power to do this. As one stands at dawn on the edge of Panggong Tso Lake in the glacial rift area of Ladakh, a light breeze stirs the surface into little lapis lazuli waves, whose crests become gilded with the rising sun. The reflections of Karakoram peaks are drawn out in the larger swirls as inverted triangles of granite and snow. Across the water the opposite shoreline is lifted up by a mirage until, reaching the edge of some dry and ancient beach, it seems the ghost of lakes long gone. The breathing of this lake is fresh and pure, its cold layers bearing little vegetation to die and choke its basin. It is a mirror into which the mind is readily drawn to receive a broader picture of reality. In its water the past lies alongside the present and the above is mirrored below. Atomic particles float freely to shape images known only in other worlds, and long-forgotten memories surface to float for a moment beside embryos of ideation in their pre-natal state.

In such lakes people like the Navaho observed the sacred whirling arms of the swastika, made up of eight powerful Yei figures who instructed them in the mysteries of healing. Generations of Tibetan seers have meditated at the edges of many such holy lakes. In 1935, after the death of the Thirteenth Dalai Lama, the Regent Reting Rinpoche went to Lhamo Lhatso lake to seek a sign that would enable him to locate the birthplace of the new fourteenth incarnation. Lying at an elevation of seventeen thousand feet, its oval-shaped basin is surrounded by massive peaks, around which the weather constantly shifts from sun to rain to hail to snow. Years before, the whereabouts of the Thirteenth Dalai Lama had been discovered there by means of a dramatic vision seen in the centre of its waters for a week by several hundred people, but on this occasion the Regent and his party split up, each to seek his own vision from different vantage points around the lake. As it happened, Reting Rinpoche alone witnessed the remarkable display of Tibetan letters indicating the place, the names and the pictures of a monastery with a turquoise-tiled house nearby.

Not every man can stand beside a lake and receive a vision, any more than can every lake throw one up. There must be certain perfections inherent in the mind of the seer, matched by the purity and receptive power of the lake, for this to occur. Both the mind and the lake must be as mirrors of the Self of all in order to reflect the loftiest and most universal visions. In the writings of Robert Crosbie several characteristics of the mind suggest the means by which human beings may perceive visions in communion with lakes. He noted that the mind, in taking the shape of the object it focusses upon, absorbs the characteristics of that thing. Being like a mirror, if the mind is covered with dust it will absorb and reflect a very distorted and dim shadow of what it sees. As spirit, with all its powers, still must act in accordance with the ideas present in the mind, the manifested progeny of human thought are often warped and crippled in their expression. The lake is also like a mirror opening to the pure spiritual energy of the sun. If it is cool and clear, in a state of optimum metabolic balance, it is capable of reflecting the essential and primordial action of spirit in matter. For the water of the microcosmic lake is analogous to the cosmic Hyle, the first primordial matter, freshly penetrated by the electric spark of *Fohat*. In its absolutely latent state this primordial matter is referred to as "the cold Virgin", a cool radiance which is colourless, formless and tasteless. But when awakened by *Fohat* it becomes the prolific "slime", the Hyle whose first born are the Akashic, the Ethereal, the Watery and the Fiery: the primal natures of the first Dhyan Chohans which, in the sensual world, are reflected as fire, air, water and earth.

Lakes of enormous depth unburdened by a vast organic load, such as Lake Baikal, are closer in nature to being a pure reflection in the world of the cool fire of the highest Akashic progeny of proto-matter. Those teeming with nutrients lend themselves to the cycle of death more rapidly and give dramatic expression in the world to the original prolific slime. Polluted lakes become breeding grounds of distortion and contamination. All the fabled monstrous births of the earliest Rounds in evolution are recapitulated in miniature within their fetid basins. They become sink-holes of ignorance and disharmony, reflecting only the darkness of death which teems in its activity beneath their surface. If such lakes have genii, they must be harbingers of pollution much to be feared, whilst the alluring lakes from whence the ethereal maid arises to tempt the passerby must surely be those dreaming pools which abound with living things and bask in petalled mist beneath the floating sky. Visions they may have to offer and magic swords as well, but they are tricky in their nature, dealing life and death with the same draught. Like the astral realm it mirrors, such a lake contains both evil and good. Only the seer of wisdom can discriminate accurately which is which. For good reason did Sir Gawain feel fear as he approached the fairy lake. He must have intuitively known that he was unprepared to discern the true nature of its potential power.

> Oh, what can ail thee, Knight at arms
> Alone and palely loitering;
> The sedge is wither'd from the lake,
> And no birds sing.

> John Keats

The lake by itself does not envision, nor would its genius ever appear, were it not for the presence of thinking man. But it is a reservoir capable of mirroring intelligence beyond what man can usually pluck from his own limited consciousness. It can reflect what man knows outside the limits of his finite awareness and cast up a vision which transcends the bonds of time and space and personal desires. It can mirror a deeper understanding of things stored in the higher astral yet unknown to worldly minds, and these sometimes may be imaged in the form of a human-like being who gestures and speaks and reveals what is known. Like the clear, unpolluted lake, the mind must become utterly pure in order to reflect the highest Akashic intelligence and perceive its presence in the world around. The human mind, which is continually affected by its environment, can easily become polluted, for it lies like a passive basin receiving the trickled effects of all that occurs around it. It needs depth and breadth and the subsequent ability to affect the climate around it to some degree. The mind that fully recognizes the radiant source of its existence is more receptive to its warming spiritual rays and freely and more fully participates in the transfer of radiant energy that operates within and through it to the other vestures. With purified concentration, channels reaching from the brain open to the astral body and from thence to the inner man, enabling that which is temporary to become a conscious part of the eternal. That this takes place within man is true, but one can see how the lake, in some cases, can play a connecting role in the process of opening the channels through the astral realm.

The mind, like the lake, has its own limno-systemic cycle. If it is deep and temperate, it emerges out of a winter's quietude full of cool, balanced thoughts which temper evenly the ways in which one perceives whatever develops. Governed by such a mind, one's actions would express a proportionality born of deep and dispassionate meditation between the highest and lowest levels of one's being. Later in the season, when the mind becomes more absorbed in the cares of the world, it tends to lose its isothermal condition and becomes increasingly stirred up and heated at its surface. A resistance to vertical mixing sets in, and it becomes more and more difficult to maintain the conscious connection between the deepest and the more surface levels. One is in danger of losing contact with the cool, undisturbed centre of one's being. With the autumn, the air over the lake becomes cooler than the water which destabilizes it, causing winds to arise. Just so does one disrupt the atmosphere and the affairs of others with an overheated mind. In Nature this is part of a repeating cycle with long-term beneficent effects, but in man such conditions are not meant to be expressed unchecked. Instead, the mind is to be taken in hand and guided wisely through its analogous cycles of involvement and withdrawal from the world. The external winds of change may clear the air and mix the layers of the mind's warm and cool waters just as it does with the lake in the autumn season, but the mixture in the mind must be consciously monitored so that only the purest reflections of solar truth are allowed to percolate throughout the whole.

A balanced use of the mind is very much like that of a lake's balanced ecosystem. The mind absorbs the rays of spiritual Teaching, causing a production of thoughts, longings, hopes, creative urges and potentials which must be put into a constructive and disinterested practice that is quite analogous to the destruction of organic matter and consumption of oxygen that must go on in the lake to counterbalance their production. If the right use of these Teachings is not enacted, a condition will evolve similar to that of the lake which is overburdened with organic growth to the point where the dying particles begin to clog its bottom, creating a growing anaerobic layer that will eventually pollute the entire system. When the mind opens itself to the pure spiritual energy of divine Teaching and is not directed by the higher will to instruct the thoughts and emotions, the sense organs and deeds, the surrounding environment will become polluted. One's relations with others, one's interaction with all sorts of objects and elements as well as the subtle matter of one's own aura, will become clogged with distorted and unnatural thoughts and desires, the monstrous progeny of imbalance which will, in turn, pollute the mind that spawned them. For the conscious mind to work in harmony with a vast, universally interacting intelligence, it must establish within itself a harmonious equilibrium between the divine solar radiation that it takes in, the resultant growth it enjoys, and the digestion and transmutation of this through daily thought and action.

To achieve this calm and sublime balance is to become like the sacred Manasarova lying placid and pure at the foot of Lord Shiva's abode. All around, the peaks of Masters arise. Like a vast range of Adepts, they loom o'er this faithful mirror and, one by one, are reflected in its open and clear water. Pilgrims struggling over the high and rocky passes draw up, tired and worn, to its shore and rejoice in their hearts to see the reflections of such Great Ones shimmering there. Coolly and with a depth of patient meditation unfathomed, such a deeply pure and azure mind reflects the heavenly abode of its Lord, who rests as the Mahayogin on the peak of Mount Kailas. Centuries may pass and still this mind never ceases its worship, never ceases to mirror the universal meditation of its Lord, until a genius grows within it which is a pure reflection of his Divine Will. Weary pilgrims who brave all trials and persist long enough to reach the lofty fastness of this sacred and pure mind may come one day. As they approach the shores of its shimmering waters, a rich reward will greet them. For the Lady of that holy lake of mind will be seen there and her words and signs will transmit to them the arcane Teaching of her Lord on high, whose fiery instructions clothe themselves in her substance and whose word garbs itself in her speech. This Lady is worth following, not into the water of oblivion or to a castle of never-ending dreams, but to the altar of reflective worship that lies cool and pure at the feet of Mahadeva.

> O Sambhu of jasmine eyes,
> Thy wild locks streaming,
> Thou art the pinnacle of my World.
> I lap in recumbent waves
> At thy blessed feet.
> O Mahadev of Crescent Brow,
> Thy bright form gleaming,
> Thou art all radiance unfurled.
> I mirror thy exalted gaze
> At thy blessed feet.

Hermes, March 1985

THE FISH

Now hear, O Brahmins, the ancient tale of Matsya the Fish,
which is holy, purifying and life-bestowing, as it was sung by the
mace-bearer, Vishnu.

Matsya Purana

Long ago there was a good and patient king named Manu who practised abundant *tapas* with what may truly be called global results. Turning his affairs of state over to his son, he diligently pursued his austerities until he attained supreme yoga. After millennia Brahmā noticed him and was pleased. He asked him to choose a boon as his prize, whereupon the king bowed low and requested the ultimate reward which would make him "the protector of all standing and moving creatures when the dissolution comes". "So be it!" boomed the grandfather of the gods, and a shower of flowers fell to earth from his hidden abode.

Sometime later the king was making sacred water offerings to the gods near his hermitage, when there fell into his hands along with the water a tiny fish, which pleaded to him for protection. Moved by compassion, Manu placed it in a small jar safe from the predations of ponds, rivers and lakes. But the remarkable fish rapidly outgrew the jar and all the subsequent containers that the concerned king could provide for it. Placed in a pond, he soon languished in its insufficient basin, and rivers and lakes likewise proved to be successively inadequate. Finally, Manu placed the enormously grown creature into the ocean itself, where its continued growth filled him with astonishment and reverential awe as he realized that it could only be a manifestation of Lord Vishnu. With this recognition, the Lord rapidly began to instruct Manu, telling him how he had fought with the demon Hayagriva, who had stolen the Vedas from the sleeping Brahmā. He taught the king their principles and the knowledge which should guide the human race during the present cycle of four *yugas*. He spoke of a coming flood which would inundate the whole world and instructed him to put all creatures and the seven Rishis of time's cycles into a boat constructed by the gods. Thus, he said, at the end of the dissolution of the world you shall be master of the creatures on earth, their all-knowing king at the beginning of the *Krita* Age.

In the *Satapatha Brahmana* the great fish saves Manu by drawing the ark until it rests upon Mount Naubandhava (Meru in the later *Puranas*), where he reveals himself to be Brahmā. In the later Puranic versions it is Lord Vishnu manifested in his Matsya Avatar who drew the boarded and ready ship across the flood by a serpent-rope attached to his horn, transferring safely to a new cycle the essential seeds and wisdom of the old. One may be cautioned not to take the Puranas too literally and to keep in mind that periods spoken of there refer to both minor cycles and *mahakalpas*. It has been suggested in various traditions that one of the keys to understanding the symbolism of the fish is to be found in the study of cycles, a subject ardently pursued by anyone wishing to unravel the mystery of the Matsya and subsequent Avatars of Vishnu. *The Secret Doctrine* points out that the last *mahakalpa* was the Padma, while the present one is the Varaha. In the series of Vishnu's manifestations, the Matsya Avatar occurred before that of the Varaha, indicating that the allegories belong to *kalpas* as well as minor cycles that have taken place since the reappearance of our chain of worlds. This is borne out by the fact that the Matsya Avatar is connected with Vaivasvata's deluge which took place on our earth during this Round. It therefore refers to a geologic period which reflects pre-cosmic events occurring on a far vaster scale.

The symbolic relation of cycles to the fish in general has been associated by some with its bobbin shape. Like the spindle of the weavers of necessity in Greek myth, the fish is thought to spin out the cycle of life after the pattern of the lunar zodiac. By others its shape has been likened to a bird whom they say drifted through the watery netherworld and periodically emerged in a cycle of regeneration and resurrection. The Chaldean symbol for this was a fish with a swallow's head. The ocean it swam through was the abyss of non-being which surrounds the world of form, the great *magna mater* that the Greeks called chaos. The fish penetrates through these waters during its life migrations and returns to its place of beginning, where it lays vast shoals of oviparous progeny destined to persist through the next generational cycle.

Its form continues though engulfed in a sea of dissolution, represented in human beings by the psychic nature. Within the aquatic gloom of this great omnipresent liquidity, the fish penetrates and asserts its fertile presence before being swallowed up by oblivion. Thus persisting, a fish is at the beginning of a cycle and at its end. In the annals of Quauhtitlan of ancient Mexico, each epoch was said to begin with the god Quetzalcoatl (the scaly, plumed serpent) as creator and end with a flood and the transformation of all creatures into fishes. The feminine matrix of life itself is sometimes referred to as the fiery Fish-Mother, who scatters her spawn in space (the ocean of chaos) where Motion (the great paternal breath) heats and quickens it until the grains form the curds of the manifesting universe.

> FISH (fly-replete, in depth of June,
> Dawdling away their wat'ry noon)
> Ponder deep wisdom, dark or clear,
> Each secret fishy hope or fear.
> Fish say, they have their stream and pond;
> But is there anything beyond?
> This life cannot be all, they swear,
> For how unpleasant, if it were!
> One may not doubt that, somehow, good
> Shall come of water and of mud;
> And, sure, the reverent eye must see
> A purpose in liquidity.
> We darkly know, by faith we cry,
> The future is not wholly dry.
> Mud unto mud! – Death eddies near –
> Not here the appointed end, not here!
> But somewhere, beyond space and time,
> Is wetter water, slimier slime!
> And there (they trust) there swimmeth one
> Who swam ere rivers were begun,
> Immense, of fishy form and mind,
> Squamous, omnipotent, and kind;

And under that Almighty Fin,
The littlest fish may enter in.
Oh! never fly conceals a hook,
Fish say, in the Eternal Brook,
But more than mundane weeds are there,
And mud, celestially fair.
Fat caterpillars drift around,
And paradisal grubs are found;
Unfading moths, immortal flies,
And the worm that never dies.
And in that Heaven of all their wish,
There shall be no more land, say fish.

Rupert Brooke

The "one who swam ere rivers were begun" looms within the mythical waters of many cultures. Some have conceived of the cosmic fish as the whole physical universe, the symbol of the progress of the world across the sea of the unformed essences of worlds dissolved or not yet manifest. Others, like the Altaic-speaking people, believed that when Ulgen created the disc of the earth upon the primordial waters, he supported it with three great fishes who could be raised or lowered by a rope attached to their gills. Held in the hand of the Bodhisattva Manjushri, a slight pulling could produce earthquakes and floods, an idea which crops up in Eastern European and Semitic lore as well. The Kirghiz notion that a bull supporting the world on his horns stands on a great fish in the world ocean is similar and suggests an interesting sequence of forms reminiscent of the Minoan bull that came from the sea. The zodiac itself holds four such pillars: the Bull, the Scorpion, the Lion and the Southern Fish, each residing at the corners of its great spiralling wheel. But it is the Fish that represents the point of transformation and cyclic change, the pillar of form which finds its base in a prior period of primordial becoming.

Among the coastal Chincha people living west of the Andes, each province worshipped a special kind of fish which they believed to have been a manifestation of the First of all Fish, who dwells in the sky. This great fish, much like that of the Hindu tradition, warns of an impending flood and instructs his devotees to build an ark which will carry them safely through the deluge. Given the widespread occurrence of this theme, it is interesting to note that the idea of a cultural hero being swallowed by a great fish is equally ubiquitous and reveals another facet of Piscean symbolism having to do with the role of saviour from dissolution and death and also the embodiment of those fearful possibilities. Like Jonah and others of the Semitic legends, many American Indian heroes had to enter into the jaws of the abyss, the great fish which ruled the powers of the deep (like the giant sturgeon which swallowed Hiawatha), from whose maw the hero re-emerged in a triumph of light over dark and watery chaos. There is a subtle cross-over between the warning, saving fish who preserves form, and the swallowing fish which appears to be one with the waters of chaos. It is like both the double-edged symbolism and the actual effects connected with the moon, with which the fish is so intimately associated. The cyclic waxing and waning to which both are related are dangerous, but they are part of a necessary process of growth through death and resurrection.

In the arcane symbolism of the ancient Middle East, a fish swimming downward represented spiritual involution, whilst one swimming upward signified the process of spiritual evolution. Depicted together, they were like the *yin* and *yang* figure of Taoism or the two fishes, nose to tail, of the Hindus, associated with the sacred *yoni*. The Akkadians believed that Tiamat, the tumultuous sea, the chaotic mother of space and the incipient watery flow, was killed by the hero Marduk, who clove her body "like a fish in two parts" and fashioned from one half the heavens, from the other the earth. He organized the world thus so that the fish above was reflected in the fish below, the one curved to enter into the world, the other poised to evolve its way out of it. *The Secret Doctrine* teaches that the fish, along with later reptiles, birds and amphibians, is the result of astral fossils of the Third Round which were stored in the earth's aura until they manifested in the Laurentian rocks of this Round, Those who preceded physical man were bisexual, becoming heterosexual only with man's separation and fall from a more ethereal state. This idea is clearly suggested by the two fishes curving up and down, circling around one another in a continual process of involution and evolution. But the fish does not merely remain as a distinct, separate link with past phases of existence, for it regularly appears in the foetal development of all vertebrates, including that of humans, where the foetus exhibits early on a fish-like shape as well as full-blown gill clefts. Thus, human foetal growth epitomizes not only characteristics of the Fourth Root Race but of the Third as well.

In this Round and on this earth as we know it, the earliest fishes began to develop between the Cambrian and Ordovician periods, leading to a Piscean explosion in Devonian times, four hundred million years ago. Jaws, destined to become a fearful symbol of destruction among later seafaring men, evolved during this time among the ancient cartilaginous fish, of which the modern shark is a living example. Bony fishes came to dominate only in the last one hundred and eighty million years, introducing the oviparous mode of reproduction so prevalent among fish today. While fish appearing after physical man were no longer bisexual, it is not the case that they became clearly and consistently heterosexual, for there is a fairly high rate of hermaphroditism among certain species (such as the bass), and changes in sex within the lifetime of an individual fish have been observed. From the standpoint of arcane symbolism it would seem that fish, though extremely long lived as a phylum, have not only evolved in a fluidic environment, but are themselves genetically fluidic, shifting gender and assuming remarkably varying forms. Fishes today make up a huge and complex group, comparable within their own ranks to all the variations within other classes of vertebrates put together.

Generally described, fishes are all those vertebrate animals which live in water and, by means of gills, breathe air dissolved in it; whose heart consists of a single ventricle and atrium; whose limbs, if present, are modified into fins; and whose skin is either naked or covered with osseous plates, bucklers or scales. They are immensely older than the Tetrapoda, being ancestral to all land vertebrates, but they do not exhibit any evidence of racial senescence. Instead, they greatly surpass all land vertebrates in number of species and new ones are constantly being discovered. This is undoubtedly because fishes live in a fantastic variety of habitats within bodies of water that are truly analogous to the endlessly transformational potential of the great astral sea out of which the manifest universe cyclically emerges. Within rivers, lakes and oceans, extreme variations of light and darkness, heat and cold, pressure, salinity, calmness and turbulence can be found. Seventy-five percent of the surface of our globe is water, and the diversity of size and shape of its Piscean inhabitants is even greater than that of insects. There are, at the very least, twenty thousand species with hundreds of thousands of subspecies flourishing around the world and at least a few of them can be found in almost all permanent bodies of water. Some types in Southeast Asia even thrive in puddles, hopping overland to another watery home when their own little abode dries up. Big ones, little ones, there always seems to be one of their kind present even in the most amazingly small pond. Let the rains come and the fish seem to sprout up everywhere.

> Calico Jam,
> The little Fish swam,
> Over the syllabub sea.
>
> Edward Lear

Throughout their long history the lives of fish have been dominated by the incompressibility of water. It has imposed upon them the general shape of the basic vertebrate: a hollow cylinder open at both ends with a vertebral column, a food canal and nerve cord running the length, the latter enlarged at the front end to form the brain. This aquadynamic shape, the method of locomotion and means of breathing, feeding and reproducing, are all adaptive responses to the fluidity, buoyancy, more constant temperature, penetrability and incompressibility of water. To move in it requires that it be displaced, shoved aside, so to speak, by a streamlined form which can wiggle through it in a serpentine motion. Along the tapering flanks of such a form, the water flows back, closing at the tail and pushing the fish forward. Thus, the fish's shape most easily penetrates the watery world, being able not only to cut through it but to use it as a means of further propulsion. Nonetheless, within the parameters of this general form, the thousands of species of fish illustrate the most dramatic variations of shape and size. The sea serpents of Aristotle and Pliny are not very fantastic-seeming when compared with oar or ribbon fish, whose heads look like those of horses, with red manes flowing in rhythm to their undulating motion. One grown to the stupendous length of fifty-six feet was cast up on the shore at Orkney in 1808!

> I never lost a little fish - yes I am
>   free to say
> It always was the biggest fish I caught
>   that got away.

Eugene Field

With whale sharks at sixty feet and basking sharks at forty, monsters of the deep seem real enough. Even the halibut can attain eight feet and a weight of four hundred pounds or more, while the sleeker, fifteen-foot freshwater *Arapaima gigas* of the Amazon can reach an equal weight. Alongside the one-half-inch goby of Luzon, such giants would appear to belong to another dimension of existence rather than to the same family. An enormous pike was captured in a lake at Wurttemberg in 1497 which had a copper ring fixed in its gill, telling that it had been put into the lake by Frederick II in 1230. Besides being two hundred and sixty-seven years old, it was said to have been nineteen feet long and weighed five hundred and fifty pounds! Whether one finds this fishy or not, the report certainly indicates that fabulous tales of Piscean splendour have flourished for a very long time. There is something, perhaps, about drawing up on a line a prize from the hidden deep that is thrilling to human beings: a conquest and discovery of a very different order from what is experienced by hunters of land animals or birds of the air. One is not quite sure what is down there, or if a giant or minnow will nibble one's bait. The uncertainty, however, has not deterred fishermen who take thirty-eight million tons of fish from the world's seas every year.

The disinterested desire to understand fish and their watery kingdom for their own sake has engaged only a small percentage of mankind. The majority who undertake this study do so in order to better exploit them for food and other products. With such a pressing motivation we have learnt a great deal about the vast migrations of albacore who travel from Southern California to Japan and back, and sardines who journey from San Diego to British Columbia over a period of six months. We know all about the wonderful cycle of the salmon, who swim upstream to their birthplace in order to spawn and die, and we catch them en route by the multitude. Sportsmen learn of thousand-pound black marlin fifteen feet long for the thrill of it, while fishermen comb the waves for eighteen-hundred-pound bluefin tuna for the fill of it. But some are simply mad for mackerel, balmy for barracuda or soft on sharks for their own sake. Their painstaking investigations have revealed wonderful details about Piscean life. From them we have learnt something of the sixth sense possessed by all fish which enables them to remain delicately in tune with all movements around them and with currents in the water. Along a visible lateral line on the fish's sides, a highly sensitized nerve canal monitors flow and is responsible for the lightning-like dart of a coral fish into a tiny crevice it cannot possibly see with its eyes. It is also responsible for vast shoals of fish being able to hold their formation in perfectly aligned schools. The studies of ichthyological enthusiasts have also revealed much about the remarkable relationships existing between parent fish and their offspring, of fish to each other in the food chain, in schools or pods and in cleaner-client associations. The bitterling emits its eggs through a tube into a mussel, where they are fertilized by the lurking male as the mussel feeds. The stickleback simply constructs a nest and drives the female into it to deposit eggs. Most mother fish nonchalantly swim off, leaving the care of the shoal of eggs to the father. The male *Tilapia* of Indonesia fasts for a fortnight while incubating the eggs in his mouth. He, like most other Piscean pops, then carries on with the job of rearing the small fry until they are able to get along on their own.

Some fry may belong to one of the several species that act as groomers of larger fish and grow up to enter into a cleaner-client relationship with them. All fish, especially large fish, acquire wounds, sores, growths and other potentially infectious problems. Cleaner-fish rid their bodies of unwanted bacterial growths and many clients obligingly take on a deeper colour so as to show up the sore spots and help them on with the job. There is a small wrasse who "goes into a customer's mouth, works over the teeth and proceeds right down to the gullet until its client signifies, by snapping its jaws a few times, that it is satisfied." One cleaner off the California coast was observed to handle three hundred clients in a matter of six hours! There was a veritable line of impatient swimmers backed up and waiting their turn, some slyly sneaking around for a second scrubbing.

And the fishes of the sea shall declare unto thee.

Job 12: 8

Fascinating as these relations may be, one might pause to wonder how they bear upon the symbolism associated with the fish. How do the migration, reproduction and social patterns of fishes relate to the mystery of the *Matsya* Avatar, to cycles or the idea found in Buddhism, for instance, wherein Buddha is called a Fisher of Men? In the *Gospel According to Matthew* (4:19), Jesus said to his new-found disciples, "Follow me, and I will make you fishers of men." Is the Fisher of Men the same Saviour as the great fish who towed the ark? Is there something about the relationship between all fishes in their cycles of generation that points to the nature of this Piscean Saviour, this man-fish, as some have called him? Or is it her? For the carp is the emblem of Kwan-Yin, who vowed never to seek salvation before all that lives had achieved their deliverance. So closely is her compassion associated with this beautiful fish in Japan that the word for love is a homophone of the word for carp.

Similar to the Buddhists and Christians, the ancient Greeks referred to Orpheus as a Fisher of Men. His disciples, like those of Buddha and Christ, were little fishes swimming in the waters of life, to be saved by one big fish. The anagram for Christ in primitive Christianity, ΙΧΘΥΣ (*Ichthys*), was the Greek for "fish", which, when spelt out, stood for the epithet "Ιησους χριστός θεου Υιός Σωτήρ" (Jesus Christ, Son of God, Saviour). Here the fish takes on a solar symbolism associated with the soul rising from the waters of chaotic matter in the Piscean form, which the Chaldeans called the Intelligent One, Ea, the father of Marduk, the purveyor of Soul upon the waters. The sign of ΙΧΘΥΣ thus relates to all world reformers. It is the sign of Jonas marking the rebirth of the sun in Pisces, the rising out of the waters of Oannes, Ea, Quetzalcoatl and other man-fish for the enlightenment of the world. They are like Thjodvitnir's fish (the sun) which swims in the River Thund (the sky) that surrounds Odin's Valhalla. Periodically they emerge from their astral realm of rest to quicken the reflected fire of spirit which lies hidden in the world of form.

Ea was the man-fish who rose out of the Persian Gulf. The Babylonians called the astrological phase from Capricorn to Pisces the Field of Ea and believed that it was in this sign that man was instructed in that which would make him truly human. The earlier Sumerians had associated this idea with the god Enki of Eridu, the lord of the manifest lower world identified with the sea. When officiating at his ritual worship, priests clothed in fish garments were believed to have the power of purification and protection attributed to the god. (Their fish headdress became the mitre of Christian bishops.) Enki became Ea of the Akkadian texts, whom Greek writers knew as Aoς in Damascius and Ωάννης (*Cannes*) in Berossus. According to the Greek record, men had lived in a lawless and bestial manner before the flood when Cannes appeared from the sea. He had the body of a fish and his feet were like those of a man subjoined to the tail. Under the fish's head he had another, a human head, from the mouth of which he spoke as he passed among men, teaching them letters, science, arts, geometry and agriculture. It is said that he instructed humanity by day but retired to the sea by night. Altogether, Cannes made four appearances as a man-fish at intervals of enormous duration (exceeding thirty thousand years) in different reigns of the pre-Diluvian kings.

In the Arthurian romance the Fisher King plays a similar role, and on the path to the Grail the rich fisherman caught a fish that satisfied the hunger of all. Here the man-fish, fisherman and fish overlap and the conception unites what may initially have appeared as three separate ideas. Seen as one complex symbol, the notion of fishing for men can be addressed in psychological terms, where the bait is cast by the fisherman into the watery depths of his or her innermost nature in order to catch (save) the soul (little fish to be saved by one great fish) which one really is. The fully conscious Adept is one with that awakened soul, being fisher, fish and subsequent Fisher of Men. Adept-Saviours are essentially solar in nature, bringing to the material darkness of the world the light of self-realization. But they descend into the world cyclically, through the cycles of coming and going associated with the tides, the moon and the reproductive generations in the watery astral realm. Through the sacrifice of the Logoic light, the pregnant astral realms are penetrated and the impulse of spiritual awakening reaches the heart of even the hardest stone. Through soma, connecting the highest spirit (cosmically and in man) with the astral nature, consciousness can soar above the physical and participate in the bliss of heaven.

> Enlil saw the eclipse of
> The hero Sin in Heaven, and
> The Lord hailed his messenger Nusku.
> Tidings of my son Sin who in Heaven
>   has been woefully darkened,
> Repeat to Ea in the Deep . . .
>
> *The Akkadian Utukke Limnuti*

Fish, Sin and *soma* together make the symbol of the Immortal Being. Sin is the moon, which is fearfully eclipsed in the incantation and whose influence is necessary for the life and growth which can lead either to enlightenment or to ignorance, evil and the wages of sin. The fish of spiritual involution, swimming downward into the water, curves like the lunar crescent of the waxing moon. It descends into the astral sea of matter, its bright scales dancing sparks of light throughout the darkness. It swims within the soup of life, eats, is eaten, cleans, is cleansed, spawns, dies and lives again. Just so, the soul descends into matter time and time again. But the time comes when the fish begins to undulate upward, curving like the crescent of the waning moon, splashing forth upon the surface like the Rishi's ark that carried the spawn of spiritual life. Its upward course was powered by the reflected light of highest Spirit, the *soma*-power coursing through the whole of Nature, making it one with the fish of spiritual evolution, the heaven-bound soul. It is from such rich occult symbolism that people have evolved their notions of sacred meals wherein fish and *soma* or wine play such key roles.

The man-fish penetrates with the undulating motion of the Logos into the invisible (to most) astral ocean that anticipates the realm of physical form. There he swims at rest and from there he emerges into the material world. He allows himself to become subject to the waxing and waning cycles of the world while retaining the powers of transmutation and endless adaptation so typical of the watery world. In his periods of rest, he can take on ideas and shapes our world has never seen. He is the arcane hermaphrodite, who can manifest in totally unexpected ways. He swims and emerges, living as a compassionate link joining the spiritual with the astral and physical realms. Disciples struggling as little fishes go through Piscean cycles over and over again. Their sixth sense begins to awaken in them not merely an instantaneous knowledge of a route to escape physical death, but an awareness of the radical unity existing within, between the self which "catches" the soul and the universal Soul symbolized by the cosmic fish, who tells of the flood and draws the essence of life and wisdom safely through to the next cycle. The tiny sliver of lunar light almost eclipsed between periods of manifestation is the umbilical thread of reflected spirit which never dies. In the darkest depths of the sea its silver curve glistens as it rhythmically undulates along. When struggling disciples learn to follow this path unerringly, like the little fry their parent, they will have conquered the astral realm and learnt to use it as a means of further propulsion. They will have come to realize the sacrificial nature of the immortal soul's path within their own heart and they will aspire to become Fishers of Men, to rise up out of the depths and become part of that sacred school which swims in the wake of the Avatar.

> Suffer little fishes
> Floundered out at sea,
> Sharks and deadly wishes
> Have made a meal of thee.
> Strike your finny course
> Up Ganga's sacred aisle
> And come onto the source
> That gave Meenakshi's smile.

Hermes, November 1986

THE DOLPHIN

As I first in the dark sea spring
In dolphin form onto the swift ship, so
Pray to me as Delphinius; whilst this altar
Shall ever be the Delphi altar, seen from afar.

Hymn to Apollo, Homer

From one end of the Mediterranean to the other, the haunting story
of a boy on a dolphin has coursed and eddied, repeatedly to surface
and be told once again. Always it is tinged with sadness. There is an
echo of a poignant longing for love and trust and a merging with pure
joyful power. They say that during the reign of Augustus a dolphin
living near Naples fell in love with a poor schoolboy. Each day the lad
would call to his friend and the dolphin would carry him across the
bay to school. There came a day when the boy was mortally stricken
with disease and could come no more. The dolphin returned daily
to their meeting place, like a mourner at the graveside, until he too
weakened, ceased to frolic around the bay and finally died. From his
death sprang more than sadness, for it was caused by marvellous
affection which is the more memorable sentiment. Perhaps for this
reason the story was often repeated, based on events recorded by
many a sober classical observer. At Naupactus, Amphilochus, Hippo,
and down the Helladic seas to the Nile Delta, the beautiful friendship
of a youth and a dolphin has been celebrated in poetry and song.
Sweet-sad lyrics tell of the boy from Iasus called Hermias, who rode
a dolphin on the open seas. Struck by a sudden storm, the boy died
whilst clinging to its back, and the dolphin carried him up on the
shore, where he expired by the side of his dead friend. People came
and marvelled. They wondered at the bond that could inspire such
sacrifice, which humans know is rare to find amongst themselves. The
Greeks have a song expressing this wonder which asks, "What is this
that they call love, what is this? Is it laughter, joy or pain? I don't know
what it is, but I love."

Mariners of the Mediterranean echo descriptions of the exuberant dolphin offered by sailors all over the world. They tell of how the dolphins play constantly around the bow of their ships, sometimes for hours on end. They rise very close alongside to breathe, making a half-snorting sigh, only to dive and tumble once again. They will glide six feet under the surface, using the large waves pushed up by the Meltemi winds as a sea toboggan. Or they will surf-ride down the Aegean with their noses protruding through the crests of the water. Being the swiftest of marine animals, they are all the more capable of helping those in need, and since very ancient times the dolphin has been seen as a guide and even a saviour of men. The dolphin is quick to help but does so with discrimination, and when its form is linked with that of an anchor, a symbol of arrested speed is indicated. The dolphin moves quickly but wisely. It hastens slowly. In the great expanses of water around this globe, dolphins have located men in trouble and saved their lives. One such was said to have saved Telemachus when he fell into the sea, causing Odysseus to choose a smiling dolphin as a shield design. The shield of Aeneas bore two silver dolphins for good fortune. Opposite each other, they are like those rendered in mosaic at Antioch, where they flank the goddess Thalassa like rudders, guides to lead on the prow of the ship across the unknown dangers of the abyss.

In the ancient world the dolphin was the guide to souls in the underworld, the saviour of the shipwrecked. The earliest Christians believed this and used the symbol of the dolphin with ship or anchor to indicate the idea of the church guided by Christ. Their identification of the dolphin with Christ went even further in that iconography which depicted the crucifixion of a dolphin pierced by a trident. But the beauty of the pagan guide who loved and died, who saved the hero and foretold the storm – this is the dolphin symbol that lives deep in the hearts of poets and those whose minds are unbounded by time. The ancient longing that wells up behind eyes looking through walls and surroundings, through centuries to the mysterious grottoes of a more vital innocence, finds this dolphin. In his sonnet "To Homer", the words of Keats reach back to lightly touch upon that archaic reality:

Standing aloof in quiet ignorance,
Of thee I hear and of the Cyclades,
As one who sits ashore and longs perchance
To visit dolphin-coral in deep seas.

Aphrodite was commonly associated with the dolphin throughout the Mediterranean world. As the Nabataean goddess Atargatis, she was the harbinger of good fortune and safe passage in the sea and in the after-life. Like her counterpart Aphrodisias, her long hair coiled around two dolphins who gracefully sprang from her head. An attribute of Isis is the dolphin, and Thetis was depicted riding naked upon one's back. This mode of divine transport was not unknown to "the Woman of the Sea", for in Tunis there is a lovely Aphrodite who, with her long sky-veil billowing out behind her, is tranquilly seated on a flying dolphin. As a pictographic seal, the dolphin appeared in Crete three thousand five hundred years before the Christian era, and the Minoan kings decorated their throne rooms with their ultramarine grace. This association with power was echoed by the medieval counts of Daufine, who used a dolphin design on their armour and gave their name (Daufin) to the heir apparent of the throne of France. The good fortune associated with dolphins passed through countless transactions within the Hellenic world in the form of coins stamped with their plunging shape. More than forty Greek cities issued such coins, whilst everywhere vases, metal work, engravings and stucco floors were fashioned to display this most auspicious motif. From as far off as Russia and Egypt, statues of Eros riding a dolphin have been found, and the soil of ancient Carthage has yielded a mysterious figure holding a caduceus whilst standing upon a dolphin.

The dolphin guides and it carries. Perhaps the most famous classical incident in which a dolphin apparently saved a man was recorded by Herodotus. He tells of the tyrant Periander who kept court at Corinth around 600 B.C. In its porticoes Arion of Methymna played his lyre and gained fame as a musician and composer. At one point Arion travelled to Sicily and made great profit from his talents before returning home to Corinth. The sailors carrying him intended to take his wealth and throw him overboard. Although he begged them to take his money and spare his life, they refused and permitted him only to sit in his full costume upon the prow whilst singing the

Orthian before he died. It is believed that the sweetness of his voice was responsible for attracting the dolphin. Whatever the cause, his cape had not yet sunk beneath the brine before he was carried up in a surge of awesome force and propelled at great speed to Cape Taenarum. From there he made his way back to Corinth to await the sailors who thought he was dead.

Two dolphins facing in opposite directions symbolize the dual cosmic streams of involution and evolution. This seems to be borne out by the strong solar and lunar characteristics which coexist in the symbolism connected with the dolphin. Closely associated with Apollo, the dolphin was believed to guide souls to their enlightenment. The Greek word *delphis* (dolphin) is related to *delphys*, which means "womb" and stands for the feminine principle. This was reflected in the relationship between the dolphin and many of the Mediterranean goddesses, and yet the dolphin was also an attribute of Poseidon and intimately associated with Dionysus. There is a beautiful cup from the early classical period designed by Exekias, who painted the godly figure of Dionysus resting upon a ship which itself looks like a dolphin. Growing around its mast is a tree with fruit and leaves hanging over the sail, and around the ship dolphins swim. This masterpiece depicts the attempted abduction of the god by sailors who were turned into dolphins for their pains, which no doubt bears a deeper symbolic meaning. It is said that the Greek myths explaining the origin of the dolphin are all related to Dionysus, and the cycle of death and rebirth has been likened to the diving and leaping dolphin coursing its way across the watery abyss.

Apollo is also a dolphin deity. Is he not called Apollo Delphinius? Legend has it that when Apollo had completed his temple near Mount Parnassus, he needed suitable priests. Spying some Cretans in a ship bound for Pylos, the great sun god leapt into the sea in the form of a dolphin and thence into the hollow of their vessel. Too large to throw overboard, the dolphin lay there, and the sailors were driven by forces beyond their control into the Gulf of Corinth and finally that of Krisa. There, as a beautiful youth, Apollo revealed himself to them and appointed them holy servants of his temple. He bade them worship him under the title Delphinius (Dolphin-Hke), and the site of the shrine, formerly called Pytho, took on the immortal name of Delphi.

As the deity guides the sun across the heavenly ocean in his golden vehicle, the dolphin leads the ship of men across the blue in watery form, and at Delphi the two meet. From the illuminated marble of Apollo's temple, the dawn reaches down and touches the slumbering depths of the sea cleft by the arc of a dolphin's curve. So close, they are the complement of each other, one above, one below.

> Dolphins have large brains.
> Possibly they will someday
> Be able to teach us what
> Brains are for.
>
> Ashley Montague

Similar to the abducting sailors who were turned into dolphins was the plight of Pharaoh's forces as they pursued the Israelites into the Red Sea. The idea of a man-fish, so revered in many religious traditions, is marvellously demonstrated in the dolphin. Whether people have thought that he was once a man or that man was once a dolphin, there is no more intelligent mammal in the ocean, and, some would argue, on land as well. Most dolphins inhabit the seas, but some, like the Ganges dolphin, live in rivers sometimes many miles from the sea. The Brahmaputra, Indus and Ganges join the Amazon, Nile, Yangtze Kiang and other great rivers in hosting this graceful sojourner. The common dolphin (*Delphinus delphis*) can reach a length of nine feet in the open seas and is distinguished from the bottle-nosed dolphin (*Tursiops truncatus*) and the beakless porpoise by its well defined narrow beak. The dolphins painted by Exekias on the Dionysian cup are a good example of this type, whilst sculptors of the Roman and medieval periods tended to favour the bottle-nosed dolphin, which grows to a length of twelve feet or more. Such awesome size seems more within familiar human proportions when one learns that dolphins have a ten-month gestation period, give birth as a normal mammal, and suckle their young for an eighteen-month period. Of course this proportion reaches beyond the human range when one notices that the new-born is three feet long and weighs twenty-five pounds, yet the loving care and discipline shown by the dolphin mother to her offspring is a model for human conduct.

Dolphins have a highly cooperative social network wherein they help each other to fish and achieve safety, and they will go to great lengths to protect a wounded or sick comrade. Since ancient times, in the Pacific and Mediterranean worlds, stories have persisted which describe how sometimes one or several dolphins gave up their lives to remain with a stricken fellow. When efforts are made to save healthy animals stranded on a beach, they refuse to be rescued and turn back to die with their injured friend.

It has often been suggested that the irresistible wail of the sirens which Odysseus heard whilst he was safely tied to the mast of his ship was really the song of dolphins. When they depicted the scene, the ancient Greeks showed the sailors with their ears plugged, their master bound fast, and dolphins leaping and gambolling around the boat. Perhaps the plaintive sounds of the dolphin lure one back through the abyssal past to a primordial mode of communication which flies in the face of separative consciousness. This could be seen as a threat to the individuating hero who must seize reason as a means of knowing and can no longer move as one with the currents of life. But the irrational force of Dionysus claims the dolphin equally with the Apollonian force of the rational, and the immense auditory specialization represented in dolphins is accompanied by a very high degree of discriminative intelligence.

Whilst the eye, which is strongly related to human powers of discrimination, is well developed in the dolphin, its outstanding characteristic is a profound audio sensitivity to changes in signal amplitude or frequency. The evolution of their hearing and sound-producing systems have involved new mechanisms as well as modifications of those possessed by their terrestrial ancestor. The entire peripheral respiratory system has been modified to facilitate sound production. Clicks and whistles are produced simultaneously and in extremely close proximity with each other and still have different beam patterns. All of these can be understood either by the dolphin using sound for echo location purposes (a minutely detailed check of its environment), or by many dolphins who carry on complex communication whilst swimming in groups. In the Black Sea, dolphins commune in whistles, each one having a unique tone and contributing to an underwater chorus of enormous variety. The bottle-nosed dolphin is exceptionally adept at learning and remembering sounds heard. They can also recognize variants of duration and frequency as derivative forms. It is this inclination that has inspired many to feel that the dolphin might well be capable of learning an imposed language. But as one observer has pointed out, why should a language be imposed upon this remarkable animal? Is it not perhaps more fruitful that we attempt to learn the meaning of its own? It is amusing to think that the intelligent "tricks" which men have taught dolphins to perform might be indulged in by them in a spirit of cheerful compassion.

Pliny the Elder told of how dolphins helped fishermen in classical times, mentioning that it was called "fishing for share". To this day, the practice continues in rivers and in the open sea. Fishermen of the Sporades catch garfish in the darkest nights of October with flares which initially attract them, whereupon the dolphins drive the fish into the net. In the Tapajoz and Irrawaddy rivers, dolphins push fish into the net, the latter being particularly revered by Burmese fishermen, each riverside village having its guardian dolphin. The dolphins of the Tapajoz can be called by Brazilian Indians with a humming tune and a knocking on the side of their canoe. Off the coast of New Zealand and Queensland, mullet were caught in a similar way. The Aborigines of Australia say that they used to call the individual dolphins by name and that they would respond to a peculiar splashing in the water made with their spears. Coming to them from beyond the waves, the dolphin would drive the mullet into nets thrown out over rocky inlets.

Man tends to think of intelligence in terms of manipulating things. Dolphins cannot do this, but in their response to the needs and desires of man they reveal an intelligence of such subtlety that people are either awed or made sceptical. One way to clear the air is with a bit of humour, a method freely used by Aesop, who wrote of the dolphin that rescued a monkey after a ship went down. Approaching Piraeus, the dolphin asked the monkey if he were an Athenian. "Oh yes," the monkey replied, "and from one of the best families." "Then you know Piraeus?" asked the dolphin.

Whereupon the monkey replied, "Very well indeed, he's one of my best friends." The dolphin was outraged with so gross a deceit and promptly took a deep dive, leaving the clever-by-half monkey to his fate. Many would argue that moral outrage was not within the scope of the dolphin and that, though clever-seeming, its acts towards man are merely the result of playfulness and curiosity. There persist, however, well documented cases of people who have been saved by dolphins at sea, including that of one woman who had fallen overboard at night in the Caribbean and was "nudged" by a dolphin away from strong currents and towards the shore. During the Second World War, many stories about dolphin rescues circulated in the Pacific. In one incident, six American airmen had been shot down and were afloat in a small rubber raft. A dolphin appeared and pushed them steadily through the open sea until they reached land. Unfortunately, they quickly discovered the island to be occupied by the Japanese, a political distinction beyond the discrimination of the altruistic dolphin.

The dolphin cannot display its intelligence by manipulating things, but with echo location he gains far more knowledge of his environment than one may imagine. The intelligence of a dolphin is lonely, almost disembodied. He floats in a watery world without the stimulus of agile, exploring fingers that can alter and formulate the surroundings. Yet in that floating world he has developed an intelligence of a very high order. Once a land mammal long ages ago, the dolphin returned to the sea where his large and highly convoluted brain slowly evolved. To quote the poetic words of Loren Eiseley, "It is as though both man and dolphin were each part of some great eye which yearned to look both outward on eternity and inward to the sea's heart."

There is indeed a special and profoundly moving kinship between mankind and the dolphin, as though they represent two specialized aspects of one self. Herman Melville expressed something of this when he wrote:

> Their appearance is generally hailed with delight by the mariner. Full of fine spirits, they invariably come from the breezy billows to windward. They are the lads that always live before the wind. They are accounted a lucky omen. If you can withstand three cheers at beholding these vivacious fish, then heaven help ye.

Always men have worked the sea with the dolphin as friend. Because he is an intelligent and altruistic partner, men have fished with him for the share. It is extremely difficult to understand how any fishing industry could, out of a greed which calls itself necessity, enter into an aggressive and dehumanizing competition with this old friend. In the second century Oppian, a Greek of Cilicia, warned:

> The hunting of dolphins is immoral and that man can no more draw nigh the gods as a welcome sacrificer nor touch their altars with clean hands but pollutes those who share the same roof with him, whoso willingly devises destruction for dolphins. For equally with human slaughter the gods abhor the deathly doom of the monarchs of the deep; for like thoughts with men have the attendants of the god of the booming sea; wherefore also they practise love of their offspring and are very friendly to one another.

Poseidon of the booming sea holds a dolphin in his right hand as his vehicle and yet it is one with him, esoterically. Some say that Poseidon became a dolphin in order to win his consort Amphitrite, whilst others have believed that the dolphin acted as messenger. For this favour Poseidon placed him amongst the immortals in heaven, where as Delphinus he lies east of Aquila on the edge of the Milky Way, occupying that portion of the sky that Aratus called the Water. This act of bringing the reluctant Amphitrite and Poseidon together is no doubt linked up with the frequent association of Eros (or Cupid) with the dolphin, and an important consequence of this was the birth of their son, Triton.

Above the waist Triton was a man, whilst below he had the form of a dolphin, a combination that links him with the idea of Cannes the man-fish as well as the Hindu notion of Vishnu-Matsya. These were Teachers of wisdom to mortals, and in the aspect of Matsya there lies a powerful example of the fish-dolphin acting as guide. Triton too assisted the transfer of human life from one age to the next at the time of the Great Deluge. Exercising control over the waters, he also acted to preserve the solar spark of wisdom culled out of a vast period of evolution. With the power of sound he allayed the rising waters. With his conch shell he blew a note that filled the deep around the world.

Thus the dolphin is instrumental in bringing about the birth of the man-fish, the saviour, and in a very real sense is itself a saviour. In the Hindu tradition the dolphin is identified with the tenth sign of the zodiac, which is Capricorn or Makara, the *vahan* of Varuna-Poseidon. The stars making up this constellation were merged by ancient seers in order to signify the meeting of water and air upon earth. This is the occult meaning of the man-fish/goat-fish associated with the mirror of mind. In this way, Makara can be seen as the *vahan* of the Universal Encompasser (Varuna-Poseidon), who fell into time and generation. The man-fish is linked to the Fall, but out of the chaos of the sea, it is said, the dragons will manifest their fruits. Clearly then, the dolphin exemplifies, as a symbol and as a living creature, a great primitive sacrifice. In this way it is linked to the five pristine Yogis called the Kumaras and to spiritual microcosmic birth. *The Secret Doctrine* suggests that these Kumaras are of the fifth order of Brahmadevas and have the soul of the five elements in them, with water and ether predominating. Because of this, their symbols were both aquatic and fiery. They are linked to the Prachetasas (the five Ministers) who worship Narayana and whose mother is the Daughter of the Ocean (Savarna-Amphitrite). In this way, they symbolize both the lunar dolphin vehicle and the manifest wisdom embodied in the solar man-fish.

With this fusion, Apollo and Dionysus are brought together. Like two dolphins circling around each other, each facing the opposite direction, like revolving teardrops in a yin-yang pattern, the two gods alternately represent involution and evolution. Both are so closely associated with the dolphin that the characterization of either as exclusively rational or irrational seems overdrawn. Rather, one might perceive a necessary blending of *Buddhi* and *Manas* suggested in their shared affiliation. Apollo takes on the guise of a dolphin to make priests of men. Dionysus rides upon a dolphin-ship and scatters those who were blind to the spiritual back into the form of the Sacrificing Ones who entered the water of the mother long ago. By this compassionate act the great god of the Mysteries afforded such persons a chance to experience a pure and selfless intelligence which is less involved in manipulating an environment than in intimately relating to it. Through hearing and producing sound, they would respond to the most minute aspects of a swirling, watery matrix in which a vast spectrum of tones endlessly resounded. Perhaps then, as dolphins, they might experience and mirror the wisdom embodied in the virgin *Akasha* which echoes throughout the heavenly ocean. As dolphins they will leap with the joy of hearing these celestial sounds and attempt, even at the risk of their lives, to share this with their human brethren.

> On the edge of the ocean
> Where the waves become sky,
> The boy rides on the dolphin,
> They leap, they dance, they fly!
> A sun splashing across the world.

Hermes, October 1981

THE WHALE

There Leviathan
Hugest of living creatures, on the deep
Stretch'd like a promontory sleeps or swims.
And seems a moving land, and at his gills
Draws in, and at his trunk spouts out a sea.

John Milton

Black clouds scudding in tendrilled bands before an alabaster moon, phosphorescent tracks scintillating over the inky deep, and a great dark shape looms out of the waves to starboard bow. A great dark shape arches like a gliding island on the sea, only to disappear silently into a world unknown to those destined merely to skim its surface and prey upon the outward forms of its mystery. Long furrows curl away from the iridescence of the leviathan's wake, ploughing to the edge of the visible world, carrying along the dreaming eye of the watcher on the bow. If he is a mariner of imagination, whose sense of wonder has not been dissipated in the noise of idle chatter, he may feel himself drawn in mind and soul along the troughs of that wake. He may shiver with the oncoming rush of the sea as, communing thus with the whale, he is enclosed by its cold darkness and sinks into its depths. Or he may remain in consciousness at his watch and ponder the true nature of this largest of all living creatures, who slips through the world's oceans so effortlessly and swims so deeply through its hidden places. In a floating kingdom of darkness where forms appear only momentarily on the lip of chaos, the whale is at home, with a form so great as to suggest the swirling formlessness in which it bathes, consumes and spews forth. It is a symbol of the deep itself, of the world encompassed by chaos wherein life meets its dissolution in death.

The idea of the whale as "the Encompasser", a symbol of the world and the grave, is a complex notion linking multiple meanings associated with death, initiation and rebirth as well as a more vague conception of dread and evil. Watching the great, dark curve of its only partially revealed immensity, a mariner or even a casual sojourner upon the deep may indeed experience intimations of all these conditions. This would not be surprising if one conceded that somewhere in the depth of the human psyche lies an awareness of the regenerative power of the ocean and its sidereal archetype, the "water" of cosmic space. The notion of an engulfing grave is merely the other side of the same coin, symbolically rendering the belly of the whale as the place of death and rebirth, whilst the emergence from its mouth signifies initiation and resurrection. The biblical tale of Jonah, and the old story conveying how a swallowed hero built a fire in the belly of a whale in order to cause it to spew him out, are examples of this. That the latter story is found in traditions as widespread as the Indo-European and the Polynesian suggests a very old and complex pattern of ideas shared in the collective consciousness of the human race.

In the Semitic tradition Jonah was the fifth of the lesser prophets of Israel, going back to around the eighth century B.C. In seeking to avoid the Lord's command that he tell the people of Nineveh that their city was to be destroyed, Jonah sailed off on a merchant ship. A storm arose, threatening the vessel, and Jonah, thinking it a divine chastisement for his disobedience, advised the crew to save themselves by throwing him overboard. It was when they finally consented to do this that Jonah was swallowed by the whale, in whose stomach he resided for three days before being vomited up onto a beach. Instead of stressing the importance of the whale in relation to the three days of initiation, Christian tradition has tended to focus almost entirely upon its monstrous and fearful aspects. The idea of the abyss or of chaos being full of potential regeneration gradually became replaced by a deep-seated dread of dissolution, loss of form and loss of identity. As the agent of chaos in this physicallized sense, the whale came to be seen as a monster to be struggled against, escaped from or vanquished.

From the depths of the sea came whales like islands, and the hideous Leviathans rising up on the sand with crocodiles twenty cubits in length. Man is before the sea like a child before a Leviathan's lair.

Old Testament

In its guise of sea monster, huge ship or even the devil whose jaws form the gates of hell, the leviathan persisted in its character of container and encompasser. Its identification with the crocodile resulted from an awkwardness in the translation of the idea of Makara or the goat-fish into some sort of recognizable animal. Egyptian lore contributed to this confusion with its reference to scaly features and other characteristics associated with dragons, but the central identity of the leviathan lies in the combined attributes of a land-going but aquatic creature, a mammal of the sea who symbolically spans the terrestrial and watery astral realms. Thus the sea gods Poseidon and Neptune had as their vehicle a giant dolphin, a member of the same cetacean family as the whale. In the ancient Vedic tradition the god of the waters was Varuna, the Lord of the Laws of Nature, who established the heavens and the earths which dwell within him. His name, coming from the Sanskrit root *var*, means "to cover" or "encompass", and his *vahan* is identified with Makara, the goat-fish, or a counterpart to the cetacean vehicle of the Mediterranean and oceanic worlds. Varuna himself, however, is much more than a counterpart to the Graeco-Roman marine gods, for he is the oldest of Vedic deities and reigns over the Waters of Space or *Akasha*. In his role of ruler and container of worlds, Varuna is well represented in the symbolism of the whale, who, like the deity, encompasses the terrestrial and celestial, death and regeneration, within its vast form. While the whale (like the dolphin) can be associated with the generation of gods who overbrood the world's oceans, it also possesses an essential nature which is directly expressive of a loftier deity, Varuna.

> He maketh a path to shine after him; one would think the deep to be hoary.
>
> *Job* 41:32

In the Hellenic tradition the true counterpart to Varuna is Ouranos who, like the older Vedic god, was degraded and caused to fall into generation. For Varuna, this fall involved an impartation of the mysteries to the sage Vasishtha, a positive-seeming result. But Varuna-Ouranos strove to confine his "children" by Aditi-Gaia as they were born so as to forestall generation. Aditi, however, is rightly called the Devamatri, from whose cosmic matrix all the suns and planets of our system were made manifest. Hesiod's *Theogony* tells us how Ouranos (Varuna) personifies all the creative powers in and of chaos, which eventually enabled the ancestral spirits of the human race to evolve primordial men from themselves. This potential power was precipitated into the realm of expression by Kronos, who mutilated his father, cutting away a part of him from the whole and thus initiating generation in time. In suffering this, Ouranos was rendered apparently impotent in time and relegated to a cosmic rulership whose effects are difficult to trace in the sequential realm of the manifest world. In the Vedic tradition the attributes ascribed to Varuna impart to his character a moral elevation and sanctity far surpassing that attributed to any other Vedic deity. Nonetheless, he too suffered a progressive displacement in the minds of later races and was relegated to a relatively impotent and rather vague upper strata of Hindu theogony, much like the Greek Ouranos whose name simply means "sky".

The mysteries of Varuna-Ouranos are more complex than these simple ideas would indicate and can be related in a powerfully suggestive manner to the little-known planet which came to be called (almost by accident) Uranus. Before attempting to investigate such correspondences, it is of primary importance to examine more closely the animal whose nature and symbolism link them all together and who, in its own right, remains for man largely a mystery. For centuries the Greeks called the whale by the name of κητος (*ketos*), which bears reference both to a sea monster and to the abyss or chaos in which it swims. Aristotle accurately described it as a viviparous, lung-possessing mammal, which drily rational observation did not dissuade centuries of writers from persisting in referring to the whale as a fish. At the beginning of the Christian era Pliny described the Physeter (whirlpool) that rose up like a column higher than the sails of ships and spouted water to sink them. He also noted the *balaenas* who came along the coast of Spain to breed. Centuries later the Norwegian *Kongespeiler* in A.D. 1250 depicted how sailors were afraid of the North Atlantic right whale, and a contemporary document, the *Speculum Regale*, described killer whales near Iceland which had teeth like dogs, peaceful baleen whales and fierce sperm and narwhals. Early Nordic sailors would not mention their names at sea for fear of danger and deprived anyone who did of food, even though they recognized as friends the baleen whales who drove the herring into the fishermen's nets.

The term "whale" bears no relation to the Greek *ketos*, which is the source of the generic zoological name of *Cetus*. It conies instead from the Old Norse *hvalr*, which is an etymological relation of both "wheel" and "to wallow". In the Old High German it became *wal* and in Old English *hwael*, referring more to the circular motion of its arching and rolling progress through the sea than to its monstrous size. Unknown to even the oldest of these latter-day namers, the earliest cetaceans, which developed eventually into the toothed whales and dolphins, or *Odontocetes*, evolved nearly forty-five million years ago during the Eocene epoch. Out of this line emerged the *Archaeocetes* who, twenty-five million years ago, sported a ball and socket joint whereby the femur articulated with the pelvis and may have possessed tibia vestiges as well, pointing clearly to an earlier terrestrial development. This is borne out in various ways by the characteristics of the modern whale, the *Odontocetes* finding their nearest relatives among mammalian carnivores, the *Mysticetes* (baleen whales) finding theirs among the even-toed ungulates such as the cow, the sheep and the camel, whose blood protein structure they share. Interestingly, the foetuses of *Mysticetes* often have teeth which disappear with the appearance of the baleen. In the embryo stage the rudimentary hind legs of all whales are initially apparent, as are the nostrils at the end of the nose which gradually migrate to the top of the head. The embryonic flippers develop like normal mammal limbs with a wrist and five fingers. The wrist disappears as the foetus grows and the digits become encased in a stiff but elastic integument, with the joint at the shoulder its only movable part.

Like carnivores on land, the *Odontocetes* hunt larger prey, one at a time, while the *Mysticetes* feed wholesale from shallow level pastures, using two or three hundred flat plates set around the edge of the upper jaw and hanging from it like an enormous, hairy screen measuring, in some cases, thirteen feet in length. A great "field" of krill (plankton) will be plowed through by the baleen whale, who simply drops its lower jaw, opening a screened cave capable of trapping enormous masses of food at a time. To obtain even a crude idea of the size of whales, one might bear in mind that the blue whale, measuring one hundred feet in length, will weigh an amount equivalent to four brontosauruses or thirty elephants or two hundred cows – that is to say, one hundred and thirty tons. Such large whales are simply the biggest by far of all the animals that have ever lived on this planet. An elephant weighing three to six tons would balance in a scale with the tongue of some *Cetis,* while the humpback whale swimming in warm Bermudan waters regularly gives a free ride to over a thousand pounds of barnacles and other parasites clustered on its head and sides. Nineteenth-century sperm whales were recorded at up to ninety-three feet with jawbones twenty-three feet long. The sight of such an aroused mass churning across the waves at a good twenty knots must have been terrifying indeed, especially when, because of being hunted so intensively, they were sometimes goaded into dramatically aggressive behaviour.

When the baleen whale lowers its underjaw while swimming through a shoal of krill, the pleated crop which covers half the length of its underbelly swells out as several tons of water are taken in. When the crop contracts, the solid food remains caught in the baleen strainer while the floods of water are ejected out of the whale's mouth. The whale then swallows the krill whole, taking it into the first of three stomachs, where it will join several tons of food taken in during the months spent in twenty-four-hour grazing near the Arctic or Antarctic seas. All whales swallow their food whole, even the *Odontocetes,* who use their teeth only to seize their prey. There is no chewing or biting – just a gulp. Whether vast seas of small shrimp-sized animals or a giant squid forty feet long taken by a sperm whale at the end of a terrible struggle thirty-five hundred feet beneath the surface of the deep, all the whale's food is swallowed whole. Offering remarkable evidence of this, and of the killer whale's voracious appetite, were the contents found in the stomach of a twenty-four-foot killer, which included the adult carcasses of thirteen porpoises and fourteen seals. Had they gone through the entire digestive cycle they would have been pulverized by the powerful muscular wall of the first stomach (or second, in the case of the *Mysticetes*) and passed on, finally, to the last, where the digestive juices do their work prior to elimination. A poignant example of swallowed evidence was found in the shape of a man who, in 1947, fell into the sea only to be swallowed by a large sperm whale. Like Jonah, he was not chewed up, but he did not manage to emerge alive after three days. His chest was crushed and it was thought that he had probably died even as he was swallowed.

> The aorta of a whale is larger in the bore than the main pipe of the water works at London Bridge, and the water roaring in its passage through that pipe is inferior in impetus and velocity to the blood gushing from the whale's heart.

> *Natural Theology*, William Paley

Some years ago two bold men, breathing a mixture of helium and oxygen in the hope of preventing bends, descended one thousand feet in a diving bell near an island off the California coast. Down they went to the greatest depth ever attempted without protective diving suits. When the bell was hoisted up, one man revived to tell what he knew of the story. The other was dying. The sperm whale, diving thirty-five hundred feet or more, experiences much greater pressures but possesses (along with other whales) a remarkably complex circulatory system which ensures pressurization of all the vital parts. The whale's *retia mirabilia* ("wondrous network"), the parts of the vascular system subdivided into plexuses of vessels, are remarkable for their profusion. Typically, a whale comes to the surface in a quick succession of blowing and inhaling, with shallow dives in between before diving deeply. It can remain under water for up to a half hour (up to two hours in the case of the sperm whale). It is believed that oxygen is stored in the myoglobin within the muscles (which function anaerobically during the dive), while the *retia mirabilia* act as a shunt ensuring that the brain is adequately supplied during the whole period of submergence. If one could imagine an immeasurably vast body encompassing the world from its airy heights to its watery depths, having complete communication to and from all points, one would of necessity construct in the mind an analogous wondrous network capable of regulating and diffusing the life-giving fluid on a scale unparalleled in lesser forms. In the whale this is writ small, and yet in so great and complex a design as to powerfully suggest the larger idea and lend credence to the feeling man has often had that the whale is somehow connected with another world, that its behaviour and intelligence cannot be explained in simple evolutionary terms.

The great sperm whales with their calls, the baleens with their trills (the low frequencies enabling the location of food, the high for communication), all manifest a lively display of intelligence not yet understood by man. Recording around sixty to seventy-five feet below the surface off Bermuda, a technician found that early in the evening there were only a few sounds, as the humpbacks seemed to be slowly tuning up. Then one began to "sing" and soon creaking and mews and whoops filled the water all around, a polyphonic choir of sounds. One night several whales surfaced near the sound technician's small boat. They watched him as he sat in the dark with his lights and wires and dials. They came very close and began to make little squeaking noises, like mice. The technician became convinced they were talking about him. Alternating voices certainly do suggest some sort of talking, as does the diversity of modulation recorded during these remarkable sessions. Sometimes there was a group sounding like children reciting a lesson, but the little mouse squeaks were heard again when the whales discovered the main boat of the expedition and other small craft associated with it. Their curiosity brought them back continually, but when a little calf began affectionately rubbing itself against the side of the main boat, its mother smartly pushed it away, spanking it with her flippers several times.

Unlike primates and even certain birds who sometimes use rudimentary tools to capture food, whales have not been thought to manipulate any sort of extension of their mouths or flippers to achieve such ends. But huge finbacks visiting along the Mexican coast surrounded a motorboat advancing slowly into a lagoon. They escorted it on both sides until the water in front of them began to boil with shoals of tiny fish, and it became apparent that the finbacks were using the sound of the boat's engine to round them up! The men in the boat had arrived there not more than twenty minutes before and were thus almost immediately put to work by these eighty-five-foot managers. Possessing marvellous hearing which picks up a very great range of sounds, including ultrasonic vibrations measured up to one hundred and fifty-three kilocycles (as compared to the human range, which falls between fifteen and twenty kilocycles), the whale experiences and expresses much of its intelligence through this sense. This would appear to be a development compensating for its poor senses of smell and sight, though it does have an excellent sense of taste and enjoys touching and rubbing. More than one whale-lover has been delighted by the presentation at the side of their vessel of a friendly, if monstrous, nose which invited patting and stroking of its barnacle-encrusted surface.

Though near-sighted (except for killer whales who have good vision), the whale's eyes are beautiful and full of life. Because of their blind spot they are careful of a diver in the water in front of them, becoming aware of him through the use of their powers of sonar. Those few divers who have actually dared to swim around and alongside a whale in the sea have remarked about its eyes, saying that "the look that a whale gives you is very different from that of a shark. A shark only glances at you. It passes with the appearance of not having seen you at all. But the whale's look is quite open. He doesn't look at you out of the corner of his eye." Though a man swimming around a whale would be like a fly buzzing around a man, slightly annoying perhaps, still whales are interested and watch divers. One diver off Bermuda said that a particular humpback came to visit him regularly while he was working on a certain job. But when they wish, they can lose a diver in ten seconds by one swish of the tail or dive straight down and vanish in a wink. No one yet understands enough about the behaviour of whales, or the complexities of their powers of intelligence and communication, to be able to predict when or why they will do such things. The more predictable patterns have to do with conception, birth and growth cycles and the vast migrations made by pods or schools of various species each year. California gray whales follow a route of five thousand miles, extending from the Bering Straits, where they feed on vast shoals of krill during the summer, to the lagoons along the Baja California peninsula, where they gather in the thousands to give birth or to mate in alternating years. The nineteenth and twentieth centuries witnessed the decimation of the great schools of Greenland and Biscayan right whales in the Atlantic and the extinction of the gray whales which used to migrate on the western side of the Pacific from Kamchatka to the South China Sea. As a result of ruthless whaling methods, other species have been extinguished or endangered, but the migration trails continue to be followed by the survivors in marvellously regular lines, those in the

Northern Hemisphere travelling from the Arctic to the equator and back, those in the Southern following a similar course in reverse.

There seem to be two basic populations of baleen whales belonging to each hemisphere, with minimal mixing between them around the equatorial belt of the globe. Sperm whales and other *Odontocetes* seem to travel more ubiquitously from forty degrees North to forty degrees South, with occasionally aggressive older sperm bulls roaming about on their own for years. *Mysticetes*, like the gray whale, have lasting ties, the mother being assisted at birth by an "auntie" who helps mind the calf well into its maturity. The act of mating for these enormous animals, being extremely difficult, also elicits assistance. Grays regularly move in pods of three (or multiples of three), so that while one male attempts to couple with his mate, a second lies across them in an effort to stabilize their buoyant, rolling bodies. Those who have witnessed this strangely moving spectacle have been deeply touched and sometimes entertained by frolicking dolphins who seem to take special joy in the occasion. Of no lesser joy, of course, is the birth of a fifteen- to twenty-ton infant who is flippered aloft by its mother for a first breath of air. One of the most remarkable instances attesting to the strong emotional ties between mothers and offspring was recorded on film when a baby humpback was liberated from a cable in which it had become badly entangled. A diver worked diligently attempting to cut the cable which was cruelly wound in and through the bruised mouth of the calf, while its mother waited a short distance off from the boat. Several hours of work were required, and even after the last binding twist of cable was cut, the youngster seemed unable to move. Desperately, the diver tugged at a loose piece that dangled from the calf s firmly closed mouth. With its removal the infant began to swim and was joined immediately by its mother, who rolled and flapped her long white flippers in the air. Together, mother and calf, they rolled and cavorted and showed every expression imaginable of relief and joy at their reunion.

Occupants of a motorboat off Baja California observed a gray whale twelve feet below, slowly moving upward. Turning on her side, she looked at them with what appeared to be a flicker of interest. She moved herself higher for a closer inspection and slipped her left flipper under the boat, raising it three feet out of the water before suddenly removing her flipper and letting it fall back to the surface with a splash. In another instance men followed a sperm whale, zig-zagging around it in an inflatable motorboat, hoping to confuse its sensitive hearing with the noise. The giant seemed paralysed. It did not dive or attempt to put on speed. Suddenly, there was a monstrous movement in the water and the launch was observed, together with its occupants and equipment, to be thrown up in the air like toys. The whale had simply grown tired of the noise and with one casual twist of its tail had gotten rid of it. He could have easily crushed the boat with his tail or mouth but he gave a measured, though effective, response instead. Such well moderated and almost thoughtful responses seem not to have been found significant by sailors of earlier centuries. Whalers of more modern times have kept alive the tales of peril and aggression, particularly regarding the sperm whale which, as the most sought-after prize of the early nineteenth century, took on many of the biblical allusions to an evil monster who operated as a devilish scourge upon the seas. There were some notorious sperm bulls known far and wide by names like Timor Tim or Don Miguel (off Chile), New Zealand Jack or the infamous Mocha Dick, whose adventures were avidly followed for thirty-nine years and who served as a model for Herman Melville's great white whale. Old bulls who had been often harpooned or maddened by the chase would sometimes jump straight out of the water to lash out with their tails or ram a large ship broadside with their massive heads. One sent the whaler *Union* to the bottom in 1807, the Essex in 1821 and the *Ann Alexander* was sunk in a few minutes in 1851. In 1902 the *Kathleen* was sunk in minutes and a fishing launch with all aboard went down off Sydney in 1963 as a result of an attack by a sperm bull.

> This high and mighty God-like dignity inherent in the brow is so immensely amplified, that gazing on it... you feel the Deity and the dread powers more forcefully than beholding any other object in living nature.

> Herman Melville

In 1957 a white (albino) sperm whale was killed off the coast of Japan. But the modern day cachalots cannot compare to the ninety-foot giants of Mocha Dick's time. Nor does man now tend to possess the vivid and deeply felt sense of the presence of good and evil in the world as in earlier centuries. In Melville's masterly tale, Captain Ahab represents an obsessive focal point for the eternal struggle between what man believes to be good and evil incarnate. To him, Moby Dick, the great white whale, represents the beast, the devil in the flesh who threatens chaos, madness and annihilation. Ahab struggles to preserve order but abandons himself to inhumanity and obsession in his monomaniacal pursuit of this formidable leviathan. In his last glimmering of humaneness he looks to his mate, Starbuck, as to his soul and cries, "Oh Starbuck; let me look into a human eye . . ." To which Starbuck answers, "Oh Noble Soul – after all, let us fly these deadly waters!" But Ahab responds, sinking again into the fatalistic clutches of his obsession, "What is it that against all natural lovings and longings, I so keep pushing . . . ?" It was truth, but with malice in it, that he saw in the white whale. In the throes of an eternal anguish he saw all that demonizes and torments and reduces conscious life into chaos in the form of Moby Dick. And chaos it was that he entered, killed in his own attempt to kill the whale, borne down into the endless deep lashed to the body of a ghostly, colourless, form-obliterating and form-dissolving monster. For Ahab, the godlike dignity and dread powers of the sperm whale became a titanic force which swept him out of the world, beyond all recognizable signs of good and evil, to a shapeless, timeless realm where human fears and longings are but unborn bubbles in a limitless sea.

> Varuna, King of hallowed might,
> Sustaineth erect the Tree's stem in the baseless region.
> Its rays, whose root is high above, stream downward.
> Deep may they sink within us and be hidden.
> King Varuna hath made a spacious pathway,
> A pathway for the Sun wherein to travel.
> Where no way was he made him set his footstep,
> And warned afar whate'er afflicts the Spirit.

Rig Veda XXIV: 7–8

Varuna the Encompasser, witness to men's falsehoods, upholder of heavens and earths, knows the secret pathways of ships and other leviathans. *The Secret Doctrine* speaks of Varuna-Ouranos as a Host which ruled over the Second Race before Kronos-Saturn ruled over the Third and Zeus-Neptune over the Fourth. The Second Race over which Varuna-Ouranos reigned was the Sweat Born, produced by the Sons of Yoga unconsciously, through asexual budding. It is said to have been endowed by the Preservers, called the Rakshasas or demons who devour. According to the *Bhagavata Purana*, Brahmā once transformed himself into the body of night, which the Rakshasas (actually Yogis and Initiates) wished to devour. Brahmā called out to them, "Do not devour me, spare me." The occult interpretation of this lies in the identification of the body of night with ignorance, but also with silence and secrecy. The Yogis (representing spiritual man) are bound to dispel ignorance by devouring it, but they are also bound to preserve the sacred and silent Truth from profanation. In the whale one can readily see an analogue to the Host or Rakshasas, who wish to devour every form but maintain the lines or pathways in both hemispheres "for the Sun [of Truth or the Law] wherein to travel". Each generation of whales maintains the same ancient course, as if they had (each particular species) a built-in magnetic compass and were annually re-establishing longitudinal lines of force around the globe. One is reminded of the *retia mirabilia*, which pressurizes and balances all parts of the whale's body as it dives through the ocean's deep, like the earth swimming through the chaos of space.

The Second Race manifested the first primitive spark of intelligence. Endowed with incarnate gods (Asuras and Kumaras, who were loath to create), it remained ethereal. But duality intervened. Prakriti (Aditi or Gaia) conceived their great potency, causing their all-encompassing wholeness to be destroyed by the resultant generation. In the Greek myth the generative part of the father was cut away by Kronos so that the host (Varuna-Ouranos) was separated from the progressively sexual modes of creation. This remoteness from physical procreation is poignantly reflected in the difficulty experienced by the whale in mating. Indeed, such an awkward and exhaustive repetition of attempts is required to ensure successful conception that one cannot help but consider the nature of the intelligence which persists in operating through the form of the whale. Is their sojourn here on earth part of a great sacrificial process wherein the Host associated with laws pertaining to our deepest ancestral nature continues to exert its influence? When thinking man took his place in the physical world over eighteen million years ago, these *Cetacea* were already evolved, already equipped with the bodily parts which would have, had they remained upon land, brought them into the mainstream of mammalian development leading to biological man. Instead, they adapted to (entered once again, perhaps) the realm of the ocean, the astral sea surrounding our globe. There, hunted and cursed, scarred and covered with the weight of barnacles, they have assumed (like the planet Uranus) a retrograde action in the evolutionary scheme of things and a horizontal position in regard to their axis or spine.

The mysterious planet Uranus got its name through what was almost a fluke (if the pun may be permitted). Though its discoverer, William Herschel, deemed it fitting to name the planet after King George III, the name was not popular. Other names were proposed but it was Uranus which immediately caught on and for reasons scientific and, no doubt, occult became the name by which the world knows it. Whatever the forces working to bring about this appellation might have been, Uranus possesses several remarkable characteristics of great interest when correlated with the symbolism associated with Varuna-Ouranos and the whale. It appears to march to a different tune from the other planets of our system. Its axis is tipped over, lying almost in a horizontal position relative to the axes of the other planets, whilst its north and south magnetic poles represent almost an exact inversion of the earth's north and south geographic poles.

Recently twentieth-century man was afforded a close-up glimpse of the Blue Giant, with its retrograde motion and its mysterious coal-black rings. It is believed that the unusual motion and position of Uranus, as well as the presence of its many retrograde satellites, are due to a terrific "war" or explosion which not only ripped away great chunks of the planet but tipped it over and set it off in its peculiarly renegade pattern. This, of course, is strongly reminiscent of the dismemberment of Ouranos by Kronos and is also echoed in the whale's adaptation to a swimming position in the sea.

Uranus, unlike Mercury, Venus, Jupiter or Saturn, is not in direct astral and psychic communication with mankind on this globe.

According to arcane traditions, it is a guardian of another (unseen) septenary chain of globes within our system. It does not depend upon the physical sun like the other planets, receiving so little of its light and hearkening to a different axis of influence. Like the whale on earth serving as the vehicle on the physical plane for the Host known as Varuna-Ouranos, so too Uranus acts as a witness and *vahan* in our solar system for an unseen ancestral Host. Covered with a deep electrically charged ocean which is heavily laced with sal ammoniac, it represents an environment not only symbolic of the waters of chaos, but chemically suited to act as a solvent, a dissolving sublimate capable of releasing the "soul" or quicksilver of substances. As the medieval alchemists knew, sal ammoniac dissolves the existing order of things, not to merely "devour" them or render them chaotic but to release a more refined and essential Truth.

> So fire with water to compare,
> The ocean serves on high,
> Up-spouted by the whale in air,
> To express unwieldy joy.

> William Cowper

Taking in gigantic draughts of the ocean and letting them out again, the whale plows its way along the sea lanes, participating on an unmatched scale in the business of alchemizing lower forms of life. Like Jonah passing three days within its belly, the triple stomach of the whale processes its food and converts it into a larger and more mysterious pattern. There is no way of knowing now how the complex ecosystem of the entire globe would be affected if whales were to disappear from its oceans. Nor is there any way we could anticipate how their absence would affect the spiritual and magnetic climate of life here. Their intelligence would indeed seem to come from afar, and man will be able to understand something about it only when he begins to be prompted by deeper vibrations within his own spiritual memory. In contemplating the life and history and all the rich symbolism associated with the whale, one moves closer to releasing such memories. The whale embodies the powers of regeneration immanent in the cosmic waters and floating unborn in the chaos of our minds. If we sense in its existence the wondrous network that binds us to the intelligence of the One Law, the wholeness of manifest life, its sojourn in this world will not have been in vain. Into the jaws of that meditation, Jonah, motivated by the fearless desire to save his fellows, entered to spend the required period before resurrection. In the fabled belly of the beast the new spiritual life is born, not to those who, like Ahab, mistake the necessary dissolution for evil and take it on as a foe, but to the patient watcher on the bow, the silent one who is willing to devour every form that ignorance takes within himself, whilst ever preserving and witnessing the Divine Immutable Law of Truth.

A mariner on the bow one night
Looked up to see the stars,
He glimpsed a line of golden light
Bound earthward from afar.
The Light dispersed upon the waves,
It marked a phosphor trail,
And where it led he strained his gaze
To see a breaching whale.

Hermes, May 1986

PARADISE

High on a throne of royal state, which far
Outshone the wealth of Ormus and of Ind,
Or where the gorgeous East with richest hand
Showers on her Icings barbaric pearl and gold. . .
As when a vulture, on Imaus bred,
Whose snowy ridge the roving Tartar bounds,
. . . Flies toward the springs
Of Ganges or Hydaspes, Indian streams . . .
That spot to which I point is paradise,
Adam's abode; those lofty shades his bower.
Now to th' ascent of that steep savage hill. . .
One gate there only was, and that looked east. . .
Heaven on Earth; for blissful Paradise
Of God the garden was, by him in the east
Of Eden planted.

Paradise Lost, John Milton

East of the plains of California lettuce farmers or of ancient Eridu: where indeed is this Eden? And did the dreamers of Sumeria look towards the rising orb with the same longing as Steinbeck's lost sons and daughters? Did their fallen state echo with a poignant cry for innocence, passed down five thousand years? Was paradise their hope, their piteous lack or their most embroidered fantasy? Or was there then and equally now a place of unsullied purity wherein the waters of truth and love flow unfettered and the lion lies down with the lamb? For gold and riches of the earth many a ship has sailed forth. But many too have launched their vessel to seek the Blessed Isle or sight the shores of Arcady. Some have risked all in pursuit of Shangri-La hidden within pinnacled shrouds, whilst others have died along forgotten Gobi tracks, lost with the sands of their shifting vision, swallowed in the thirst of their dreams. Has mankind always suffered such longings? Has it ever transferred its bliss to a jewelled garden hovering in the world just beyond its reach?

One of the most intriguing passages to be found in literary archives is that in which Christopher Columbus announced to his royal patrons his supposed discovery of the ascent to the gate of the long lost Garden of Eden. He described an island mountain from whose summit he believed the mighty rivers of Eden came rushing to the sea. Though he felt certain that no one could ever reach this peak without the permission and assistance of God, he was confident that it was indeed the terrestrial paradise and he wrote of the "Mouth of the Dragon" which would have to be braved in approaching it. Navigating just off the coast of Venezuela, Columbus thought that he had reached the fabled Land of Ind (the Indus) which did, indeed, lie east of Eden. But while he mistakenly discovered a new world, Mogul rulers of the fabled land itself were preparing to build pleasure gardens patterned after that which bloomed in the paradisaic poetry of Islam. Set within the confines of a walled square, the four rivers of the world streaming within the carved sandstone channels of such cantons of delight as Shalimar or Naseem Bagh, they would enable at least the consorts of privilege to enjoy a daily blessing of paradise on earth.

Golden Age memories abound in the secret corners of the human unconscious. The idea of paradise is universally stamped in the deepest consciousness of the human race. Often conceived as a walled garden, it has also been sought in a New Jerusalem or, as in the case of the Maori and Celtic peoples, in an Avalon under the sea. Many traditions have persisted in identifying paradise as an island floating on the ocean or surrounded by a lake and rivers. Others have emphasized the mountain at its centre. All point to a condition of primordial innocence or hard-won perfection as prerequisite to their entrance, the former suggestive of a Golden Age state, the latter of a spiritual goal. In the centre of the gardens of paradise there is a tree of life, from whose roots spring the four rivers that extend out in the direction of the four cardinal points. Commonly, this tree grows at the heart of a fountain or lake often situated at the top or base of a perfectly formed mountain. Such gardens are always enclosed or surrounded by something which makes entry very difficult. But within the enclosure all is at peace, animals and human beings speaking one language and all living in harmonious accord. The wall may be invisible and the gate unseen by all except one who has the eyes to see it. Whether called the Promised

Land, El Dorado, the White Isle, the Green Isle, Shamballa, Arcadia, the Elysian Fields, Eden, Olympus or Jerusalem, they are all believed to be somehow accessible, somehow within the reach of the heroic few who strive mightily to find them.

The Greek term *paradeisos* was first used by Xenophon, who borrowed it from the Persian word *pairidaeza*, which modern scholars say simply means "around" (*pairi*) "mould" (*diz*), pinpointing the wall enclosing the garden. This lack-lustre etymological designation could be happily set aside, but for now it is more relevant to note the importance of the idea to the ancient Persians and the fact that they, as well as the other peoples of Mesopotamia and the mountainous plateau to the north, had always looked eastward for its location. The old Semitic description spoke of the four rivers, naming the Nile, the Euphrates, the Indus and the Phison or Ganges, and spoke of Hawilah (India), the "gold-bearing land". Within the heart of Asia itself people such as the Yakuts of Siberia described paradise as the dwelling place of the first man, the place of the tree whose crown is the tethering post of God, They believed that the first man approached the tree to learn the purpose of his life. A female visible within its trunk responded to his unspoken question and told him that he was to become the father of the human race. Among the neighbouring Buriats it was said that a snake called Abyrga waited at the foot of the Zambu tree which rose out of the milk sea of Narvo, from whence sprang the four rivers. Striking parallels spring to mind between these ideas and the story of the goddesses associated with the Yggdrasil tree (under whose roots the serpent Nidhogg abides), causing one to ponder the connection between Siberian and Eddie mythologies. But the similarities persist as one travels even further afield. One is driven again and again to wonder where the idea may have found its genesis, or if it is simply a very complex but universally impressed archetype whose basic elements express themselves repeatedly according to geographical and cultural peculiarities.

> And the Lord God planted a garden eastward in Eden; and there he put the man whom he had formed.
> And out of the ground made the Lord God to grow every tree that is pleasant to the sight, and good for food; the tree of life also in the midst of the garden, and the tree of knowledge of good and evil.

And a river went out of Eden to water the garden; and from thence
it was parted, and became into four heads.

Genesis 2: 8–10

Paradise might never have been conceived by anyone had it not
been for the deep sense that it has somehow been lost. The bliss and
innocence associated with it continue to be seen only in children, who
never question their state of being but invariably grow up to suffer a
sense of alienation from the wholeness of those happy days. Just as
in the Siberian Altaic myth which tells of how there was no sun or
moon before the first man ate the forbidden fruit of paradise, so too
the child eats of the knowledge of good and evil and loses the carefree
bliss of ignorance. The Cheyenne described how this happened to
Sweet Medicine, who lived in a paradise of naked innocence before
reaching understanding and becoming the father of their race. Once
lost, there is nothing left to do but to strive to regain it. All cultures
are rich in heroic tales of how it may be regained, and even the
labyrinth followed on behalf of scientific discoveries seems to be only
another instance of such striving. For has not modern man pinned
his hopes upon technology to deliver him the bliss and general sense
of shared abundance he so deeply craves? The pathways, be they
physical, intellectual or metaphysical, are all pursued out of the same
longing. For one man the way may lead to wealth or power, which he
believes will buy him the bliss of paradise on earth; for another the
search may mean worldly summit after summit climbed, or turning
within in order to seek out a Mount Analogue. A common theme is
the difficulty and danger encountered in this striving. Apparently,
paradise lost is not easily regained and many are the dragons or
serpents to be encountered in the effort.

An Icelandic myth tells of the bridge to paradise that crosses the
Ganges in India and which, it relates, is guarded by a terrible dragon.
The hero Eirek, deliberately wading into "the maw of the dragon" with
his sword in hand, finds himself (an instant later) liberated from the
gloom of the monster's interior and safely in paradise! How poignant
it is that this theme, so similar to the Australian belief that one must
be swallowed by a great serpent and spit up again in order to enter
into the timeless state of the gods, should be echoed so confidently

in Columbus' reference to the Island of Paradise and the Mouth of the Dragon nearby. One wonders if he looked upon the setting with the awed anticipation of one considering the possibilities of an actual quest culminating in initiation, or whether he was merely playing with words and symbols, hopeful of lending greater significance to his discoveries. In truth, the struggle between abdication from a personal quest conveniently supplied by the doctrine of vicarious atonement, and a genuine desire to believe in paradise even here in the world, seemed to have been warring in his breast. Columbus, like so many of his age, had already bitten the bitter crust of scepticism which would progressively sour in subsequent centuries, but he still retained the innocence of true belief, the simplicity of a child let free to explore the world.

In the misty dawn of June 18, 1767, the frigate HMS *Dolphin* under Captain Samuel Wallis found itself near the shore of what appeared to be a dream. Beyond a shrouded turquoise lagoon, tier upon tier of lushly wooded peaks arose above pillared coconut palms drooping and swaying in myriad-fingered grace over stands of jewelled blossoms and black volcanic sand. Towards the ship came hundreds of beautifully carved canoes "full of tall, brown, conspicuously handsome men", who gazed at them with eager curiosity. The scurvied and unwashed sailors, months out from the dingy dockside taverns of England, gaped and marvelled and wondered if they had discovered paradise. In the six weeks that they stayed in what would eventually become known to the world as Tahiti, many of them came to believe it. So simple and trustingly generous were the islanders, so good natured and free of disease or want, the sailors were overwhelmed. Even the most cynical of them came to think that they were far happier in their way of life and their idyllic surroundings than they or any other European had ever dreamt of being. This awareness was shared by every subsequent group of Europeans who visited the island. Sadly, it did not prevent them from conducting themselves in ways that ensured the complete destruction of this happy way of life. But even as the natives were being brow-beaten with doctrines of private property and original sin, the idea grew in England and on the Continent that a paradise on earth had been found.

On the eve of his departure for Tahiti, Paul Gauguin painted what he imagined he might find there: a childlike Eve picking fruit from a tree in paradise. He described a later such subject, saying that "the riddle hiding in the depths of her childlike eyes is still incommunicable to me. . . . She is Eve after the Fall, still able to go about unclothed without being immodest, still with as much animal beauty as on the first day, ... Naïvely she searches her memory for the "why" of times past and present. Enigmatically she looks at you." By Gauguin's time much of the carefree ease of everyday life had been badly curbed through the offices of French political and ecclesiastical authority. A century earlier Louis de Bougainville had rhapsodically recorded how he felt "transported into the garden of Eden. . . . Everywhere we found hospitality, ease, innocent joy and every appearance of happiness." Gauguin was fated to seek out the remnants of this under the censorious eye of civilized opinion-makers who had decided that paradise should not be confused with the morally questionable happiness of savages. Despite this prejudice, the idea of paradise in the Pacific lingered, and a steady trickle of artists, poets and writers made their way there from European and American spiritual ghettos to seek a draught from the fount of eternal and innocent perception they hoped to find.

> Mamua, when our laughter ends,
> And hearts and bodies, brown as white
> Are dust about the doors of friends,
> Or scent a-blowing down the night,
> Then oh! then, the wise agree,
> Comes our immortality.
> Mamua, there waits a land
> Hard for us to understand.
> Out of time, beyond the Sun,
> All are one in Paradise.

> Rupert Brooke

Apart from the happy ease of life, visitors from the grim world outside the South Seas also noticed a childlike quality about the native people. When sailors were flogged as punishment for infractions of rules aboard various ships, the Tahitians wept at the cruelty and begged the officers to desist. But even more at the heart of their simplicity was their inability to live beyond the moment. With little concern for the past or the future, they continued to repeat experiences in a changeless cycle shared by all and passed down from generation to generation. Millennia before, they had set out upon the ocean from Southeast Asia. When they happened upon an island which pleased them, they settled down to a life usually peaceful and always uneventful. Alone through the ages, they ceased to imagine a world beyond the neighbouring islands, and with the climate barely changing through the seasons, they scarcely took note of time. In a world overbrooded by an impersonal Deity with lesser gods and spirits closer at hand, they had no concept of a devil or a hell and felt required only to show reverence to gods through kindness and unselfishness with each other. Possessing everything communally, they knew no envy or avarice but worked and played together in a way that made laughing banter out of both. Thoughtful visitors watched and marvelled at their lack of questioning, their lack of doubt and indecision, of introspection or self-conscious creativity. Was this the innocence of paradise, the bliss of a Golden Age? If so, then how had the rest of the world to account for the development of discriminating intellect and individuation that had been accompanied by such heightened powers of reasoning as well as increased mental suffering? Did the South Sea Islanders represent a human ideal or had they yet to go through the pain of self-conscious realization? By the time people seriously asked the question, their innocence and their way of life was already a thing of the past.

> I am as free as Nature first made man,
> Ere the base laws of servitude began,
> When wild in woods the noble savage ran.

> John Dryden

In his inspired epic on the fall from paradise, Milton described Lucifer's arrival at the zenith of the outermost shell of the globe where, directly beneath the stairway leading to heaven, he saw an orifice permitting a passage to the seat of paradise on the way down through the starry orbs to earth. Milton's Heaven of Heavens is quite different from paradise, "where redeemed souls may choose to dwell", and both seem to be either side of an orifice associated with the pole-star lined up with the North Pole of the earth. Many traditions have hinted at a linking pillar or column between the celestial and terrestrial paradise, and some have envisioned the linking axis running from the celestial through the terrestrial paradise down through the globe to the realm of Hades associated with the South Pole. Milton seems to have intuited such a connection when he described how Satan could view the three gates leading to heaven, earth and hell simultaneously. All this would strongly suggest a northerly location of an earthly paradise, and indeed there is no dearth of support for such an idea.

The Chinese, in speaking of the inferior gods surrounding paradise, seem to have been describing the Pleiades that circle the pole-star, while in the Hindu tradition the sacred Ganga is said to travel seven times around Meru in its descent from the abode of the Seven Rishis of the Great Bear. In terms of the Hindu *varshas*, Bharata describes the subcontinent above which rises the Himavat and a series of *varshas* culminating in that of Illavrita, which rests at the top of the world. Here, according to the Puranas, Sumeru rises, its four faces of Brahmā marking the cardinal points from whose "mouths" flow the four rivers. Sumeru, the "beautiful axis", is opposite Kumeru, its "infernal" counterpart, easily suggesting a polar location for those whom the Greeks called the Hyperboreans. In the latter tradition the idea of Hyperborea, the *ultima Thule*, fascinated early writers including Homer, whose description of Odysseus' voyage includes a visit to the Ὀμφαλὸς Θάλασης (North Pole) as well as to the underworld. Called the "navel" of the world, the Ὀμφαλὸς literally means a "mountain rising", and though its emblem can be found at such sacred places as Delphi, the archetypal form was believed to rise at the umbilical point where the terrestrial and celestial worlds are generationally connected.

A year of mortals is a day and a night of the gods, or regents of the universe seated around the North Pole.

Code of Manu

It is difficult to warm up to the notion that paradise could rest in the icy North but strong arguments do seem to favour it. Where else on the globe could a year of mortals be experienced as a day and a night? One of the most convincing ideas is that which places the axes of these various worlds in alignment, whether one wishes to imagine an actual terrestrial paradise or one hovering midway between heaven and earth. In considering other locations on the globe, one wonders if they are simply analogues that have lived vividly in people's minds and even shifted from time to time with migrations and new ideas. Or are there truly sacred places in the world, perhaps closer to the equatorial belt than we would think, where one might suddenly find oneself in the presence of eternal bliss and innocence? In the Semitic tradition Eden is usually identified with the Plain of Eden in Babylonian times. Could it have been located at Eridu, a city of magical virtues containing a famous oracle tree? Was this the place that inspired Enoch's dream, or was that dream drawn only from the Akashic realm where timeless bliss commands? All the myths of creation, paradise, the Fall and the Flood found in the Semitic tradition are of Babylonian origin and can possibly be traced back further through the Sumerians.

It is likely that the name of the Akkadian capital, Akkad, provided the inspiration for the Greek term "Arkadia" and acted as a channel through which these ideas flowed into the western Mediterranean. But this would merely be a relatively recent transmission and many other linguistic and symbolic clues point to an older, more easterly, origin. The earlier non-Semitic Sumerians might have brought such ideas with them when they came into Mesopotamia from India around 4000 B.C. For it is among them that the story of the god Yaw who planted a garden in Eden to the east seems to have first originated.

> Paradise was in the Orient . . .
>> higher than any other land upon earth . . . .
> Shut off from the habitable world
>> by vast mountains that cannot be crossed. . . .
> Some say that Enoch and Elias
>> are still in that Paradise.

> > > > St. Thomas Aquinas

It is, perhaps, significant that in China and Southeast Asia the Pure Land of paradise is assigned to the west. None of the Asian peoples of the Far East looked out over the Pacific in hopes of glimpsing its sacred tree and mountain. Like an enclosing ring, the myths and lore of people throughout Asia, Siberia, the Middle East, eastern and northern Europe, all point to a location somewhere near the Himalayas or in Central Asia to the north. If the evidence for a super-terrestrial paradise at the North Pole is strong, that for the location of a worldly paradise somewhere in the Himalayan region is overwhelming. A few scholars have drawn some interesting connections between names like Sumeru and Sumer, pointing out that the ancient Sumerians are believed to have come from the upper Indus River, whose name, Yav-Ya, simply means "River of God". The cuneiform writing on certain seals from the Harappan civilization as well as from Sumer tell of Kanwe, a Brahmin priest-enchanter, and of the great mountain Meru. Harappan records were later substantiated by Alexander the Great and Aristotle, who both spoke of an Indus-Nile hydrographic system wherein the Indus and the Ganges swung variously through Lemuria and Arabia to feed into the Tigris and the Euphrates as well as the Nile. This, it could be argued, might account for the inclusion of the Mesopotamian rivers in the four originating from paradise. Other linguistic evidence traces the name Eden back to the Sanskrit *Gau-Edin* associated with the vale of Kashmir. This is particularly fruitful, as a proliferation of closely related words seems to have spun off into Tibet (*Gan-Edin*), Egypt (*Gin-Aden*) and Persia (*Gan-Hedon*) through the Sumerian-Akkadians (*Gu-Edin*), The Greeks, picking up the term *Hedon* from the Persians, gave the world the idea of "hedonism", coming from their word for pleasure, an interesting if rather double-edged cultural transmission.

While *Gan-Hedon* refers to a "garden of pleasure", *pairidaeza* is assumed merely to emphasize its surrounding wall. There is, however, a much more significant possible origin for this latter term. The ancient Parthians, using the word "Parada" for "Bharata", referred to Kashmir as the Land of Parada and called its kings by that name. In the Indian epics Kashmir was considered to be the home of the wise Maga who carried their arcane teachings to the four corners of the world. According to Indo-Sumerian records, these were Tire worshippers, the

Magi of the East who brought their religion to the Middle East long before the time of Zarathustra. Tradition claims that they travelled to far distant lands and that their influence was responsible for the striking similarities in paradise myths as far flung as Scandinavia and Japan. In any event, the name for the Celtic Elysium, *Mag-Mar*, is certainly suggestive of a reference to them if not to their actual presence.

> This land is cut off from the rest of the world, and is flowing with golden rivers and lotus lakes, adorned with precious jewels. ... It is situated near Kailas and the source of the great rivers.
>
> *Mahabharata*

This is the Land of Uttarakuru, the Land of the Blessed so beautifully described in the *Mahabharata*. The great classical Sanskrit poet Kalidasa wrote of it in the "Cloud Messenger", sketching in limpid words a mount-encircled lake wherein clouds like heavenly wings in reflection floated. "Now on the mountain's side", he penned, "behold the city of the gods impend. . . . Thy goal behold where Ganga's winding rill skirts, like a costly train, the sacred hill." Of Kailas the poet writes, and Lake Manasasarova at its foot. Just as the Yambo tree of life was said to grow to the south of Mount Meru, so also the soma tree was said to grow in the middle of the lake south of Mount Kailas in the trans-Himalayan chain. It is difficult to know whether the upper Indus associated with the possible home of the Sumerians refers to the Land of Parada (Kashmir) or to the Himalayan valleys southwest of Mount Kailas. That a mythical and religious connection exists between Kailas and Meru there can be no doubt.

It is also clear that the four great holy rivers of the world have been thought to have their source in Manasasarova Lake. Given the barrenness of the Himalayan valleys leading towards Kailas, it would seem plausible that, in more recent millennia at least, the Garden of Paradise was indeed identified with Kashmir, while its mountain and lake was and still is believed to be represented by holy Kailas and Manasasarova.

Manasasarova is the holiest place in the world. In its centre dwells
a divinity in human form. In its bosom grows a tree with a thousand
branches and a double crown . . . overshadowing the whole world.

From the Bon tradition

The four rivers of paradise in the trans-Himalayan tradition are
the Indus, the Ganges, the Tsanpo (Brahmaputra) and the Sutlej. They
flow from the mouths of the four sacred animals: the lion, the cow, the
horse and the elephant. In the Semitic scheme the Nile answers for the
Indus, and the Tigris and Euphrates for the Tsanpo and Sutlej. The
sacred animals are once again represented, the Phison (or Ganges)
pouring forth from an angel's instead of a cow's mouth, and the Nile
being associated with the lion, as would seem consistent if the reports
of Alexander the Great and Aristotle are to be given any weight. Of
no small interest is the physical fact that the Indus and the Sutlej
do indeed take their source at Kailas, while the Tsanpo makes its
beginning but a short distance away. The Ganges flows with roaring
freshness from Gomuck Cave (the Cow's Mouth) on the southern side
of the Himalayas, removing its immediate source from the Kailas
range, but the glacier from which it gathers its force is but a cloud
itself, barely shifted from the mirror of Manasasarova's waters. Thus
in the mundane world the reflection of an ideal realm is impressed. It
is not difficult to understand why so many have risked life and limb
and even sanity in order to seek out the sacred precinct in which this
is believed to reside. The harrowing journeys over icy and desolate
mountain passes, the close calls with bandits, starvation, altitude
sickness and madness – none of these things have deterred those
whose eyes ever seek for paradise. Over the next mountain pass, over
the next range – surely it will be found there!

Neither by taking ship,
Neither by any travel on foot,
To the Hyperborean Field
Shalt thou find the wondrous way.

Pindar

It is in the heavenly lake of the soul that the tree of soma grows. And the mountain within rises up above it between thine eyes, Lanoo. There on that mountain of paradise Shiva dwells. Locked in meditation he bears within his cosmic mind the timeless, pure innocence of unsullied and eternal Truth. There, above the storms of longing, the obsessions with finding paradise in the world, He resides in perfect calm. O poor humanity, poor wayfarers who trudge the roads and seaways waiting for the vision to burst suddenly upon their senses. How many lives have been spent in this search and how little it has garnered. But do not doubt of paradise, for it surely exists. Like Lucifer in Milton's poem, man can mount to the gate of the celestial world and there view the entrances to heaven and paradise and hell. One may find this at the foot of Kailas or within one's closet in secret, for that which exists in the realm of archetypal ideation finds its reflection in the world. What is critical and requires the highest powers of discrimination is the ability to recognize the noumenon mirrored in the reflection and to avoid being caught in the psychic rapture of the image itself. A wise man avoids the paradise of the physical senses because he knows it is short-lived indeed. He avoids also the paradise of the astral senses with its sweetly dreaming *devachan*. The paradise he seeks is the bliss of unwavering Truth, the pinnacled state of ever being consciously one with that which is in harmony with every intelligent monad in the cosmos. He is the tree in paradise whose fruitful wisdom lies beyond good and evil and from whose watered roots flow forth the rippling echoes of the Divine Word.

> To the gate of Paradise I would go
> Where first I glimpsed its peak,
> Where first its light shone on my soul
> O Kailas of my dreams,
> I came to thee!
> And my heart discovered speech.

Hermes, March 1986

KRISHNA:

"It is even a portion of myself which, having assumed life in this world of conditioned existence, draweth together the five senses and the mind in order that it may obtain a body and may leave it again. And those are carried by the Sovereign Lord to and from whatever body he enters or quits, even as the breeze bears the fragrance from the flower. Presiding over the eye, the ear, the touch, the taste, and the power of smelling, and also over the mind, he experienceth the objects of sense. The deluded do not see the spirit when it quitteth or remains in the body, nor when, moved by the qualities, it has experience in the world. But those who have the eye of wisdom perceive it, and devotees who industriously strive to do so see it dwelling in their own hearts; whilst those who have not overcome themselves, who are devoid of discrimination, see it not even though they strive, thereafter. Know that the brilliance of the sun which illuminateth the whole world, and the light which is in the moon and in the fire, are the splendor of myself.

The Bhagavad-Gita, Ch. XV

978-0-9793205-1-4
0-9793205-1-8

Made in the USA
Middletown, DE
27 February 2016